THEOLOGY
OF THE BODY

for Teens

Leader's Guide

Jason & Crystalina Evert
and
Brian Butler

ASCENSION
PRESS

West Chester, Pennsylvania

Nihil obstat: Rev. Robert A. Pesarchick, S.T.D.
                    Censor Librorum
                    April 17, 2007

Imprimatur: +Justin Cardinal Rigali
                    Archbishop of Philadelphia
                    April 20, 2007

Except where otherwise noted, Scripture verses contained herein are from the Catholic Edition of the Revised Standard Version of the Bible, copyright 1965, 1966 by the Division of Christian Education of the National Council of the Churches of Christ in the United States of America. Used by permission. All rights reserved.

Quotations from Pope John Paul II's General Audiences on the Theology of the Body, indicated by a date reference, are taken from the weekly English edition of *L'Osservatore Romano*.

Ascension Press
Post Office Box 1990
West Chester, PA 19380
Orders: 1-800-376-0520
www.AscensionPress.com

Cover design: Devin Schadt

Printed in the United States of America

ISBN: 978-1-932927-87-0

This book is dedicated to John Paul II

(dare we say, "John Paul the Great"), our hero,

not only for teaching us the Theology of the Body,

but for showing us how to live it. We thank God

for his faithfulness to his vocation and for

his daily intercession on our behalf.

ACKNOWLEDGMENTS

We would like to thank the following people whose support and encouragement helped bring this project to fruition:

- Our **spouses**, for their patience and support throughout this project, and for their amazing love which reveals Christ to us on a daily basis.

- **Mark Hart**, for his great help on this project, and for his humor and ability to bring "head knowledge" to the hearts of teens.

- **Siobhan McCarthy Nye**, for her insights, inspiration, and patience in the development of the vision, and for keeping us focused on the feminine genius.

- **Matthew Pinto**, for guiding us in this project, and everyone at Ascension Press for their pleasant, helpful, and hardworking approach.

- **Christopher West**, for helping us and so many others to better understand and appreciate the Theology of the Body. We are especially grateful to him for the expertise he shared with us on this project.

- **Randy Hernandez**, for his honest advice that helped this program to stay real and approachable.

- Everyone at **Dumb Ox Productions**, Inc., for challenging and helping us to bring Christ to young people in an engaging, faithful, and convincing manner. We are particularly grateful to: Kelley and Courtney Brown, for their helpful insights and critiques of multiple drafts; Jason Angelette, for his passion for the Theology of the Body and his helpful consultation and input; Roy Petitfils, for his solid ideas and encouragement; Chris Baglow, for his theological expertise and constant support; and Lisa Butler, for doing more excellent office management than any good wife and mother needs to do.

- **Cory Hayes**, for his philosophical insights and overall valuable input on this project.

- Our **parents**, for passing on the Faith to us and for their constant love and support.

- All of our **family and friends** who have supported us through their prayers and encouragement.

- **The Holy Trinity**, for creating us, redeeming us, and sanctifying us. May all glory be to the Father and to the Son and to the Holy Spirit, as it was in the beginning, is now, and ever shall be, world without end. Amen.

CONTENTS

LEADER'S INTRODUCTION TO THE
THEOLOGY OF THE BODY FOR TEENS CURRICULUM

Welcome to the *Theology of the Body for Teens* curriculum!

In this leader's guide you will find a wealth of activities and resources to help you bring Pope John Paul II's landmark teaching known as the Theology of the Body to your teens in a way that engages both their minds and hearts. The curriculum is both catechetical and evangelistic. We have made a great effort to make it accessible to the average student as well as interesting for those who are ready for an intellectual challenge. The curriculum also features a series of optional exercises within each lesson designed to create the best learning experience for your students.

Each chapter can be approached either as a single lesson (60 minutes) or two lessons (100-120 minutes). Whether it takes you one hour or two depends on the time you spend in discussion, which activities you choose, how quickly your students engage the program, and the amount of reading you have the students do outside of class time.

If you are already familiar with the Theology of the Body, you will notice that we have diverged somewhat from the original order of John Paul II's catechesis. This departure is intentional, as we believe our approach will be more easily embraced and understood by teenagers. We have not changed the teaching, but merely modified the order in which John Paul presented it. It also should be noted that since this curriculum is an introduction to the Theology of the Body specifically for teens, we have focused mainly on chastity and vocation, two areas of study that are particularly beneficial for teens. We realize the Theology of the Body is much larger in scope than what we have presented in this program.

There are twelve lessons in the curriculum. The structure of each lesson in this teacher manual is as follows:

Overview: A quick summary of the entire lesson.

Objectives: A list of what the student should know and be able to do by the end of each chapter.

Opening Prayer with Scripture: Using Scripture as the centerpiece, we have offered you two different opening prayers in each chapter. This is for two reasons: First, to give you a choice, and second, to provide for you two separate prayers, should you opt to spread each lesson over two learning sessions.

Icebreaker: An optional, attention-grabbing visual or physical activity that creatively helps to lead students into the topic covered in the lesson. We encourage you always to pray the Opening Prayer prior to doing the Icebreaker.

Two Minute Drill/Verbal Review: A set of quick questions designed to facilitate two-to-three minutes of oral review of the content in the previous lesson. Only the questions are in the student manual; the questions and answers are in the teacher manual.

Story Starter: A dramatic story that helps capture the attention of students and draw them into the topic of that chapter.

Bridging the Gap: A few paragraphs that connect the story to the lesson and prepare the students for the material they are about to cover.

To The Core: The main body of the teaching of the lesson.

Comprehension & Discussion Questions: Interspersed throughout the curriculum, a mix of questions ensures reading comprehension. It also offers meaningful points of departure for discussion or opinion writing/journaling.

Notes & Nuggets: Additional information for the teacher's "notes" and some "nuggets" (ideas) for teaching the lesson.

Words of Wisdom: Short quotes generally from Scripture, the Catechism, Pope John Paul II, a saint, or another learned person.

Did You Know: Interesting and relevant facts and statistics pertaining to each lesson.

You Decide: A match-up of ideas, pitting the words of a popular song (or movie, etc.) against the beauty and truth of the words of Pope John Paul II, a saint, or some other wise person, or a passage from Scripture.

Digging Deeper: A call-out box that explores the topic at hand in a deeper, more focused manner than the rest of the chapter. Some of these sections are more nuanced or theologically rich and may have a few more theological terms in them, but they are excellent ways to understand the material in a deeper way, for those who are ready.

Science & the Theology of the Body: Though not found in every chapter, this section aims to bring scientific facts about the body into union with the purposes for which God created it. The information presented here demonstrates that science and faith are not opposed to each other but rather are complementary.

Live it Out: This is another call-out box, a practical section to help teens "apply" the teaching to their lives. It is packed with real-life examples, words of encouragement, and practical advice.

Application: This is usually a tangible way to help your students apply (or further and more tangibly explore) their comprehension of the lesson.

Movie Clips/Songs: This is a list of movie and song ideas that you can use to better unpack the topic at hand. The movie clips are intentionally short (for the most part) so as to be an "aid" to the lesson, not to take the place of it. They are conveniently noted by their exact time code according to the DVD versions, saving you the time of having to watch through the whole movie searching for the clip. If you have a VHS version, you can still use the DVD time code notation as an approximate guide for finding the clip in the movie. Each clip has a short explanation as to how it connects to the topic at hand.

The songs can be used as closing reflections or opportunities for journaling, etc. They are noted by the artist/band of the recording, along with the name of the CD on which the song appears. Many of the songs are also available through iTunes, if you want to download them instead of buying the whole CDs.

Work It Out: A list of three to six assignments generally ordered in such a way that they *ascend* in difficulty (#1 being easiest, #6 the hardest). After the assignments, there is usually a list of a few projects that entail more work, greater attention, and more time. Many of the projects are meant for group work.

Closing Prayer: A short prayer, asking for the intercession of a particular saint whose life reflected the value of the topic in that specific chapter.

Glossary of Key Terms: Throughout the curriculum, we have **bolded** key terms within each of the chapters. All of these key terms are arranged alphabetically in the glossary at the end of each chapter. While most are defined within the body of each chapter, all bolded terms are specifically defined in the glossary.

In His Own Words: This is a collection of relevant quotes from John Paul II, appearing only in the teacher manual, as some of them are fairly dense. They will enhance your own understanding and give you a richer appreciation of the material, which should enhance your teaching.

Note: Page numbers in this Leader's Guide match those of the Student Workbook. Blank pages preceding chapters, however, have been omitted here (i.e., pages 4, 50, 126, 158, and 178). As such, leaders will notice a break in page sequence at these points in the Leader's Guide.

THE KEY TO SUCCESSFUL TEEN RELATIONSHIPS

Whether or not you have a team of volunteer adults and peer ministers helping out, it is essential for you (and/or for them) to form good relationships with the teenagers. Being a teacher of teens, surely you not only know this but probably are good at it. Still, a reminder on the importance of this never hurts.

The relationships that your students form with you at the beginning will be a foundation upon which you can build trust. In our society, it is no longer enough to teach solid doctrine and smile at our students. As teachers, we need to earn the right to be heard. We live in a skeptical age and are also competing against an intoxicating pop culture. We teachers need to be engaging to compete with the influences that dominate our teens' lives. This also means we must be genuine and take the time to really get to know our students. We must invest beyond our comfort zones to meet them in their world. One way to do this is to take an interest in their lives by attending their sporting events, plays, recitals, etc. This takes time, which the students realize is precious to you. In turn, they realize you want to know them. In return, they will become more open to what you have to say. Once they begin to trust you, you can act like the apostle Andrew did with Peter, bringing them directly to Christ (see Jn 1:42).

It is also vital to invest time into relating to your teens outside of the classroom, even if it is just talking after class or in the parking lot. It does not mean you need to be their "buddy" or that you should descend into teenage immaturity. Talking with teens and sharing time with them outside of class shows that you care. Teens want meaningful relationships with adults. Remember: you need to "earn the right to be heard" by these teenagers. If you invest your time in cultivating relationships with them, you are bound to see better results than you thought possible. Throughout years of teaching and youth ministry, we've seen tremendous fruit come from investing time with teens outside the classroom.

Learn Their Names

A great classroom experience usually begins with the simple gesture of learning your students' names. It may take some time to memorize them, especially if you have 100-200 students, but when you look in a teen's eyes and remember his or her name it speaks volumes to that student. It is a simple but powerful way to say you care.

An Environment of Dignity

Though it may be obvious to some, the environment you set in your classroom is a major factor in helping students to accept the truths you are teaching. The environment begins with your demeanor and the way that you speak to your students. If you are pleasant and genuine in your approach to teens, you send a positive message to them.

Once you have set the tone of respect for your students, it's important to demand respect from them–not only for you, but for each other. At the core of the Theology of the Body is the truth that we are all made in the image and likeness of God, and we all have dignity. The way you allow students to treat each other in class will witness to them the degree to which you believe what you are teaching about dignity. When teenagers get comfortable, they sometimes get jovial and sarcastic. It is easy to unintentionally let them cross the line of respect with each other, even if only in a "joking" sort of way. You can expect to see some immaturity at times, especially since you are dealing with subjects of a sexual nature. Be careful with your students in these instances, calling them to a higher level of maturity. Do so in a manner that is firm, yet charitable.

The more consistently you demand and uphold respect for every single student, the more they will relax. They will come to see that your classroom is a sanctuary from the rest of their life, hopefully a place where Christ can begin to heal their wounds. If you set rules of respect and then do not enforce them, you may create a situation worse than if you never had rules to begin with. (For new teachers who may not have worked with teens before, be aware that they are particularly keen about "fairness" and will quickly pick up on any inconsistency on your part.)

The "Co-ed" Question

As you read through this manual and plan the implementation of this program, remember the unique opportunities that segregating boys and girls affords. We realize that, for many, splitting boys and girls into separate groups or separate classes is not a viable option. But if it is an option, consider that group discussions about chastity in same-sex settings can often be more frank, more comfortable and achieve more depth. Of course, if segregation is not an option, co-ed settings will provide a balanced perspective of both genders. Rest assured that this curriculum will be effective in whichever setting you use it.

A Message of Hope and Healing, Not Condemnation

When teaching or preaching about morality—especially sexuality and God's plan for chastity—there may at times be a temptation to correct or admonish teens for their improper, disrespectful or outlandish views. Preaching condemnation or emphasizing a religion based upon rules is not only ill advised, but it is in direct opposition to the heart of John Paul II's teaching of love, truth, and freedom. His approach was one of existential personalism. He taught the Theology of the Body through those personal appeals to human experiences that everyone understands. This methodology, along with the compelling content, is one more reason your students will connect with this teaching. Their hearts will be awakened and set free to love.

While your teaching and explanation of this material is important, your life example—your own incarnation of this Theology of the Body—will be equally, if not more important. This is why Pope Paul VI said, "Modern man listens more willingly to witnesses than to teachers, and if he does listen to teachers, it is because they are witnesses."[1]

Teenagers need witnesses of the truth. Teens *want* role models who will challenge them to be more than they thought possible and support them in their journey towards authentic love and freedom. Despite the challenges that come with teaching teenagers, take hope in knowing that John Paul II believed in our young people enough to entrust them with a "stupendous task" at the end of the Jubilee Year:

"Yet again, the young have shown themselves to be for Rome and for the Church *a special gift of the Spirit of God*. Sometimes when we look at the young, with the problems and weaknesses that characterize them in contemporary society, we tend to be pessimistic. The Jubilee of Young People, however, changed that, telling us that young people, whatever their possible

ambiguities, have a profound longing for those genuine values which find their fullness in Christ. Is not Christ the secret of true freedom and profound joy of heart? Is not Christ the supreme friend and the teacher of all genuine friendship? If Christ is presented to young people as he really is, they experience him as an answer that is convincing and they can accept his message, even when it is demanding and bears the mark of the Cross. For this reason, in response to their enthusiasm, I did not hesitate to ask them to make a radical choice of faith and life and present them with a stupendous task: to become 'morning watchmen' (see Is 21:11-12) at the dawn of the new millennium."[2]

As you begin teaching *Theology of the Body for Teens*, may the Holy Spirit inspire and strengthen you to rise in faith to this great challenge and privilege: helping your students to learn their purpose in life and to live it out faithfully.

Thank you for joining us in the New Evangelization of our young people. You have been and will continue to be in our prayers. John Paul the Great, pray for us!

Veni, Sancte Spiritus!

– Jason & Crystalina Evert and Brian Butler
  Pentecost Sunday, June 4, 2006

1 Pope Paul VI, Address to the Members of the Consilium de Laicis (2 October 1974): AAS 66 (1974), p. 568
2 *Novo Millennio Ineunte*, 9

INTRODUCTION

It had only been a week into his sophomore year of high school when Nick first spotted Kristen in the gym on campus. Although he didn't have the chance to meet her that afternoon, he eagerly awaited an opportunity to find someone who knew her. He had seen her from time to time, and wondered who she was and whether or not she had a boyfriend. Whenever he'd see her on campus, a lump would form in his throat, and he'd make a conscious effort not to trip or walk into anything as she passed by.

Nick's big day finally arrived when he noticed some of his friends sitting with Kristen in the cafeteria. Pretending like he hardly realized her presence, he took a seat with his friends and displayed his impeccable etiquette for the first time; he finally kept his mouth closed while chewing. She must have been impressed because from that day on she began to smile in his direction and offer a friendly "Hi" whenever they passed each other on campus.

In the fall of junior year, Nick and Kristen shared a history class together and their acquaintance grew into a friendship. They began studying together, and it wasn't long before their mutual attraction was obvious. They talked on the phone, stayed up late instant messaging each other, and enjoyed meeting one another's friends at school and social events. Kristen decorated Nick's locker with notes of congratulations when he was chosen as the tailback for the varsity football team. Nick was there to sit in the front row with her family when she got a leading role in a school play.

They went to a winter "formal" dance together and, by the end of their junior year, the two were inseparable. Soon, thoughts of "forever" started to rise up in their hearts, and even conversations about where they might go to college seemed influenced by their relationship. As they grew closer emotionally, intellectually, and spiritually, they also desired to grow closer physically. Often, after a late night of studying, they'd lose interest in the textbooks, and would find themselves leaving the desk in favor of the couch.

Once in a while, they'd go too far, and have "the talk," agreeing that they needed to slow things down. But it seemed like the more often they'd have the talk, the sooner they would fall back into the same things they agreed to avoid.

During class, Nick would often find his mind wandering to what they did the previous evening, or what might happen that upcoming weekend. When they were alone, he'd often initiate affection, but he knew something wasn't right. After one particularly intense evening, he sent an email to a friend, explaining the guilt he was feeling: "Sometimes afterwards, I feel as though I was just taking something from her. I mean I know I didn't, because I didn't force her to do anything. But it's not like she always wants to before we start. I just keep on pushing the envelope until she wants to."

Little did he realize Kristen's conscience was also bothering her. Her family upbringing had taught her to look for "true love," but hadn't been so clear on how to find it. Kristen had once asked her older sister, who was engaged, how she could know she had found true love. "You'll just know," was the answer she got. Now, she felt close to Nick and thought maybe she even really loved him, but she wasn't sure how to express that. She enjoyed the feeling of closeness, but she was afraid that the physical stuff was becoming the center of the relationship. She talked to some of her friends, and they told her it wasn't a big deal as long as she and Nick loved each other. But she wasn't totally convinced. One night, after going "too far," Kristen wondered aloud to Nick if he really liked her, or if he was only interested in her body. They both felt torn between the pleasure their bodies wanted, and the innocence their relationship was losing.

To make matters more difficult, Nick was raised in a family where the only advice he received about his sexuality was "Don't do it." After a few months of dating Kristen, he would often think to himself, "Then what am I supposed to do with all these desires if marriage is still years away? Ignore them?"

No answers came. He had been taught rules, but no reasons. As a result, boundaries just felt like burdens. Repressing his sexuality seemed unhealthy (not to mention, impossible) and so he began to question why God would impose such unfair laws. But at the same time, he sensed that his lust was starting to suffocate their love. He cared deeply for Kristen, but it seemed as if he only had two options: suppress all his desires, or give in to what felt natural. When given a choice like this, one could see why he wanted to throw his faith aside.

Plenty of us have felt confused in similar ways. In the words of one musician, "Life in Lubbock, Texas taught me two things: One is that God loves you and you're going to burn in hell. The other is that sex is the most awful, filthy thing on earth and you should save it for someone you love."[1]

Sound familiar?

When you hear about "the Catholic Church's teaching on sexuality," what comes to mind? Maybe it's something like this: "Give up everything you really want and follow all these miserable rules or you're going to hell."[2]

If you can relate to this, then you'll be relieved to learn that the Theology of the Body is not a list of rules. Rather, it's a map that answers these questions, among many others:

- "Who am I?"

- "What is my purpose in life?"

- "Why did God make me a male or a female?"

- "How can I find true happiness here on earth?"

• "How can I find love that really satisfies me?"

The Theology of the Body helps us learn to receive God's love so we can give and receive it with others in our lives. Instead of seeing the body as bad or dirty, and treating our sexual desires like they should be repressed or ignored, the Theology of the Body reveals *that our body and its desires actually point us to the meaning of life!*

This revolutionary teaching, given to us by Pope John Paul II, says that our bodies are holy and good! Instead of dwelling on the consequences of impurity, it shows the deeply satisfying freedom that comes from having a pure heart.

Basically, it's what Nick and Kristen struggled to understand but were never taught.

In this curriculum, *Theology of the Body for Teens*, you will discover the beauty and purpose of your sexuality, and why it is such a major part of our ability to love. You'll learn that the Church actually teaches and believes that human sexuality is really important, and good, and beautiful. It is actually meant, in a sense, to point us to heaven (More on this bold statement later).

In the Theology of the Body, you'll also learn four things that Jesus' love on the cross and sexual love in God's plan actually have in common. You'll also learn about heaven, how to get there, and how to experience a taste of it here on earth. You'll learn all this and much, much more!

Read, think, pray, and ask your teacher lots of questions. The curriculum you are studying will help you figure out how to *express* your sexuality properly without repressing it. Through this material, you will finally understand more about the meaning of your life, God's plan for your sexuality, and a course of action that leads to freedom and happiness—and believe it or not, God *does* want you to be free and happy!

So, if you wish to find love and be free, hear the good news: the truth will definitely set you free—free to love and live like never before. God's plan for life and love is so profound and beautiful that, once it is revealed to us, we'll never look the same way at the relationship between a man and woman.

When we see the truth about our bodies and the truth about sex, we change our lives not as a result of persuasion, guilt, fear of pregnancy or disease, or because we have to, but because God's view of love is everything that the human heart longs for. But it's not enough that we long to receive this kind of love. We must learn how to give it.

OBJECTIVES At the end of this lesson, the teens should know and be able to:

• Explain that God loves us and desires to have an intimate, personal relationship with us.

• Show how our bodies teach us profound truths about the reason for our very existence as well as our purpose in life.

• Define "theology" and "Theology of the Body."

• Explain that our bodies are very good, as they were created by God and all that God creates is good.

• Demonstrate that God designed us for communion with Himself and with each other.

• Explain how our bodies make visible the invisible mystery of God.

• Identify that the reason for our existence is to be united in an eternal relationship of love with God in heaven.

• Explore opportunities for a deeper relationship with God and others.

Notes & Nuggets: Prayer is the key to success of any faith-based program. And prayer should not be a one-time thing as you teach. Please consider praying for and with your students every day that you present this material to them. Remember this little adaptation of an old teacher's axiom: Proper prior prayer preparation prevents poor public pedagogical performance!

Today, pray that your students will be open to seeing that God created them for a specific purpose: to love and to be in communion with Him. In a society filled with broken families and extraordinary wounds from sexual sin, pray that your students' hurts and doubts about the possibility of real, loving communion would be overcome by God's grace.

Chapter One

Created for Love

Have you ever wondered why the subject of sex is part of nearly every TV show, advertisement, song, and movie? And the sex shown or sung about is usually glorious—with no pain inflicted on those involved.

Rarely do we see the pain that comes, for example, from selfishness. Did you ever think about what society would be like without selfishness in relationships? If everyone simply loved the other as he or she wished to be loved, we would have virtually no pain, no problems in relationships. Imagine, for example, if marriages never ended in divorce. Think about the pain that both parents and kids would be spared.

Confusion reigns, and it is leading to some seriously broken hearts. People today seem more confused about the meaning of love and the purpose of sex than perhaps ever before. Many people are searching for the meaning of life and love but don't realize that the answer is actually right in front of us; the key to finding that love we're all looking for (even if we don't know it) is hidden in God's original design of our bodies and souls. Yes, you read that correctly. This Catholic curriculum is stating that God has actually hidden in our design as "male and female" a key to the secret of love.

ICEBREAKER (optional): "Hacky Sack" Name Game

Have the teens form a circle. The person with the Hacky Sack should state his or her name and toss the Hacky Sack to the next person in the circle. The receiver should state the name of the previous person plus his or her own name. Continue until each person in the circle has been included and all names have been learned. After each person has gone once, he or she can make longer throws across the circle to others if they can remember that person's name. They should say it aloud as they throw to the receiver. If you don't have a Hacky Sack, use some other item, as long as it is safe to throw (a Koosh Ball, a stuffed animal, an eraser for the blackboard, etc.).

To add a wrinkle to this introductory game, have each person also make some physical sign that can be identified with his or her own name. Have participants recall aloud those names that have been introduced already before saying their own.

For example: Billy likes basketball so he says his name while simulating a basketball jump-shot; then the next teen, Jason, has to say Billy's name while simulating his jump shot, then adding his own symbol. Jason is in Junior ROTC, so he says his name and salutes as his symbol/gesture. Jill then says Billy's name while simulating a jump shot, says Jason's name while saluting, and then says her own name while giving the "peace sign" to signify her peaceful nature, etc.

Teens must pay attention to names, but they also learn a small gesture with which to identify each other. With groups of more than fifteen, the game gets harder and takes more time. However, remember to be patient. Investing time at the beginning is worth it if it can help the teens become familiar with each other and the safe environment you are trying to establish. At the very least, they can learn the name of the person sitting near them and already know one thing about them.

As the leader of the group, give them a few examples before you start. You should also go first to help break the ice. If you can, try to go first and last to show them that you are paying attention to them and want to connect with them. Do your best to recall all of their names and symbolic actions. (Hint: Study your roster or sign-up sheet of names a few times to familiarize yourself with each teen's name.)

Here's a quick explanation. You'll notice that this theme repeats itself many times throughout the *Theology of the Body for Teens* curriculum. If you can grasp this early, you'll understand the lofty (but awesome) concepts in the pages and discussions ahead. Here goes: Our sexuality is a gift through which we can choose to be generous or selfish. Society has flipped the idea of "self-giving" on its head. In fact, many "love stories" portrayed in the modern culture could more appropriately be called "lust stories." Why is this important? Because "love" involves being generous —like God—while "lust" is sexual desire that is selfish—apart from the love of God. Not to be confused with sexual attraction (which is good), lust is almost purely self-seeking. As renowned youth leader John Crudele succinctly says, "Love seeks to give; lust seeks to get."

Are You Obsessed, Too?

Many people in the world think that the Catholic Church is obsessed with the topic of sex, saying that it has all these "rules" about it. In reality, it's our culture that is obsessed with sex. Think about it. The next time you're in a supermarket, look at all the magazines near the check-out counter. Virtually every one will be dominated with headlines about sex. Or, better yet (maybe, worse yet), think of the various shows on primetime television on any given night: they are loaded with sexual content that is either explicit or implied. The view of sex put forth by much of the world actually robs humans of **dignity**. The real problem, though, is that we often come to think about sex as the world does, instead of in the way that God intended.

The Call to Love as God Loves

We humans are called to love one another. We are not called to dominate or oppress or use others, but to respect them as persons made in God's image and likeness. This call to love is actually "stamped" into our very bodies. The physical union of man and woman in the sexual act (also called the "marital act" because it is intended to express marital love) is actually meant to be a foreshadowing of the union that we will all experience in heaven. That heavenly union is not a sexual one, to be sure, but it is real—more real than anything we have (or will) experience here on earth. It's a perfect union between God and mankind—for eternity.

This union was also foreshadowed in the book of Genesis, the first book of the Bible. In it we read about God's original plan for unity with our original parents, Adam and Eve. But confusion reigned and there was a rupture—a breaking—between God and man. Because of this rupture, lust became a reality. A "twisting," if you will, took place in our hearts. Instead of seeking the good of others, we desire to seek our own good, often at the expense of someone else's dignity.

Yet God created us for union with Him. He gave us an "echo" in our hearts of the love that He intends for us all. Pope John Paul II's Theology of the Body is an attempt to identify and find that love that God intends for us. If you seek, you will find it. It simply takes work on our part along with God's amazing grace.

Did you know?

The government spends 12 dollars to promote safe sex and contraceptives for every one dollar spent on abstinence.

OPENING PRAYER

Leader: In the name of the Father, and of the Son, and of the Holy Spirit. **Amen.**

(Option #1)

Leader or Reader #1: Read Genesis 1:1-2, 25-28a, 30b, 31a

"In the beginning, when God created the heavens and the earth, the earth was a formless wasteland, and darkness covered the abyss, while a mighty wind swept over the waters.

God made all kinds of wild animals, all kinds of cattle, and all kinds of creeping things of the earth. God saw how good it was. Then God said: 'Let us make man in our image, after our likeness. Let them have dominion over the fish of the sea, the birds of the air, and the cattle, and over all the wild animals and all the creatures that crawl on the ground.' God created man in his image; in the divine image he created him; male and female he created them. God blessed them, saying: 'Be fertile and multiply; fill the earth and subdue it, and so it happened. God looked at everything he had made, and he found it very good."

Leader or Reader #2: Lord, as You created us in Your image and likeness, we know that You created us out of love and for love. You created us for a union of love with each other just as You created us to be together forever with You. Lord, help us to be open today to learn, to live, and to love like You. We ask all this as we pray together: Our Father, who art in heaven, hallowed be Thy name. Thy kingdom come, Thy will be done, on earth as it is in heaven. Give us this day our daily bread, and forgive us our trespasses, as we forgive those who trespass against us. And lead us not into temptation, but deliver us from evil. Saint (patron saint of your church or school), pray for us. In the name of the Father, and of the Son, and of the Holy Spirit. **Amen.**

(Option #2)

Leader or Reader #1: Read John 10:10, 15:11

"I came that they may have life, and have it abundantly… These things I have spoken to you that my joy might be in you and your joy may be full."

Leader or Reader #2: Jesus, You have created us for love. You made us for Yourself, and our hearts will not be at rest until they rest in You. So, open our minds and our hearts, so that this hour of study may be an hour of prayer. Help us to let go of those things that keep us from receiving the joy You wish to give us today and always. **Amen.**

notes

STORY STARTER:
Words and Wounds of the Heart

- "I gave in to him because I thought it would make him like me more. But the next day, he acted like he hardly knew me."

- "My parents got divorced when I was four, so I never really had a dad. Now my mom is with this other guy, but he gets drunk all the time and they fight a lot."

_____

_____

_____

_____

_____

_____

_____

- "I've been hooked on porn for years and I don't know how to get rid of the stuff."

- "I had too much to drink and slept with this one guy. Now I got a call from the clinic and they said I have an STD that can't be cured."

- "No one has ever seemed interested in me. I hate my body."

- "You always hear about the guys using the girls, but after I gave my virginity to my girlfriend, I found out she was cheating on me."

Could you imagine a world in which there was no divorce, sexual abuse, rape, sexually-transmitted diseases, depression, eating disorders, guilt, addictions, cutting, cheating, or pregnancies before marriage?

It's hardly imaginable. But if we all long for such a world, then why do we all live in such a different one? If we were made for love, why does it seem so hard to find? And if we want love, why do we so often settle for the counterfeit of lust?

The twelve chapters in this workbook will set out to answer those questions and will show that the answers are not as far away as you may think.

Did you know?

The U.S. actually has the highest divorce rate in the Western world, followed by the U.K, and Canada.[i]

COMPREHENSION & DISCUSSION QUESTIONS

notes

1. Have you ever felt like the teens quoted above?

2. Do you have friends who are having trouble with more than one of the issues discussed in the quotes above?

3. Do you think that many teens look at the broken relationships around them and lose hope for their own futures?

4. Can you name some ways that sexual behavior seems to be out of control in our culture?

5. What is the best advice you have ever heard to solve these problems?

6. How has the sexual confusion of our society influenced your view of sex and love?

Notes & Nuggets: For Beginning Teachers

You can approach the following material in a few different ways as you move through the curriculum. The first option is to use the following Bridging the Gap and To the Core sections as "notes" from which you can present the information in your own way.

Another option is to pick teen volunteers to read the following paragraphs in small groups and answer the related comprehension and discussion questions. You probably already know that it's not a good idea to force kids to read. You don't want your desire to have them read make them uncomfortable, and thus, somehow cause them to be less open to you and the healing truth found within this beautiful teaching of John Paul II. Be patient with those students who do not seem to want to participate out loud through reading or discussion (for whatever reason). Give them some space, but don't write them off. It is easy to fall into the extreme of either pushing hard on those teens or ignoring them altogether in favor of those extroverts who really help the classroom experience. Continue to make eye contact with them and gently encourage them to step out of their comfort zones.

Remember that you are a witness of God's love as much as you are a catechist of Catholic teaching. This material is intimately tied to relationships, and that does not exclude your relationship with your students. If you have a good relationship with them, they will be more open to receive the truth in the teaching that you are presenting. In time, they may do just that.

BRIDGING THE GAP

So why is there so much pain and suffering in the world today? It all started with one simple choice: when Adam and Eve chose to go with their own plan instead of God's plan. Their **original sin**, which you will learn more about in the coming chapters, affects us all. Instead of wanting to do what's right, we often desire to do the wrong thing. This tendency to sin is called **concupiscence**.

Concupiscence is not something that affects only a select group of people; it affects every single one of us as members of a society that is damaged and hurting from the effects of sin. Just look at all the broken families, broken hearts, sexual abuse, addictions, infidelity, and shame and regret in people's lives. This is what **despair** looks like in a society that thought it found **sexual liberation** and freedom by using sexuality in whatever way it wanted. Consider how all this has brought us to where we are today.

In the second half of the twentieth century, the mass media grew stronger and stronger in their influence on society. You could say they became a primary teacher of young and old alike. Television and movies degenerated quickly from mere sexual suggestion to more sexually-explicit material. As some observers have noted, we are experiencing the "frog in the pot" scenario. You may be familiar with this example. If you take a frog and put it into a pot of boiling water, it will immediately jump out. However, if you place the frog in room-temperature water and then slowly heat the water, the frog will continue to adjust to the rising temperature and not know that it is in danger. It will stay in the ever-increasingly hot water until it finally dies. This describes very well the moral swamp displayed in our modern media. We have gradually become desensitized to the increase of explicit sexual content in our media. The result of all this is that our country is plagued by a seriously warped understanding of marriage and the role that sex should play in relationships.

Lust is "disordered desire for or inordinate enjoyment of sexual pleasure" (CCC 2351). It is sexual desire apart from God's love that selfishly seeks one's own pleasure at the expense of another. Lust often dominates our culture. This domination can easily lead to apathy, or lack of concern, on the part of many. Apathy then leads to a lack of motivation to change. We begin to settle for less than true, good, and beautiful relationships. These are heavy words, we know. They almost sound dismal. A natural question one would ask is, "Is there any hope?" Are we all doomed to suffer broken hearts and marry people who will commit to us only as long as it is convenient? Where is God in all this mess?

God is with us, and there is hope! The good news is that life and sexuality were not always the way we find it now. Jesus tells us, "In the beginning, it was not so" (Mt 19:8). In fact, in the beginning, love had its way and lust *didn't even exist.* To learn more about how to solve the problem of lust and sexual confusion, we must go back to the beginning to see how God created sexuality. In doing

Did you know?

One in three girls is sexually abused by the time she's eighteen years old.[ii]

Did you know?

About 40 percent of all children in the United States will live with their single mother (never-married or divorced) and her boyfriend at some point before their 16th birthday.[iii]

Did you know?

Every day, 8,000 teenagers in the United States become infected with a sexually transmitted disease.[iv]

Notes & Nuggets: The "Wednesday audiences" are the Pope's weekly addresses to visitors gathered in St. Peter's Square. John Paul II used these opportunities to give reflections on Scripture, to greet visitors from around the world, and to teach the faith.

Notes & Nuggets: It's no secret that many high school students are suspicious of the stories found in the book of Genesis. Whether through secular or catechetical misinformation and disorientation, many teens believe that Adam and Eve weren't real people. Some of them lump the story of original sin into the same mental compartment that holds other catechetical missteps, such as the Exodus story being a gross exaggeration based upon the probability that a few Israelites escaped Egypt with the help of some coincidental natural phenomenon. To put all this into context and to give yourself the greatest handle on how to approach the book of Genesis and the truth found within it, we recommend you review the *Catechism of the Catholic Church,* paragraphs 355-421.

For your students, it may be helpful to offer the following analogy: Consider the difference between the approach that an optometrist takes when he looks into a woman's eyes, and the way that same woman's husband looks into her eyes. Both men look into the same eyes and have vastly different approaches and appreciations for the depth and beauty of the woman's eyes. One is looking with the eyes of a scientist; the other is looking with the eyes of a lover. This is analogous to how we can and should look at the book of Genesis.

The Church looks at Genesis differently than secular historians. While historians search for precise information detailing a chronological account of the events in Genesis, the Church looks to Genesis for the truth that it imparts about all of humanity, which is rooted in the story of Adam and Eve. In short, the Church is looking for the "truth behind the words." That said, it is also important to remember that Jesus referenced the reality of the story of Adam and Eve, even if He didn't refer to them by name (Mt 19:4-5).

so, we will discover the true purpose of our sexual gifts. We will see what went wrong and find the hope that will lead us back to true love and happiness.

 TO THE CORE

Pope John Paul II (1920–2005) dedicated 129 of his "Wednesday audiences" during the first six years of his papacy (1979 to 1984) to a series of talks about the human body and sexuality. These addresses were later compiled into book form, creating the first major teaching of John Paul II. This teaching is called the **Theology of the Body**, and an international surge of interest has followed its proclamation.

The Theology of the Body explores the meaning of our bodies and of sexual desire as it relates to the purpose of our existence. Philosophers have asked questions about the meaning of life for thousands of years. If you've ever wondered, "Who am I? What is my purpose in life? What is love all about?", you are asking very good questions. Answering these questions was a major goal of John Paul II through his teaching of the Theology of the Body. After all, he was not just a great pope but also a great philosopher.

So, what is **theology**? Theology may be understood as the study of God. St. Anselm, an eleventh-century philosopher, theologian, and archbishop, called it "faith seeking understanding." The word theology can be broken down like this: In Greek *theos* means "God" and *logos* means "word." Logos was also defined by the ancient Greeks in other ways that relate to "science" and "study." (Notice that our modern words which have "-ology" at the end of them refer to some type of study: biology, archaeology, radiology, psychology, etc.) So, the Theology of the Body is the study of God as revealed through our bodies.[1]

By looking at the creation of Adam and Eve in the book of Genesis, we begin to find the answers to our questions about the purpose of life.

Love Equals Communion

In Genesis 1:26-31 we learn that when God made man and woman it was "very good." They were made in his "image and likeness." We may hear that phrase often but let's consider what it means: The Bible says "God is love" (1 Jn 4:8). Now, when love is present, it is never in isolation. This is why a person can't marry himself. Rather, whenever you have love, you must have a lover, a beloved, and the love between them. There must be a communion of persons, united in love. A communion of persons is created when two or more persons give themselves to one another in love. So, in the case of God, you have the Father, the Son, and the fire of love between them, which is the Holy Spirit.[2]

As a "communion of persons," God created humans to participate in heaven and on earth in God's love. This means that God created us male and female

"Then God said:
'Let us make man in our image,
after our likeness.
Let them have
dominion over
the fish of the sea,
the birds of the air, and the
cattle, and over all the wild
animals and all the creatures
that crawl on the ground.'

God created man
in his image;
in the divine image
he created him; male and
female he created them."
– Gn 1:26-27

Notes & Nuggets: To help your students further understand how our bodies act as visible signs of the invisible, help them through this quote from John Paul II. Write it on the board, and then create a list on the other side of the board of things that we know are real but that are invisible to the naked eye. Challenge them to offer examples, and include the following in your list:

"INVISIBLE" THINGS:

- Thoughts
- Feelings
- Gravity
- Wind
- Heat/Cold
- Trust/Faith
- God (keep for last)

After compiling the list, pick out a few and point out that these are all things we cannot see. They are "invisible," but there are signs that help us to know they are all real; though we cannot see them, we can see their effects. Draw arrows from the list on the left to a new list of corresponding signs of the invisible realities.

For example, we cannot see gravity, but we all know it exists, because whenever we throw a ball, it lands on the ground again. We can't see the wind, but we can see trees bending from it and houses destroyed by it in hurricanes. Feelings of fear, courage, pain, sadness, and joy are all very real, but they are invisible in themselves; instead, we see visible signs of them: smiles, frowns, crying, laughing, etc. Now make the connection to God. He is invisible, but our visible bodies tell us something about the invisible mystery of God.

You may want to finish with this example: since God is invisible, He has given us bodies to help one another learn about Him. The fact is that the authors of this program can type these words, and God has enabled you to read with your eyes, transmit the information to your brain, and therefore understand more about God and all that happens through the use of our bodies.

precisely so that we could image His love by becoming a sincere gift to each other.[3] Giving this sincere gift to one another creates a communion of persons, through which we share God's love with each other.

COMPREHENSION & DISCUSSION QUESTIONS

1. What is *theology*?

2. What was the goal of John Paul II in his teaching of the Theology of the Body?

3. What do you think our society believes and teaches us about the meaning of our bodies?

4. Where in Scripture does it say that our bodies are very good?

5. Why do you think some people believe our bodies are bad?

6. How is a *communion of persons* formed?

The Catechism of the Catholic Church *teaches us that "God himself is an eternal exchange of love…and He has destined us to share in that exchange"* (CCC 221).

Not Meant to Be Alone

When God said that Adam and Eve were made in His image and likeness, one thing this meant was that they were designed for love. But when Adam was created, he was without Eve. But even before Eve was created, Adam knew something was missing. As a result, God said, "It is not good that the man should be alone" (Gn 1:18).

Since we're made in God's image and likeness, the Church teaches that, "Man can fully discover his true self only in a sincere gift of self."[4] In order to give to someone else, one must not be alone. *Someone else* is there for communion. This total gift of self can be seen in the married life or in the **celibate life**, which is *choosing* to forego earthly marriage so as to devote oneself entirely to the marriage of Christ and the Church. In both cases, marriage and **celibacy**, we are called to make ourselves living sacrifices. In the words of Blessed Mother Teresa, "Life is not worth living unless it is lived for others."

John Paul II's vision of the body is a key to understanding the meaning of our lives. This short quote summarizes his view of the body as a visible sign that points to things that are invisible:

> The body, in fact, and it alone is capable of making visible what is invisible: the spiritual and divine. It was created to transfer into the visible reality of the world the mystery [of God]… and thus to be a sign of it.[5]

Although we cannot see God, our bodies reveal many amazing truths about Him, because we are made in His "image and likeness." For example, just as a

sacrament makes a spiritual reality (grace) visible, the body makes our call to love visible. This is what John Paul II refers to as the **sacramentality of the body**. Just as a sign on the side of a road points you to something in reality, our bodies point us to the meaning of life. Our bodies and their desires are very good signs of God's existence, of His love for us, and of our call to love others!

More Than Human Love

But God is not simply calling us to love one another. Our most intimate human love actually points us to the love that we were ultimately created for: union with God (here and in heaven). It may be hard to believe that God desires an intimate relationship with you, especially if you've been through a lot of suffering in your life. You may not even believe that God loves you. But don't forget that the man who gave us the Theology of the Body, John Paul II, was no stranger to suffering and death. First his sister died, then his mother, then his brother, then his father, and then many of his friends … all by the time he was twenty years old. As a young man, he witnessed the brutality of the Nazis in World War II and was forced to take a deep look at the heart of man and the meaning of life. Through his prayer, personal suffering, and study, Pope John Paul II learned that God had not abandoned man. Rather, he saw that God has a plan of hope and freedom for each one of us.

COMPREHENSION & DISCUSSION QUESTIONS

1. What does John Paul II mean by the *sacramentality of the body*?

2. How do you think our culture views the body? List three examples.

3. Give your own example of a *visible reality* that points to an *invisible one*.

4. What is your deepest question about life?

DIGGING DEEPER: Who am I?

Have you ever heard the expression, "Know thyself"? If you have seen the movie *The Matrix,* you may recall a scene where Neo (Keanu Reeves) is first introduced to the Oracle. In this important meeting, the Oracle points to a phrase carved on a piece of wood hanging over her kitchen door which reads, "Know thyself." The advice would become a turning point in Neo's life. It should be a turning point in our lives, too.

notes

APPLICATION: GOD LOVES PLAY-DOH

Provide the teens with Play-Doh or another type of modeling clay. Ask them to sculpt their concept of God and their relationship with Him. Remind them that God is a "communion of persons" and that He created us to share in His eternal exchange of love. Encourage them to be honest and to create something that represents their present (and possibly future) relationship with God. Take the time to create your own model prior to class that day. Share your model with your students, describing its meaning before they begin modeling their own. Then, as they begin modeling, move around to help give ideas to those teens who seem "stumped." If time allows, have them all share what they created and why.

The goal is to have teens create scenes that may bring comments and explanations wherein they honestly let you know where they see themselves in their walk with the Lord. It is important to remember that there are no "wrong answers" here. If the teens are honest, then whatever they depict–assuming it is not improper or vulgar–is acceptable. You may find students coming up with symbols or comments like these:

- "My relationship with God is on and off, so I made a light switch"

- "My relationship with God is supposed to be one of communion, but I don't think I'm there yet, so this is me still walking up the aisle."

- "Here's me and there's God over there–the maze between us shows that I want to get closer to Him, but I can't figure out how yet."

- "This broken-down car represents me without God. I'm on empty; but I'm heading to the gas station, which is Mass, where I know God is going to fill me up with His grace."

- "This is me in a chapel praying, and there is God outside the Church. You'll notice He has no ears, because God never answers my prayers."

- "This is me helping at a soup kitchen, and this is little Sally who comes every Saturday to get food. When I serve her, I feel like I can see God in her eyes. I feel closest to God when I help others."

- "This is a ball of clay that represents the world. There's nothing else in my picture because I'm an atheist and don't believe God exists."

- "This is my grandmother saying her rosary in her rocking chair. This is me doing a puzzle, trying to figure out if the stuff my parents and grandma teach me is real."

- "This is me with a big smile because I just came out of reconciliation. I feel closest to God after that."

- "This is my brother lying dead from cancer. This is me walking away from the Church because I don't believe in a loving God anymore."

As a teacher, pay very close attention to what your students do with this activity. It may give you helpful hints about their world, their beliefs, their struggles, and their sources of either joy or pain. Remember to watch for these particulars, which may give you hints about how to best minister to them throughout the program:

- Did the picture focus more on themselves or on God?

- Did they make God out to be someone far away and unapproachable?

- On what characteristics of God did they focus? Did Jesus enter the picture at all?

- Was their picture generally hopeful or filled with despair or confusion?

The idea of knowing ourselves opens up to us an ocean of questions about the purpose of our existence. Such questions have captivated man since ancient times.

Who am I? Where have I come from? Where am I going? John Paul II, who often thought about these questions, called them "fundamental questions which pervade human life … These are the questions which we find in the sacred writings of Israel … in the poetry of Homer and in the tragedies of Euripides and Sophocles … in the philosophical writings of Plato and Aristotle. They are questions which have their common source in the quest for meaning which has always compelled the human heart. In fact, the answer given to these questions decides the direction which people seek to give to their lives."[6]

The question must now be turned to you, "Who are you?"

Even if you have not given this question much thought, you are in some way already answering it. Your actions say much about who you understand yourself to be. What answer have you made and where is your path leading you? Your path is probably leading you toward the desires of your heart. The truth is that, "God has placed in the human heart a desire to know the truth—in a word, to know Himself—so that, by knowing and loving God, men and women may also come to the fullness of truth about themselves."[7] To confirm this truth, just think about how angry it makes you feel when someone lies to you. You don't want lies. Your heart desires the truth, even if you do not consciously realize that you desire it.

You may wonder what your body and sexuality have to do with knowing yourself. Well, consider how the desire of your heart to know the truth is actually expressed on a daily basis. Your *body* expresses your very essence (your person) as well as your desires. This is why John Paul II taught that through the lens of love and God's plan for sexual union, we can rediscover "the meaning of the whole of existence, the meaning of life."[8] He is saying that, through and in our bodies, we can learn the meaning of existence. That's a powerful statement, and it is why we have written this program.

If our hearts desire the truth, and Jesus is revealed as "the truth" ("I am the way, the truth, and the life"—see John 14:6), then our hearts ultimately desire Jesus. Christianity is not afraid to proclaim that the ultimate knowledge of self lies in the mystery of the "Word made flesh,"[9] Jesus Christ. He is true God and *true man*, the one in and through whom everything was made, revealing to us "who" we are and "why" we are here. Using one of John Paul II's favorite phrases from the Second Vatican Council, "it is Jesus, the Son of God, *who fully reveals man to himself* and brings to light *his most high calling*."[10]

notes

It is Jesus who first calls to us, saying "know thyself." He challenges us to learn the truth of our existence and to direct our lives toward the purpose of the loving communion for which we have been created. He knows that our fulfillment cannot be found in lies but in truth. God, who is a perfect communion in the blessed Trinity, created us to be in communion with Him. This relationship with God "is defined by that unique fact that the more deeply I abandon myself to Him, the more completely I let Him penetrate my being, the more powerfully He, the Creator, gains authority in me, the more *I become myself.*"[11]

So, the great command to be given is to *become who you are*. In the movie trilogy, *The Lord of the Rings*, this call is given directly to Aragorn in the *The Return of the King*. Aragorn is the heir to the throne of his kingdom, but he has not accepted responsibility for it yet. When in the midst of the greatest challenge facing Middle Earth, Lord Elrond has re-forged the sword of the king, he presents it to Aragorn with the words, "Put aside the 'ranger.' *Become who you were born to be!*" Just like Aragorn, if we set aside the lies that we have believed about ourselves and embrace the reality of our life in Christ, we can claim and proclaim with boldness the truth of who we really are.

Read these inspiring words of John Paul II and see if they speak to you, even as a faint echo in your heart:

> It is Jesus that you seek when you dream of happiness; He is waiting for you when nothing else you find satisfies you; He is the beauty to which you are so attracted; it is He who provoked you with that thirst for fullness that will not let you settle for compromise; it is He who urges you to shed the masks of a false life; it is He who reads in your hearts your most genuine choices, the choices that others try to stifle.

> It is Jesus who stirs in you the desire to do something great with your lives, the will to follow an ideal, the refusal to allow yourselves to be ground down by mediocrity, the courage to commit yourselves humbly and patiently to improving yourselves and society, making the world more human and more fraternal.

> *– Pope John Paul II, World Youth Day, Rome 2000*

You Decide

In whose vision of life do you think true happiness is found?

Weezer, from the song "Tired of Sex"

"I'm tired, so tired. I'm tired of having sex. So tired. I'm spread so thin. I don't know who I am. Monday night I'm makin' Jen. Tuesday night I'm makin' Lyn. Wednesday night I'm makin' Catherine. Oh, why can't I be makin' Love come true?"

vs.

Pope John Paul II

"The person who does not decide to love forever will find it very difficult to really love for even one day."

Understanding the propulsion system on a space shuttle…

Having a working knowledge of the new tax laws governing foreign trade…

Knowing how to properly care for a beached whale…

These are not situations that the average person really needs to know much about. To be ignorant of any one of these facts—or millions of others like them—does not render one stupid or lazy. That being said…

Knowing how to shut off the water to an overflowing toilet…

Knowing how to perform the Heimlich maneuver on a person who is choking…

Knowing how to ask for the nearest clean restroom in a foreign country…

These are all situations in which a little bit of knowledge can go a long way. To be ignorant in one of these moments could be disastrous—or at least messy.

Sure, if you *wanted* to learn about the physics of a shuttle launch, or the ramifications of changes in tax laws, or how to take care of a whale, you're usually just one book, one click, or one seminar away. Again, these issues might be interesting, but they really are not necessary to the average person's everyday happiness. You can choose to remain ignorant when it comes to several areas of life and your world will just keep on spinning.

But remaining ignorant on "the purpose of your life" is an entirely different matter. Knowing your purpose in life and living it out will determine your future on earth as well as your eternity after death. That's an amazing concept worthy of your attention.

As you study this curriculum, you will have a choice each day of whether to be open-minded as you read. You'll also have the choice of whether to be open to change in your life. If you have an open heart, you will grow in wisdom and knowledge before God and man. The truth you find in these pages will bring challenges, but also great satisfaction. And remember that God will never offer you a challenge without also offering you every grace needed to overcome it.

In short, if you take what you learn in this workbook and apply it, in a practical way, your life is going to change … for the better. This is a crash course in love, in truth,

and in authentic freedom. In these "live it out" sections, you will be offered encouragement and practical ideas of things you can do with your body that will have an everlasting impact on your soul. That will help the "head knowledge" you gain on these pages become "heart knowledge" you retain for life.

So, what is the goal of your life? What is it supposed to be? The answer is actually quite simple—it's living it that is the challenge. The answer is "to love." God calls us to this. This is what Christ lived. This is what the Holy Spirit makes possible. This is what the saints achieved.

But only after you have accepted the love of God can you share that love with others, freely and purely. So, here's your chance—your "Love 101" course starts today. Learn how to receive the love of God, and to allow that love to transform your life into something beautiful. (And guys, this is absolutely for you, too. Love is an extremely masculine thing. If you're looking for the ultimate challenge, try laying down your life—in big and small ways—for another. And then try doing it day in and day out. You'll find if you get married, for example, that the test of a real man involves "dying to yourself" every day. We'll say more about this later.)

If you ask, "Why am I here?", know that God created you to love and to be loved. As Christ said, "Love one another, even as I have loved you" (Jn 13:34). Want to know God's expectations for you? Consider Micah 6:8: "What does the Lord require of you but to do justice, and to love kindness, and to walk humbly with your God?"

God loves you more than you love yourself. Doubt it? Read John 15:13: "Greater love has no man than this, that a man lay down his life for his friends."

The verses listed above are to be prayed through…that's how you will start to *live it out* in a real, practical way.

Here's one final idea before we move forward: next time you see a crucifix, consider the fact that you have a God who loves you so much that He would rather die than spend eternity without you.

Notes & Nuggets: If you have the opportunity to take your teens to a church or adoration chapel, this prayer and journal activity would be an excellent, prayerful way to begin a time of quiet reflection or adoration of the Blessed Sacrament. This is also a great time for you to dedicate your teaching of the Theology of the Body to God through prayer before the Body of Christ in the Eucharist.

Notes & Nuggets: Explain up front to the students whether you intend to read their journals or not. Most states have laws that bind you as a teacher (if you collect the journals) to read them in their entirety. If you are not sure of the laws in your state, check with a counselor at your school or the pastor at your parish. In addition, if there is anything within the journal that incriminates the student or someone else in a crime, suggests suicidal tendencies, or hints of abuse of any sort, you are bound by law to report it to the proper authorities. You may choose to check the journals during class (without collecting and reading them), to see that they have been done. There are benefits to reading the journals, but with that reading comes much responsibility.

MOVIE CLIP/SONG SUGGESTIONS

MOVIE CLIPS:

1. ***The Return of the King:*** Show the segment between 1:15:48 and 1:17:35. (Note: The time code we are providing here is from the second disc of the extended version.) Frodo and his best friend, Sam, are on a mission together. Frodo has had to carry the burden of the ring and just can't go on. Sam tells him that he can't carry the ring for him, but he can carry Frodo. It could be said that their friendship resembles the relationship between God and His creation. God created us with a purpose, and while He will not accomplish our mission for us, He is always there offering us grace. He is a faithful friend ready to help us at every turn.

2. ***Signs:*** Show the segment between 1:25:56 and 1:39:28. (Note: This scene is a little scary.) This clip can be used to convey the section about finding one's purpose in life. Mel Gibson's character finds out the truth about his purpose in life.

3. ***The Day after Tomorrow:*** Show the segment between 1:44:03 and 1:50:23. This scene demonstrates the power of family love. Dennis Quaid's character vows against all odds that he will find his son. His son never doubted that his father would come to rescue him.

SONGS:

1. ***Not Home Yet*** — Steven Curtis Chapman *(Greatest Hits)*

This song stresses the need to remember we are not home until we are in heaven. Contemporary.

2. ***Meant to Live*** — Switchfoot *(The Beautiful Letdown)*

The singer wonders what life is about as he explains that we are meant to live for heaven. Hard/ Alternative Rock.

3. ***Wait for Me*** — Rebecca St. James *(Transform)*

A call to one's future spouse to "wait" for the right time for love: marriage. Note: This song is extremely popular with girls. Pop/Contemporary.

PRAYER & JOURNAL ACTIVITY

→ **Read:** Quietly and slowly read the following meditation.

Everyone longs to give himself or herself completely to someone, to have a deep and committed soul relationship with another. We want to be loved thoroughly and unconditionally. But God says:

Wait until you are satisfied, fulfilled, and content with being loved by Me alone, with giving yourself totally, unreservedly to Me alone.

I love you, my child. But until you discover that only in Me is your satisfaction to be found, you will not be capable of the perfect human relationship that I have planned for you. You will never be united with another as you desire to be until you are united with Me, exclusive of anyone or anything else, exclusive of any other desires and belongings.

I want you to stop planning and stop wishing, and allow Me to give you the most thrilling plan that exists—one that you can't imagine. I want you to have the very best. Please allow Me to bring it to you.

Just keep your eyes on Me, expecting the greatest things.
Keep experiencing that satisfaction knowing that I AM.
Keep learning and listening to the things I tell you.
You must be patient.

Don't be anxious.
Don't worry.
Don't look around at the things others have.
Don't look at the things you think you want.
Just keep looking to Me, or you will miss what I want to give you.

And then, when you are ready, I will surprise you with a love far more wonderful than you could ever dream. You see, until you are ready, and until the one I have for you is ready ... until you are both satisfied exclusively with Me and the life I have prepared for you, you won't be able to experience the love that exemplifies your relationship with Me ... and this is perfect love.
(Anonymous Prayer)

Pray: Take a few minutes to reflect silently on what God is saying to you in your heart.

Respond: Use your journal to respond to this amazing love that God has for you. If it helps you, read through the meditation again (written from God's point of view) and respond to each of the sections.

"Chastity is a difficult, long-term matter; one must wait patiently for it to bear fruit, for the happiness of loving kindness which it must bring. But at the same time, chastity is the sure way to happiness."

– Pope John Paul II

4. *Voice of Truth* — Casting Crowns *(Self-titled release)*

This one is about believing Jesus, the "voice of truth" above all other doubts and lies. Contemporary/ Rock.

5. *Dangerous Wonder* — Curtis Stephan *(Sacred Revolution)*

This song helps us to rejoice in the fact that we are made in the image and likeness of God. Pop/ Rock.

6. *Big Enough* — Chris Rice *(Past The Edges)*

This is about facing doubt, having lots of questions and asking God about them. Folk/Easy Listening.

7. *I Still Haven't Found What I'm Looking For* — U2 *(Joshua Tree)*

Journey of searching near and far, knowing what Jesus did and still not being convinced it is what we need. Suggestions in the song are made that connect sexuality with eternity. His "burning desire" is more than just a physical thing. He knows he is meant for more, but he is confused. Pop/Rock.

7. *God of Grace* — Adam Watts *(Noise Inside)*

Our God is a God of grace and love and He is there whenever we need Him. Pop/Rock.

8. *God is Love* — John Reuben *(Are We There Yet?)*

God is love and love is God. If we focus on Him we will be love. Hip-Hop Ballad.

Notes & Nuggets: This project is only a possibility if you can break teens into groups and have access to video cameras. It will be worth the effort as the teens will really enjoy this exercise. Get permission from your parish or school to have video cameras on campus.

Notes & Nuggets: We chose to ask the Blessed Mother for her intercession because she beautifully exhibits for us the teaching of John Paul II on the Theology of the Body. She made a perfect gift of herself through her body, and she was perfectly pure. She is a model for holiness for us all.

WORK IT OUT

Assignment #1: Draw a picture, write a poem, or write a song that creatively helps others realize why men and women do not make sense without the other—the two were made for union with each other. What would the world be like if there were no women? What if there were no men? Creatively include the text of Genesis 2:24 at some point in your creation. By the simple realization of our need for each other, we can also recognize that we were made for communion with each other.

Assignment #2: Use the terms from the glossary at the end of the chapter and go online to create your own crossword puzzle or word search that other students could use to help them better learn the many definitions in this chapter.

Assignment #3: Dig into the primary text of Pope John Paul II's Theology of the Body from November 14, 1979, which focuses on man imaging God through the communion of persons. Write a summary essay of the address.

❖

Project #1: Create your own "man on the street" video. Go to your cafeteria or a school sporting event to ask the following question: What is the meaning of life? After taping ten responses from people in different age groups, get on camera yourself and give a verbal summary of what you heard. Then give your own one minute answer to the same question.

CLOSING PRAYER

Leader: In the name of the Father, and of the Son, and of the Holy Spirit. **Amen.**

***Leader or Reader #1:* O Blessed Virgin and Mother Mary**, please pray with me that I, like you, can live a life of perfect love. Help me to live a life worthy of returning to the One Who created me in love and for love. Please pray that I, like you, will live as a sinless and perfect vessel of the Holy Spirit.

Leader or Reader #2: Let us pray together: Hail Mary, full of grace, the Lord is with you. Blessed are you among women, and blessed is the fruit of your womb, Jesus. Holy Mary, Mother of God, pray for us sinners, now and at the hour of our death. Amen. Saint (patron saint of your church or school), pray for us. In the name of the Father, and of the Son, and of the Holy Spirit. **Amen.**

IN HIS OWN WORDS

- **On the Body in "Theology":** "Through the fact that the Word of God became flesh, the body entered theology through the main door. The Incarnation and the redemption that springs from it became also the definitive source of the sacramentality of marriage … " (April 2, 1980).

- **On imaging God in the Communion of Persons**: "Formed in the image of God, also inasmuch as they form a true communion of persons, the first man and the first woman must constitute the beginning and the model of that communion for all men and women, who, in any period, are united so intimately as to be one flesh" (November 21, 1979).

- "Man becomes the image of God not so much in the moment of solitude as in the moment of communion. Right 'from the beginning,' He is not only an image in which the solitude of a person who rules the world is reflected, but also, and essentially, an image of an inscrutable divine communion of persons" (November 14, 1979).

- **On Intimacy & Nakedness:** [Gen 2:25] "According to this passage, the man and the woman saw themselves, as it were, through the mystery of creation. They saw themselves in this way, before knowing that they were naked. …They see and know each other with all the peace of the interior gaze, which creates precisely the fullness of the intimacy of the persons" (January 2, 1980).

- **On Original Happiness:** "Happiness is being rooted in love. Original happiness speaks to us of the beginning of man, who emerged from love and initiated love. That happened in an irrevocable way, despite the subsequent sin and death … This beginning can also be defined as the original and beatifying immunity from shame as the result of love" (January 30, 1980).

- "The revelation and discovery of the nuptial meaning of the body explain man's original happiness" (January 16, 1980).

- **On the Sacramentality of the Body:** "The sacrament, as a visible sign, is constituted with man, as a body, by means of his visible masculinity and femininity. The body, and it alone, is capable of making visible what is invisible: the spiritual and the divine. It was created to transfer into the visible reality of the world the mystery hidden since time immemorial in God, and thus be a sign of it" (February 20, 1980).

- **On Communion and Marriage:** "Against this vast background we understand fully the words that constitute the sacrament of marriage, present in Genesis 2:24: 'A man leaves his father and his mother and cleaves to his wife, and they become one flesh'" (February 20, 1980).

- "Therefore, in his original situation man is alone and at the same time he becomes male and female–unity of the two. In his solitude he is revealed to himself as a person, in order to reveal, at the same time, the communion of persons in the unity of the two … In the unity of the couple he becomes male and female, discovering the nuptial meaning of his body as a personal subject" (January 13, 1982).

Glossary
of Key Terms

Celibacy (celibate life): Freely choosing to forego earthly marriage "for the sake of the kingdom of heaven" (Mt 19:12), that is, for the sake of the heavenly marriage of Christ and the Church. Celibate people "consecrate themselves with undivided heart to the Lord and to 'the affairs of the Lord'" (CCC 1579, 1 Cor 7:32).

Communion of persons: The "common union" between two or more persons who give themselves to one another in love; they see in each other the image and likeness of God and want the best for the other. John Paul II refers to the unity of Adam and Eve as the "prototype" for the communion of persons, through which man and woman become more fully the image of God.

Concupiscence: The "inclination to sin" that is present in all humans, inherited through the sin of Adam and Eve, and against which we must struggle to resist "by the grace of Jesus Christ" (CCC 1264). While it inclines us to sin and comes from sin, concupiscence itself is not a sin.

Despair: The opposite of hope, despair is the resolve to give up pursuing whatever was initially pursued. In the case of relationships in our culture, many people despair, thinking that the possibility of finding loving, faithful relationships is impossible. But with God there is always hope, and in Him we find the keys to building loving, life-giving relationships that last.

Dignity: The inherent and unchanging value of all persons as a direct result of their being created by God in His image and likeness.

Love: A decision to "will the good of another" person (St. Thomas Aquinas, as quoted in CCC 1766). John Paul II echoes this same definition in much of his writing on love, and adds that love involves a sincere gift of oneself to others.

Lust: It is "disordered desire for or inordinate enjoyment of sexual pleasure" (CCC 2351). It is sexual desire apart from God's love—a selfish desire that seeks one's own pleasure at the expense of another.

Original sin: The first sin of mankind against God, when Adam and Eve chose to disobey God's command and do what they wanted instead. This choice affected all of humanity, giving us all a tendency to sin, a disordered desire to break God's law, and a world prone to suffering and struggles of all kinds—including death.

Sacrament: A sacrament makes a spiritual reality visible to us. It is an outward sign "instituted by Christ and entrusted to the Church by which divine life [grace] is dispensed to us" (CCC 1131).

Sacramentality of the body: The inherent ability of the body to act as a visible sign of God's invisible love.

Sexual liberation: The common term for escaping sexual "rules" so as to do whatever one wants with his or her sexuality. In reality, this liberation is not sexual freedom but an excuse to use sexuality as a form of recreation, often leading to the slavery of sexual addiction and a life of emptiness and broken relationships.

Theology: The study of God, or "faith seeking understanding" (St. Anselm). The word comes from the Greek words *Theos* (God) and *logos* (word). Theology is its own science of faithful study, seeking to understand God and His word.

Theology of the Body: A study of God and the purpose of our existence, as discovered and revealed through our bodies.

OBJECTIVES At the end of this lesson, the student should know and be able to:

- Define and explain the nature of love.
- Identify the differences between self-donating love as *"giving"* and self-indulgent "love" as *"using."*
- Explain the difference between abstinence and chastity.
- Recognize chastity as a way to happiness.
- Recognize love as the only proper attitude (or response) toward another person and explain why.
- Test the quality of a relationship based upon the difference between "giving" and "using."
- Differentiate between love and lust.

Notes & Nuggets: Pray today that your students would be open to seeing that many of their ideas about love may be shallow or misdirected. Pray also that you would be able to be a model of authentic love for them, and that your love would attract them to want to learn more.

Notes & Nuggets: It may be a good idea to explain to your students that many analogies will be used throughout this curriculum, as well as throughout your own teaching. It is important to understand, though, that the point of using an analogy is to make use of a simple idea or word picture that is easy to grasp so that your students can make deeper connections. Analogies help us make the complex simpler. That said, analogies used to describe the attributes and actions of God always fall short because there is no way for a finite concept to fully contain an infinite God. In fact, St. Thomas Aquinas said that we can say more about what God is not (*via negativa*) than we can in describing what He is (*via positiva*).

For example, when we say God's love is like an ocean (meaning it is "deep" and "wide"), the reality is that God's love is actually more unlike an ocean than it is like it. But the word picture helps us to understand the concept that God's love is vast and stretches beyond the parameters in which we place it. But do not assume that your students will understand this concept. Explain it to them. This is especially important when applying the analogy of spousal union to God and His love. God is not sexual. But our sexuality does reveal something of His divine mystery.

Love Defined:
Giving versus Using

Imagine a coach who says to his players, "If you don't feel like coming to practice, then don't come. Do whatever feels right." The team would soon become a confused bunch of people who share a love for their sport but also a total lack of commitment to it. Such a free-wheeling approach to the sport would lead to division within the group and a loss of common vision and cooperation. On the night of their big game, the players would run the wrong plays, miss their assignments, make mental mistakes, and suffer as a team. Once the focus becomes the *pleasure of the individuals* instead of the *success of the team*, the players certainly will *not* achieve the cohesive teamwork that usually brings victory.

✻

Deep in our hearts, each of us wants to give and receive love, but most of us don't know *how* to do this. In the first chapter, we established that many people today have a confused idea about love and the purpose of our sexuality. One major reason for this confusion is that we make so many decisions because they "feel good" and not because they are rooted in truth. Basing decisions primarily on feelings can cause real problems, as feelings are fleeting and can easily change from one moment to the next. Truth, however, is stable and reliable.

In order for people to love one another properly, they must first desire what is good for the other person. In this chapter, you will discover what authentic love looks like and learn the difference between "love" that is *self-seeking*—that is actually lust—and real love that is *self-donating*.

(optional): "Telephone"

Introduce your teens to the simple and classic game of "telephone." Preface the game by explaining the monumental importance of listening carefully in this game. Set the rule that the phrase sent through the "human telephone line" may not be repeated. It is to be said only one time, then repeated to the next person. You start the game by sending out the first message with something silly like, "There's a bee in your ear. Can you feel it?" (or make up your own silly phrase). Keep in mind that the more ridiculous the statement, the harder it becomes to get it right because there is no logic to it. Based on the success of the group, move on to harder phrases such as, "Mrs. Piggy drives with her feet on the dashboard and her hands out the sunroof" or "My shoes are leaking motor oil and I'm hungry for some alligator." Finally, let the teens make up their own crazy phrase. To keep things from getting out of hand after you turn it over to them, make sure you are the first one that the "creator" of the new line has to send his or her message through on the chain.

- **COMPETITIVE TWIST:** To make it into more of a competition, break the students into two groups and pit them against one another with the same phrase. See which team can send the message through the quickest and with the most accuracy. Set your own point system for number of words that arrive correctly to the end of the line as well as certain points for quickness against the clock (you can time it with a stopwatch or digital watch to be exact).

- **DISCUSS:** At the conclusion of the game (or later in the lesson), you can make the connection to the concept of love. The connection is that love involves not only receiving but giving in a right manner. Obviously, it also takes teamwork– working toward a common good together. This is love. Was the game easy? Neither is love.

TWO MINUTE DRILL — VERBAL REVIEW:

1. What is theology?
   Answer: It can be simply defined as the study of God, or as St. Anselm taught, "faith seeking understanding."
2. What can Pope John Paul II's Theology of the Body teach us?
   Answer: By reflecting on the human body, its origin, and its purpose, we can learn God's purpose for our lives and ultimately find true love and happiness.
3. What does JPII mean by the "sacramentality of the body"?
   Answer: The body is a visible sign for us of invisible realities concerning God and the deepest meaning of our existence. Our bodies make the invisible love of God visible.
4. Why did God create us?
   Answer: He created us freely out of love. He made us for loving communion with each other and destined us to be in a loving relationship with Him forever in heaven. In other words, He created us to share in His own eternal bliss.

OPENING PRAYER

Leader: In the name of the Father, and of the Son, and of the Holy Spirit. **Amen**.

(Option #1)

Leader or Reader #1: Read Philippians 2:5b-11

"Christ Jesus, ... though he was in the form of God, did not count equality with God a thing to be grasped, but emptied himself, taking the form of a servant, being born in the likeness of men. And being found in human form, he humbled himself and became obedient unto death, even death on a cross. Therefore, God has highly exalted him and bestowed upon him the name which is above every name, that at the name of Jesus every knee should bow, in heaven and on earth and under the earth, and every tongue confess that Jesus Christ is Lord, to the glory of God the Father."

Leader or Reader #2: Father, help us to examine our hearts. Help us to love others as You love them, and not see people as a means to our own ends but, rather, as unrepeatable human beings endowed with a God-like dignity. Help us learn to give ourselves as You desire us to give. We ask this in your name, Jesus. **Amen**.

(Option #2)

Leader or Reader #1: Read Philippians 2:5b-11 (above, in Option #1)

Leader or Reader #2: Lord, as You emptied Yourself for us upon the cross, teach us to give ourselves totally to You and to others. Help us to sacrifice for those we love, to say "yes" to the generosity of the Holy Spirit at work in us, and "no" to every temptation of selfishness. Let us pray together the prayer of St. Francis of Assisi:

> Lord, make me an instrument of your peace.
> Where there is hatred, let me sow love;
> where there is injury, pardon;
> where there is doubt, faith;
> where there is despair, hope;
> where there is darkness, light;
> and where there is sadness, joy.
>
> O, Divine Master,
> grant that I may not so much seek
> to be consoled as to console;
> to be understood as to understand;
> to be loved as to love;
> for it is in giving that we receive;
> it is in pardoning that we are pardoned;
> and it is in dying that we are born to eternal life.
> **Amen.**

Need a Review of Lesson 1? Look to next page.

STORY STARTER: Searching for Happiness in a "Hook Up" World

**Verbal Review
of Lesson 1**

1. What is theology?

2. What can Pope John Paul II's "Theology of the Body" teach us?

3. What does JPII mean by the "sacramentality of the body"?

4. Why did God create us?

It was my senior year of college and I went on a study abroad program to beautiful Costa Rica, a peaceful country in Central America. One weekend we traveled to the Eastern coast to a port town called Limon, a town filled with drug trafficking, rampant alcohol abuse, loud reggae music, and wild parties. I was behaving myself rather well, and I made it through our first night there without getting into trouble. Since money was tight, we decided (unwisely) to rent one bamboo hut for the ten of us who were traveling together. Everyone had sleeping bags, and when we got in a little after midnight, we all settled in and prepared to go to sleep, except Jenny.

Jenny was a spunky girl with cool blue eyes that sparkled with playful mischief. When she laughed, everyone did. She skipped along more than she walked through her days, and her energy made me feel truly alive. She loved people and could light up a room with her smile. On this particular night, Jenny won the attention of two guys who were tourists from the East Coast of the United States. As I watched them flirting together, I could tell these were not the kind of guys who were going to ask her to go to church with them on Sunday. They were on the prowl. They thought Jenny was cute and they really wanted to "get to know her better." They drank beer, hugged her, and laughed with her for a few hours, and I was relieved when Jenny came back with us to the bamboo hut. But as I slid down into my sleeping bag, Jenny got up and whispered to me that she was going back out. I could smell the sweetness of the new perfume she had just put on, and my heart sank.

"Now?" I protested. "It's almost 1:00 a.m. and we're in a foreign country! Don't go out now."

"I'm just going to have some fun," she replied, but she paused for a moment, as if thinking it over again.

"C'mon, Jenny, don't do this!" I quietly pleaded as my other friends went to sleep. "I don't think they're the kind of guys you should be going out alone with."

"I'm a big girl," she said sarcastically with a smile, "I'll be back later." With that, she disappeared into the Costa Rican night.

I said a prayer, quickly fell asleep and then awoke at 4:00 a.m. when Jenny stumbled next to me in the darkness. She was quietly whimpering like a puppy that had been abandoned. I sat up and helped her find her sleeping bag, but sleep was not the answer for her that night. There, on the edge of the Atlantic Ocean on a dirt floor in a bamboo hut, Jenny put her head on my shoulder and cried. I didn't have the heart to even ask her what had happened. I didn't want to make her relive it. But I knew. She had been used and discarded.

notes

To this day, something in my gut tells me that she was not raped, but that she was certainly tricked, used sexually, and then tossed aside. They had gotten what they wanted, and she had been deceived, believing that they actually cared about her. They hadn't wanted to *give* her anything; they only wanted to *take*. They just wanted to *feel good*. Perhaps she thought they actually cared about *her—the person*—instead of just her body. Maybe she had hoped for love. Or perhaps she was just looking to have some fun, and ended up feeling the regret of using another and having been used. Either way, now she felt empty.

In frustration over the whole event, I clenched my fists with anger in the dark. I was angry at all men who took advantage of others. I didn't want to be associated with the male gender that night. I didn't want to be a part of any group that would rob a girl of her dignity, even if she had consented to being robbed. For the longest time, I could say nothing, and she could only cry in my arms. Finally, I whispered in her ear, "There is a better way, Jenny. There is a better way. Jesus loves you, and there is a better way."

– Brian Butler

COMPREHENSION & DISCUSSION QUESTIONS

1. Should the guy telling the story have tried harder to help Jenny before she went out? What could he have done?

2. What are some signs that someone may be a "user"?

3. What are some signs that someone can be trusted?

4. Why do you think Jenny went back out?

5. Do you think that some people get addicted to using others?

6. Have you ever felt used by someone in any way, instead of respected and loved?

7. Was Jenny's desire for love and acceptance unreasonable?

8. Why is using someone—sexually or for any other reason—such a serious sin?

9. Name three reasons why you think people allow themselves to be used.

10. How have guys and girls in our culture learned to use one another differently?

11. How can we make better decisions in this area?

23-L

BRIDGING THE GAP

The fact that there is a whole lot of "using" going on in today's high school relationships probably is not news to you. But have you ever thought about doing something about the using that you witness every day? What personal choices can we make to live a more sacrificial life—one in which others are respected—instead of simply making choices because they "feel good"?

Some teens aren't always sure how to differentiate between someone who *loves* and someone who *uses*. First, we must see that although there are many ways to love and give of ourselves, there are just as many ways to deceive, to use, and to live selfishly.

Many of the things we learn as children come from imitating what we see others doing, especially those in our families. Learning to love can be difficult when so many of us do not have excellent examples to learn from. This is a major reason why so many misunderstand what love really is. Without a "Love 101" course, we have to rely on our life experiences.

Hopefully, you are able to recognize that our culture has not helped us much with this concept of love. Sadly, our media was bombarding us with messages of sexual permissiveness before we even knew what sex was. Even worse, the culture and the media have been inviting us to "explore" our sexuality even before we understand sex at all.

The truth is that God made us to desire sex, and that is a good thing. Our sexual desire is not merely a hormonal reaction in our bodies, but a deeply rooted attraction to the beauty we see in others. Our sexual desire is a gift from God, who put the desire for union with another in us. God created us male and female so that we can learn to make a sincere gift of self to another. The union between man and woman is intended for marriage, which is a foreshadowing of the union that will ultimately satisfy us—the union with God in heaven. When teens start dating at thirteen, fourteen, and fifteen years old, they are often entering a ten- to fifteen-year period of dating, since most people don't marry until their late twenties or early thirties. Chastity is a challenge even when you are not dating. Spending ten to fifteen years in search of a spouse is a whole lot of time to stand on the edge of a cliff without ever falling off. In other words, our desires for union are very good, but we must respect them and learn to channel them into genuine love.

One of the discussion questions on the previous page asked you to discuss how guys and girls have learned to use one another differently. There are many different ways of using other people. For example, a guy may be praised in the locker room as a "pimp," a "player," or a "groomer" because he uses girls for getting sex. Meanwhile, a girl may "hook up" to try to find love, acceptance, social status, or mere physical affection. In either case, the pressure and the "using" often goes both ways.

Did You Know?

Many teens become sexually active because they want to show how much they like the other person. But did you know that 61 percent of teen sexual relationships end within three months, and 80 percent end within six months?[i]

Consider this teenager's experience of quick sexual pleasure which led him to emptiness: "I finally got a girl into bed (actually it was in a car) when I was seventeen. I thought it was the hottest thing there was, but then she started saying that she loved me and was getting clingy. I figured out that there had probably been a dozen other guys before me who thought that they had 'conquered' her, but who were really just objects of her need for security. That realization took all the wind out of my sails. I couldn't respect someone who gave in as easily as she did. I was amazed to find that after four weeks of having sex as often as I wanted, I was tired of her. I didn't see any point in continuing the relationship. I finally dumped her, which made me feel even worse because I could see that she was hurting. I felt pretty low."[1]

The heavy rock band, Offspring, sums up the situation in their song "Self-Esteem," when the lead singer hollers, *"Now I know I'm being used/That's OK, man, cause I like the abuse/I know she's playing with me/That's OK cause I got no self-esteem."* This way of using is so common in our world that many teenagers have come to expect it, to seek nothing more, and to hope for nothing deeper. This cycle of using others is an empty one that ultimately satisfies no one. It leads not only to confusion about love and sex in the teenage world but also to many adults thoughtlessly entering marriage.[2] However, there is hope. Get ready to learn about the better way!

 ## TO THE CORE

A popular men's magazine recently displayed several female models on the cover. Above the women was the headline: "The women we love!" The editors of the magazine were making the claim that the readers actually "loved" the women on the front cover because of their beauty. But could the readers of the magazine truly *love* these women? After all, the readers really didn't know these women personally; they had never even met them.

We often confuse love with simple attraction. This usually becomes a problem when the attraction fades away. Or, we may engage in deeply intimate acts with someone because our attractions are so strong—only to find out that we couldn't stand the idea of being with that person for the rest of our lives. What is it that draws a man and a woman together and sustains them when physical attraction is no longer there?

What is Love?

People talk about finding "true love," but what is it? Pope John Paul II explained: "For **love** is not merely a feeling; it is an act of will that consists of preferring, in a constant manner, the good of others to the good of oneself."[3] In other words, you can't judge the value of love by the intensity of the emotion. It's not enough to feel attractions or simply to want love. We must strive to know

notes

Notes & Nuggets: LOVE versus LUST Showdown

Before diving deeper into what love is all about, you may want to do a pre-test with your teens to figure out where they are in their understanding at this point. Write "LOVE =" in large letters on one side of the board and then "LUST =" in large letters on the other side of the board. Tell the class you are going to take a vote to see how they would define the two words on the board.

Ask your students to complete the following statements, while you circle the word for which most students vote. Undoubtedly, the right words of description will win the vote. If, by chance, they pick the words that do not match, then you have an opportunity to teach them the nature of love and lust.

LOVE = Committed or Uncommitted?

= Faithful or Unfaithful?

= Life-giving or Lifeless?

= Life-long or Temporary?

LUST = Generous or Selfish?

= Deep or Shallow?

= Sensitive or Insensitive?

= Pure or Impure?

After associating the right words with each term, review the following with your students:

- Love gives to the other.
- Lust uses the other.
- Love treats another person like a person!
- Lust treats another person like an object.
- Love cannot exist apart from its source, God.
- Lust is sexual desire apart from the love of God.
- Love is honest and life-giving to all persons involved.
- Lust is devious and ultimately destructive to all persons involved.
- Love seeks to do what is best for the other.
- Lust seeks to please the self.

what is best for the other, and then make an actual commitment of our wills to bring about this "good" for the other. A great place to begin learning how to love is to understand John Paul II's insights in his book ***Love and Responsibility***.

Like the Theology of the Body, *Love and Responsibility* grew out of a series of lectures that John Paul II gave from 1958 to 1959 (long before he was pope) when he was still known as Karol Wojtyla, a priest and professor at Catholic University in Poland. In this book, he defines love and links it to the virtue of chastity, saying that "chastity is the sure way to happiness."[4]

Chastity and Happiness

What exactly is chastity and why can it bring happiness? **Chastity** is the virtue that directs our sexual desires and attitudes toward the truth of love. (A **virtue** is a firm habit of doing what is good.) To view chastity as a positive virtue we must see that it is much more than **abstinence**, which means "not having sex."

Chastity falls under the cardinal virtue of **temperance**, which is the virtue of controlling and moderating our desire for pleasure, enabling us to enjoy pleasure in good things the way that God intends. But chastity is not merely learning to control one's desires. It is really about learning how to love another rightly. As seen in the title *Love and Responsibility*, John Paul II showed that a life of chastity is one that loves responsibly and purely, embracing the responsibility that comes with love, rather than running from it. Chastity says "yes" to the demands of love, while also fighting the selfish desires of lust. Only then can we say "no" to choices that actually rob us and others of their dignity.

If we bottle up our sexual energy and attempt to ignore it (as chastity is often caricatured by some in our culture), it can lead to repression, which is actually an unhealthy response to the sexual gift. **Sexual repression** can sometimes lead to a "slingshot effect," when a person allows himself or herself to get out of control and into reckless sexual behavior. So neither repression nor indulgence of lust is the proper response to the sexual gift. Neither is what God would intend for us. What He does call us to is a healthy chastity, through which we acknowledge the power of our sexual desires and guide them with the deeper desire to love. Chastity is seen and lived as a life-giving virtue; it leads to happiness. This is why the Church teaches us that, "man ... cannot fully find himself except through a sincere gift of himself."[5]

"Chastity means the successful integration of sexuality within the person and thus the inner unity of man in his bodily and spiritual being" (CCC 2337).

As we've shown, love is not just about feeling good, although this is a part of love. Love is an active decision. It is a decision to give oneself to another and to do so totally. John Paul II uses the term **total self-donation** for this type of giving.

26-L

COMPREHENSION & DISCUSSION QUESTIONS

1. What is the name of the book that Pope John Paul II (Karol Wojtyla, at the time) wrote in the late 1950s about love?

2. What is *love*?

3. What is *chastity*?

4. What is the difference between *chastity* and *abstinence*?

5. What do you think it means when the Church says, "man … cannot fully find himself except through a sincere gift of himself"? (GS 24)

6. What is *total self-donation*?

Humans Deserve Only Love

Now that we have seen what love is, let's look at to whom love is directed. John Paul II said that, "the person is a 'good' toward which the only proper and adequate attitude is love."[6] This understanding is the basis of John Paul II's teaching about love, and he calls it the **personalistic norm**. That's a fancy way to say that human persons deserve only the best—they deserve love, and we should never treat anyone with less than love.

"The greater the feeling of responsibility for the person the more true love there is."
– *Pope John Paul II*

Of course, real love is not one-sided; thus is it not only about giving, it is about receiving as well. It takes humility and gratitude to warmly receive another's love, allowing them to give of themselves freely. Think of how hard it would be to love someone who always criticized the way you gave of yourself. You might feel like a child who uses his underdeveloped artistic gifts to lovingly draw a picture of his parents, who then say, "We don't look like that! That's awful!" Thus, love must involve a mutual relationship between persons and love must be in keeping with what is genuinely good for another. According to John Paul II, there are three aspects of love that can be summarized as follows:

a. **Love as Attraction:** Recognizing the good of another person; seeing the inner and outer beauty of another person.

b. **Love as Desire:** Wanting a good for yourself; desiring goodness and happiness.

c. **Love as Goodwill:** Willing (or desiring) the good of another person.

It is this last part that we will discuss further in this chapter as our general definition of love: willing the good of another person. Love is not selfish, it is generous. Willing the good of another is closest to the love with which God loves us. The word used to describe this type of love is **agape**.[7]

Willing the Good of Another

Love means that you do what is best for your beloved. So, what does this mean for our relationships? If you are a guy, consider the following: Research of more than 10,000 women revealed that the earlier a woman becomes sexually active, the more likely she is to experience the following:

- out-of-wedlock pregnancy
- single motherhood
- STDs
- multiple sexual partners
- breakups
- abortion
- poverty
- depression
- divorce

The research showed that the longer a woman delayed sexual activity, the greater the quality of life she enjoyed. Now obviously this doesn't mean that people who have lost their virginity at a young age are doomed to have a miserable life. But, the fact remains that the consequences of early sexual activity in most cases are very bad for women. So, if a young man really loves a girl, he would do what is best for her. He would not expose her to these risks—even if she willingly consents to a sexual relationship. He would guard her body, as well as her soul, which is also placed in danger when God's plan for sexual love is rejected.

Likewise, out of love for the guy, a young woman would not risk causing him to experience many of the same consequences. She also would not give a guy sex for the sake of feeling loved. Together, the two of them should do what is best for each other, no matter how strong the temptations may be. This isn't easy, but real love never is. Perhaps that's why it seems so rare.

Loving versus Using

This is the greatest commandment that Jesus gave us: "Love one another, even as I have loved you" (Jn 13:34). How is it that Jesus loved us? He *gave all* of himself for us as He willed us to be saved. He *gave* his own life so that we might live. This is the essence of those home-made "John 3:16" posters we see at football games: "For God so loved the world that he gave his only Son, that whoever believes in him should not perish, but have eternal life" (Jn 3:16).

John Paul II teaches that the opposite of love is not hate. Rather, it is the *using* of persons. This philosophy of using people for one's own gain is called **utilitarianism**. However, it is important to realize that most people who live this way don't do so intentionally. Although it is clear that some deliberately lead sinful lives, most people simply have been taught incorrectly, often by watching the bad example of others. They focus on maximizing their pleasure and minimizing their pain, pleasing themselves at the expense of others. While desiring good things for oneself is good, if love ends there, it becomes a lifeless form of selfish

You Decide

Which of the following people do you think has the better understanding of love as self donation?

50 Cent, from his song, "Just a Lil' Bit"

"All (I) really need is a lil' bit. Not a lot baby girl, just a lil' bit."

vs.

St. John Chrysostom

A young husband should say to his bride: "I have taken you in my arms, and I love you, and I prefer you to my life itself. For the present life is nothing, and my most ardent dream is to spend it with you in such a way that we may be assured of not being separated in the life reserved for us."

Notes & Nuggets: You can use the following "love test" as a springboard for a discussion about teen relationships and how they match up with God's plan for real love. We recommend letting the students work individually to take this test silently. As they take it, there will probably be a lot of guilt and then resolve for several of your teens. Because of this, we recommend you allow them time to do this within a class setting so you can facilitate a discussion, offer them hope, and speak of God's healing grace.

It is possible to use these questions for a group discussion, but use your discretion because many of them are very personal and could turn the discussion into dead silence or a group confession, neither of which you want. If you opt for a group discussion, use the questions from the generic list for guys and girls. You may want to speak more generally about the questions that are specific to each gender (unless you teach in a class of only guys or only girls, which is actually the preferred method according to most chastity educators, including the authors of this program. In this case, go deeper according to what you perceive to be best for them).

survival. God's love doesn't bring heartache, depression, guilt, or loneliness. God's love is life-giving. This is a major part of the test to discover the real basis of your relationships.

COMPREHENSION & DISCUSSION QUESTIONS

1. What is the *personalistic norm*?

2. What are the three aspects of love that John Paul II focused on in *Love and Responsibility*?

3. Of the three aspects of love, which do you think come more naturally? Which are harder to learn?

4. What is *utilitarianism*? Share some real-life examples of it (sexual and non-sexual).

(LOVE TEST)

"ARE YOU A USER OR AN AUTHENTIC LOVER OF OTHERS?"

For Guys & Girls:

○ YES   ○ NO   Do you spend quality time with his or her family?

○ YES   ○ NO   Do you honor the rules that his or her parents set up?

○ YES   ○ NO   Are you honest with *your* family about him or her?

○ YES   ○ NO   Do you long to do what is the best for him or her?

○ YES   ○ NO   Has the relationship brought you closer to friends, family, and God?

○ YES   ○ NO   Could you see yourself possibly marrying him or her?

○ YES   ○ NO   Would he or she make a good father or mother?

○ YES   ○ NO   Do you go to church with him or her?

○ YES   ○ NO   Do you pray for each other?

Notes & Nuggets: If you decide to discuss the questions that are specific to guys and girls, be sure to give them encouragement, extending hope to them and reminding them that God has a great plan for their lives. The desires that He put in their hearts–to be loved and to be happy–are good. Just because the teens recognize patterns of using in their lives or in the lives of those they care about does not mean that the patterns must continue. Encourage them to stand up in truth and love, and to honor and respect one another, rather than disrespect and use one another.

In addition to the unhealthy relationships that teens find themselves in is the major struggle with pornography that many teenagers face, especially guys. You should point out that pornography is a form of utilitarianism. Through lust, pornography divides the body from the person. Suddenly, a person becomes "pieces and parts" to be desired rather than a whole person to be loved. As you encourage your teens with the message of chastity and purity, you may want to ask them the rhetorical question: If a person forms a habit of acting selfishly when they are alone, how hard will it be in a relationship to transition back to generously loving another? (This is an important topic that we will explore in a much deeper way in Chapter Six.)

Remind your teens that God wants us to help one another find true freedom and joy. He does not want us to simply rely on coping mechanisms that, while attempting to "protect ourselves," actually hurt ourselves and others. In other words, God does not want us to merely survive the teenage years and to escape high school without having sex. God wants us to be happy and to be free. Share with your students Jesus' words about His truth which will set us free (Jn 8:32). He did not say that the truth would make us miserable. Explain that you know that a change of perspective or lifestyle can cause a certain sadness of heart but that, with Jesus, we need not despair. He has promised to work out all things for our good (Rom 8:28). He can turn our patterns of using and being used into opportunities for redemption and new life.

○ YES   ○ NO   If the two of you have already been sexually active, would you stay together if he or she no longer wanted to have sex?

○ YES   ○ NO   Do you set clear boundaries about what you won't do physically?

○ YES   ○ NO   Do you avoid situations where you're likely to go too far?

○ YES   ○ NO   If his or her family knew everything about your relationship, would they approve?

○ YES   ○ NO   Do you dress and speak modestly to help him or her stay pure?

How many of your answers in the last set were honestly "yes"? The more "yes" answers you honestly gave, the more your actions resemble those of a person who exhibits characteristics of authentic love! You may want to read these questions from time to time, allowing them to encourage you to keep your priorities straight and to continue to rise to the challenge of loving as God loves.

For Guys:

○ YES   ○ NO   When you see an attractive girl, do you automatically imagine doing sexual acts with her?

○ YES   ○ NO   When it comes to your speech, are you respectful around girls you want to impress, but you sound like Howard Stern when you're with the guys?

○ YES   ○ NO   Do you look at your girlfriend (or any girl) and try to think of ways to get her to have sex with you?

○ YES   ○ NO   Do you ask or hint to your girlfriend that you want to sleep with her, hoping one day she'll say yes?

○ YES   ○ NO   Do you tell your girlfriend you love her, hoping that she will be inclined to be sexually active with you?

○ YES   ○ NO   Do you get mad at your girlfriend if she doesn't want to be physical in any way?

○ YES   ○ NO   Do you cheat on your girlfriend?

○ YES   ○ NO   Do you gently push her to go further than she wants during times when the two of you are physically intimate?

○ YES   ○ NO   Do you think to yourself, or say to others, "I'll go out with her, but I probably wouldn't marry her"?

○ YES   ○ NO   Do you often think about engaging in sexual acts with girls?

○ YES   ○ NO   Do you find yourself trying to spend time alone with girls, rather than spending time together with them in group settings?

○ YES   ○ NO   Do you find that you "agree" with your girlfriend to avoid fights so that you can get physically intimate with her?

○ YES   ○ NO   Do you look at pornography?

○ YES   ○ NO   Do you find that you listen or "put up" with your girlfriend (or any girl) to increase your chances of becoming physically intimate with her?

○ YES   ○ NO   Do you want to get out of the relationship if she doesn't want to get physically intimate with you?

Notes & Nuggets: It is particularly important to recognize that many girls feel starved for true affection (especially in the divorce culture in which many grow up) and this manifests itself in their accepting utilitarian relationships. Also note that many of them feel "stuck" in such relationships.

To be sure, there are *elements of love* at work in those relationships, however distorted they may be. The famous Catholic apologist G.K. Chesterton once said, "Every man who knocks on the door of a brothel is really seeking God." The same logic holds in teenage sexual relationships. The two involved in such relationships are seeking a deeper truth-communion and love. Even though they are doing so in illicit manners, the fact remains that they are actually searching for love.

Take this opportunity to encourage girls not to settle for anyone who treats them less than the glorious creations that they are. They are beautiful and they deserve to be loved, not used. Encourage them to change their own patterns of using, and to take responsibility for their lives instead of acting like victims, which is also prevalent among teenage girls. Strongly encourage them to demand change in the behavior of those whom they date should patterns of using be present. Support them through their decision to drop any relationship with any guy who is using them, rather than respecting them and loving them rightly.

On utilitarianism, John Paul II says, "Anyone who treats a person as the means to an end does violence to the very essence of the other" (p. 27). He later writes that "treating a person as a means to an end ... the maximization of pleasure, will always stand in the way of love" (p. 40).

For Guys: *(Cont.)*

○ YES　　○ NO　　Do you talk to your friends about what you did or plan on doing sexually with your girlfriend?

○ YES　　○ NO　　Do you dance in a way with your girlfriend (or any girl) that would make the girl's dad want to shoot you?

How many of your answers above were "yes"? The more "yes" answers you honestly gave, the more clearly your behavior is that of a "user." The good news is that once you recognize this, you can ask God for strength and can commit to become an authentic "lover" of persons instead.

For Girls:

○ YES　　○ NO　　Have you done sexual acts or compromised your dignity to make a guy more interested in you?

○ YES　　○ NO　　Do you sometimes give in to a guy's sexual advances out of a fear of rejection or to avoid arguments?

○ YES　　○ NO　　Do you sometimes dress immodestly to get attention?

○ YES　　○ NO　　Do you talk about impure things with your girlfriends?

○ YES　　○ NO　　Do you flirt with guys when you have no intention of dating them?

○ YES　　○ NO　　Have you ever flirted with a guy who was dating someone else?

○ YES　　○ NO　　Have you flirted with another guy while you were dating someone else?

○ YES　　○ NO　　Do you flirt in a sexual way?

○ YES　　○ NO　　Do you cheat on your boyfriend?

○ YES　　○ NO　　Do you settle for being a "friend with benefits," hooking up with no commitment?

○ YES　　○ NO　　Do you put up with degrading sexual jokes in order to not seem prudish?

○ YES　　○ NO　　Do you spread gossip about sexual acts others have done?

○ YES　　○ NO　　Do you rush into relationships or always say "yes" when someone asks you out?

○ YES　　○ NO　　Do you fall back into the same sexual mistakes, relationship after relationship?

○ YES　　○ NO　　Do you justify doing sexual acts because you feel "in love" or "ready"?

○ YES　　○ NO　　Do you talk about or look at impure images online?

○ YES　　○ NO　　Do you read materials that have a distorted approach to love and sexuality?

○ YES　　○ NO　　Do you tolerate your boyfriend looking at pornography?

○ YES　　○ NO　　Do you stay in unhealthy relationships because you're afraid of being alone?

○ YES　　○ NO　　Do you dance in a way that invites guys to lust after you?

Notes & Nuggets: In order to help the teens grasp the power and depth of these quotes from C.S. Lewis and John Paul II, you may want to write them on the board and have your students copy them into their notebooks or the margins of the workbook. In addition, you may want to break each statement down and have the students share their insights on what each means. Help them with your own examples to see how love is more powerful than lust. The Resurrection of Easter Sunday is a fitting and powerful response to the death and pain of Good Friday. Share with your students the Bible verse: "O death where is your victory? Where is your sting?" (Hos 13:14; 1 Cor. 15:55)

Growing Out of Lust and Into Love

If the preceding test strikes a nerve, you're not alone. The questions you just answered are not meant to condemn or accuse you. Rather, the test is meant to be a "wake-up call" to alert you to the fact that there is a better way to live and interact with members of the opposite sex. It doesn't matter where you have been or what you have done. What matters is what you choose today and what you choose for your future. Remember that all things are possible in the strength of Christ (see Phil 4:13).

If you're feeling right now that you need to learn how to give and receive love better, join the rest of the human race. Loving people rightly—and not using them for our own ends—is not easy in this culture, which celebrates the "quick fix" and "satisfy me now" attitude. Though lust may seem overwhelming at times, it is no match for the beauty of authentic love. This should give us reason for great hope. It is also why C.S. Lewis once wrote, "Lust is a weak, poor, whimpering, whispering thing when compared with that richness and energy of desire which will arise when lust has been killed."[8]

While you may be tempted to despair because learning to love and be loved rightly is difficult, remember that it is especially during your teen years that you can learn to love as God does. Just because your relationships may seem to be dark now does not mean that the sun will not rise on them tomorrow, if you allow God's love to fill your heart and your relationships. God can and will make clear your entire purpose for living. This is what John Paul II meant when he wrote, "Man cannot live without love. He remains a being that is incomprehensible for himself, his life is senseless, if love is not revealed to him, if he does not encounter love, if he does not experience it and make it his own, if he does not intimately participate in it."[9]

COMPREHENSION & DISCUSSION QUESTIONS

1. What did C.S. Lewis write about lust?

2. Why did John Paul II say that humans cannot live without love?

3. Share stories about people you respect because they love as God intends us to love—in a true and life-giving manner. What is so attractive about their lives?

notes

_____

_____

_____

_____

_____

_____

_____

_____

_____

_____

_____

_____

_____

_____

_____

_____

_____

_____

_____

DIGGING DEEPER:
Chastity Frees Us to Love

"Chastity can only be thought of in association with the virtue of love. Its function is to free love from the utilitarian attitude."[10]

When you hear the term "chastity," what comes to mind? Odds are it's the word "NO!" Here's how you might imagine a typical conversation between a student and a teacher:

Student: Is it OK for my girlfriend and me to …
Teacher: NO.
Student: Well, what if we just …
Teacher: NO.
Student: But what if we really …
Teacher: NO. NO. NO. Just don't. Be good boys and girls. Hold hands and go to a pumpkin patch together, then play board games with her family, and be home by 7:00 p.m. Otherwise you'll get her pregnant, die of an STD, and go to hell. Class dismissed. Have a fun weekend!

While this is *not* a fair picture of religion teachers, it *is* a fair representation of the way many teens view the concept of chastity. With such negative ideas associated with the word, it's understandable why Pope John Paul II said that the word "chastity" needs to be rehabilitated.

Purity "consists in quickness to affirm the value of the person in every situation, and in raising [sexual reactions] to the personal level."[11]

If people understood the true purpose of chastity, they would see that it has nothing to do with fear or prudishness. Nor is it a repression of sexual desires. Rather, chastity is an exercise of the will, to choose what is good. It is a refusal to allow the desire for pleasure to displace the call to love. Pleasure is not a bad thing, but when a person pursues enjoyment at the expense of another, love is abandoned.

This is why John Paul II tells us that chastity can only be thought of in association with love. When love is present, the man and woman have a sincere desire to do what is good for the other. Therefore, when it comes to teenage dating relationships, chastity frees the couple from using each other as objects, and thus makes them capable of authentic love.

When lust takes precedence over love, "pleasure is the end, and all else—the 'person,' that person's 'body,' 'femininity' or 'masculinity'—is only a means to it," according to the pope.[12] Instead of trying to do what is best for the other, the other person is seen as a means to achieve pleasure. John Paul II described such actions as those of an "egoist," who is "preoccupied to the exclusion of all else with his own 'I,' his ego, and so seeks the good of that 'I' alone, caring nothing of others."[13] Such a person may take an interest in another, but only for the sake of sexual gratification. When the urge is satisfied at the other's expense, all interest disappears until desire is aroused again."[14]

For the egoist, chastity is seen as an obstacle. It serves no purpose but to threaten his or her lifestyle. Because lust is directed at finding an outlet, chastity appears repressive.

While it's easy to label *others* as being egoists, we often refuse to admit the same tendencies in ourselves. Instead of admitting the weakness within all of us, we make rationalizations. For example, a person might say, "Well, I'm not using my girlfriend (or boyfriend). We really love each other, and both agree that we're ready for sex. There's no pressure, and it's not like all we do is have sex."

However, if the couple is sexually active and unmarried, they are not doing what is best for each other. They may have genuine feelings, but if they refuse to sacrifice for the good of the other, then they become users: two people who agree to use and be used.

This approach to relationships is common but still full of errors. It mistakes sensual feelings and reactions for love. With such a misunderstanding, chastity is viewed as the enemy of love. The couple fears that living chastely will actually separate them, when in reality, such sacrificial love will ultimately unite them much more closely than sex ever would have done.

Because the demands of authentic love are so challenging, every man and woman is tempted to turn away and make up his or her own rules when it comes to sexual relationships. One way that people do this is by diminishing the value of purity. Pope John Paul II explains: "The fact is that attaining or realizing a higher value demands a greater effort of will. So in order to spare ourselves the effort, to excuse our failure to obtain this value, we minimize its significance, deny it the respect which it deserves, even see it as in some way evil, although objectivity requires us to recognize that it is good."[15]

Simply put, many people pretend that chastity is harmful because they do not want to change their lives. They distort the value of chastity because they would much rather light-heartedly pass it by. As Pope John Paul II says, it allows the person to "recognize as good only what suits him, what is convenient and comfortable for him."[16]

But love is not about comfort and convenience. If we long to find the love we have been created for, we must be willing to put others before ourselves. As one husband said, "Winning this battle takes faith in Christ, dedication, commitment, honesty with ourselves and others, and a willingness to make sacrifices and deny our own selfish desires. But love is not afraid of those things; love is those things."[17] Once we understand this, we will be able to understand why Pope John Paul II said that "only the chaste man and the chaste woman are capable of true love."[18]

notes

APPLICATION

Love versus Lust Race

Break teens into groups of three to five. Secure copies of three or four different magazines with which the teens are familiar. Include one additional Catholic magazine in the batch. Give a selection of magazines to each group along with scissors and a print out of 1 Corinthians 13:1-13. Next, write the following phrases on the board:

a. "What is love? It is willing the good of another."

b. "What is lust? It is sexual desire apart from God's love. It is "disordered desire for or inordinate enjoyment of sexual pleasure.""

c. Any selected verse, or group of verses, from 1 Corinthians 13.

Basically, this is a scavenger hunt — a word search through magazines to create the designated phrase. Explain to the groups that their task is to quickly look through the text of their magazines, to find every word in whichever phrase (or phrases) you assign them.

The winning group is the one that first finds each word, cuts them out individually, and arranges them (with proper punctuation) in the correct order on a sheet of paper.

MOVIE CLIP/SONG SUGGESTIONS

MOVIE CLIPS:

1. **Armageddon:** Show the segment between 2:08:04 and 2:14:46. (Note: Be aware that this scene contains one profanity.) Bruce Willis' character takes the place of Ben Affleck's character and is willing to die to let him live to go home to his fiancée, Grace, who is the daughter of Bruce Willis' character.

2. **Bruce Almighty:** Show the segment between 1:22:55 and 1:30:45. The main character in the movie, Bruce, finds out that his ex-girlfriend, Grace, has always prayed for him–even when he was a jerk. After finally giving in to God's will in his life, Bruce meets God and proves that he really wants what is best for Grace.

3. **Star Wars:** Show the segment between 1:29:53 and 1:32:54. Obi-Wan allows himself to be struck down so the power of good will increase and Luke Skywalker and the others will be saved.

4. **The Princess Bride:** Show the segment between 1:22 and 5:17. This clip includes a few scenes where Wesley responds to Buttercup's every request with "as you wish," which she eventually learns means "I love you."

5. **The Last of the Mohicans:** Show the segment between 1:33:09 and 1:40:40. A British soldier offers his life in the place of a woman he loves and the man who has been his rival. This is a clear example of willing the good of another (Note: There are subtitles in this scene).

SONGS:

1. **Sometimes Love** — Chris Rice (*Deep Enough to Dream*)

This song is all about sacrificial love and how it is necessary to give for another. It is reflective of Jesus' example: "Sometimes love has to drive a nail into its own hand." Folk/Acoustic Ballad.

2. **Love** — Curtis Stephan (*Sacred Revolution*)

Defining what love means through 1 Corinthians 13. Contemporary.

3. **I'll Give** — Smalltown Poets (*self-titled*)

This is a song about giving all we have and not holding anything back. It is really about giving to God. Modern Rock.

4. **I Believe** — Blessid Union of Souls (*Home*)

This song artistically hits the nail on the head regarding the "personalistic norm." It deals with racism and concludes that love is the answer. Persons should be loved. Rock/R&B.

5. **This Man** — Jeremy Camp (*Live Unplugged*)

This song basically asks, "Would you take the place of Jesus if you could?" He gave us so much. Rock Ballad.

6. **Give it Away** — Michael W. Smith (*Change Your World*)

Another song explicitly about love as giving and sacrificing for others. Contemporary.

"So," you might ask, "when it comes to dating, how am I supposed to live out the truth of love?" This is a good question. How are you, practically speaking, to proclaim Christ with your body in a culture that often mocks such a commitment to virtue? How do you stop "using" in a very *user-friendly* culture at your high school, and later at college? How do you create an environment that helps you to live this out and protects you from using others or being used? What are some positive things you can do to avoid making mistakes in your ongoing pursuit of purity?

Well, consider these five ideas:

The "Five Directives" of Dating, Mating, and Waiting

1. **Offer your relationships to God.** God *is* love. If you want *love* to be at the center of your friendships and dating relationships, then you want *God* to be at the center of your friendships and dating relationships. So offer every night to Him from the start, whether you're out with friends or on a date. Instead of excluding Him, *invite* Him into the center, to guide you in all things and teach you how to love.

2. **"Christian, know thyself."** This ancient spiritual advice is critical if you are to avoid unnecessary temptations. It means understanding your own gifts and strengths, but also, your own weaknesses and limitations. For example, a guy and girl with a mature level of purity should be able to be alone together and not sin. We are not animals who can't control ourselves. Still, if you know that being alone will pose a strong temptation to sin, then *do not be alone.* Knowing yourself well and practicing good discipline in this area will leave you without regrets.

3. **Be more social.** Group dating might not seem as "romantic," but there are good reasons to recommend it. For one, it is a great way to meet other people. And also, there is strength in numbers, so find some friends and hang out in groups instead of just with your date. Plus, it is important to maintain friendships with lots of people rather than focusing only on your dating relationship.

4. **Go "face first."** Remember the old saying that refers to the eyes as "windows to the soul." Challenge yourself to use the "face first" principle and to look others in the eyes. This will serve as a good reminder to acknowledge the soul of the person you are speaking to, and not just ogle at a person's body, reducing them to body parts. When you see someone walking toward you in a hallway, at the mall, or on the street, you can employ the "face first" principle, helping you view the whole person through a lens of dignity. You should easily be able to describe a person's face if you have been truly looking in their eyes and respecting their dignity. This is especially useful on dates. Looking at members of the opposite sex in their eyes instead of only at the rest of their bodies is the fastest way to both uphold their dignity and to convey trust. It's also important to dress in a way that draws the attention of others to your face instead of elsewhere. We are called to see the *whole* person rightly; one of the best ways to practice seeing the bodies of others rightly is to start "face first."

5. **Be real.** On your next date or the next time you are talking to a member of the opposite sex, talk about the important things in life. Ask about their belief in God, thoughts about life and death, dreams and aspirations, and most embarrassing moments. This isn't just to gather information. This is to give you more insight into the soul beneath the skin—the child of God present in the other person—who is created for far more than sex. Don't talk about yourself "the way you want to be seen." Talk about the real you, and try to find out with whom you are really hanging out.

We may complain that it is difficult to live a pure life, but the reality is that we have more control over our situations than we like to admit. By following these five tips, it will be much easier to find happiness through chastity by expressing our sexuality the way God intended.

Notes & Nuggets: Here are a few examples for you to see what this assignment might look like:

Example #1: *40 Days & 40 Nights* – The main character decides to give up sex, pornography and masturbation for the forty days of Lent. In the process, he meets a cool and wonderful girl whom he cares about, but near the end of the movie decides to abandon his quest for purity and lies to his girlfriend. Then after they make up, they have sex.

Redeemed Version: Have the main character tell the truth to the girl and deliver the line "Treating a person as a means to an end … will always stand in the way of love!" Have her leave him, causing him to suffer and question himself and his faith. In the end, have her come back to him and have them reconcile, talk things through, and decide to journey together in purity.

Example #2: *The Notebook* – The movie makes many great points about love, but in the end, justifies having pre-marital sex as it misses out on a key component of love: willing the good of the other even if it involves sacrifice. The movie greatly values *love as attraction*, and also honors *love as desire*, but it neglects *willing the good of the other*, thus making the "love" between the main characters an act that is ultimately empty and selfish, but in a "nice, feel good" sort of way. This could subtly deceive people into thinking love is mainly about feeling passionate and feeling good.

Redeemed Version: In the real movie, they decide to have sex while still in high school. The guy delivers the classic pre-cursor line "We don't have to do this if you don't want to" before having sex. Change this scene so that at the height of their temptation, he leans over and says, "I want to love you like no other guy ever has … and I love you enough to wait for you." Rewrite the climactic scene which portrays the guy having passionate sex with someone else's fiancée (then making her his own wife). Instead, without offering her sex, have him purely and creatively offer her a life of love and commitment just before she marries the other guy whom she does not love. (Deliver the key line here!) Then have her choose him for his virtue instead of because of strong feelings that were enhanced by the "fit of passion."

Notes & Nuggets: In the closing prayer, we chose to ask St. Andrew's intercession because he was a martyr who made a total donation of himself to God.

WORK IT OUT

Assignment #1: Think of two books or movies that you like that clearly show love as "giving" rather than "using." Write them down and give a short summary of why you like them. Next, find two books or movies that you like that clearly show confusion about love and instances where people have used others, seeing them as objects rather than persons. Finally, be creative and offer a suggestion for the writers or directors of each "false love" story and give ideas of how they could have been moral and more helpful to society (but still successful) by recreating their tale.

Assignment #2: Approach your grandmother, grandfather, or another elderly or wise person whom you admire. Thank them for being a good example of what it means to love. Tell them about what you have been learning in this course or read them a quote from John Paul II and discuss it with them. Ask them to share their secret to building a lasting love, to create their own list called the "Top Three Ways to Love" or share their favorite quote about love. Later, share their quote and/or their top three answers with the class.

Assignment #3: Think of a movie you've seen that promotes the *using* of others and rewrite its climactic scene in the way you think John Paul II would have done it. Cast characters from your class and make it into a three-minute skit. Be sure that at some point, whether at the climax of the story or as comic relief, some character delivers the line, "Treating a person as a means to an end ... will always stand in the way of love!" Finally, have the class guess the name of the original film that you have rewritten.

Assignment #4: Dig deeper into the primary text by reading either pages 34-44 of *Love and Responsibility* (Ignatius Press) on John Paul II's critique of utilitarianism, or read John Paul II's audience from October 10, 1984 (see www.ewtn.com/library), which focuses on the power of love between men and women as sharing in the love of God. Write a summary essay on one of these readings.

❖

Project #1: Serve It Up Like Jesus. While it is sometimes hard to serve others, some of our greatest challenges arrive when we are presented with the task of serving another completely on their terms. For this project, you will choose the person or persons whom you want to serve, and give them two or three hours of your time. The catch is that you must ask them what they would like for you to do, and then, no matter what they ask you (so long as it is moral and does not jeopardize your health), you will do it. For example, the lady across the street or a family member may ask you to go to the grocery store with her. No matter what the task (and how hard it may be), the key is to serve completely on their terms, not yours. When you are finished, write a summary reflection on your experience. Reflect in particular on what it was like to "donate yourself to another" and "will the good of another" completely on their terms, with no strings attached.

CLOSING PRAYER

Leader: In the name of the Father, and of the Son, and of the Holy Spirit. **Amen**.

All: St. Andrew, please pray with me that I, like you, would be willing to make a total self donation of my mind, body, and soul as a witness to the Gospel, and that it would remain upon my lips now and forever. **Amen**.

IN HIS OWN WORDS

- **On Sexual Morality:** "Sexual morality is within the domain of the person. It is impossible to understand anything about it without understanding what a person is, its mode of existence, its functioning, its powers. The personal order is the only proper plan for all debate on matters of sexual morality" (*Love and Responsibility*, 18).

- **On Self-Control:** "In order to succeed in mastering this impulse and excitement, the personal subject must be committed to a progressive education in self-control of the will, feelings, and emotions. This education must develop beginning with the most simple acts in which it is relatively easy to put the interior decision into practice" (October 24, 1984).

- **On the Battle for Purity:** "The truth of original sin explains a very basic and very widespread evil–that a human being encountering a person of the other sex does not simply and spontaneously experience 'love' but a feeling muddied by the longing to enjoy" (*Love and Responsibility*, 161).

- **On Who Can Love:** "Thus also only the chaste man and the chaste woman are capable of true love. For chastity frees their association, including marital intercourse, from that tendency to use a person which is objectively incompatible with 'loving kindness,' and by so freeing it introduces into their life together and their sexual relationship a special disposition to 'loving kindness'" (*Love and Responsibility*, 171).

- **On Utilitarianism:** "The principle of 'utility' itself, of treating a person as a means to an end, and an end moreover which in this case is pleasurable, the maximization of pleasure, will always stand in the way of love" (*Love and Responsibility*, 40).

- **On The Personalistic Norm:** "This norm, in its negative aspect, states that the person is the kind of good which does not admit of use and cannot be treated as an object of use and as such the means to an end. In its positive form the personalistic norm confirms this: the person is a good toward which the only proper and adequate attitude is love" (*Love and Responsibility*, 41).

- **On Chastity Affirming the Person:** "The essence of chastity consists in quickness to affirm the value of the person in every situation" (*Love and Responsibility*, 171).

- **On Chastity and Happiness:** "For this reason, chastity is a difficult, long-term matter; one must wait patiently for it to bear fruit, for the happiness of loving kindness that it must bring. But at the same time, chastity is the sure way to happiness" (*Love and Responsibility*, 172).

Glossary
of Key Terms

Abstinence: The action of self-control that avoids (or abstains from) something. In this case, abstinence means not engaging in sexual intercourse.

Agape: The Greek term for divine, unconditional love; the manner in which God loves us.

Chastity: The virtue that directs all our sexual desires, emotions, and attractions toward the dignity of the person and the real meaning of love. It falls under the cardinal virtue of temperance. Chastity is saying "yes" to the demands of authentic love.

Love as Attraction: Recognizing the good of another person; seeing the inner and outer beauty of another person.

Love as Desire: Wanting a good for yourself; desiring goodness and happiness.

Love as Goodwill: Willing (or desiring) the good of another person.

Love and Responsibility: A book by Karol Wojtyla (later John Paul II) that explains the importance of living a life that accepts responsibility and, therefore, results in loving others in a responsible manner.

Personalistic norm: The principle that recognizes that the only proper and adequate attitude toward human persons is love. The opposite of love is to use a person as a means to an end.

Pornography: Pictures or stories created with the direct intention of arousing lust in the viewer or reader.

Sexual repression: The unhealthy attempt to ignore (or bury) sexual desires rather than embracing them and allowing God to reorder what is disordered in them for the good of oneself and others.

Temperance: The virtue that enables us to take pleasure in the good gifts of God in the balanced way that He intends; one of the four cardinal virtues under which all other virtues come forth.

Total Self-Donation: The total giving of oneself for the good of another.

Utilitarianism: The philosophy of maximizing pleasure and minimizing pain, often at the expense of others. When applied in relationships, one ends up using a person for one's own gain. If one's goal for sex is pleasure, the other person becomes a means to that end.

Virtue: A firm habit of doing what is good. In its fullest sense, it is not only doing, but delighting in and desiring what is true, good, and beautiful.

OBJECTIVES At the end of this lesson, the student should know and be able to:

- Relate the creation accounts of Genesis to modern situations and consequences.
- Recognize the beauty of God's original plan as evident in the blessings of love, innocence, and fertility.
- Explain that God made man and woman in His own image and likeness, and that we are all created "good."
- Recognize the meaning of our existence as revealed through the one-flesh marital union of our bodies, the sexual relationship.
- Define the original experiences of man: nakedness, solitude, innocence, unity, happiness.
- Recognize the amazing benefits of a life in which lust, shame, and selfishness do not dominate.
- Identify Satan as the enemy of God whose purpose is to twist and destroy the good that God has created.
- Explain how original sin entered the world and resulted in a host of damaging consequences.
- Compare and contrast the original world of life and love with the world after the Fall.
- Demonstrate an understanding of humanity's roots in both worlds of "original man" and "historical man."
- Show that God allows us to choose Him in total freedom, and that we will experience great joy in our relationship with Him.
- Analyze the "nuptial meaning of the body" and develop practical conclusions based upon this reality.

Notes & Nuggets: We suggest praying today that your students might come to understand the reality that original sin has made our world a far more difficult place to live in than God originally intended. Pray that their hearts will recognize the beauty of God's original plan and be open to learning how they can allow Christ to redeem their desires. You may want to pray a Divine Mercy chaplet, a decade of the Rosary, or some other prayer for your teens today.

TWO MINUTE DRILL — VERBAL REVIEW:

1. What is chastity?
   Answer: The virtue that orients all our sexual desires, emotions, and attractions toward the true dignity of the person and the real meaning of love. It falls under the cardinal virtue of temperance. Chastity is saying "yes" to the demands of authentic love.

2. How did John Paul II define love?
   Answer: It is willing the good of another person.

3. What is the personalistic norm?
   Answer: It's a fancy way to say that human beings deserve only the best—they deserve love, and the only proper way to treat someone is with love, not use.

4. What is lust?
   Answer: Lust is sexual desire apart from God's love. It is a selfish desire to please oneself. Lust treats people as objects.

5. What is the name of the selfish philosophy of using people for one's own gain?
   Answer: Utilitarianism.

Chapter Three

Naked Without Shame

In the beginning, God created Adam and Eve to be pure and holy, setting them to live in a perfect world. They did not have problems like we do today, and their relationship with each other was filled with a pure love, a pure generosity, and a pure passion. God blessed them with fertility and gave them the tremendous gift of caring for all of His creation. Theirs was the first marriage, a union in which they were "naked without shame." In fact, there was no such thing as shame (or embarrassment) because there was perfect love. There was no need to cover themselves because there was no fear of being seen as an object to be used. They saw in their naked bodies the call to be a gift to each other. This unity, peace, and perfection would soon be shattered once they turned from God and committed the original sin.

ICEBREAKER (optional): Lost in the Garden

This activity is an attempt to playfully recreate the idea of what happened when Adam and Eve committed the original sin.

STEP 1: Match up guys and girls so that each has a partner. (If the numbers don't match up perfectly, you can have some teens wait for a second game.) Let them get together for a moment to meet and exchange names, especially if they do not know each other. Tell them to introduce themselves to each other by replacing their first name with "Adam" (guys) and "Eve" (girls). As they meet their Adam or Eve, ask them to answer this question: **"If you could go anywhere in the world for one day, where would it be? Why?"** Tell them they must answer the first question in one or two words, and then the second question in one simple sentence. For example: "Colorado. Because I love to ski." Or "Rome. Because I want to meet the pope."

STEP 2: Split up the couples and place them at opposite ends of a large room (or outside) so that all the guys are single file at one end, and all the girls are single file at the other end. They should be facing each other (similar to the game "Red Rover"). Once they get to their positions, blindfold each participant. After they are all blindfolded, physically move them around into a different order so that they are no longer at the same place in the line and no longer directly across from their partner.

STEP 3: Next, say this: "The point of the game is to find your partner. The tricky part is that we now have (# of) people named Adam and (# of) named Eve. In a few moments, each "Eve" will find her "Adam," the one with whom you shared your vacation dream. Adam, you must stay stationary, not moving at all. And, because you both ate the forbidden fruit, you must be blindfolded."

STEP 4: You, the teacher, are God. Your job is to roam the garden while playing a flute, recorder, or some other instrument that all the Adams and Eves can hear. You don't have to know how to play, you just need to have something with which you can make a sound for all to hear. (Singing a song could work as well, but amidst the voices of the students who will be searching for each other, it will be hard for them to hear you, unless it is a very small group.)

STEP 5: During the preparation process, share the following rules with your students:

- **Rule #1: No peeking.** No peeking out from your blindfold in any way. To lessen the temptation, keep your eyes closed, too.

- **Rule #2: You may only call your spouse by their new name.** This means that you may not call your spouse by any other name or nickname than the one they now have: Adam or Eve. As you search for them, you may not say anything else other than their new name. This means you must listen carefully for the voice of your spouse.

- **Rule #3: You may not purposefully touch your spouse until you are absolutely sure that you have found them.** If you are unsure if you are speaking to your spouse because you do not recognize his or her voice, you should ask him or her the question: "If you could go anywhere in the world for one day, where would it be? Why?" Only when you are sure you have found them can you hold his or her hand and walk together to find God.

- **Rule #4: You must work together.** You must find God together because He is the only one who can take off your blindfolds. As you look for Him together hand-in-hand, you may call out to God together; you are bound to find Him quicker.

- **Rule #5: Embrace with grace.** You may not hug your spouse until God has taken off your blindfolds. Only then may you express your joy at finding your spouse and finding God by hugging your spouse as God gives you His blessing. The first couple to hug each other (and to simultaneously be hugged by God) wins. (The first couple to find God wins.)

- **Optional Rule #6 — To make it easier:** If an Eve is having trouble, she may call out for God's help. This is her only lifeline and can only be used once. If she chooses to use it, she may hold up her hand and cry, "God help me!" At this point, the person designated as God will come to her aid and point her in the direction of where her real spouse is in the room. This can only be used once, and can only be used by Eve. But, choosing to do this will cost Eve 10 seconds that will be added to the end of her time. (To have this option "God" (you) must know who is matched up with whom—be sure to write it down!)

STEP 6: Once spouses have finished, they must move to the side of the room to watch the fun, but they should not interfere. Let people play until they find their spouse and God.

(Continued on next leader's page)

OPENING PRAYER

Leader: In the name of the Father, and of the Son, and of the Holy Spirit. **Amen**.

(Option #1)

Leader or Reader #1: Read Psalm 139:1b-6, 13-17 (NAB)

"O LORD, you have probed me, you know me: you know when I sit and stand; you understand my thoughts from afar. My travels and my rest you mark; with all my ways you are familiar. Even before a word is on my tongue, LORD, you know it all. Behind and before you encircle me and rest your hand upon me.

Such knowledge is beyond me, far too lofty for me to reach … You formed my inmost being; you knit me in my mother's womb. I praise you, so wonderfully you made me; wonderful are your works! My very self you knew; my bones were not hidden from you, When I was being made in secret, fashioned as in the depths of the earth. Your eyes foresaw my actions; in your book all are written down; my days were shaped, before one came to be. How precious to me are your designs, O God; how vast the sum of them!"

Leader or Reader #2: Lord, we thank You for all of the blessings we have mentioned, especially for the dignity and goodness of our bodies. Help us to use our bodies to praise You, to rejoice in You always, and to give You thanks each day. **Amen**.

(Option #2)

Leader or Reader #1: Read Proverbs 3:5-8, 13a, 18

"Trust in the Lord with all your heart and do not rely on your own insight.
In all your ways acknowledge him, and he will make straight your paths.
Be not wise in your own eyes; fear the Lord and turn away from evil.
It will be healing to your flesh and refreshment to your bones.
Happy is the man who finds wisdom …
She is a tree of life to those who lay hold of her;
those who hold her fast are called happy."

Leader or Reader #2: Lord, help us not to rely on our own understanding of our bodies or our desires. Help us to trust You completely and to be open to learn from You about your wonderful creation, each person here with us today. May your Word bring us healing, renewal, wisdom, and happiness. **Amen.**

Need a Review of Lesson 2? Look to next page.

Icebreaker: Lost in the Garden (Cont.)

POST-GAME DISCUSSION

In this game, there are many obvious parallels to Scripture and real life. Ask the students to make the connections. If they have trouble, help them along:

- When Adam and Eve sinned, it blinded them. Their "spiritual" eyes were closed and they could no longer see each other the way they had before.

- Life was much more difficult. There was failure and frustration.

- Suddenly communication became more difficult.

- There was the constant temptation to disobey God's instructions. (How bad did you want to peek from under your blindfold?!!)

- It was harder to hear God's "voice," as suddenly there was confusion with everyone calling out in frustration and not being able to see.

- Asking for God's help may have seemed like it was going to hurt your chances of winning, but those who do it early in the game usually find their spouses much quicker—just like those who ask for God's wisdom find peace and happiness quicker than those who try to live life on their own.

- Those who listened well to their spouse in the very beginning had a better chance of winning. In real life relationships, while talking to another is sometimes more fun, it is careful listening that shows one truly cares. This is what helps bring confidence and trust into good relationships.

- Seeking God together was the key to winning. Asking God to bless your relationship together by praying and receiving the sacraments is the best way to receive grace and to achieve a life of chastity. This is how to make love strong!

- When God hugged the spouses, He gave them grace to love one another properly. He also gave them the clear vision needed to make the relationship blossom into a successful and happy marriage that would last.

STORY STARTER: The Two Bishops

In the early Christian Church, several bishops were gathered outside a cathedral in Antioch, when a beautiful prostitute passed by on the street. Upon noticing her, the crowd of bishops looked away to avoid being seduced. Bishop Nonnus, however, stared intently at her, and then said to his fellow bishops, "Did not the wonderful beauty of that woman delight you?" The bishops remained silent. Nonnus insisted, "Indeed it delighted me," but he wept for her. When the prostitute saw how the bishop looked at her, she was caught off guard. No man had ever looked at her with such purity. He was not lusting after her, but rather saw something in her that she did not even see in herself. The simple purity of that one bishop's glance marked the beginning of her conversion to Christ. She soon returned to find him, and today, we know this former prostitute as St. Pelagia.

There is great power in the way a man looks at a woman, just as there is great power in the way that a woman dresses for a man. What this bishop possessed was something called "positive purity." He was not afraid that the sight of her body would force him to lust. Rather, her body revealed his call to love her properly. He didn't see a prostitute walking toward him—he saw a potential sister in Christ. Though he lived many centuries before Pope John Paul II, he truly lived out the future pope's words when he said that God "has assigned as a duty to every man the dignity of every woman."[1]

But what about the bishops who looked away from the oncoming prostitute? It can be said that they had "negative purity." They were right to avoid the occasion of sin—by turning away from what, for them, would have been a serious temptation—but God ultimately wants to transform our hearts so that we aren't afraid we will lust every time we see an attractive person. This is the freedom exhibited by Bishop Nonnus and offered to all of us. Similarly, God offered St. Pelagia freedom and gave her the grace to help her grow out of the habit of allowing herself to be used. No matter where we have been or what we've done, purity is possible! It may seem difficult to attain, but all things are possible with God.

COMPREHENSION & DISCUSSION QUESTIONS

1. How can the way a girl dresses affect the way a guy views her?

2. Do you think it is really possible to be able to look at a woman the way Bishop Nonnus looked at the prostitute?

3. Why do you think that Bishop Nonnus wept?

4. Compared to the way other men would look at a prostitute, how do you think the way Bishop Nonnus looked at the prostitute made her feel?

Verbal Review of Lesson 2

1. What is chastity?

2. How did John Paul II define love?

3. What is the personalistic norm?

4. What is lust?

5. What is the name of the self ish philosophy of using peo ple for one's own gain?

notes

_____

_____

_____

_____

_____

_____

_____

_____

_____

_____

_____

_____

_____

_____

_____

_____

_____

_____

Notes & Nuggets: At this point, we suggest having students read the text of Genesis 2:4-25. If you read it with them, you can use the following two ideas to break up the reading. Get your teens fired up about this reading! Get excited! If straight reading and discussion is not the best method for your students, try using one of the methods below that will help them learn best:

1. "PLAY" IN THE GARDEN: You can easily make the reading more relevant and fun by creating simple narrative "scenes" or a short play out of this reading. Have fun with it, but don't get elaborate with props or costumes as this may distract from the insights the teens will gather from the reading. As "the director" of the play, feel free to stop it at any moment to teach your teens more about what is going on. You can also help the characters realize the rich meaning of their actions, which the average theater goers (Bible readers) may miss.

2. GET DRAMATIC: Do a dramatic reading of the account. Encourage teens to be respectful but to be dramatic as they read. If you want, you can play the voice of God yourself (do your best James Earl Jones impression!) to add some spice and help them stay interested. Again, feel free to stop and teach throughout the reading.

BRIDGING THE GAP

As we approach the book of Genesis, you might be thinking, *"I know that story. If Adam and Eve hadn't messed it all up, we'd be OK."* Or maybe you don't care and think that Adam and Eve have no connection to your life whatsoever. Though you have likely heard of **original sin**, which was the first human offense against God, you may not know much about Adam and Eve's life *before* "the Fall," i.e., before they disobeyed God. We can learn much from their entire story, particularly the period of their experiences before their first sin, which John Paul II calls **original man.**

The original sin of Adam and Eve plunged humanity into a new world filled with selfishness, suffering, shame, lust, and death. This is why the bishops struggled to look at the prostitute with dignity. In the beginning, there was no such struggle. In this chapter, we look to our first parents to learn more about what perfect love looks like and how humanity began its journey from peace to pain, from love to lust. If we can understand the beauty of God's original plan and the stark reality of original sin, we can appreciate the amazing benefits of following God's plan for our lives rather than our own.

TO THE CORE

We discussed in the first chapter how God created us, and how he found mankind (and, therefore, our bodies) to be "very good" (Gn 1:31). Moving on to the **second creation account**, God creates man and woman last and gives them dominion over all of creation. John Paul II described Adam's first experience with the animals as one of **original solitude.**

It was in this state that Adam realized he was alone, not having a suitable companion. He saw that he was fundamentally different from the animals. Not only was man without woman (and woman without man) but he was alone in the visible world as a *person.* The spiritual aspect of Adam's nature set him apart from all the other creatures. He had a **spiritualized body** that was unique in the visible world. Adam longed for a true companion.

"For the scientist who has lived by his faith in the power of reason, the story ends like a bad dream. He has scaled the mountain of ignorance; he is about to conquer the highest peak; as he pulls himself over the final rock, he is greeted by a band of theologians who have been sitting there for centuries."

– Robert Jastrow, Ph.D., *God and the Astronomers*

Naked Without Shame

God knew it was not good for Adam to be alone, so He created Eve. At this point, everything was still pure, including the heart of man. Adam experienced sexual desire in a totally pure way. So, when Adam first saw Eve, there wasn't any confusion between love and lust. When he saw her body, he didn't want to use her. He saw and experienced his call to love her. This may be hard to

imagine because many of us have been led to believe that sex itself is bad or "dirty." But when God originally designed us, sexual desire was the desire to love in the image of God. In other words, sexual desire was a pure desire to give to the other. Sexual desire was an expression of the person who desired to make a gift of self (a self-donation) to another person. In the beginning, the **original nakedness** of Adam and Eve was a peaceful state because there was no struggle to love. It was natural for Adam and Eve to be naked and to love rather than lust after each other. According to Pope John Paul II, their nakedness, combined with **original innocence**, allowed Adam and Eve to be **naked without shame** (Gn 2:25).

"Jesus came to restore creation to the purity of its origins" (CCC 2336).

COMPREHENSION & DISCUSSION QUESTIONS

1. What is original sin and how did it affect all of humanity?

2. Why do you think original sin has had such a major effect on human sexuality?

3. To whom does John Paul II refer as *original man*?

4. What was *original solitude*?

5. What was *original nakedness*?

6. Why do you think shame is associated with the body so much today?

Adam proclaimed, "This at last is bone of my bone and flesh of my flesh" (Gn 2:23) because Eve was a person he could love as a companion. Adam and Eve were innocent and trusted in the other's unconditional love. This is the difference between being "naked without shame" and being "**shameless.**" While "naked without shame" refers to nudity that exists within the context of innocence, purity of heart, and freedom, being "shameless" in today's society refers to flaunting the body without inhibitions or conscience; it's what's left when sex loses its sacredness and mystery. When we act shamelessly, sex becomes a recreational activity instead of a wonderful gift to be cherished.

"Shame is a tendency, uniquely characteristic of the human person, to conceal sexual values sufficiently to preserve them from obscuring the value of the person as such."
– *Pope John Paul II*

The Nuptial Meaning of the Body

Because of the purity of their hearts, Adam and Eve's naked bodies revealed their call to make a gift of themselves to each other. This is what Pope John Paul II called the **nuptial meaning of the body**. In the physical design of their bodies, Adam and Eve saw that their bodies literally fit together; they knew they were made for a communion that is sacred. God made them as a gift for each other and, by giving themselves to one another, Adam and Eve were able to mirror the very life of God. They desired to unite in a bodily way, which would not

only join their bodies, but their *persons* as well. This initial experience of perfect unity between the man and woman is what John Paul II called **original unity**.

Included in this original unity was a complete integration of the soul and body. Adam and Eve, our first parents, experienced a profound unity of will and desire. Their bodies responded in perfect accord with their wills, thus allowing them to love each other rightly and easily. Their sexual desire sprang from an authentic love. Later, original sin would plunge us all into a state of conflict and dis-integration. No longer would our bodies respond with complete order to our wills.

The second chapter of Genesis concludes with a core teaching about how marriage came to exist: "Therefore a man leaves his father and his mother and cleaves to his wife, and they become one flesh" (Gn 2:24). It is only here, however—after marriage has been described—that Genesis tells us "the man and his wife were both naked, and were not ashamed" (Gn 2:25). It is this participation without shame in the sacrament of marriage—instituted by God—that not only brought Adam and Eve unity, but also **original happiness.**

The happiness of Adam and Eve came in living and loving in marriage as God loves: freely, totally, faithfully, and fruitfully. These four descriptions of God's love can be briefly described like this:

• **Free**: God's love is freely given to us.

• **Total**: God's love is complete and He gives all of Himself to us, withholding nothing.

• **Faithful**: God never abandons us and never stops loving us.

• **Fruitful**: God's love brings us life. Jesus died for us so that we could have new life.

We will discuss these four concepts with more detail in Chapter Seven, but for now, remember that God's love for you is a perfect and all-encompassing love.

"Since a woman does not find in herself the sensuality of which a man as a rule cannot but be aware of in himself, she does not feel so great a need to conceal 'the body as a potential object of enjoyment.' The evolution of modesty in woman requires some initial insight into the male psychology."
– Pope John Paul II

"Only true love ... is capable of absorbing shame ... True love is a love in which sexual values are subordinate to the value of the person"
– Pope John Paul II

COMPREHENSION & DISCUSSION QUESTIONS

1. Why was Adam lonely in the beginning?

2. Was it God's original plan for Adam and Eve to be unhappy?

3. What kind of sexual desire did Adam experience in the beginning?

4. What is the *nuptial meaning of the body*?

5. What is the difference between being *naked without shame* and being *shameless*? Give a modern example of each.

Notes & Nuggets: Here, we suggest reading Genesis 3:1-7 aloud with the students, using the text below as an explanation of the Scripture.

Family of Love

After God created man and woman in His own image and likeness (Gn 1:27), He gave them His first command: "Be fruitful and multiply" (Gn 1:28). So, God wanted Adam and Eve to enjoy sexual intercourse, which He had given to them as a wonderful gift to give each other. Through their union, they experienced a deep meaning of their life and also came to the realization that, from their love, new life was born. This new life is a dim reflection of the love that proceeds from the Father and the Son, which is the Holy Spirit. Remember, the Trinity is a communion of persons, a family of love. So, too, is an earthly family a communion of love.

As great as this love, peace, and happiness may sound, why are there so many people who are so confused about the body, sex, and their beautiful purposes? Why are there so many marriages that do not grow into pure families of love? The truth is that the confusion and pain is nothing new. Actually, it all began with—and is a bad fruit of—an original lie.

The Big Lie

notes

We read in Genesis that the serpent encouraged Adam and Eve to question the motives and generosity of God. The serpent tricked Eve into thinking that she was missing out on something—that God wasn't a trustworthy and loving Father. She fell for this lie and so did Adam, who did nothing to defend or protect her. They both would eat the fruit from the tree of the knowledge of good and evil, in direct defiance of a command of a loving God.

Satan wanted them to believe that God was holding out on them and that He really didn't want them to be happy. In other words, he convinced Adam and Eve that if God had things *His* way, they would live miserable lives. Following His laws would bring sadness, not joy. The essence of the sin of Adam and Eve was the lack of trust in God. They wanted to decide for themselves what was right and wrong. They chose to serve their own wills over the will of God.

The original lie is still alive and well today. How often do we doubt the goodness of God and feel the need to break away from Him in order to satisfy our desires? How often do we want to decide what is right instead of trusting God and following His ways? We often grasp at what feels like love, only to discover that it was a counterfeit. We're left with regrets, and we may even come to doubt that love is possible. After Adam and Eve sinned through **pride** and disobedience, a rupture was formed between body and spirit. At that moment, Adam and Eve both realized that they were naked, and their original state of innocence was shattered. Fear and lust entered the picture.

Although some people would like to think that original sin is simply a quaint religious idea, its effects are hard to dispute. From that moment on, humanity launched into the era that John Paul II calls **historical man**, which we are still living in today. In some way, the first man and woman represent all humanity

44-L

and our tendency to sin. We all suffer from darkened intellects, weakened wills, and disordered appetites resulting from original sin. We are all prone to selfishness, anger, impatience, and a host of other faults. But, thank God, there is hope. His name is Jesus.

COMPREHENSION & DISCUSSION QUESTIONS

1. What was the sin of Adam and Eve?

2. In whose image and likeness were Adam and Eve made?

3. Where does the impulse come from to disbelieve those who know more than we do?

4. What is it that makes us want to obey ourselves rather than those appointed to guide us?

DIGGING DEEPER:
Naked Without Shame?

"Only the nakedness that makes woman an object for man, or vice versa, is a source of shame. The fact that they were not ashamed means that the woman was not an "object" for the man, nor he for her." – John Paul II, February 20, 1980.

Imagine visiting the world-famous San Diego Zoo and seeing hundreds of animals hiding behind trees and rocks because they finally realized that they were all naked. The elephants have taken cover, the monkeys have escaped to the treetops, and the fish have darted back into the coral.

The absurdity of such an idea should make us wonder: Why are humans the only creatures on earth who experience shame? Some may argue that it's because of prudish religious laws. Others explain that shame comes from a dislike of one's body, fearing that it isn't attractive. Both of these theories have some merit. After all, some people have been misled in the name of religion to think the body is bad and should, therefore, be covered. Others cover their bodies out of insecurity.

But these answers fail to explain why people from every culture on the planet, including non-Christian cultures, experience shame in one form or another. It also fails to explain why no model would wear a bikini on the runway when it was first invented in France in 1946.[2] In fact, the fashion designer had to hire a stripper to debut the outfit! Since the other models had no reason to be insecure about their bodies, what was causing their sense of shame?

notes

In order to understand the real cause of shame, we have to go back to the beginning. As we've already discussed, Adam and Eve were created by God as something very good—in their nakedness. This is why Michelangelo painted nude figures on the ceiling of the Sistine Chapel. Years later, perhaps out of a prudishness, Church leaders commissioned painters to cover Michelangelo's nudes with loin cloths. These alterations remained for centuries until Pope John Paul II ordered most of them to be removed. He knew that the paintings were not done to arouse lust, but rather to reveal the glory of Creation. In fact, he defined purity as "the glory of the human body before God."[3] As the Church has always taught, the human body is considered something very good.

Sadly, many people today harbor a sense of hatred for their own bodies. Eating disorders, cutting, and even steroid use are often symptoms of self-loathing. Because we are bombarded by a culture that expects every man to have six-pack abs and every girl to wear a size zero, most of us feel inadequate. We must realize, however, that pride, which manifests itself in our comparing ourselves to others, is the root of all inferiority. Instead of trying to meet the expectations of the world, reflect on the fact that God does not make garbage. You may think it's absurd that your body is "very good," but that is only because you have not yet seen what God sees in you. God knows your body isn't "perfect" according to the world's standards. But that's OK with Him, because He knows the world is confused. You're not the problem, and it's time that you begin to see the goodness of your body.

In the beginning, Adam and Eve had no difficulty seeing the goodness of their bodies. Since their hearts were pure, they were able to look upon each other's bodies and see their call to self-donating love. Another term for this is "integrity." They experienced a perfect unity of body and soul, which enabled them to live in truth and goodness in their thoughts and actions. Because of the purity of their hearts, they were able to be seen in their nakedness without any fear of being used by the other.

However, with original sin came shame. With the Fall of man came the weakness of lust. And, now that lust was present, a defense mechanism was needed. Shame would be the means of self-defense against being looked at as an object. Because Adam and Eve were no longer able to see each other as God saw them, the selfless love that had come so naturally to them was now tainted with urges of selfishness and lust.

Some people seek to deal with shame by becoming shameless. In other words, they learn to feel no remorse for their desire to use another person, or to be used themselves. They make no effort to overcome this selfish urge with selfless love. This usually happens because they have numbed their consciences. Take, for example, the stripper who wore the first bikini on that modeling runway in France in 1946. She wasn't willing to wear it simply because she was "comfortable with her body," but because she had lost her sense of shame. She had lost her understanding that the sexual values of her body would distract lustful men from her dignity as a person. On the other hand, the models

APPLICATION: God is the Magnet

To visibly demonstrate the sacramentality and complementarity of the body in the relationship between Adam and Eve (and therefore, echoing in the heart of every person today), you may choose two students to help make a word picture before the class. You (the teacher) and student #1 will serve as both Adam and Eve (in other words, "everyman" and "everywoman"). Let's assume for the sake of this application that you are Adam and student #1 is Eve. Position student #1 (Eve) in front of you and face each other. Position student #2 directly behind student #1, also facing in the same direction, toward you. Designate student #2 as "God"–the creator of the universe. Both you (Adam) and student #1 (Eve) are, of course, part of God's creation.

You should only be able to see student #1 from your vantage point. God is "invisible" to you because He is behind student #1. Make the point that God has put the desire within each of us to be with Him. He has, in a sense, put a massive magnet in each of us that is attracted to Him. Act out this analogy by being "pulled" toward God (because of the magnet within you). But who is between you and God? Student #1 is. Make the point that God created Adam and Eve (and all of us) with bodies so that we could see our call to love and better "see" Him through one another. Despite being invisible to the eye, we can actually see Him in and through others. In each of us is an inherent attraction to God and this attraction is, here on earth, most often expressed in our yearning to be with another. Being with another is a deep desire we all have, and it actually foreshadows our desire for union with God. But often we forget the Creator and focus only on His creation. If we can put on Theology of the Body "lenses," we will see that visible persons, created by God, point us to the invisible mystery of God and His love.

Next, ask your students to propose ways that God's plan for us (to live out our call to love one another) can be blocked or even destroyed. They may not immediately understand that the devil, sin, pride, lust, and selfishness can block and even destroy our ability to "see" God. In other words, when we misuse our bodies through sin, we can actually blind, wound, or otherwise shackle ourselves. Explain that since the body expresses the person, when the person becomes destroyed, so

does our image of God. In other words, if we cannot see persons for who they are, we see only bodies and we lose the view of persons as integrated beings of body and soul. It is a true integration of body and soul that shows forth the image of God, since we are all created in His image and likeness.

Allow your students to come up to the board to write out examples of this disintegration, or break them into groups of three to four people and let them brainstorm their own lists. Then invite the class back together and have your teens share their answers in a large-group class discussion. Here are some examples that you might share to get their minds flowing:

- **Abortion:** By killing innocent babies and destroying their bodies, we literally destroy persons and exterminate visible signs of God's love.

- **Racism/Prejudice:** By acting as if some humans are not created equal, we buy into the lie that only some people show the face of God–that not all people are signs of our call to love. In Chapter Two, we explained that the opposite of love was not hate, but rather the "using" of another. Through the institution of slavery, which is an extreme form of racism, we are engaging in perhaps the most aggressive form of treating humans as objects, not recognizing that they, too, are endowed with the extraordinary gift of a human soul and human dignity.

- **Pornography:** By focusing on mere parts of the body or sexual actions that others can do for and with us, we actually rob persons of their dignity and, ultimately, of their humanity. These persons become objects for our use and, therefore, we do not recognize them as persons to be loved and as visible signs of God's love. Pornography robs men and women of their ability to see one another as God intended us to see each other: as signs of His invisible love. Pornography also stifles our ability to love like Him.

- **Prostitution:** Blending elements of pornography and racism, prostitution forms a type of slavery in which men and, more commonly, women are treated as sub-humans whose only purpose is to physically gratify others. People become commodities that can be bought for pleasure, instead of loved as persons. Amazingly though, in this desire to use another, we are actually seeking something which, at its root, is

(Continued on next leader's page)

who refused to wear the outfit felt a natural reflex to conceal the mere sexual value of their bodies; somehow they inherently knew their dignity, and they were eager to avoid what was shameless.

So what does this mean for you?

When the time comes for a husband and a wife to reveal their sexual values, how can they be naked without shame? Or when it is time for a priest to instruct a couple preparing for marriage, how can he avoid falling into the "bodies are bad and sex is dirty" error? Pope John Paul II tells us that only true love is capable of absorbing shame. This means that shame is "swallowed up by love, dissolved in it, so that the man and woman are no longer ashamed" of sharing themselves and their sexuality with each other.[4] He said "Sexual intercourse between spouses is not a form of shamelessness legalized by outside authority."[5] On the contrary, when a husband and wife understand each other's value as persons, they are safe. There should be no shame because they are making a total gift of themselves in life-giving love. After all, what could be shameful about loving as God loves? Also there should be no room for shame because there should be no room for selfishness. Simply getting married doesn't guarantee that sexual union will be a true act of selfless love, but it is an absolute prerequisite for that possibility.

Because of the redemption that is offered to us in Christ, our hearts can be renewed. Because Christ's death on the cross won for us the grace not only to be saved, but also to transform our fallen inclinations, a husband and wife can again experience something of that original nakedness without shame. They can experience the authentic, safe, self-donating love that we are all seeking.

LIVE IT OUT: Winning the Tug-of-War

"I do not understand my own actions. For I do not do what I want but I do the very thing I hate...So then it is no longer I that do it, but sin which dwells within me...So I find it to be a law that when I want to do right, evil lies close at hand" (Rom 7:15, 17, 21).

Can you relate to what St. Paul was writing about in the verses above? You knew what you were supposed to do but, for whatever reason, you simply could not live up to the mark? Your dad told you when you were eleven years old to stop bothering your younger sister in the back of the car, but you couldn't resist picking on her. Your mom told you to get your homework done before you played any more X-Box, but you snuck in a few games. Or you knew you shouldn't gossip about a particular friend, but you just couldn't help it. This sums up so much of the Christian experience: we know that we are supposed to live a certain way but our hearts, minds, and bodies fight against "the law."

You might be saying to yourself right now, "Hey, what I've read so far is all fine and good, but it ain't *realistic*. This is just too hard to live." You wouldn't be the first one to think that way, and you won't be the last.

(Cont.)

good. As we mentioned before, the famous Catholic author G.K. Chesterton once said, "Every man who knocks on the door of a brothel is a man looking for God."

Chesterton's point was that because each of us, in our very core, desires union with God (and is attracted to Him just as a magnet is attracted to metal), we seek Him. Sometimes, though, this desire gets twisted because of the culture around us or due to habits formed through our own bad choices.

In the case of men visiting a brothel, they seldom find God in such sordid pursuits. In fact, such persons most often fall deeper into sexual addiction, and further away from the two essential truths about the human person: (1) that we have extraordinary value as persons; and (2) that we should never be used as objects for another's mere pleasure.

MOVIE CLIP/SONG SUGGESTIONS

MOVIE CLIPS:

1. **The Two Towers:** Show the segment that falls between 1:38:37 and 1:41:04. (Note: The time code shown here is from the Extended Version.) Smeagol and Gollum (two personalities of a character with schizophrenic tendencies) argue about whether the master, Frodo, really cares about him, will take care of him, and is trustworthy. This is a perfect comparison for the "questioning of the gift" that John Paul II discusses when Adam and Eve did not trust God.

2. **The Empire Strikes Back:** Show the segment that falls between 1:49:16 and 1:54:05. Darth Vader tempts Luke Skywalker to join the Dark Side.

3. **The Lion, the Witch, and the Wardrobe:** Show the segment that falls between 26:40 and 35:59. This is the scene in which Edmund follows Lucy into the wardrobe and bumps into the White Witch in Narnia. She tempts him with sweet food as well as appeals to his pride. He succumbs and enters a new realm of concupiscence.

SONGS:

1. **Wonderful Maker** — Jeremy Camp *(The Carried Me Project)*

This song focuses on the beauty of God's creation and the goodness of God as a truly wonderful maker. Contemporary Praise/Worship.

2. **Undo Me** — Jennifer Knapp *(Kansas)*

This song is all about human nature being depraved and sinful, and the struggle we must make to love. She's asking the Lord to "undo" the damage of Original Sin. (Note: Although this is a good song, Catholic theology does not go to the extent of traditional Protestant theology in saying we are "totally depraved." Catholic theology contends that we are "deprived"— we were made good and are still essentially good, but have an orientation toward sin.) Folk Rock.

3. **I Belong to You** — Superchic[k] *(Last One Picked)*

Sometimes life brings pain, but God is there no matter what. Pop Ballad.

4. **Everytime I Fall** — Jaci Velasquez *(On My Knees)*

Just when you think God is not there, He will lift you up. Pop.

LIVE IT OUT: *(Cont.)*

You might feel like a character in a cartoon when you try to "live out" chastity or tame your sexual temptations: there's an angel on one shoulder telling you to be good and a devil on the other saying, "Go ahead. It'll be fine." When it comes to living a holy life, you might feel like there is a huge tug-of-war going on in your soul between God and the devil, or between your body and your soul. That's the battle between the "flesh and spirit" that St. Paul writes about in his letter to the Romans. This is another effect of original sin. It's called concupiscence, and it's the tendency toward sin. And it also clouds our judgment and skews our thinking.

Here are three things you can try to help you along when you feel like you're being pulled toward the "mud pit" in this spiritual tug of war:

1. **Iron sharpens iron**. You've heard since you were little that the friends you choose make a huge difference in your life. Well, it's almost always the truth. The Bible tells us that having a good friend can help us to stay sharp—to stay alert and aware—when it comes to growing in our faith. "As iron sharpens iron, so man sharpens his fellow man" (Prov 27:17, NAB). If you are feeling tempted to do or watch something impure, a friend to whom you are accountable can help steer you away from a certain choice. When you get hit with a major temptation and you're feeling weak, call your friend and ask him or her to pray for you. While these ideas might seem a little extreme, ask yourself if your purity is worth it. God would say, "Yes, it is worth all of these things and more."

2. **Remember God's promise.** Read and commit 1 Corinthians 10:13 to memory: "No temptation has overtaken you that is not common to man. God is faithful and he will not allow you to be tempted beyond your strength, but with the temptation will also provide the way of escape, that you may be able to endure it." Now, *that* is some Good News! God has promised to give us the grace—any time—to pull us out of any temptation. We also read in Romans 5:20, "Where sin increased, grace abounded all the more." Trust in the promises of the Lord, He will not leave you abandoned.

3. **Sing loud or be quiet.** Get out of your box. Do something different to solve the problem. You may think it's weird to sing to God, but challenge yourself to lift your heart to God in a new way by singing. Or, better yet, don't just sing … worship. St. Augustine said that when you worship God with song, you pray twice. Sing at Mass if you usually don't. Or if you normally do, sing louder. If you're not ready to sing the words at Mass, don't tune out. *Pray* the words.

If you really aren't ready to worship out loud, then be quiet. Make a visit to a nearby chapel or find your favorite quiet place and, in silence, soak in God's love. This is especially powerful if the Blessed Sacrament is present. You can engage in what the Church calls Eucharistic Adoration, where we silently sit in the presence of the Lord. In the silence—standing, sitting, kneeling, or even lying prostrate—slow down your body and allow God to speak to your heart. Worship Him "out loud" in the quiet of your heart. The Scriptures speak volumes about the need for worship—not for God's sake, but for our own sake. God, in His word, encourages us to offer our whole bodies in praise and worship of Him. When you join the movement of your soul (prayer) to the movement of your body you have begun to heal that rupture, that great divide between body and spirit discussed earlier.

There is no escaping the fact that life is a tug-of-war, but it doesn't have to become a war that you lose. You don't have to approach the mud pit. Every time you resist temptation, moving toward God and away from selfishness, you grow a little bit stronger and a little bit holier.

Remember, the devil is not afraid of you, but he is petrified of the presence of Christ within you. The only way for you to win this spiritual tug-of-war is not to pull harder, it's to let go … and let God.

Notes & Nuggets: In the closing prayer, we pray through the intercession of St. Francis and St. Clare of Assisi who, both lived simple lives and abandoned all the world had to offer in order to live in poverty and receive all that God had to offer them.

WORK IT OUT

Assignment #1: Reflect upon Adam's experience of original solitude and compare it to the loneliest time in your own life. Write a reflection on the similarities and differences between your own solitude and Adam's original solitude.

Assignment #2: Write a "letter" of at least one page to someone (famous or otherwise) who dresses shamelessly. In your letter, explain to the person the difference between "naked without shame" and "shameless." Explain why being "naked without shame" in its fullest context can only truly exist in marriage. Do not mock or condemn the person. Write the letter with an abundance of charity. Help the person see the beauty of living and dressing chastely. (**NOTE:** In order to be the super-student of John Paul II and his call to engage the culture with a New Evangelization [see chapter 12 glossary], go the extra mile to share the Good News with an actual person. Ask your teacher to help you polish up your letter and prepare it for actual delivery to a friend in need. Then, find the person's address and mail the letter to him or her. If you get a response, consider sharing it with the class.)

Assignment #3: Write a "Back to the Future" poem or story. Imagine that you and another person are actually Adam and Eve and living in the Garden of Eden. Then imagine that you know all the information that you know today about the temptation of the devil (the snake), the Fall, and the baggage that comes with original sin. Here's the catch: You have this knowledge but your spouse does not—and there's only one week before the Fall takes place. You have a job to do: *avoid the Fall!* Write a creative, pure, and humorous message to your spouse in the Garden that pledges your love and simultaneously attempts to avoid the upcoming "Fall."

Assignment #4: Use your knowledge from the first three chapters—especially the concepts of creation, love, lust, pride, innocence, and freedom—to analyze the biblical poetry found in the Song of Songs. What is the point of the story? Is there any shame in their love? Is it similar or dissimilar to people being sexually "shameless" in our society? How? Write an essay of your analysis.

Assignment #5: Write a song, poem, or rap that creatively teaches the popular culture about the "nuptial meaning of the body" and its significance. Get creative but stay honorable. Be sure to include words such as "pure," "heaven," "sign," and "giving." The more terms you can creatively use (such as "naked without shame" and "original unity"), the better!

Assignment #6: Cross reference Genesis 2:24 with Ephesians 5:31. Examine the rest of Ephesians 5 to see how St. Paul's idea of marriage has "fleshed out" the ideas found in Genesis. Write an analytical essay that details your findings.

CLOSING PRAYER

Leader: In the name of the Father, and of the Son, and of the Holy Spirit. **Amen.**

All: Sts. Francis and **Clare of Assisi,** please pray with me that I, like both of you, would be willing to leave behind any and all worldly desires that might lead me away from God. **Amen.**

IN HIS OWN WORDS

• **On Genesis:** "Following the contemporary philosophy of religion and that of language, it can be said that the language in question is a mythical one. In this case the term 'myth' does not designate a fabulous content, but merely an archaic way of expressing a deeper content" (November 7, 1979).

• **On Original Innocence:** "Historical man tries to understand the mystery of original innocence almost by means of a contrast. … He tries to understand original innocence as an essential characteristic for the theology of the body, starting from the experience of shame. In fact, the Bible text itself directs him in this way. Original innocence, therefore, is what 'radically,' that is, at its roots, excludes shame of the body in the man-woman relationship. It eliminates its necessity in man, in his heart, that is, in his conscience" (January 30, 1980).

• **Original Experiences:** "Speaking of original human experiences, we have in mind not so much their distance in time, as rather their basic significance. The important thing is not that these experiences belong to a man's pre-history (to his 'theological prehistory'), but that they are always at the root of every human experience … They are so intermingled with the ordinary things of life that we do not generally notice their extraordinary character" (December 12, 1979).

• **Original Nakedness:** "Only the nakedness that makes woman an object for man, or vice versa, is a source of shame. The fact that they were not ashamed means that the woman was not an 'object' for the man nor he for her" (February 20, 1980).

• **On Original Sin:** "Questioning in his heart the deepest meaning of the donation, that is, love as the specific motive of the creation and of the original covenant (see Gn 3:5), man turns his back on God-Love, on the Father. In a way he casts God out of his heart. At the same time he detaches his heart and almost cuts it off from what 'is of the Father.' Thus, there remains in him what 'is of the world'" (April 30, 1980).

• **On Shame:** "Man is ashamed of his body because of lust. In fact, he is ashamed not so much of his body as precisely of lust. He is ashamed of his body owing to lust. He is ashamed of his body owing to that state of his spirit to which theology and psychology give the same name: desire or lust, although with a meaning that is not quite the same" (May 28, 1980).

• **On Absorption of Shame by Love:** "On the contrary, affirmation of the person influences the emotions in such a way that the value of the person is not just abstractly understood but deeply felt. This is the point at which love is psychologically complete, and sexual shame can be thoroughly absorbed. A man and woman can become 'one flesh'—in the familiar words of the Book of Genesis (2:24), with which the creator defined the essence of marriage—and that oneness will not be a form of shamelessness, but only the full realization of the union of persons, which results from reciprocal conjugal love" (*Love and Responsibility,* 184).

Glossary
of Key Terms

Historical Man: The period that begins with original sin and ends when Christ returns. Historical men and women are simultaneously fallen and redeemed in Christ.

Naked Without Shame: Nakedness that exists within the context of innocence and pure freedom, apart from lust. This is what Adam and Eve experienced before the Fall.

Nuptial Meaning of the Body: The marital meaning of the body. " ... the body's capacity of expressing love, that love precisely in which the person becomes a gift and ... fulfills the very meaning of his being and existence" (January 16, 1980).

Original Happiness: A happiness that was rooted in the perfect gift of love that was initiated by God, received in love, and shared in love.

Original Innocence: The state of Adam and Eve prior to their knowledge of sin, when their minds, hearts, and bodies were perfectly innocent.

Original Man: The era of humanity in the "original experiences" before the Fall, up until the original sin of Adam and Eve.

Original Nakedness: The first experience of Adam and Eve when they were naked without shame. Before original sin, lust did not even exist and all sexual desires were pure.

Original Sin: The first sin of Adam and Eve, when they distrusted God's plan and chose their own will over the will of God.

Original Solitude: The original state when Adam realized he was alone because he was without a true companion; it also refers to the human experience of being alone in the world as a person, as someone fundamentally different from the animals.

Original Unity: The initial experience of perfect unity between man and woman as they lived in perfect communion with each other and gave themselves to each other through the mutual gift of their bodies.

Pride: The original sin that caused Adam and Eve to prefer themselves to God. This is the root of all moral evil in the world.

Second Creation Account: The second telling of the creation of the world in the book of Genesis. The first account focuses on the grand scale of the creation of the world, while the second account focuses on the creation of man and woman as the climax of all creation.

Shameless: In today's society, this term refers to flaunting the body without inhibitions or conscience. Acting shamelessly reflects a false notion of sexual freedom.

Spiritualized body: The human body not only as living with a soul, but also being a dwelling place of the Holy Spirit, through the grace of redemption.

OBJECTIVES At the end of this lesson, your students should know and be able to:

- Explain eschatological man as the experience of full redemption in the perfect marriage of Christ and His Church in heaven.

- Express a view of God whose mercy and forgiveness can heal the imperfection, hurts, and sins of our lives.

- Demonstrate that Jesus offers us hope that we can overcome and heal from the pain and regret of our pasts.

- Experience forgiveness and reconciliation with God through a free encounter with His mercy in the sacrament of reconciliation.

- Explain that God has revealed to us the meaning of our existence through the nuptial meaning of the body.

- Recognize that God wants an eternal union with us beyond anything experienced on earth—a "marriage" relationship with us in heaven.

Notes & Nuggets: Pray for your teens to repent of their failings and to receive the healing power of Jesus so that they can forgive others and forgive themselves for the way they have lived in the past.

We also strongly suggest that, as part of this lesson or following it, you arrange for a priest to be available for the teens to have an opportunity for the sacrament of reconciliation. This is one of the best ways to bring hope and redemption down from being distant, abstract ideas and to make them practical and life-changing realities. Of course, it is always wise to attempt to secure a priest who has the natural gift of making teens feel comfortable and welcomed back to God's family (rather than chastised) through the sacrament. Even without such a priest, the grace of the sacrament can still be an effective and affective part of their understanding and experience of hope and redemption.

Chapter Four

Hope and Redemption in Christ

Through the Fall, our first parents (Adam and Eve—**original man)** chose themselves over God and began the course of **historical man**, the period of human history between the Fall and the end of time. Instead of perfect peace and happiness of paradise, our world is filled with pain and suffering. While Satan's plan is to lie, destroy, and separate, God's plan is to love and restore. He accomplished this through His only Son, Jesus, the Way, the Truth, and the Life, who was sent to redeem the world from the destruction and death brought on by original sin. Just as Jesus rose from the dead on Easter morning, God can and does bring new life to people, marriages, and families that seem spiritually dead.

In Jesus Christ, God offers us a hope and redemption that often seem impossible to us. In Jesus, the tide of sin can be reversed and defeated. Contrary to what society sometimes tells us, life with Christ is a full one. Unlike sin and deception, which promise the world but deliver only death, God offers us a way to perfect peace and happiness.

God also wants us to go to heaven. As our redeemer, Jesus is our invitation, our ticket to get there. In fact, by His sacrifice He gave Himself totally for us so that we could enjoy a union with Him in heaven—an amazing marriage of perfect love between Christ and His Church. This is the life of **eschatological man** and the purpose for which we were all created.

ICEBREAKER #1 (optional): Crumpled Bill Demonstration

This simple visual exercise can be a good bridge for your lesson. Pull out a crisp twenty dollar bill, show it to your students, and ask them if they would like to have it. Next, crumple it up a bit and show it to your students again. Ask them if it's still valuable and if they still want it. Then, put the twenty-dollar bill on the floor and jump on it. You may even have a few of your big and tall students stomp on it as well. Then, pick it back up and open it again. Ask them again if the bill is still valuable. Ask them exactly how much it is worth. When they say its original value has not changed, make the analogy that today you will be exploring the nature of hope and redemption. Subtly place the crumpled bill into your pocket and quickly explain that no matter how worthless they may feel or how many times they stomped on themselves or allowed others to trash them, each one of them is still a person of great worth ("of inestimable value," as John Paul II says). Then, from your other pocket, pull out another crisp and new twenty dollar bill. After this, have one of your students read (or re-read if you just used it for the prayer) Revelation 21:3-5, paying particular attention to the phrase, "all things new."

ICEBREAKER #2 (optional): "Adam's Fall"

This is a simple re-creation of the old "trust fall." Break teens into pairs and place one teen facing away from the other. Teen #1 (Adam) must stand straight as a board and fall back without bending his or her body, trusting that Teen #2 (Jesus) will actually catch him or her before hitting the ground. This takes a tremendous amount of trust. We recommend only doing this icebreaker if you have mattresses, pillows, or some sort of cushioning below the teens. Be sensitive to those who may be overweight and do not want to participate. If they are secure with themselves, let them do the trust fall, but be sure to assign them someone (or two people!) strong enough to catch them.

The simple symbolism is: Adam falls, but Jesus, through His death and resurrection, "catches" him and his whole family, making it possible for us all to have hope and redemption. Through the Fall, we did not drop out of the reach of God's mercy. Jesus' death on the Cross is the safety net that caught all of humanity and, through His sacrifice, gave us an opportunity at redemption.

TWO MINUTE DRILL — VERBAL REVIEW:

1. What is the state of longing that Adam experienced before God gave him Eve?
   Answer: He experienced loneliness among all the animals that were unlike him. John Paul II called this original solitude, which Adam and Eve also experienced as the only material creatures who were *persons*.

2. What does it mean to say that Adam and Eve were "naked without shame"?
   Answer: When Adam and Eve first saw each other, there wasn't any confusion between love and lust. In their nakedness, they rejoiced with a pure attraction to both the beauty of their bodies and their entire beings.

3. Why did God create us?
   Answer: He created us because He loves us and He wanted to share His life with us–to be in communion with us forever in heaven.

4. What was the essence of Adam and Eve's original sin?
   Answer: They believed the lie that God was not a good Father. They doubted the gift of God and disobeyed His rule, which was there to protect them.

5. Why does original sin matter so much to us?
   Answer: It was through this act that the family of Adam and Eve, and all creation, was plunged from a life of purity, love, and grace into a darkened state brought about by sin. God's plan was life. Original sin brought us suffering and death.

OPENING PRAYER

Leader: In the name of the Father, and of the Son, and of the Holy Spirit. **Amen.**

(Option #1)

Leader or Reader #1: Read Romans 8:14-15

"For those who are led by the Spirit of God are children of God. For you did not receive a spirit of slavery to fall back into fear, but you received a spirit of adoption, through which we cry, 'Abba, Father!'"

Leader or Reader #2: Loving Abba Father, You have created us for Yourself and called us to Yourself. You have freed us in a most powerful way and Your Spirit is upon us. We ask You to grant us the grace not to resist Your grace. May we not fall back into the darkness, but remain with You in the light, where there is warmth, comfort, hope, redemption, and the fullness of love. Lord, help us to be open today to accept Your forgiveness and Your grace to begin anew.

We ask all this as we pray together: Our Father, who art in heaven, hallowed be Thy name. Thy kingdom come, Thy will be done, on earth as it is in heaven. Give us this day our daily bread, and forgive us our trespasses, as we forgive those who trespass against us. And lead us not into temptation, but deliver us from evil. Saint (patron saint of your church or school), pray for us. In the name of the Father, and of the Son, and of the Holy Spirit. **Amen.**

(Option #2)

Leader or Reader #1: Read Revelation 21:3-5 (NAB)

"I heard a loud voice from the throne saying, 'Behold, God's dwelling is with the human race. He will dwell with them and they will be his people and God himself will always be with them (as their God). He will wipe every tear from their eyes, and there shall be no more death or mourning, wailing or pain, (for) the old order has passed away.' The one who sat on the throne said, 'Behold, I make all things new.' Then he said, 'Write these words down, for they are trustworthy and true.'"

Leader or Reader #2: Jesus, please help us to understand our eternal purpose as sons and daughters and to live our lives in the new life that You offer to each of us. Renew our purity and our belief in our self-worth so that we might draw near to our goal of eternal life with You. Help us bring others along with us on our journey by offering them the same hope that we find in Your amazing love. **Amen.**

Need a Review of Lesson 3? Look to next page.

STORY STARTER: The Room

In that place between wakefulness and dreams, I found myself in the room. There were no distinguishing features except for the one wall covered with small index card files. They were like the ones in libraries that list books by author or subject in alphabetical order. But these files, which stretched from floor to ceiling and seemingly endlessly in either direction, had very different headings.

As I drew near the wall of files, the first to catch my attention was one that read "Girls I Have Liked." I opened it and began flipping through the cards. I quickly shut it, shocked to realize that I recognized the names written on each one.

And then without being told, I knew exactly where I was. This lifeless room with its small files was a crude card-catalog system for my life. Here were written the actions of my every moment, big and small, in a detail my memory couldn't match.

A sense of wonder and curiosity, coupled with horror, stirred within me as I began randomly opening files and exploring their content. Some brought joy and sweet memories; others a sense of shame and regret so intense that I would look over my shoulder to see if anyone was watching. A file named "Friends" was next to one marked "Friends I Have Betrayed."

The titles ranged from the mundane to the outright weird. "Books I Have Read," "Lies I Have Told," "Comfort I Have Given," "Jokes That Made Me Laugh." Some were almost hilarious in their exactness: "Things I've Yelled At My Brothers." Others I couldn't laugh at: "Things I Have Done In My Anger," "Things I Have Muttered Under My Breath At My Parents." I never ceased to be surprised by the contents. Often there were many more cards than I expected. Sometimes fewer than I hoped.

I was overwhelmed by the sheer volume of the life I had lived. Could it be possible that I had the time in my years to write each of these thousands or even millions of cards? But each card confirmed this truth. Each was written in my own handwriting. Each signed with my signature.

When I pulled out the file marked "Songs I Have Listened To," I realized the files grew to contain their contents. The cards were packed tightly, and yet after two or three yards, I hadn't found the end of the file. I shut it, shamed, not so much by the quality of music, but more by the vast amount of time I knew that file represented. When I came to a file marked "Lustful Thoughts," I felt a chill run through my body. I pulled the file out only an inch, not willing to test its size, and drew out a card. I shuddered at its detailed content. I felt sick to think that such a moment had been recorded.

An almost animal rage broke on me. One thought dominated my mind: "No one must ever see these cards! No one must ever see this room! I have to destroy them!" In an insane frenzy I yanked the file out. Its size didn't matter now. I had to empty it and burn the cards. But as I took it at one end and began pounding it on the floor, I could not dislodge a single card. I became desperate and pulled out a card, only to find it as strong as steel when I tried to tear it.

Defeated and utterly helpless, I returned the file to its slot. Leaning my forehead against the wall, I let out a long, self-pitying sigh. And then I saw it. The title bore "People I Have Told About My Belief In Jesus." The handle was brighter than those around it—newer, almost unused. I pulled on its handle and a small box fell into my hands. I could count the cards it contained on one hand.

Verbal Review of Lesson 3

1. What is the state of longing that Adam experienced before God gave him Eve?

2. What does it mean to say that Adam and Eve were "naked without shame"?

3. Why did God create us?

4. What was the essence of Adam and Eve's original sin?

5. Why does original sin matter so much to us?

"Our sins are nothing but a grain of sand alongside the great mountain of the mercy of God."
– St. John Vianney

And then the tears came. I began to weep. Sobs so deep that the hurt started in my stomach and shook through me. I fell on my knees and cried. I cried out of shame, from the overwhelming shame of it all. The rows of file shelves swirled in my tear-filled eyes. No one must ever, ever know of this room. I must lock it up and hide the key. But then as I pushed away the tears, I saw Him. No, please, not Him. Not here. Oh, anyone but Jesus.

I watched helplessly as He began to open the files and read the cards. I couldn't bear to watch His response. And in the moments I could bring myself to look at His face, I saw a sorrow deeper than my own. He seemed to intuitively go to the worst boxes. Why did He have to read every one?

Finally, He turned and looked at me from across the room. He looked at me with pity in His eyes. But this was a pity that didn't anger me. I dropped my head, covered my face with my hands and began to cry again. He walked over and put His arm around me. He could have said so many things. But He didn't say a word. He just cried with me.

Then He got up and walked back to the wall of files. Starting at one end of the room, He took out a file and, one by one, began to sign His name over mine on each card.

"No!" I shouted rushing to Him. All I could find to say was "No! No!" as I pulled the cards from Him. His name shouldn't be on these cards. But there it was, written in red so rich, so dark, so alive. The name of Jesus covered mine. It was written with His blood. He gently took the card back. He smiled a sad smile and began to sign the cards again. I don't think I'll ever understand how He did it so quickly, but the next instant it seemed I heard Him close the last file and walk back to my side. He placed His hand on my shoulder and said, "It is finished."

I stood up, and He led me out of the room. There was no lock on its door. There were still cards to be written.

"Though your sins are like scarlet, they shall be as white as snow; though they are red like crimson, they shall be like wool."
(Is 1:18)

＊

By Joshua Harris. (Originally published in New Attitude *magazine; ©1995 New Attitude. Used also in the book* I Kissed Dating Goodbye.*)*

COMPREHENSION & DISCUSSION QUESTIONS

1. What is the overall point and symbolism of the story?

2. What are the "cards" that you have written that you would be eager to show to Jesus?

3. What can you do to create more cards of goodness, purity, and love, and stop "writing" the ones that would embarrass you before Christ?

4. What do Jesus' words "It is finished" symbolize in the story and for our own lives? When have we heard Him say those words before?

5. What connections do you see between the story and the sacrament of Reconciliation?

6. Do you believe that Jesus loves you enough to write His name over all of your "cards" of sin?

7. How can Jesus help you turn from shame and hurt to forgiveness, peace, and hope?

8. What does the word "redemption" mean to you in your own life? Why do we need it? Why is it sometimes hard to accept?

 ## BRIDGING THE GAP

Imagine a wedding reception taking place thousands of years ago. The bride, in preparation to meet her groom, adorns herself with jewels and a beautiful gown. And what's the groom doing? He's burning, engraving, or tattooing her name into the palm of his hand, as a sign of his complete faithfulness to her. This ritual may sound a bit extreme when compared to the simple exchange of rings we see today. But this was the custom for certain people in the Old Testament, and some cultures still practice it today.

Regardless of how strange the wedding tradition seems, you know the bride had no doubts about her groom's devotion to her. Just as this mark would remain on his body for the rest of his life, so, too, would she belong to him, and him to her. It was in this historical setting when God said to us, "I have called you by name, you are mine... Behold, I have graven you on the palms of my hands" (Is 43:1; 49:16 NAB).

Jesus did more than tattoo Himself to remind us of His love and devotion. As the story of Jesus and the young man with the index cards so beautifully showed, Jesus gave all of Himself for us. He allowed Himself to be nailed to a Cross, giving His own blood so that our sins would be wiped away and our lives could be spared. But there are "still cards to be written," and we are the authors of what will go on those cards.

Often, people assume that when they sin and fall away from God, He hates them. But unlike us, God does not hold grudges. We're the ones who pull away from Him, but He remains faithful. In this chapter, you'll learn that regardless of what you've done, He still waits for you, offering hope, healing, and redemption.

Did You Know?

The media portrays teen sex without regrets, but a survey of 1,000 sexually active teens across America revealed that two-thirds of them wish that they had waited longer to have sex (77 percent of girls and 60 percent of boys).[1]

Notes & Nuggets: "A Modern-Day Prodigal Son"

One Option: Instead of just reading or discussing the story of the Prodigal Son from Luke 15: 26-41, recreate the story in a modern-day context. You can do this from two different angles. The first one requires simple dialogue while the second gets your students more physically involved.

Modern-Day Reading: Simply read the story of the Prodigal Son but stop often to allow your students to make modern day analogies or comparisons as to how it would happen now. For example, when the young son squanders his inheritance on a life of recklessness, stop and let them fill in the blank as to what that would be today. (What kind of car would he buy? Where would he go? What would he do there?) When the father throws the party for the son, let them say what type of posh clothing would be comparable for the robe today, what upscale restaurant the father may have cater the party, etc.

Skit/Role Play: Let your teens make a skit out of the story, but using the language and circumstances of modern times.

STEP 1: Have your students read the story in small groups, using a few of your own guide questions if you think they need it.

STEP 2: Then, give them time to come up with a modern-day version of the Prodigal Son story. Let them perform their skits for the class.

STEP 3: Engage your students in a discussion about forgiveness, using some of the questions provided on the next page.

TO THE CORE

We've all heard the story of the Prodigal Son in Luke 15, in which one son leaves the house of his father in order to spend his inheritance on loose living. When the son decides to return, the father sees him at a distance and runs to meet him. In the same way, God does not wait for us to become perfect before He begins to love us. No matter how far we feel from Him, if we simply respond to His grace and turn our hearts back to Him, He runs to us. We can walk a million miles away, but all we need to take is one step back, and there He is, waiting for us with open arms.

As Blessed (Mother) Teresa of Calcutta said:

> The devil may try to use the hurts of life, and sometimes our own mistakes—to make you feel it is impossible that Jesus really loves you … This is a danger for all of us. And so sad, because it is completely the opposite of what Jesus is really wanting, waiting to tell you. Not only that He loves you, but even more—He longs for you. He misses you when you don't come close. He thirsts for you. He loves you always, even when you don't feel worthy. When not accepted by others, even by yourself sometimes, He is the one who always accepts you. Only believe—you are precious to Him. Bring all you are suffering to His feet—only open your heart to be loved by Him as you are. He will do the rest.[1]

COMPREHENSION & DISCUSSION QUESTIONS

1. How and why does Jesus want all that we have—our bodies and souls—even our imperfections?

2. What do you think are the main reasons that people struggle to believe they are precious to God?

3. Name the primary reasons that you think prevent people from turning back to God? How are these connected to the answers to question #2 above?

4. List ways to overcome—and help others to overcome—these obstacles that prevent us from experiencing the peace of reconciling and reuniting with God.

"As far as the east is from the west, so far does he remove our transgressions from us."
(Ps 103:12)

Christ Forgives and Redeems Us

If you have struggled with **sexual addictions**, painful memories of abuse, lustful thoughts, self-hatred, or anything else that seems impossible to heal or over-

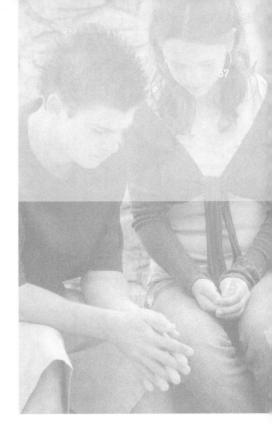

come, God wants to set you free. When we return to God, He not only forgives our sins, He offers us a new heart. Christ did not die and rise from the dead so that we could repress our sexuality and simply "try our best not to think about sex." He did not come to simply **redeem** our souls and then leave us with a bunch of coping mechanisms to battle temptation. Thankfully, He came to redeem every part of us, including our bodies and our desires.

Christ came to offer us victory and freedom. Sadly, instead of claiming this victory, we often complain that purity is too difficult. By doing this, we are actually emptying the Cross of its power and meaning. We are reducing our redemption to some quaint religious idea that sounds good but has no real power to change us. By doing so, we fail to experience its life-changing effects.

God Heals and Cleanses Us

So what do we need to do? First, realize that purity is a gift from God and that He will give it to those who ask for it. So begin right now with the prayer of David, who said, "Create in me a clean heart, O God, and put a new and right spirit within me" (Ps 51:10). As soon as you are able, take advantage of the sacrament of Reconciliation. Jesus promised us that He would be with us until the end, and one of the ways He is present to us right now is in the sacraments. You may be reluctant to go to confession out of fear or embarrassment. But take the advice of St. Augustine, who had plenty of struggles with purity in his youth. He said, "What could be hidden with me, even if I were unwilling to confess it to you? I would be hiding You from myself, not myself from You."

St. Augustine knew that God is **omniscient**, which means He knows everything. He sees all, both your strengths and weaknesses. If you haven't been to confession in a long time, now is a great time to go. Have courage. Pope John Paul II said to the young people, "In order to see Jesus, we first need to let Him look at us!"[2]

If you're too ashamed to go to a particular priest, then go to a different one. The important thing is that you are honest with the priest and sincerely desire to turn from your wrong choices in the past.

Often, the biggest thing holding us back is our disbelief that God can actually make us a new creation. When Jesus was approached by blind men in search of healing, he asked them, "Do you believe that I am able to do this?" (Mt 9:28). He waited for their response of faith before giving them the gift of sight. In the same way, we must trust that Christ has not come to condemn us but to save us.

If you approach God with true sorrow in your heart in the sacrament of Reconciliation, it doesn't matter which priest God uses to give you **absolution**. Jesus will welcome you back with open arms and give you a clean slate, along with extraordinary graces to stay strong in the faith.

"I have swept away your transgressions like a cloud, and your sins like mist; return to me, for I have redeemed you. ... I will not remember your sins."
(Is 44:22; 43:25)

COMPREHENSION & DISCUSSION QUESTIONS

1. What do many of us do that "empties the cross of its meaning"?

2. In order to experience the real effects of redemption of our sexuality, what is the first thing we must recognize?

3. What is often the biggest thing holding us back from having a clean heart?

4. What do you think are some practical reasons that absolution can have such a positive effect on our thinking?

"Have patience with all the world, but first of all with yourself."
– St. Francis de Sales

The Resurrection of the Body

There are plenty of misconceptions about heaven and our participation there. But this is because the wonders of heaven are beyond our imagination. St. Paul tells us that "no eye has seen, nor ear heard, nor the heart of man conceived what God has prepared for those who love him" (1 Cor 2:9). While many people think the body is merely a carrying case for our souls, this is literally *not* the case. Remember, each human is a composite—a full union—of body and soul. Heaven is not only for our souls; it is for our bodies *and* souls.

If you are looking for an "out-of-body experience," you will get one when you die, but it will only be for a while. At the end of time, at **the resurrection of the body**, our souls will be *joined* with our bodies in heaven. This is the truth we proclaim at the end of the Creed during Mass.

The Church realizes that this truth is not accepted by everyone, but it is a major part of our belief in the afterlife. This is why the *Catechism* states, "'On no point does the Christian faith meet with more opposition than on the resurrection of the body.' It is very commonly accepted that the life of the human person continues in a spiritual fashion after death. But how can we believe that this body, so clearly mortal, could rise to everlasting life?" (CCC 996). We can look straight to Scripture for the answer to this question, as Jesus ascended *body and soul* into heaven: "… he was lifted up and a cloud took him out of their sight … 'Jesus, who was taken up from you into heaven'" (Acts 1:9,11). What does this have to do with you? St. Paul speaks about the life of Jesus being at work in our mortal flesh and reminds us that "He who raised the Lord Jesus will raise us also with Jesus and bring us with you into his presence" (2 Cor 4:14). At the end of time, we will enjoy heaven *with* our bodies, not without them.

59-L

No Tears in Heaven

Once we do make it to heaven, God Himself will be with us and will wipe away every tear from our eyes (see Rev 21:4). In eternity, we will experience the fullness of Christ's redemption, and when we are rejoined with our bodies, they will be our **glorified bodies** (see 1 Cor 15:35-58). We won't experience illness, pain, or death, and there will be no more suffering. Our knowledge will be perfected, and our desires will be purified so completely that we will no longer feel torn between sin and God, as we do now. Even St. Paul felt this conflict when he said, "I do not do the good I want, but the evil I do not want is what I do. ... I see in my members another law at war with the law of my mind" (Rom 7:19, 23). Thankfully in heaven, we'll be freed from this tension within ourselves. Pope John Paul II called this final stage of our perfection **eschatological man**. This term comes from the word *eschaton*, which refers to the end times, or the end of the world as we know it.

Heavenly Marriage

The main reason that the life of eschatological man will be different from life here on earth is that our union with God will be complete. The **nuptial meaning of the body** not only points us toward our union here on earth, but also toward a participation in a heavenly marriage. Remember that **nuptial** is another word for "marital," "spousal," or "conjugal." Eschatological man will surely be married, but not to another human as on earth. Our heavenly marriage will exist in the sense that we are all members of the Church, the bride of Christ. Recall that when the Sadducees asked Jesus about marriage in heaven, He said, "For in the resurrection, they neither marry nor are given in marriage" (Mt 22:30). Jesus was not saying that marriage does not exist in heaven, but that in the resurrection, marriage will not be between only a man and a woman. Instead, it will be a single reality that we all participate in together: the marriage of Christ and the Church. It is there that we will experience an intimate union not only with Christ, but with each other in the **communion of saints**. The *Catechism* sums it up like this: "For man, this consummation will be the final realization of the unity of the human race, which God willed from creation. ... Those who are united with Christ will form the community of the redeemed, 'the holy city' of God, 'the Bride, the wife of the Lamb'" (CCC 1045).

COMPREHENSION & DISCUSSION QUESTIONS

1. Which Christian doctrine does the *Catechism* say meets more opposition than any other?

2. What type of body will we have after the resurrection of our body? Why is this so?

3. What is *eschatological man*?

4. What does the word *nuptial* have to do with heaven?

5. What did Jesus teach about marriage in heaven?

6. How will our participation in the *communion of saints* be different in heaven from what we experience of it here on earth?

Union of Christ and the Church

Now, if there will be a heavenly marriage, it is logical to ask whether there will be sex in heaven. The answer is "no" and "yes." There will be no conjugal (sexual) relations as we humans experience here on earth. This is *not* because sex is "bad" or "unworthy" of the kingdom. Let's remember that God created sex, and all that He created is good! Recall that the primary purpose of the sexual relationship, on the natural level, is (a) to bring about unity between a husband and wife, and (b) to bring about new life. On the supernatural level, the marital embrace is intended as a symbol or foreshadowing of the union that all of us will have with God in heaven.

Once we are in heaven, the unity that sexual relationships bring to us here on earth will no longer be needed. Here's an example: Let's say you wanted to drive from New York to Florida. On the way you would see a series of signs that would say: "1,000 miles to Florida," "500 miles to Florida," and "ten miles to Florida." Those signs point you to the reality you will soon experience: Florida. Once in Florida, you would not see any more signs because you would be there. (There will not be a "0 miles to Florida" sign.) Well, similarly, once we are in heaven, there is no need for the foreshadowing of divine unity that sexual relations are here on earth.

Furthermore, since we will reach our purpose and fulfillment in heaven, where all things will be brought to completion, there will be no further need for additional human beings. So the other primary purpose for sexual relations here on earth, the bringing forth of new life, will be unnecessary.

Although there will be no physical sexual relationships in heaven, we will retain "sex," if we mean by this "the differences between the sexes." We will retain our gender in heaven (see the "woman" in Rev 12:1). In heaven, we will still be male or female. Your sex (or gender) is eternal, but sexual intercourse on earth is merely a shadow of the greatness of our eternal exchange of life and love with God heaven.

The marriage of Christ and His Church has a time of "courtship" before it—our union with Christ begins here on earth. If heaven is a marriage, then your marriage preparation starts now. The more honest we are with ourselves, the more seriously we should ask the question, "How am I getting to know Jesus?"

notes

APPLICATION

Option #1: Sacrament of Reconciliation

This would be a great point to take the teens to a church or chapel and offer them the opportunity to receive the sacrament of reconciliation. Be sure to provide your teens with a good Examination of Conscience and ample time for them to go through it (at least five to ten minutes). Another good idea is providing them all a typed version of an Act of Contrition, as many may not know how to make one. Just having an Act of Contrition in their hands gives them one less reason to be worried or fearful. If your teens have not been to confession in a while (and chances are that this will be the case for at least some of them), for their benefit, do a quick review of the process of the confession: what they should say, what they can expect the priest to do, etc.

If you cannot arrange for multiple priests to hear confessions and the process is going to take a while, it is helpful to give the teens something else to read or write as they wait before and after their confessions. Otherwise, invite them to pray in an adoration chapel before and after their turn in confession.

Option #2: "My Response to the Cross"

Role Play: As you are teaching your teens, abruptly excuse yourself and leave the room, saying you need to use the restroom. After only walking outside the door and being gone for five to ten seconds, burst frantically back into the room as a crazed character with a strong foreign accent. The essence of the role play is that a man died for one of your teens this morning, and you are desperately trying to find the teen to tell him or her the story of what the man did for him or her. The most critical part of the entire activity is threefold:

1. You are ridiculously passionate and in the students' faces about the amazing event you witnessed this morning.

2. You must pick the RIGHT student to approach. Your choice should be someone that you know is polite and mild-mannered. DO NOT pick the extreme extrovert in the group. Preferably you don't want to pick a "teacher's pet" either. You want someone who is generally liked by his or her classmates, and one who you know will not "take over" or "shut down" in the middle of this experience.

3. Even as you remain in character, keep tight control over the whole group so that extreme reactions (and the center-of-attention/thorn-in-your-side teen who wants to spoil your point) do not break the experience into something trivial.

Note: If you are not comfortable with acting in such a dramatic way in front of your teens, ask someone else who is more comfortable to burst in on your session with the following role play. (If you really can't make this a dramatic scene, then you can take the truth of the exercise and work it into your lesson.) When done well, it is extremely effective. The script is easy to follow, and goes something like this:

Character: *(out of breath, crazed, wide-eyed)*: Hello, my friends! My name is Mr. _____ (insert an odd foreign name) and I am looking for a certain man (or woman)... his (or her) name is _____.

Insert the student's last name and intentionally murder the pronunciation in your thick accent, but close enough so that they know for whom you are asking. For example, if the teen's last name is "Leftwich," say, "I am looking for a man named 'Leftorwichie'" or some such intentional mispronunciation. Remember, you don't know these teens. You've never seen them before. Move intentionally in the wrong direction in the room so that teens must point out the student. If they hesitate, say, "You do not know this man? He is not here?!" Then move quickly to the student pointed out.

Character *(urgently)*: You are this man!? *(Wait for a nod of confirmation.)* I have to tell you something very important!

Don't wait for a response from the teen. Rattle the next part off really fast — you're so crazed and excited you can barely stand it.

Character: Just this morning I was in the marketplace minding my own business when a man step into the street, hold a machete above his head like dis *(wildly brandish the imaginary machete above your head)* and he say, "I want to kill _____"(insert name again). He was looking for you! I say to myself, I don't know who this _____ is, but he must be a bad guy, no? Just then, he said it again, louder this time, "I want to kill _____."

(Continued on next leader's page)

Could you imagine getting engaged to someone you didn't know? What about marrying someone who wasn't really committed to you, or left when things got tough? We should seriously ask ourselves if this is how we want to treat our relationship with God now.

Hope of Every Day

Recall that as a result of original sin, "human nature is weakened in its powers; subject to ignorance, suffering, and the domination of death; and inclined to sin" (CCC 418). As we wait for the full redemption of our bodies in heaven (see Rom 8:23), we are in a constant battle between sin and obedience. But the battle is ours to win. John Paul II says that in Christ we hold the "**hope of every day**," which helps us to live in freedom and to defeat "evil with good" (Rom 12:21). This means that Christ offers us grace to begin anew now, and this newness of life in him points us to the fullness of redemption in heaven. The amazing truth is, "Christ has set us free" (Gal 5:1). After using and being used, there is still hope and freedom to start over. God waits for us to open the door to Him.

"His mercies never come to an end; they are new every morning."
(Lam 3:22-23)

COMPREHENSION & DISCUSSION QUESTIONS

1. Will there be sex in heaven? Explain.

2. What is the *hope of every day*? Why is this good news?

DIGGING DEEPER:
The Greatest "Catch-22" in History

God loves you so much that He would rather die than risk spending eternity without you.

Do you believe this statement above? Read it again, pray about it, and ask yourself, "Do I really believe this?"

This is the reality of the cross and the reality of God's unyielding love. God loves *you* so much (not just "the world" in a general sense, but *you*, personally and intimately) that He would rather take your sin upon Himself than write you off or risk losing you forever to a place where you are separated from His love—hell.

If you don't agree with this statement, it either means you don't believe Jesus was God, don't believe you are a sinner, or don't believe that the cross of Christ and the mercy of God are bigger than your sin.

(Cont.)

Be sure to be close, nearly invading the teens' personal space as you relate the story. When appropriate, look around to connect your wild eyes with the students around him or her as you tell your tale.

Character: Suddenly, another man stepped out of the shadows and he said "My name is Mr. Timmons. I know this _____. He (or she) does not deserve to die ... I will die for him (or her)!"

Get emphatic, as if maybe they are not believing you.

Character: This is what he said! This happened this morning! The guy with the machete, he stepped forward and said, "Are you sure?!"

Brandish the invisible machete above your head again, and then, nodding your head, continue.

Character: "I am sure," he said. Then, he stuck his neck out like this *(stick your neck out)* and FOOM! *(swiftly swing your invisible machete down upon Timmons' imaginary neck)* He cut off his head!

At this point, pause briefly and stare expectantly at the teen. When he or she says nothing, go on ...

Character: What do you say to this man?

Predictably, ninety percent of the time the teen will respond with a sheepish "Thanks" or "Thank you." For the purpose of the activity, this is EXACTLY what you want them to say. Then, incredulously jump all over them!

Character: THANKS??!!! This man give his life *for you!* I saw it myself! His head rolled down the street—and all you say is thanks??!!

Start mumbling about Americans needing to learn to be grateful and head toward the door ...

Character: I pray that one day you will understand what it means to give a life for a life! *(Exit into the hallway or other room still muttering to yourself.)*

Pause for ten seconds. Then re-enter the room as yourself, as if everything is normal and you are returning from the bathroom. Attempt to begin the lesson again, though hopefully they won't let you. If they don't say anything, just ask them why they are looking at you so funny. Then ask them if something happened while you were out of the room. Draw them into telling you what happened as if you have no idea. Then ask them how

many times a day or times a week they look at a crucifix. Get some answers and then ask how many times each day or each week they actually think about what that crucifix means. Finish by consoling the student who was the "victim" of the skit, saying that we would all react to the news as he or she did. We look at this amazing sacrifice and we are either shocked or overwhelmed, and we often live as people who are giving the very inadequate response of "thank you" to Christ's action. Finally, lead them into a journal assignment by finishing with something like this:

"How inappropriate is just saying 'thanks'? If someone had physically saved your life today, wouldn't you do more than say thanks and pat them on the back? Chances are you would wish you could have gotten to know them and would want to give back to their family in some way. This is how it is with Jesus, except He is alive. You can get to know Him. You can make your life a "thank you" to Him. And you can give back to His family, the Church. But all that is your decision. What is **your response** to Jesus' death on the Cross? Are you ready to accept the redemption that He offers you? More than just accepting new physical life, will you accept the new spiritual life He's offering to you?"

(NOTE: Resist the temptation to allow the teens to write in their journal later. It absolutely works best if it immediately follows the dramatic role play. If there is not time for them to finish in class, at least let them start it there. To add a reflective mood to their journaling, you could quietly play the song "How Could You Say No?" (Steve Angrisano on his CD, "You Are the Way.").

Option #3: *Dare You to Move* — Group Skits

Find the lyrics to the song *Dare You to Move* (by Switchfoot, on the album *The Beautiful Letdown*), and share them with your teens as you listen to the song together. Break them into groups of five or six and allow them to create their own skits that tell the story of redemption and grace to which the song refers. Let them get creative in portraying the tension spoken of in the song between our unredeemed selves and how "salvation is here" for us in Christ. The catch is that the skit must have no words and must speak for itself visually as the song tells the story in a musical and lyrical way. Depending on your time restrictions, allow the teens to perform their skit before the group while the song plays as a soundtrack in the background.

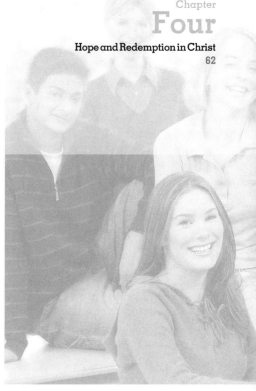

Whether you admit you have sinned has no bearing on the fact that you have sinned, as all of us have done (see Rom 5:12). How "bad" you think your sin is has no bearing on the fact that sin equals spiritual death (see Rom 6:23). How merciful God is has no bearing on the fact that God is also *just*; don't mistake God's mercy for weakness.

God is too just to simply dismiss a person's sin. God upheld "His end" of the covenant. He loves us perfectly. It is we who fail in the relationship, not God. Because God is just, He cannot simply "dismiss" sin. It requires an offering, a blood offering to be exact. If God just wrote off sin, then we couldn't trust God or any of His promises (over 4,000 promises in the Bible). Imagine the ramifications of that for a minute. If God doesn't uphold the covenant broken in the Garden of Eden by Adam and Eve (and broken over and over again by His children since), then God is a liar and we can't take Him at His word. If God is a liar, then Jesus isn't God and He didn't rise from the dead. But, remember that Jesus said, "Destroy this temple and in three days I will raise it up. When therefore he was raised from the dead, his disciples remembered that he had said this; and they believed the Scripture and the word which Jesus had spoken" (Jn 2:19, 22). Additionally, if God is a liar, this would mean we have no forgiveness and no chance at heaven, no chance at eternal life with God. If God is a liar, then heaven doesn't exist; when you die, you die. Remember the famous verse, John 3:16? It says, "For God so loved the world that he gave his only son, that whoever believes in him might not perish but have eternal life." If this Bible verse and the one above are not true, then God is a liar.

But God is not a liar. He promised us in the Garden of Eden, after the original sin of Adam and Eve, that He would send us a redeemer (Gn 3:15). Christ is that Redeemer. Christ is your Redeemer. And that leads us to the greatest "catch-22" in the history of creation. Here is what that means: While God is too *just* to dismiss your sin, God is too loving to dismiss you. So, God came up with a plan, the greatest plan in history, to ensure that you have a shot at eternal life, a plan that both cleanses your sin (with blood) and opens the door to salvation.

Your redemption is more than just forgiveness; it is adoption. It is God, your Father (Mk 14:6) saying, "I've seen your sin and I'll take your place. I've seen your sin and I love you anyway. And, not only am I going to save you but I'm actually going to adopt you as my child." This means that through sin we had become "aliens"—foreigners who no longer enjoyed the close, family-type of relationship with God that humanity once had. St. Paul tells us it is through Christ that our loving Father adopts us as His children (Eph 1:5). We're no longer "aliens"—we are in God's family. He is our Father who loves, protects, and provides for us.

God loves you so much that He would rather die than risk spending eternity without you. He has gone to extraordinary lengths (redemption and then adoption) to secure our love and our eternity with Him. And so, the next time you think your sin is too big for God, think again.

notes

Notes & Nuggets: This journal activity could be done while the students are waiting before and after their opportunities for the sacrament of reconciliation.

Sitting on the steps in front of a church, I pondered if I should actually go in to the adoration chapel. Based upon what I had been doing at a party one hour earlier, I felt like I had no business being there. Yet something was tugging at me. Perhaps it was God calling me toward Him, or maybe it was just the fact that my lifestyle left me feeling so dissatisfied and hollow. Looking back, now I see that it was both.

So, I decided that if I had tried everything else in high school, I might as well try God. I walked into the chapel and knelt before the Blessed Sacrament. There was no flash of lighting or voice from heaven. Actually, I was thinking about the elderly lady sitting in the corner, wondering if she could smell the aroma of pot on me. There was pure silence. I was alone with Him.

At first, it was hard to look up at the Eucharist. I just buried my face in my hands, and debated if I should just leave. I didn't feel like rattling off memorized prayers. So, I just looked up and said, "God, Here I am ... in my sin. I'm not hiding anymore. If you want me out of this, I need You to help me." I felt torn between the life I had known for years and a God I hardly knew. His invitation was clear, but my future seemed so uncertain. All He was saying to me was: "Let go and trust me."

From that moment, I understood that God does not just want my goodness. He wants the ugly. He doesn't like sin, to be sure, but in order for Him to embrace me and have a relationship with me, He wanted to embrace me exactly as I was, even with all of my faults. For years, I had thought that I would need to become a saint in order for Him to love me. So I always kept Him at a distance.

It is precisely when you feel most torn between God and sin that you need to be still and let Him love you. Only when you understand your value in His eyes will you be able to change. You won't be motivated by shame, guilt, or fear, but because you know you deserve love. Knowing His love for you will give you the motivation to love yourself. Knowing His forgiveness of you will help you forgive yourself.

But if you do not find your worth in how God sees you, where will your value come from? Will you measure your value by what you look like or what people think of you? Will you seek your worth in your athletic ability, your intelligence, or how much money you make? Pope John Paul II said that man has been created "for his own sake." What this means is that your value cannot come from what you do or from anything outside of you.

Regardless of your past, God has a plan for your life. You don't need to earn His love. You just need to let Him give it to you. No matter what you have been led to believe, you are lovable. It does not matter where you've been or what you've done. All that matters now is where you go from here.

– Crystalina Evert

CLOSING JOURNAL ACTIVITY

Here is a real opportunity for you to respond to the grace of Jesus. Write a letter addressed *directly* to Jesus. This letter should be the most honest thing you have ever written. If you do not believe that Jesus loves you or that He died for you, that's OK; still, write a letter that tells Him exactly how and why you feel that way. Whatever you write, devote at least two paragraphs to reflections on the following questions:

1. What is keeping me from wanting to enter more deeply into a relationship with You?

2. Regardless of the opinions of others, am I open to getting to know You, Jesus?

MOVIE CLIP/SONG SUGGESTIONS
MOVIE CLIPS:

1. **The Shawshank Redemption:** Show the segment that falls between 1:51:38 and 2:00:27. This is the part when Andy breaks out from the tunnel into the field and the water, symbolizing baptism, redemption, and new life.

2. **The Passion of the Christ:** Show the segment that falls between 1:05:49 and 1:07:53. This shows Jesus saving Mary Magdalene from being stoned to death. He offers her a new life. You may also want to read the story from Scripture: Jn 8:1-11.

3. **The Passion of the Christ:** Show the segment that falls between 1:14:50 and 1:19:19. Mary runs to Jesus, who has fallen, and Jesus looks at her through His suffering and says, "Behold, Mother, I make all things new."

4. **The Day After Tomorrow:** Show the segment that falls between 1:44:03 and 1:50:23. This scene demonstrates the power of familial love. Dennis Quaid's character vows against all odds that he will find his son. His son never doubted that his father would rescue him.

SONGS:

1. **Dare You to Move** — Switchfoot (*The Beautiful Letdown*)

Dares us to move from sin to forgiveness, from concupiscence to redemption. Very popular song on mainstream radio and in the movie "A Walk to Remember." Alternative Rock.

2. **Refine Me** — Jennifer Knapp (*Kansas*)

Beautiful, simple, and prayerful request for God to refine our desires into what will please Him. Acoustic/Soulful.

3. **New Day** — Janelle (*New Day*)

Upbeat pop song about the new life we have in God's love, which washes away the past, allowing us to focus on the brand new day He give us. Pop/Contemporary.

4. **Worlds Apart** — Jars of Clay (self-titled)

This song is all about allowing Jesus to break down our world and to redeem us from our sin and pride. A beautiful and penetrating look at sin and the opportunity for redemption. Acoustic Rock.

5. **Hold Me Jesus** — Rich Mullins (*A Liturgy, a Legacy & a Ragamuffin Band*)

Whenever there is a crisis of faith, Jesus is always our answer. This song not only acknowledges Jesus as the answer, but asks Him to hold us close and to help us surrender our lives to Him. Acoustic/Soulful.

6. **My Hope Is You** — Third Day (*Offerings: A Worship Album*)

This song is all about putting our trust in the Lord. He is our hope. Southern Rock.

7. **Beautiful** — Bethany Dillon (self-titled)

Though sometimes we don't feel beautiful, God tells us different—He tells us the truth. Acoustic/Worship

8. **L. A. D. I. E. S.** — Flame (self-titled)

This song makes the point that Jesus has always had a special place for women–very close to His heart. Hip-Hop.

notes
_____
_____
_____
_____
_____
_____
_____
_____
_____
_____
_____
_____
_____
_____
_____
_____
_____
_____
_____
_____
_____
_____
_____
_____
_____
_____

CLOSING JOURNAL ACTIVITY *(cont.)*

3. Am I open enough to allow You to transform me?

4. How can I more fully give myself to you, Jesus, in my everyday life right now?

Now, if you are open, ask Jesus for the hope, healing, and transformation that He offers; ask Him to help you to be open to His grace. Ask Him to give you eyes to see simple and concrete ways in which you can allow Him to come into your heart.

WORK IT OUT

Assignment #1: Take all of the things you learned in this chapter to create your own list of "Top Five Hope and Redemption" quotes. Take the truths you've learned today and make up a few quotes that would grab other teens' attention and make them think differently about hope and redemption in Jesus Christ. To get your mind rolling, here are a few examples that may give you some ideas:

- "Maybe redemption has stories to tell. Maybe forgiveness is right where you fell. Where can you run to escape from yourself?" (Switchfoot/ "Dare You to Move")

- "Hope is a good thing, maybe the best of things. And no good thing ever dies." (The film *The Shawshank Redemption*)

- "The shortest distance between pain and peace is the distance from your knees to the floor."

Assignment #2: Create your own "Top Five Obstacles to Redemption" by brainstorming a list of difficult experiences in your life and the lives of your family and friends. What do those who struggle to accept Christ's hope and redemption have in common? In other words, what keeps people from saying "Yes" to Christ's love and forgiveness? Stay focused and edit all of your insights down to only five of the most common obstacles that you see in the lives of teenagers. Then go back and create your own "Top Five Paths to Redemption" that would be good ways for teens to overcome temptation and the five obstacles you just listed.

Assignment #3: Dig into the primary source. Get online and read John Paul II's general audience from July 21, 1982, entitled "The Mystery of the Body's Redemption." Outline this talk and write a summary paragraph of it.

Assignment #4: Find the six paragraphs in the *Catechism of the Catholic Church* that reference "redemption." Read them all and then write a list of at least five points that you learned.

Notes & Nuggets: In this closing prayer, we ask St. Elizabeth Ann Seton for her intercession, remembering a life filled with trials but never despair. "Mother Seton" lived as a wife and mother of five children until her husband died when she was only twenty-nine. She converted to Catholicism and soon began founding schools and educating children, beginning with her own relatives. Later, when her children were older, she took vows of chastity and obedience and began a religious order, the American Sisters of Charity. In a letter to her good friend, Julia Sitgreaves Scott, she wrote "Faith lifts the staggering soul on one side, hope supports it on the other, experience says it must be and love says let it be" (March 26, 1810). Knowing that your teens will encounter struggles and trials as they try to accept Christ's offer of redemption and healing, lead them in asking St. Elizabeth Ann Seton to pray for them to remain steadfast in faith and hope.

❖

Project #1: Read selections from St. Augustine's *Confessions*, and notice his struggle with purity and his view of the body. (You may particularly want to check out book two, chapters one through three, and book three, chapter one. The text of *Confessions* is available on multiple websites online.) Write a one-page summary of your reading and then write a paragraph of your own "Confessions." This is not meant for you to confess your sins on paper, but to analyze your own views of the body, your sexual urge, and the redemption that Christ offers to you.

Project #2: Look up "Manichaeism" in a Catholic encyclopedia and write a report summarizing this heretical view of the body and the Church's response to it. You can also find an online version of a Catholic encyclopedia at: *www. newadvent.org*

Project #3: Search through the writings of some early Church Fathers, looking for their sayings and teachings on the idea of redemption in Christ. Compare the ideas of Sts. Augustine, Athanasius, Ambrose (and even later teachers, such as Aquinas) and compare them to the theology of the early Protestant theologians, Martin Luther and John Calvin. Write a detailed paper highlighting the similarities and differences, particularly in the area of being "deprived" versus being "depraved," and what that means for us when it comes to the redemption of our bodies on earth and in heaven. *(For starters, visit www. newadvent.org and www.catholic.com.)*

 ## CLOSING PRAYER

Leader: In the name of the Father, and of the Son, and of the Holy Spirit. **Amen.**

(Option #1)

→ *All:* **St. Elizabeth Ann Seton**, please pray with me that I, like you, would always trust, hope, and rest in the love of God, remaining mindful of His promise of redemption in the face of death or despair. **Amen.**

(Option #2)

Leader or Reader #1: Read Romans 12:9-12
  "Let love be genuine, hate what is evil, hold fast to what is good; love one another with brotherly affection; outdo one another in showing honor. Never flag in zeal, be aglow with the Spirit, serve the Lord. Rejoice in your hope, be patient in tribulation, be constant in prayer."

Leader or Reader #2: Lord, thank You for your total love for us, no matter what we've done or how far we've strayed from You. Help us to rejoice in the hope that You offer us. Thank you for being a loving Father and welcoming us back home, even when we don't deserve it. **Amen.**

IN HIS OWN WORDS

- **On The Redemption of the Body:** "However, the redemption of the body is expressed not only in the resurrection as victory over death. It is present also in Christ's words addressed to historical man, when they confirm the principle of the insolubility of marriage as a principle coming from the Creator himself, and also when, in the Sermon on the Mount, Christ called man to overcome concupiscence, even in the uniquely interior movements of the human heart" (July 21, 1982).

- **On The Hope of Every Day:** "Here it is a question not of the eschatological hope of the resurrection, but of the hope of victory over sin, which can be called the hope of every day. ... Man and woman, bound in marriage, must daily undertake the task of the insoluble union of that covenant which they have made between them. But also a man or a woman who has voluntarily chosen continence for the sake of the kingdom of heaven must daily give a living witness of fidelity to that choice, heeding the directives of Christ in the gospels and those of Paul the Apostle in First Corinthians. In each case it is a question of the hope of every day, which in proportion to the normal duties and difficulties of human life helps to overcome 'evil with good' (Rom 12:21)" (July 21, 1982).

- **On Resurrection of the Body:** "Furthermore, the resurrection is the reply of the God of life to the historical inevitability of death, to which man was subjected from the moment of breaking the first covenant and which, together with sin, entered his history" (January 27, 1982).

- **On Resurrection as Redemption:** "Redemption is the way to the resurrection. The resurrection constitutes the definitive accomplishment of the redemption of the body" (January 27, 1982).

- **On the Spiritualization of Eschatological Man (in heaven):** "The conclusion can be drawn that the degree of spiritualization characteristic of eschatological man will have its source in the degree of his divinization, incomparably superior to the one that can be attained in earthly life. ... Participation in divine nature, participation in the interior life of God himself, penetration and permeation of what is essentially human by what is essentially divine, will then reach its peak, so that the life of the human spirit will arrive at such fullness which previously had been absolutely inaccessible to it" (December 9, 1981).

Absolution: The action of a priest as a mediator of grace, standing "in the person of Christ," concluding the sacrament of Reconciliation. Absolution cleanses us from our sins through Christ's loving mercy and gives us strength to start anew.

Communion of saints: We already enjoy this communion here on earth with each other (the Church Militant). In spirit, we are connected with those who have died and are still being purified in purgatory (the Church Suffering). In prayer, we have communion with the saints in heaven (the Church Triumphant), who intercede for us before God (see Rev 5:8). In the Resurrection, we will experience a fullness of communion as human members of the Church, sharing eternity together as persons perfectly integrated in bodies and souls.

Eschatological Man: The final stage of our perfection, achieved in the resurrection at the end of time, where we'll be freed from any tensions between the flesh and the spirit within ourselves, because we will be perfectly united with God and with one another in the communion of saints.

Eschaton: The final reality of man's existence, when Christ returns and our bodies are raised.

Glorified body: The perfected state of the resurrected body as it will be at the end of time; it will be radiating the glory of God.

Historical Man: The period of human history between the Fall of Adam and the end of time, where man struggles against concupiscence to love as God does, but also experiences redemption in Christ.

Hope of every day: The daily hope of victory over sin which is available to us through Christ, who helps us overcome "evil with good" (Rom 12:21).

Nuptial: Another word for "marriage-like," "marital," or "spousal."

Nuptial Meaning of the Body: The marital meaning of the body; "…the body's capacity of expressing love, that love precisely in which the person becomes a gift and… fulfills the very meaning of his being and existence" (January 16, 1980).

Omniscient: Literally, "all knowing." A quality of God, meaning that God knows everything there is to know.

Original Man: The period of man's existence as God created him (lived by Adam and Eve) prior to original sin. The original experiences of Adam and Eve in purity and happiness "echo" in the heart of every man and woman and are always "at the root of every human experience" (December 12, 1979).

Redeem: To pay off a debt through the exchange of something of equal or greater value than the debt owed. Through original sin, an infinite debt was owed to God, thus, only an infinite exchange could be made—this is why God sent His own Son, Jesus, to redeem and save us.

Redemption: The ransom of humanity from the slavery of sin to a new life of freedom through the sacrificial death of Jesus Christ on the cross.

Resurrection of the body: The joining, at the end of time, of the bodies of the saved with their souls in heaven, at which point they will participate bodily in a face-to-face encounter with God within the marriage of Christ and the Church.

Sexual addiction: A compulsive and frequent habit of seeking sexual pleasures, including fornication/intercourse, pornography, cybersex, masturbation, and other sexual behaviors.

OBJECTIVES At the end of this lesson, the student should know and be able to:

- Define "freedom."
- Explain that man is created for freedom.
- Demonstrate that freedom is possible only in choosing the good.
- Explain how Christ has set us free and what this freedom requires.
- Explain that freedom allows man to participate in authentic love.
- Compare and contrast authentic freedom with the cultural view of freedom.
- Explain that "being free from the law" means being free of the "internal constraints" of sinful desires.
- Explain how the sacrament of reconciliation can help us in our quest for freedom.

Notes & Nuggets: Pray today for the Holy Spirit to set your teens free from all the ways, small and large, that they have allowed themselves to become enslaved to their passions, forfeiting freedom for fleeting pleasure. Pray that the truth of Christ and His hope will set them free. We suggest praying a Divine Mercy chaplet, a decade of the Rosary, or some other prayer for your students today.

Truth and Freedom

Freedom is the ability to *desire* and *choose* the good. It means accepting the responsibilities of authentic love. This idea differs greatly from the common understanding of freedom, which is "being able to do whatever I want, whenever I want." Sometimes we think the more choices we get to make, the greater freedom we have. When we reduce freedom to the shallow notion of "doing whatever, whenever," we overlook the opportunity to experience the deeper meaning of love, which brings authentic freedom. Sure, we all enjoy having options, but freedom cannot be reduced to a wide variety of choices or the absence of boundaries. Instead, real freedom comes from recognizing the truth and choosing to live in it, through Jesus Christ, who is the Truth (see Jn 14:6).

To experience real freedom, we must remember two very important facts: *who we are* and *how we are called to live*. We have been told that we are God's children, made in His image and likeness, but what does this mean? It means we were made to love, and love always rejoices in the truth (see 1 Cor 13:6). Knowing and accepting this reality can help us understand the origin of our freedom.

In the beginning, Adam and Eve abandoned the truth and accepted a false view of freedom. Thus, they fell into sin, plunging the world into an identity crisis over who we were created to be. God promised to send a Savior to the world who would set us free from the evil one and his deceptions that bring us into slavery (see Gn 3:15). It is Christ who reveals the truth of our identity to us and sets us free so that we might choose Him, choose life, and have it to the full (see Jn 10:10).

ICEBREAKER #1 (optional): The Truth about Skittles*

Step #1: Show the students a jar of pre-counted Skittles. Begin by asking the students how many Skittles are in the jar, keeping track of who has the closest and the furthest answers from the correct figure. Without telling them the correct answer (nor who is the closest or furthest), ask them which student should receive the prize (a small bag of Skittles).

Step #2: Let the students attempt to explain who the winner of the game should be and why. Eventually, tell the class the correct number of Skittles. After the noises of excitement and disappointment subside, attempt to give the prized bag of Skittles to the person who was *furthest* from the real answer. Protests will ensue. Let the real winner try to explain why he or she should get the prize, rather than the person whose guess had been the furthest from the actual number in the jar.

Explanation: The analogy can now be clearly drawn that there is one and only one truth in the world—*objective* truth. The student's *subjective* opinion about the number of Skittles in the jar does not change the *objective* reality.

TWO MINUTE DRILL — VERBAL REVIEW:

1. When man reaches heaven, what is this period of his existence called?
   Answer: Eschatological man

2. Name three differences between historical man and eschatological man. Remind the students that historical man includes all the people between the Fall of mankind and the end of the world–which, of course, includes us.
   Answer: Eschatological man:
   a) experiences no pain (historical man does)
   b) experiences no concupiscence (historical man does)
   c) is in full union with Christ in heaven (historical man is not in heaven yet)

3. What is the hope of every day?
   Answer: Each day, the Lord offers us new help and new grace that allow us to start anew and to progress further toward heaven and our quest for full redemption.

4. What is the redemption of the body?
   Answer: It is the time when our bodies will be fully "spiritualized" and essentially re-created, bringing our intellects, our wills, and our bodies back into perfect union, ridding us of concupiscence and perfecting our ability to love (see 1 Cor 15:35-58.). It begins even now but will only be complete in the eschaton.

* This activity originally appeared in The *Da Vinci Outreach Teachers Guide* by Roy Petitfils and Matt Hebert (Copyright ©2006 Ascension Press and Dumb Ox Productions. Used with permission.)

OPENING PRAYER

Leader: In the name of the Father, and of the Son, and of the Holy Spirit. **Amen.**

(Option #1)

Leader or Reader #1: Read Galatians 5:1

"For freedom Christ set us free; so stand firm and do not submit again to the yoke of slavery."

Leader or Reader #2: Lord, You have created us for a specific reason. Help us to be free of all that keeps us from understanding what it means to be human. Free us from all that prevents Your glory from radiating through us. Lord, help us to be open today to learn, to live, and to love like You.

We ask all this as we pray together: Our Father, who art in heaven, hallowed be Thy name. Thy kingdom come, Thy will be done, on earth as it is in heaven. Give us this day our daily bread, and forgive us our trespasses, as we forgive those who trespass against us. And lead us not into temptation, but deliver us from evil. Saint (patron saint of your church or school), pray for us. In the name of the Father, and of the Son, and of the Holy Spirit. **Amen.**

(Option #2)

Leader or Reader #1: Read John 8:31-32

"Jesus then said to those Jews who believed in him, 'If you remain in my word, you will truly be my disciples, and you will know the truth, and the truth will set you free.'"

Leader or Reader #2: Loving Father, we wish to abide in Your word. Let us dwell in Your truth–the truth of who You are and the truth of who we are. Give us the grace to follow You, to know the truth, and to live in the freedom for which You have set us free. Help us to be open today to learn, to live, and to love like You.

We ask all this as we pray together: Our Father, who art in heaven, hallowed be Thy name. Thy kingdom come, Thy will be done, on earth as it is in heaven. Give us this day our daily bread, and forgive us our trespasses, as we forgive those who trespass against us. And lead us not into temptation, but deliver us from evil. Saint (patron saint of your church or school), pray for us. In the name of the Father, and of the Son, and of the Holy Spirit. **Amen.**

Need a Review of Lesson 4?

STORY STARTER: "Free" and Empty

Just like you, we (the authors of this program) all struggled to understand the nature of true freedom at one point or another. Consider Jason and Crystalina's experiences when they were in high school:

Crystalina:

"Get out of my life!" I screamed and slammed my bedroom door shut. I was so sick of my mother telling me how to live that I couldn't wait until I turned

Verbal Review of Lesson 4

1. When man reaches heaven, what is this period of his existence called?

2. Name three differences between historical man and eschatological man.

3. What is the hope of every day?

4. What is the redemption of the body?

eighteen so I could finally move out. I was tired of her guilt trips and constant nagging about what she thought about my relationship with Andre.

I had been in relationships before, but this one was different. We really cared about each other, and since he also came from a broken family, we could relate on many levels. He was a little older than I was, and I was relieved to date a guy who was more mature than most of the boys I knew at our school.

When it came to the sexual stuff, I respected the fact that he'd never push things too far and that he said he was willing to wait until I felt ready. Six months into the relationship, we started sleeping together and I hid it from my mom as long as possible. Eventually, she found some of my birth control pills and went through the roof. I was equally angry with her for invading my privacy and trying to take away my freedom by throwing her religious rules in my face.

But as much as I thought I was fooling my mom, I was only fooling myself. At the time, I thought lying to her and sneaking off with Andre was an expression of my freedom. But if I was so free, then why was I so afraid to leave him, even when the abuse started? If I was so free, why did my hand always tremble when I flipped over a pregnancy test? How could it be that I was doing exactly what I wanted, but I felt so unfulfilled?

Jason:

I sat in the passenger seat of my friend's Volvo as he took his time in the "adult" bookstore. Realizing that I had a Confirmation class to attend later that evening, I started to think that perhaps I hadn't made the best choice of friends. But we had been hanging out for years, and I didn't feel like making the effort to find new friends.

At least fifteen minutes had passed when he bolted out of the store and got in the car so quickly you would have thought he just robbed the place. He peeled out of the parking lot and drove away without saying a word. On his face was a miserable expression, and I couldn't resist asking, "What happened in there?"

He didn't reply. We pulled up to a stop light, and he leaned his head back and closed his eyes. He mumbled, "I've never felt so sorry for someone in my life." Apparently, he paid for some kind of peep show in the store to see a woman behind glass. With his voice filled with pity and guilt, he quietly said, "Her eyes looked so sad."

Lest you think that his guilt was stemming from an old-fashioned, prudish, religious upbringing, I should add that he never went to church. In fact, his mother even paid for him to have a subscription to *Playboy!* Hugh Hefner promised in one of his first issues of the magazine that *Playboy* would free a generation from guilt about sex.

But here was my friend, and the guy was totally empty. *This* was freedom?

Did You Know?

Many young people think that becoming sexually active will make them happier, but did you know that sexually active teenagers are more likely to be depressed and to attempt suicide?

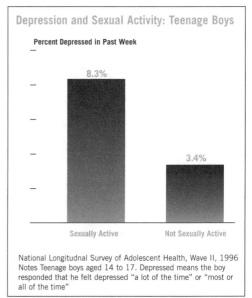

Depression and Sexual Activity: Teenage Boys

Percent Depressed in Past Week

8.3% (Sexually Active)

3.4% (Not Sexually Active)

National Longitudnal Survey of Adolescent Health, Wave II, 1996 Notes Teenage boys aged 14 to 17. Depressed means the boy responded that he felt depressed "a lot of the time" or "most or all of the time"

Source: www.Heritage.org/research/family/cda0304.cfm

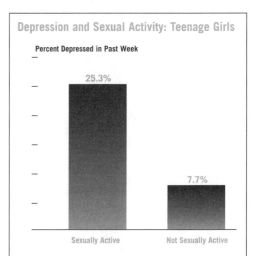

Depression and Sexual Activity: Teenage Girls

Percent Depressed in Past Week

25.3% (Sexually Active)

7.7% (Not Sexually Active)

National Longitudnal Survey of Adolescent Health, Wave II, 1996 Notes Teenage girls aged 14 to 17. Depressed means the girl responded that she felt depressed "a lot of the time" or "most or all of the time"

Source: www.Heritage.org/research/family/cda0304.cfm

COMPREHENSION & DISCUSSION QUESTIONS

1. What are the differences between living in freedom and living in slavery?

2. If the people in the stories on the previous page had viewed their bodies as valuable gifts to be given in love, how might this have changed the way they acted?

3. If you have a well-formed conscience, what does guilt signify about whether your actions are free or not?

4. If fear exists within a relationship, what does this say about the freedom of those involved?

BRIDGING THE GAP

Imagine you just bought a brand new car. It is a beautiful day, so you go cruising around to show off your new car to a couple of friends. After a while, the "low fuel" light comes on. You pull up to a gas station and look at the different fuel options.

Now, you know your car is designed to run on unleaded gasoline only, but you begin to feel *restrained* that you must choose a certain kind of fuel and feel *limited* by the car company telling you what to do with *your* car. "This is *my* ride. They're taking away my *freedom*," you mumble under your breath. Besides, you've heard some cars can go 300,000 miles on diesel fuel. "Maybe the diesel will help my car last longer," you think to yourself.

In defiance, you say, "I'm going to put diesel in my new car because this is my ride and nobody can tell me what to do with it." The fuel nozzle won't fit properly, but you're determined. You run inside the gas station, buy a funnel and begin to fuel up your car the way you want. Gallons of diesel pour into the brand new car and a smile of victory sweeps over your face.

But what happens when you try to drive away? How "limited" and "restricted" will you feel when the car stops running in the middle of a busy intersection? The point here is that there is such a thing as **objective truth**, a reality that we cannot change or decide for ourselves. In this case, if a car is designed for unleaded fuel, you can subjectively decide that the car will run on diesel fuel. Your subjective decision will soon prove to be a bad one, because it was not based in the reality (the objective truth) of the car needing unleaded gasoline to work properly. Your goal was to be free to do what you pleased, but freedom without boundaries is a recipe for disaster.

Just as we cannot change or decide the reality of the way a car works, neither

Notes & Nuggets: The nuanced point to make here is that the husband or the father needs to desire and choose the good if he is truly going to be free in the way God intended. He places limits on his next choice because he would not be free in that choice.

is morality something that is subjective. God created us to choose between good and evil, not to determine what they are.[1]

We must understand the truth of our freedom and then use it *responsibly*.

TO THE CORE

Most people might define freedom as being able to do whatever you want, but this is only partly true. In most states, if you are sixteen, you are free to drive. However, the only way for this freedom to exist is if it has boundaries. That sounds contradictory, but imagine a country where you were free to drive, yet there were no traffic laws. Nobody had to take a driver's test. There were no speed limits, and you could drive on whatever side of the road you desired. Initially, this might sound like fun, but it would create chaos (accidents, traffic jams, drunken driving, etc.). This is the same with regard to the freedom for which we have been created.

Defining Freedom

So, what exactly is freedom? **Freedom** is the ability to desire and to choose the good. If you truly love a person, you are making a decision to live your life in a way that places certain boundaries or restrictions on yourself. For example, if a husband loves his wife, he should freely choose not to flirt with other women. Instead, he should choose the good of his wife and their marriage over the temptation to commit adultery. If he loves his children, he should freely choose not to neglect them by acting like a bachelor and staying out with friends every night. With love comes responsibility, which puts the commitments of love into action. But this does not ruin love any more than tying a string on a kite ruins its ability to fly. If you were to cut the string, the kite would crash. The same happens with love. In the words of Pope John Paul II, "Freedom without responsibilities is the opposite of love."[2]

Freedom of the Heart

So freedom is not about escaping rules, responsibilities, or **external constraints**. Authentic freedom involves accepting and living out the truth of who we are (children of God) and for what we are created (love and communion). Freedom entails living without **internal constraints** on our hearts.

Consider this example. Bridget loves to go to the ballet. She not only loves the dancing, but the music and the costumes as well. Bridget decides to bring her friend, Elizabeth, to her favorite ballet, *Swan Lake*. A few minutes into the performance, Elizabeth takes out her cell phone to call her boyfriend. She's hungry and figures she'll go get a Coke® and some popcorn while she's on the phone. She stands up and asks Bridget if she would like anything. Bridget

"If the Son makes you free, you will be free indeed."
(Jn 8:36)

notes

Notes & Nuggets: In his book, *Theology of the Body Explained* (Pauline, 2003), Christopher West explains the thought of John Paul II on freedom from the law by noting, "In this view, at the heart of liberty is the freedom to choose the good, not to create it. True freedom is liberation not from the external 'constraint' that calls me to good, but from the internal constraint that hinders my choice of the good. The truth sets us free. And the truth is that the Son of God took on flesh and died and rose again to free us from all that hinders our capacity to love as He loves" (p. 488).

pulls Elizabeth back down into her seat, shushes her, and whispers, "You can't use your cell phone or eat in the middle of a performance! It's not allowed." Elizabeth had no idea. She just knew she was hungry and wasn't that interested in the ballet.

Although Bridget's mother had to teach her the rules of the ballet when she attended her first performance as a little girl, Bridget grew in her appreciation and love of the ballet and now naturally focused on the art before her. She did not need the rules of being quiet, not eating, or not using her cell phone because she cared for the art of ballet so much that any other desires paled in comparison to her enjoyment of the ballet itself. The same could not be said for Elizabeth.

So being truly free does not entail merely obeying the law or abiding by external constraints. People who are truly free are not held back nor bothered by internal constraints—they have no desire to break the external constraints (the law), so they don't need them. This is real freedom, when our hearts are redeemed and *our* desires come into conformity with *God's* desires. Then we are able to desire and to choose the good, and ultimately we desire and choose God.

"If freedom is not used, is not taken advantage of by love, it becomes a negative thing and gives human beings a feeling of emptiness and unfulfillment."
– *Pope John Paul II*

Selfishness Leads to Misery

Being free to love without internal constraints is only possible through the grace of God giving us pure hearts. Once we choose God and allow Him to transform our desires, then the moral life becomes a life not about rules, but about love. We obey God's commands not because we *have* to but because we *want* to. If we reject the calling to purity and truth (and seek love while pretending to be "free" to do whatever we want), we often end up empty. We have been made to become a gift to others and, by doing so, to love as God loves. If we live for ourselves, we miss the point of our existence. And living in this way leaves us unfulfilled.

A good example of being unfulfilled is the young man from the story earlier in this chapter, who drove away from the adult bookstore bewildered and depressed. He had missed the whole point of freedom. In his desire to be free, he had become a slave to his weakness of lust. That's why he felt so empty.

When his conscience stung him with a sense of pity for the woman, he was beginning to see the truth about her. He realized that she was worth much more than the money he had paid to see her. Had he not realized this truth, he would never be free to love her—or any other woman, for that matter. How could anyone have the ability to receive another person without knowing the greatness of the gift that is being exchanged?

COMPREHENSION & DISCUSSION QUESTIONS

COMPREHENSION & DISCUSSION QUESTIONS

1. What is freedom?

2. Why is freedom so tightly connected to truth?

3. What is the difference between "internal" and "external" constraints (or laws)?

4. How can someone become free of the "internal constraints" of lustful desires?

5. Why do you think so many people have sexual addictions?

6. Why do most of those same people keep their sexual addictions "in the dark"?

notes

God Respects Our Free Will

Imagine Dave, a high school junior, is nervously awaiting his prom. The girl he wants to take to the dance, Samantha, is the most amazing girl he's ever met. She's beautiful, smart, genuine, and just fun to be around. A week before the prom, Dave finds out that Samantha is not yet going with anyone to the dance. He gets up the courage and asks her to go with him, but she politely says "No, thanks." Dave is determined and selfish (and maybe a few sandwiches short of a picnic), so on prom night he drives over to her house and knocks on the door. When Samantha answers, he pulls a rope out from behind his back, ties her hands together, and literally drags her to the prom. Although Samantha and Dave are at the prom together, she certainly didn't come freely, of her own choice. Her free will was taken from her, and this robs the relationship of any real meaning.

Unlike Dave, God is not selfish. God wants us to *freely choose* Him (the ultimate Good). God does not want to force Himself on us. He does not want to trick us into knowing, loving, and serving Him. Our freedom is the key to our ability to love! When we freely choose God, which is itself a grace from Him, we are participating in His love and sharing in His life. He gives us **free will**, and it is through the use of our free will that we have the capacity to desire the good and choose it. In this way, we participate in true freedom, which brings us perfect happiness.

What is the relationship between free will and the pursuit of freedom? Man is created in the "image" and "likeness" of God. Thus, as St. Irenaeus said, "man is rational and therefore like God; he is created with *free will* and is *master over his acts*." Our free will differs from God's free will in that ours has been **deprived** of much of its strength through the Fall and is now imperfect. We still have the

dom. But this is exactly why Christ died on the Cross—to redeem our desires and set us free from the internal constraints of sin. Christ is our way to freedom.

There are times when we truly *feel* forced into doing some things or "restricted" from doing other things that, in reality, are for our own good. For example:

1. Is a child's freedom violated when he or she only wants to eat hot dogs and his or her parents "make" him or her eat vegetables and other nutritious foods?

2. Is a person's freedom violated when he wants to kill someone and a policeman prevents the murder from taking place?

3. Is a person's freedom violated when he is about to be struck by a car and someone pulls him to safety?

One's freedom is not being taken away in any of these three instances; we are simply being guided for our own good.

"*The more one does what is good, the freer one becomes. There is no true freedom except in the service of what is good and just. The choice to disobey and to do evil is an abuse of freedom and leads to 'the slavery of sin'*" (CCC 1733).

COMPREHENSION & DISCUSSION QUESTIONS

1. What did St. Irenaeus say about our being created in the "likeness" of God?

2. Define free will. Explain how it is connected to freedom.

3. Have you ever felt pressured in a relationship to the point that your free will was stolen from you?

4. Have you ever viewed God as a miserable rule maker? If so, what would help you to better see God as a Good Shepherd who loves and protects you?

Freed From Slavery, Free For Love

Freedom always has certain truths intimately tied to it, and without these truths, we lose our freedom and our purpose. One of these truths is the fact that freedom exists for the sake of love. While we all have the desire to love and to be loved, at times that desire becomes disordered and turns into lust. Remember, lust is the desire to love that has become twisted and self-seeking instead of self-giving. Instead of being a *participation in divine life* through authentic love, lust *separates us from the love of God*. Lust is not self-*donation*; it is self-*gratification* at the expense of another.

Just as the desire to love can be disordered and manifested as lust, the desire

for freedom can be disordered and manifested in *slavery*. If you are not free to control your own sexual desires, how can you be free to love? Living in the truth means daily observing our desires and placing them in the hands of God, allowing Him to cleanse and renew us. Each day is another step toward freedom or away from it. So our choices of friends, movies, parties, etc., all contribute to our progress toward being able to worship God with our lives—with every free action—in "spirit and truth" (Jn 4:23).

Christ Sets Us Free

You are probably familiar with the words, "The truth will set you free." But this quote from Scripture loses its meaning if we do not come to know what Christ is saying in the words that immediately precede the more well-known part of the sentence. Christ says, "*If you continue in my word, you are truly my disciples, and you will know the truth and the truth will make you free*" (Jn 8:31-32). The great news is that Jesus did not merely give us commands, He also gave us ways to become free, namely the sacrament of Reconciliation.

This sacrament is a gift from Jesus to us out of His love, a gift that can truly set us free. Not only do we become spiritually cleansed of our sin, but we also become more accountable for our actions before God and man. This increased accountability helps us to desire to choose the good not only to please God, but also to support each other—the body of Christ—by using our freedom to walk with others toward heaven.

"Man longs for love more than for freedom—freedom is the means and love is the end."
– *Karol Wojtyla*
(Pope John Paul II)

For the truth to set us free it must be "the" truth. This truth is also more than simply learning what is right and what is wrong. It is about *being with* Jesus. It is about following Him and being faithful to Him, which is also remaining faithful to who we are.

Christ has set us free so that, with Him, we can truly say "yes" to Him and His truth. Doing this also enables us to experience the authentic freedom for which we long. In the movie *Braveheart*, Mel Gibson's character, William Wallace, says that every man *dies* but not every man truly *lives*. Freedom is really living. Living in the truth sets us free and opens our hearts to be the men and women we have been created to be.

APPLICATION

Option #1: LEGOS® WITHOUT A CLUE

This simple LEGO® construction project will help students recognize how order and truth enhance one's freedom rather than hurting or limiting it. Instead of cramping their freedom, students will learn that order and truth provide an opportunity for freedom and the opportunity to become who they've been created to be.

Setting Up:

First, pre-select your student groups (three to five people per group). Before class, empty LEGO® packages into separate sandwich bags and include instructions. Be sure that the LEGO® construction project is fairly complex. You don't want the project to be too easy. Also, be sure to vary the amount of instructions per LEGO® group:

> *1/3 of groups receive total instructions

> *1/3 of groups receive just some of the instructions (you must cut away sections)

> *1/3 of groups receive NO instructions at all

NOTE: The above "set up" steps are essential to the entire success of this project. Be sure to give the varying amounts of directions to the different groups, otherwise the teaching moment will be lost.

STEP #1: Split your groups and explain that they will need to build a specific car or boat, etc., with their LEGOS®. The type and design of the project will depend on the pieces they receive. Most important: *Explain that every group of LEGOS® is intended for a specific model and will perform its best only if modeled to its exact intended design.*

STEP #2: Pass out materials to each group, explaining that they'll receive *no further instructions from you (or any moderators)*. They must rely on their group members and any instructions that they *may* have. Tell them that the teams are spaced out so that no one can spy on the instructions that other groups may have. To make things a little more interesting, get each team a different LEGO® item to construct, but do not tell them each group has a different object. After every team gets all the necessary materials, tell them they have fifteen minutes to put together their specific assignment.

STEP #3: As questions arise as to why some groups are missing all or parts of their instructions, simply explain the following:

"I did not give all of the instructions to you simply because I want to make sure you have a good time and are able to be creative with how you choose to build that specific model. I don't want to take away your freedom for creativity or hinder your fun!" Then, say no more.

STEP #4: While observing, take notes and write down specific quotes of various students as they express excitement or frustration throughout the project. Write at least one quote per group on a notepad as you survey the class progress.

STEP #5: Call "Time is up," leaving at least fifteen to twenty minutes to wrap things up.

STEP #6: Have one person from each group present the finished product to the class. Have this group representative explain the amount of instructions, if any, that his or her group had available for consultation, including any comments made or frustrations the group experienced in the process. At the end of each presentation, share some of the quotes you recorded from the group members while they were assembling the LEGOS®. This will give more detail and entertain the group as well!

FOR DISCUSSION:

1. Who experienced more freedom in this activity? Was it the group with all the directions, some of the directions, or none of the directions? Explain your answer.

2. How important was it that you needed all the directions to build your project?

3. If it is so important and necessary to have direction for just putting LEGOS® together, don't you think it is just as important to follow those "instructions" that God has given us so that we can enjoy the fulfillment for which we were created?

CONCLUSION:

Explain the relationship between this scenario/activity, and the "order, truth, and freedom" that we were given by God to live. Without any order, we don't feel peace or experience real freedom to live, because we do not have the necessary guidelines needed to reach the goal of heaven. And so we struggle through trial and error, unable to reach our potential. We cannot fully live the life for which we were created and designed.

(Continued on next leader's page)

COMPREHENSION & DISCUSSION QUESTIONS

1. What does truth have to do with freedom? Can freedom actually exist without it?

2. Can one experience freedom if truth is not tied intimately with it? Why or why not?

3. Explain the role that rules play in games. Do you think that rules take the fun out of games? Why or why not?

4. We have mentioned that freedom involves not simply the absence of external barriers but also of internal barriers that prevent us from choosing the good. In light of this understanding of freedom, where in your life do you not feel free?

5. What is lacking in the idea that freedom is only "the ability to do whatever you want"?

DIGGING DEEPER:
Sometimes Truth Hurts

> *"For the time is coming when people will not endure sound teaching, but having itching ears they will accumulate for themselves teachers to suit their own likings, and will turn away from listening to the truth and wander into myths. As for you, always be steady, endure suffering, do the work of an evangelist, fulfill your ministry."*
>
> *(2 Tim 4:3-5)*

"Once the truth is denied to human beings, it is pure illusion to try to set them free. Truth and freedom either go together hand in hand or together they perish in misery."[3]

To understand the marriage of truth and freedom, we must recognize a basic principle called **objective truth**. Objective truth is the reality of how things are. This is entirely different than someone's opinion, which is *subjective*. Opinions are fine as long as we understand they are *subjective* and not equal to objective truth.

It might seem fair and fun to let people have their own opinion and make their own decisions based on what they think or feel. But let's face it: some things are always true. Molesting children, raping women, murdering Jews in gas chambers, and holding black people in slavery are all examples of intrinsically evil actions. Hopefully, you would agree that these acts are *always* wrong.

But often our emotions get the best of us. Feelings can lead to conclusions that have nothing to do with the truth.

Take pride, for example. We all like to be right, and we all want to believe that we have the truth. This is why it is so hard to change someone's mind during an emotional argument. When heightened emotions are present during debates, some people cannot seem to admit that their belief is wrong, either because they simply do not see the truth—for a variety of intellectual reasons—or

(Cont.)

When we pick and choose only a few instructions, similar conflicts and frustrations arise. Why? Because there are gaps in our understanding of who we were created to be.

In summary, we need order. We need to know and be aware of the truth, which helps us to understand the totality of who we are. Knowing and following this truth provides us the freedom to truly live, not merely survive. God's commands for us are not just arbitrary "do's and don'ts." They are a framework of loving guidance from our Father, who wants our good even more than we do. Through His instructions, He guides us toward the love, destiny, and fulfillment that our hearts long for: union with Him in heaven.

Option #2: Freedom of Choice in Scripture

Have your students read the following passage from Sirach and answer the questions, either in small groups or individually. Then have them plan to discuss their answers together as a group:

- Sirach 15:11-20

Say not: "It was God's doing that I fell away"; for what he hates he does not do. Say not: "It was he who set me astray"... he does not let it befall those who fear him. When God, in the beginning, created man, he made him subject to his own free choice. If you choose, you can keep the commandments; it is loyalty to do his will. There are set before you fire and water; to whichever you choose, stretch forth your hand. Before man are life and death, whichever he chooses shall be given to him. Immense is the wisdom of the Lord; he is mighty in power, and all-seeing. The eyes of God see all he has made; he understands man's every deed. No man does he command to sin, to none does he give strength for lies.

Small Group Discussion Questions:

1. Does God cause man to fall away from doing what he should?

2. Does God want man to stray from Him and do wrong?

3. What does it mean that God made man "subject to his own free choice?"

4. With the imagery of fire and water, what do you think God is telling us about the choices we make?

5. God is all about man's free choice, because God created us with free will. But what does He tell man

to do with this free will and why?

6. What does it mean that if man chooses life, he will receive life, and if he chooses death, he will receive death?

7. What is the difference between a tyrant and a loving father who guides his children with clear rules?

8. God is awesome, and His love, power, and knowledge surpass everything we could possibly imagine. However, sometimes His plan for us and all of creation can be very confusing. Sometimes, bad things happen, and people lose faith and hope in God's love and even in His existence. What do you think God would tell someone who is suffering from something very traumatic? What do you think He would tell you if you are confused or struggling right now?

9. Reflection: Read this passage again and write a short prayer using what you have learned from it.

Option #3: Freedom to Play (SKIT)

We may not realize this, but every time we play a game we subject ourselves to some kind of rules and regulations. These rules are given to us not to make the game less fun or boring, but to give the game structure and order. These rules provide the game with a clear purpose of what to do, how to play and, of course, how to win. And the crazy part about it is, these rules allow for the fun to take place. The challenge increases when there are many players on a team. Each person has a responsibility to play their position well and to play as a team. The old saying, "There is no 'I' in TEAM" helps us to remember not to look selfishly at our role in the game. Let's consider the game of football. To play a game, the players cannot be selfish and simply "do their own thing." They must obey the rules and the structure of the game in order to play the game well.

CAST:

- Coach
- Football players:
  - Receiver
  - Quarterback
  - Center
- Optional: Two more offensive linemen and some on defense

(Continued on next leader's page)

because their pride keeps them from admitting it. Often, they imply that truth is "relative" by saying things such as, "What's true for you may not be true for me."

Along the same line of thinking, consider the "I'm just kidding" syndrome. It's one of the most aggravating and hurtful habits of our culture. When joking around and hurting someone's feelings, instead of quickly saying "sorry" and asking for forgiveness, we act as if it is the other person's fault for getting hurt. And so we respond with, "I was just *kidding*." But what is the truth in this situation? The truth is that we crossed the line of decency and we should apologize to the person we offended. This, however, would take humility—admitting we were wrong—and likely involve some awkwardness. So we deny the truth and say we were kidding. "It's *your fault* for being sensitive," we imply.

Sometimes we are afraid of the truth and so we pretend to not know it or even deny it completely. We don't want to admit we are wrong because we know the truth may call for a change in our lives. When things get intense and our consciences start to bother us, we may drop the conversation or even verbally attack the other person who is presenting the truth. This is usually code for: *what you're telling me makes me uncomfortable and I don't want to believe it, so leave me alone and let me believe what I want.*

When truth is abandoned or denied, then lies and falsehoods take the place of reality. Reality is reduced to an illusion. An illusion is something that *seems* to be true but is not. The *illusion* of reality can trap people into a life without freedom. This, of course, can be a major problem for such a person.

John Paul II explained the problem this way: "Once the idea of a universal truth about the good, knowable by human reason, is lost, inevitably the notion of conscience also changes." Instead of admitting there are some things that by their nature are good or evil, "there is a tendency to grant to the individual con-science the prerogative of independently determining the criteria of good and evil and then acting accordingly."[4]

Living this way inevitably will lead one to decide that God made some "mistakes" regarding what *is* and *is not* good for humans. Soon enough, people are creating their own morality based upon their preferences and convenience and not at all based upon what is actually good or evil. Whether we trick ourselves or we trick someone else—through lives based on fiction that poses as fact—the truth is that no one lives happily ever after.

In John Paul II's very first encyclical, he wrote the following concerning the relationship of truth and freedom:

> Jesus Christ meets the man of every age, including our own, with the same words: 'You will know the truth, and the truth will make you free.' These words contain both a fundamental requirement and a warning: the requirement of an honest rela-tionship with regard to truth as a condition for authentic freedom, and the warning to avoid every kind of illusory freedom, every superficial unilateral freedom, every freedom that fails to enter into the whole truth about man and the world.[5]

(Cont.)

OPTIONAL PROPS:

- Football (any kind can work)
- Whistle, hat, clipboard, with "plays" written on a sheet of paper for the coach
- You can dress up the players in big t-shirts and put balloons on their shoulders under the shirt. Put black strips under their eyes (electrical tape would be funny), and have the receiver put on a pair of gloves.

SKIT:

Coach: "Time out!" *(Coach motions for the players to come to him. All players run up to the coach and take a knee.)*

Coach: "OK, guys. This is an important down for us. It's third and four, and we need to make that first down if we want to stay alive in this game. Are you with me?!"

Team: *(All nod their heads solemnly and focus in on Coach).*

Coach: Good. First, we're gonna' run a pass play. Where's Billy?

Billy the Receiver: Right here, Coach.

Coach: (Pulls him close to him.) Look, son, this play is directed to you. I want you to run a five-yard slant, and Jimmy is gonna' hit you in the middle of the field. Like I've told you all week, their defense is weak in the middle, and it's a sure first down for us. If we make this first, we'll get a fresh set of downs, and then we can take a few shots at the end zone. Can you do this?

Billy the Receiver: Sure I can, Coach.

The team runs off to the field.

Jimmy the Quarterback: OK! (He looks to Billy.) I'll be looking for you in the middle, so get there quick! (Jimmy turns to the offensive line) Guys, all I need is three seconds. Dig in this last time for me, OK?

Offensive lineman: We'll handle 'em, but you better get rid of the ball. Don't dance around back there like a ballerina.

As the offense is walking into position, Billy the Receiver faces the onlookers and begins to speak. As he begins to speak everyone freezes in place.

Billy the Receiver: "A five yard slant? Who wants to run a five-yard slant when we're down by five points and on the fifty yard line? I can smoke this cornerback. I wanna' run a 'Hail Mary!' And that's what I'm gonna' do. When the ball is snapped, I'm gonna' zip down that sideline and I'll be wide open in the end zone, ready to catch the pass. I'll make a touchdown and win this game. Coach will be so proud of me.

As he moves back into position, everyone else unfreezes and lines up. The center snaps the ball, Jimmy (the quarterback) drops back quickly and throws the ball in the middle of the field where Billy is supposed to be .

Coach: Billy! What are you doing?! Who do you think you are?! Who's team are you playing for, anyway?!

Making the connection:

What we see here is a great example of selfishness and disorder at its worst. The receiver lost sight of his role, and instead of being open for the pass, he closed himself off. Let's look at some of the roles in this skit.

A deeper look at the players:

- The coach is the person who is put in charge of guiding and directing his team.
- The players freely chose to be part of the team. To be a player means to play the game according to the rules. It also means to serve the team and to train as well as one can with respect to the position.
- The game has been designed to be played a certain way. It has certain rules, and these rules, instead of taking the fun out of the game, actually make it enjoyable.

What happened:

The receiver was not being a good player. He selfishly wanted something that was not for him to decide. Instead of following the coach's play to help the team, he let down his teammates, the coach, the fans, and even himself. His freedom as a receiver was not in making up his own plays and trying to be the coach but being a receiver who follows direction and guidance from the coach. When the team works together, that is when great things happen. He lost sight of the point of the game and focused only on one part he wanted to play on the team.

(Continued on next leader's page)

Notice that he did not refer to "the many truths." Instead, he clearly refers to *"the whole truth about man and the world"*—to one truth—an objective truth that everyone must recognize in order to experience "authentic freedom." John Paul II proclaimed that if people live with a false notion of freedom, they are not living in truth at all. This first encyclical, *Redemptor Hominis (The Redeemer of Man)*, in many ways laid the foundation for the rest of John Paul II's work and teaching because it focused on Jesus Christ—the Redeemer of man, the Way, the Truth, and the Life.

If we desire to live in true freedom, let us follow the lead of John Paul II and the famous anthem that he repeated throughout his entire pontificate: "Christ, the final Adam, by the revelation of the mystery of the Father and His love, fully reveals man to himself and makes his supreme calling clear."[6]

Just as it would be ridiculous for a person to claim it is not raining as he or she stands soaking wet in a thunderstorm, it is just as foolish for one to deny the objective truth of who we are—the truth that Christ reveals to us—and that our purpose is to make a free gift of ourselves in love and find ultimate freedom in heaven for eternity.

(Truth Quiz)

To help discover what areas of your life need to be renewed in the truth of Christ, make an honest attempt with this true or false quiz.

1. ○ **T** ○ **F** Flirting is innocent fun, even when it involves sexual innuendos.

2. ○ **T** ○ **F** It is OK to have sexual conversations online, as long as you don't act on them.

3. ○ **T** ○ **F** There is nothing wrong with posting provocative pictures of yourself online as long as you are wearing clothes.

4. ○ **T** ○ **F** It is OK to look at pornography because you are not actually having sex.

5. ○ **T** ○ **F** It is OK for a married couple to look at pornography to keep the spark alive.

6. ○ **T** ○ **F** It is OK to masturbate because you are not involving anyone else.

7. ○ **T** ○ **F** It is OK to think about your boyfriend or girlfriend in a lustful manner as long as you don't act on it.

8. ○ **T** ○ **F** It is OK to engage in sexual acts as long as you are not going "all the way."

9. ○ **T** ○ **F** As long as you are in love, and are planning to get married, it is OK to have sex before marriage.

10. ○ **T** ○ **F** Your future spouse wants you to have sexual experience before you get married.

notes

_____
_____
_____
_____
_____
_____
_____
_____
_____
_____
_____
_____
_____
_____
_____
_____
_____
_____
_____
_____
_____

(Cont.)

Sometimes we lose sight of who we are and to what we are called. Let's take this analogy in the skit just a step further.

A deeper look:

- God: is the good coach who wants us all to "play" and wants us all to "work together" in the "family" to which He has called us.

- Man and woman are created for a specific reason with a specific purpose. We do not create our own happiness or our own purpose, but we do discover that God is a loving Father who has amazing things in store for us. We must understand that to "play" the game of life, we must follow the "rules" that God, the author of the game, gave us.

- Life: We are not meant to go through life by ourselves doing any old thing we want. We are called to be in communion with God and with others. This communion takes place when we live out truthfully the freedom that we have be given. We must hear the call that God has placed in our life and live out that call. This means we must be open to "receive" God's will for us in our lives. Only then will we play the game correctly and obtain the victory for which our hearts long. In other words, only when we live in the truth of freedom that Christ has given us can we receive the gift that man is called to in heaven.

MOVIE CLIP/SONG SUGGESTIONS

MOVIE CLIPS:

1. *The Truman Show:* Show the segment that falls between 1:01:01 and 1:08:07. This scene shows an interview with the producer of the TV show who has lied to the main character, Truman, his whole life. He is confronted by a former cast member and attempts to defend himself. A great exploration of the connection between truth and freedom is in this segment.

2. *The Truman Show:* Show the segment that falls between 1:22:19 and 1:35:55. The producer of the TV show tries to prevent Truman from seeing the truth when Truman finds out his whole life has been based upon a lie.

3. *Ever After:* Show the segment that falls between 1:44:23 and 1:46:15. The segment shows the main character, Danielle, being released into freedom from captivity after being objectified by her captor.

4. *The Shawshank Redemption:* Show the segment that falls between 1:51:38 and 2:00:27. This is the part when Andy (Tim Robbins) breaks out from the tunnel into the field and the water. This scene could be compared to baptism, freedom, redemption, and new life.

5. *Braveheart:* Show the segment that falls between 1:12:25 and 1:18:53. This is the famous speech William Wallace makes before a big battle. "Run and you'll live. At least for a while ... and dying in your beds, would you trade all the time between this day and that for one chance—just one chance—at freedom? ... They may take our lives, but they can never take our freedom!"

6. *The Passion of the Christ:* Show the segment that falls between 38:52 and 48:06. This is the exchange between Jesus and Pilate concerning the topic of "truth." Pilate asks Jesus the question, "What is Truth?" Pilate then discusses the nature of truth with his wife.

SONGS:

1. *Shackles* - Mary Mary (*Shackles — Praise You*)

The truth will set us free. All we have to do is embrace it. Pop/Hip Hop.

2. *Irene* - Toby Mac (*Momentum*)

God will be there to carry you even when you feel like giving up. Hip Hop.

3. *The Life You Give* — Curtis Stephan (*Sacred Revolution*)

Deciding to not settle for anything less than the life that God gives us, we are encouraged to fight through lies to live in the truth. Contemporary/Rock.

4. *Free* — Steven Curtis Chapman (*Signs of Life*)

Story of an incarcerated man who finds interior, spiritual freedom in prison. A powerful song of how we find authentic freedom in Christ. Acoustic/Contemporary.

5. *Say Won't You Say* — Jennifer Knapp (*The Way I Am*)

A call goes out for God to show His love to her. As echoes of love and freedom resound in her own heart, she then calls out to God in love, gratitude, and freedom. Soft Rock/Pop.

You may remember the famous words of Patrick Henry, "Give me liberty or give me death."

You may not be so bold in your words as Mr. Henry (yet), but you do desire freedom. Everyone does. In fact, our desire for freedom is something God places in the heart of every human, just as He also gives us the desire to be loved and the desire to be happy. So, at this point, you may be asking, "So, how exactly can Christ set me free in my mind and body regarding my sexuality?" Scripture tells us to "be transformed by the renewal of your mind" (Rom 12:2). We must seek the truth of Christ and allow His truth to fill our minds and hearts, washing away the lies that we have begun to believe. A life of freedom in mind and heart is not only possible, it is guaranteed when we allow Christ to renew us.

But in order to achieve this renewal, we must recognize the lies of the world for what they are: deceptive half-truths that lead us away from Christ, who is the Truth.

Obviously, in an objective reality in which God is God (and you are not), and in which the Gospel is lived out as truth (which it is), each one of the answers in the "Truth Quiz" on page 78 is *false*. Regardless of how anyone seeks to justify his or her actions or seek "loopholes" with the objective truth that exists, the truth cannot be subject to personal opinion, individual bias, or personal beliefs. Truth is bigger than all of that. Those who belong to Christ belong to the truth.

As Christ Himself reminded Pilate (and us), "Everyone who belongs to the truth hears my voice" (Jn 18:37).

Most likely one or a few of the phrases in the quiz on the previous page challenged you or made you want to debate, argue, or justify your thoughts or actions. If they did, it's likely that you have been affected by moral relativism, in which the lines of morality are blurred. Conversely, God's truth is not blurry. In fact, it's quite clear, as proven by these Scripture verses:

1 Thessalonians 4:3-5 "For this is the will of God, your sanctification: that you abstain from immorality, that each one of you know how to control his own body in holiness and honor, not in the passion of lust like heathen who do not know God."

Colossians 3:5 "Put to death therefore what is earthly in you: immorality, impurity, passion, evil desire, and covetousness, which is idolatry."

1 Corinthians 6:13 "The body is not meant for immorality, but for the Lord and the Lord for the body."

2 Corinthians 7:1 "Let us cleanse ourselves from every defilement of body and spirit, and make holiness perfect in the fear of God."

Take some time to pray these Scriptures. Open your heart to God as you meditate upon these verses. If you approach God with a pure and open heart, He will recreate what needs re-creation, and perfect that which needs perfection.

Finally, as you live out the truth of the Gospel, ponder these words from the late Archbishop Fulton Sheen:

> The root of all our trouble is that freedom for God and in God has been interpreted as freedom *from* God. Freedom is ours to give away. Each of us reveals what we believe to be the purpose of life by the way we use that freedom.

For some, the purpose of life appears to be pleasure. Others may live for popularity or success. By the way you use your freedom, what do you reveal to be the purpose of your life?

> **Notes & Nuggets:** In the closing prayer, we ask for St. Patrick's intercession because he was a bold promoter of freedom. St. Patrick was captured and sold into slavery, along with thousands of others. Later in his life, after he had escaped, he wrote his *Letter to the Soldiers of Coroticus*, in which he protested British slave trading. St. Patrick knew the truth and he knew that it was worth the struggle to attain freedom.

IN HIS OWN WORDS

• **On the Truth of the Body:** "On the basis of Christ's words in the Sermon on the Mount, Christian ethos is characterized by a transformation of the conscience and attitudes of the human person, both man and woman. This is such as to express and realize the value of the body and of sex, according to the Creator's original plan, placed as they are in the service of the communion of persons, which is the deepest substratum of human ethics and culture" (October 22, 1980).

• **On "Safe Sex" as a Loss of Truth:** "So-called 'safe sex,' which is touted by the 'civilization of technology,' is actually, in the view of the overall requirements of the person, radically not safe, indeed it is extremely dangerous. It endangers both the person and the family. And what is this danger? It is the loss of the truth about one's own self and about the family, together with the risk of a loss of freedom, and consequently a loss of love itself" (*Letter to Families*, 1994).

• **On the New Law as a Means to Freedom:** "If the whole law (the moral law of the Old Testament) is fulfilled in the commandment of charity, the dimension of the new Gospel ethos is nothing but an appeal to human freedom. It is an appeal to its fuller implementation and, in a way, to fuller "utilization" of the potential of the human spirit" (January 14, 1981).

• **On Purity and Truth:** "Purity is a requirement of love. It is the dimension of its interior truth in man's heart" (December 3, 1980).

• **On Human Freedom as a Gift:** "Human freedom belongs to us as creatures; it is a freedom which is given as a gift, one to be received like a seed and to be cultivated responsibly. ... Freedom then is rooted in the truth about man, and it is ultimately directed toward communion" (*Veritatis Splendor*, 86.1).

WORK IT OUT

Assignment #1: Think of a time when you or someone you knew stubbornly would not listen to what was true. Draw a cartoon strip that depicts this event. Try to tie in the authentic elements of freedom in a funny way. Then write a few paragraphs specifically explaining the cartoon strip and its point.

Assignment #2: Read Exodus 3:4-10; 16:1-3; and 17:1-7. Reflect on a time when you had to endure some kind of hardship or struggle for the sake of what was true or important. Write an essay on what you learned—or wish you had learned—from this experience.

Assignment #3: Reflect on a time when you or someone you know overcame the temptation to abuse freedom, and successfully chose the good. Write an essay about the experience, the rewards that came with exercising freedom properly, and how it affected those around you.

Project #1: Pick a local community issue in which the truth is being obscured or abandoned, possibly leading to a loss of freedom for someone (young, old, handicapped, poor, vulnerable, etc.). Do some investigating and interview a few people who know more than you do about the issue. Then write a letter to the editor of the local paper or to a leader in local government asking for justice regarding the issue. Use the truth creatively as your weapon, but try not to use it angrily; the truth speaks loudly and powerfully by itself. Use your mind and your pen to make a difference.

CLOSING PRAYER

Leader: In the name of the Father, and of the Son, and of the Holy Spirit. **Amen.**

All: St. Patrick, please pray with me that I, like you, would have the courage to live a life that echoes truth and promotes freedom for all. **Amen.**

Glossary
of Key Terms

Deprived: This term refers to humanity's loss of the grace of original innocence. Through original sin, we were deprived of the perfect integration of our bodies and our wills. Though human nature is still good, we struggle to choose God's will over our own.

External constraints: The laws of God or society that protect us from abusing our free will and hurting ourselves or others.

Freedom: The ability to desire and choose the good.

Free will: The gift given to us by God that allows us to choose between good and evil. This God-given ability allows us to be the authors of our own choices, thus allowing us to determine our own destiny.

Internal constraints: Distractions or disordered desires within us that steer us away from choosing the good.

Objective truth: Reality as it is, apart from what we think or feel about it.

OBJECTIVES At the end of this lesson, the student should know and be able to:

- Demonstrate ways the body can speak both truths or lies.
- Judge the truthfulness or untruthfulness of sexual behavior(s).
- Analyze the "language of the body" as the "language of love" spoken within marriage.
- Explain how pre-marital sex, adultery, pornography, and contraception all constitute lies of the body.
- Name examples of non-sexual body language.
- Explain that the Holy Spirit is the Creator of life in the one-flesh marriage union.

Notes & Nuggets: Pray today for your teens to come to understand the power they hold in their bodies and the responsibility that comes with that God-given power. Also pray for their humility, as this is needed if one is to discern the new language we are called to speak with our bodies. We suggest praying your own private and unscripted prayer to Jesus, the God who took on flesh and taught us so much through His own language of the body. May He help you as you reach out to your students and witness to the truth with your own body.

TWO MINUTE DRILL — VERBAL REVIEW:

1. What is a good definition of freedom?
   Answer: The ability to desire and to choose the good.

2. Define free will.
   Answer: The capacity to choose one's own deeds. God created man and woman like Himself—as rational creatures with free will. This gift of free will makes humans the masters over their own acts.

3. Give an example of challenging responsibilities of love that bring about "a good" and, thus, more freedom.
   Answer: For example, returning home from a date on time, even when it is not convenient or "fun." This creates respect between you, your date, and his or her parents. It then results in more trust and greater freedom for all the persons involved.

4. Why is truth so connected to freedom?
   Answer: God designed us for certain purposes that, if honored and followed, lead to our fulfillment and, subsequently, to true freedom. Just as putting diesel in an unleaded car ruins the car, ignoring the truth of our call to love destroys our freedom.

5. What does "freedom from the law" mean?
   Answer: It means that, because of a purified heart, a person no longer desires to break the law, and, thus, does not need the law. Through Christ's grace, we are freed from "internal constraints," allowing us to abide by the law out of love rather than merely out of obligation.

Chapter Six

Language of the Body

By God's design, the body is capable of speaking its own language. This reality means, however, that we can speak a language of truths or lies—not only with our mouths but with the very actions of our body. Simple things like a smile, a nod of the head, or a wave of the hand all act as signs that convey a message even if no words are said. When people express love sexually, they speak some of the most powerful language of the body. For example, the act of intercourse is meant to proclaim, "I give all of myself to you and to you alone."

In this chapter, we will examine the **language of the body** and show that the proper language it *should* speak is a **language of love**, which rejoices in always telling the truth.

ICEBREAKER (optional): Body-Spelling Charades

This game is most exciting when done as a competition between two teams, but it can certainly be effective if done with only one group. It also works best in a room with a lot of space; moving desks around probably will be necessary.

Break your group into two equal teams, with perhaps ten to fifteen students each. If available, line up chairs on each side of the room with plenty of floor space in the middle. Have a few members from each team stand on the chairs (two or three for each side, looking into the middle). The remaining members of each team should stand in the middle, facing their teammates who are on the chairs. Upon your signal, those standing on chairs should either leave the room or cover their ears as you give the direction to the rest of their team. You say a word, such as "lake," and the teams need to try use their bodies to spell out the word "lake" on the floor. The people standing on the chairs must "read" (or guess) as quickly as they can the word their teammates are trying to spell.

To make the game easier, assign each team a designated leader to help coordinate the "body-spelling" effort. To make the game harder, do not allow the "spellers" to say any letters out loud, and make it so that each team is only allowed one guess (this will make them concentrate on figuring it out, rather then just yelling out guesses). Instead, mandate that their communication to one another be only with gestures. You can complicate things even more by making them do all capital letters, all lowercase, or capitalizing the first (or first and last) letter of each word. Start the game with easy words and progress to harder and longer ones, depending on how many people are on each team. The fewer people on each team, the shorter the words need to be for this game to work. Here are a few suggestions of some terms and related words found in this curriculum.

- FALL
- FRUIT
- SIN
- POPE
- HOPE
- BODY
- IMAGE
- LOVE
- FREE
- GARDEN
- TOTAL
- PURITY
- SHAME
- ORIGINAL
- CHASTITY
- FREEDOM
- INNOCENCE
- ESCHATOLOGICAL (for extra credit!)

Here's another twist to this game. Get the teams to create objects instead of words (i.e. stop sign, football, sunglasses, chalice, pretzel, the Chi-Rho symbol, etc). Later on in the lesson, you can make the connection to the material by referring back to this "language of the body," reminding students again in a tangible way that the body shows forth the message or truth of the person.

OPENING PRAYER

Leader: In the name of the Father, and of the Son, and of the Holy Spirit. **Amen**.

(Option #1)
Leader or Reader #1: Read Ephesians 4:22-25
"Put off your old nature which belongs to your former manner of life and is corrupt through deceitful lusts, and be renewed in the spirit of your minds, and put on the new nature, created after the likeness of God in true righteousness and holiness. Therefore, putting away every falsehood, let everyone speak the truth with his neighbor, for we are members of one another."

Leader or Reader #2: Lord Jesus, help us to resist all temptations that keep us from speaking the whole truth with our mouths, minds, hearts, and bodies. Make us strong in Your grace so that we can be honest in word and deed, with pure hearts that follow after You. **Amen**.

(Option #2)
Leader or Reader #1: Read Matthew 5:33, 37
"Again you have heard that it was said to your ancestors, 'Do not take a false oath, but make good to the Lord all that you vow'...Let your 'Yes' mean 'Yes,' and your 'No' mean 'No.' Anything more is from the evil one."

Leader or Reader #2: Father, thank You for sending Your Son to set us free. Help us to know the truth and to be committed to speaking it, both in word and in deed. We do want to be free. Help us to live truthfully in freedom.
Amen.

Need a Review of Lesson 5?

STORY STARTER:
A Deceptive Appetite

When an Alaskan Eskimo becomes aware of the presence of a wolf in his territory, he is forced to protect his herds and family. But rather than face the wolf, the hunter uses the animal's own appetite to bring it down. He begins by slaughtering one of his smaller goats and pouring its blood over the blade of a knife. The weapon is left to freeze in the arctic temperatures, and once the first coating of blood is set, more blood is placed on the knife. This process is repeated until the entire blade is covered with frozen blood.

Before nightfall, the Eskimo hikes outside of his property and buries the handle of the knife in the ground, leaving the blade protruding from the snow. Since wolves can smell blood from miles away, it doesn't take long for one to track the scent, find the knife, and begin cautiously licking the frozen blood. As the taste excites the animal, it begins to lick more aggressively.

Verbal Review of Lesson 5

1. What is a good definition of freedom?

2. Define free will.

3. Give an example of challenging responsibilities of love that bring about a "good" and, thus, more freedom.

4. Why is truth so connected to freedom?

5. What does "freedom from the law" mean?

Before long, parts of the blade are exposed and the wolf's tongue is nicked. But since its tongue has been numbed by the icy blood, the animal is unaware of the damage being caused. As the blood of the goat is cleaned off the blade, it is replaced with the warmer blood of the wolf. In an excited frenzy at the taste of the fresh blood, the animal licks all the more ravenously until it becomes faint. Within hours, the wolf will die of blood loss.

This trap resembles the allure of sexual sin. A person experiences satisfaction without initially seeing the consequences. We feel like we are getting away with doing a particular act—only for a while, that is. The pleasure offers us an escape from loneliness and a brief relief from the emptiness we often feel. But before we realize it, the damage has been done to us. This is similar to the allure of sin: It promises us everything and gives us little or nothing in return. In fact, the whole power of temptation rests on the deceptive promise that living for ourselves will give us more joy than if we live for God.

The challenge we face as Christians is that we need to unmask the lies given to us by the modern culture and then have the courage to choose what will actually satisfy us.

COMPREHENSION & DISCUSSION QUESTIONS

1. Can you think of a time when you were deceived by an empty promise?

2. Can you think of a time when you were deceived by another person's language of the body? What did you feel like after you realized you had been deceived? Have you ever done this to someone else?

3. What would motivate a person to tell a lie with his or her body?

4. Describe a time when someone told you the truth with the language of his or her body. How did this make you feel?

5. Why do you think some people believe that lies with the body are not the same as verbal lies?

6. How much of your time do you spend learning the language of the body from the television set?

7. Twenty years ago, the average adolescent in the United States saw 14,000 sexual references on TV each year.[1] Do you think television has gotten more wholesome since then? Why or why not?

8. Is the language of the body we see portrayed on TV and in the movies generally speaking truth or lies?

You Decide

Which of these people do you think has a better perspective on loving relationships?

Lou Bega, from the song "Mambo Number 5"

"A little bit of Monica in my life. A little bit of Erica by my side. A little bit of Rita's all I need.

A little bit of Tina's what I see. A little bit of Sandra in the sun. A little bit of Mary all night long.

A little bit of Jessica here I am. A little bit of you makes me your man."

vs.

Blessed (Mother) Teresa of Calcutta

"Love, to be real, must cost—it must hurt—it must empty us of self."

Did you know?

The average high school student watches more than twenty-one hours of TV per week,[i] and listens to three to four hours of radio per day.[ii] That's significantly more time than he or she will spend in the classroom.

BRIDGING THE GAP

There are so many ways to grab someone's attention these days, but none is more popular than splashing sexual images, lyrics, innuendos, jokes, stories, or actions into our lives. We have become conditioned by all of these messages showing the "language of sexuality" and may no longer question the truth of these messages. As the hungry wolf was tricked into thinking the bloody knife would satisfy his hunger, we are often tricked into thinking our deepest desires will be met by sexual pleasure. One of the keys to satisfying our deepest desires is to learn the language of the body and learn to "speak it" well.

TO THE CORE

notes

Without having to say a word, the body is capable of speaking its own language. This "language of the body" can be something positive like a hug, or negative like a not-so-friendly gesture on the freeway. Since the body is capable of speaking, it is also capable of lying. For example, consider when Judas kissed Jesus while betraying Him (see Mk 14:45). Judas' body said one thing, but his heart clearly said another.

Pope John Paul II taught that the language of the body is not only a language of love but a language of divine love. The love of God is unconditional. Remembering that we are created in the image and likeness of God, this language of divine love is the body's "native" language. It's the language our bodies were created to speak: the truth.[1]

The Promises of the Body

When it comes to sex, people often speak a lie with the language of their bodies without even realizing it. For example, after the lead character in the movie *Vanilla Sky* slept with a woman, she said to him, "Don't you know when you sleep with someone ... your body makes a promise whether you do or not?" Odds are, he was not intending to lie to her. But she was right. He had "spoken" a promise with his body that he had not intended.

Whether we know it or not, the true language of sex says, "I am completely yours. I belong totally to you." But this is often not what people really mean to say. Consider the situation of two teens having sex. They are physically doing the same thing as a married couple, but they do not mean what their bodies are saying because they have not made the marriage commitment. A married couple has made a commitment in front of the Church and many witnesses, freely offering their whole lives to each other until death. On the other hand, two teenagers who are dating or "hooking up" have given no promise of life-long commitment. Therefore, they are not making a total gift of self to each

other. In the end, people may choose to have sex (because God gave us free will), but no one is free to change the meaning of sex.

The language of sex is only true when it speaks of marital love. Even if the dating or "hooking up" couple's intentions are good, their act is still a lie expressed in the language of their bodies. They may hope to get married one day, but they do not yet belong to each other in the eyes of God because they have not made the commitment through the means that He has established. They have made no promise to be faithful to each other until death. They don't need to get a civil divorce if they break up (although they may feel like they do). The bottom line is this: they are not husband and wife. They want one of the great joys of marriage—sexual relations, also known as marital relations—without the responsibilities and without the commitment. Isn't it interesting that one of the traditional names for sex in marriage is "the act of marriage"? The fact that sex expressed marital love was so well understood that we, as a culture, simply referred to it as "the marital act." Today, this definition is barely known because sex has become such a casual, accepted behavior of unmarried people. When unmarried people have sex, it actually mocks and cheapens marriage.

COMPREHENSION & DISCUSSION QUESTIONS

1. What is the *language of the body*?

2. Why did John Paul II call divine love the body's "native" language?

3. What do you think is the biggest influence on people learning to speak the language of the body?

4. What does the body "say" through sexual intercourse?

5. Why are unmarried people incapable of freely expressing ("saying") the full meaning of sexual intercourse?

Marriage carries with it many responsibilities, but few are more foundational than the importance of telling the truth. While most people eventually get married, we often hear that half of marriages end in divorce. One of the major causes of divorce is infidelity. What many teenage couples do not realize is that by speaking the truth with their bodies now—through purity and self-control—they are actually training themselves in the faithfulness that is the bedrock to future marital stability.

Notes & Nuggets: Sign Language of the Body

Break your teens into groups of four or five. Have them brainstorm different kinds of non-vulgar forms of body language (nods, smiles, sign language, high fives, hugs, pats on the back, kisses, hand holding, handshakes, "thumbs up," winking, opening a door for someone, etc.) Whichever group can come up with the most within one minute gets a prize. You can use this as a small way to back up your teaching that says there are many ways to speak the truth with our bodies that are not sexual. Encourage your teens to be consistent and truthful with the way they speak the language of the body, even when it is not sexual.

Notes & Nuggets: On the topic of contraception, John Paul II wrote, "Thus the innate language that expresses the total reciprocal self-giving of husband and wife is overlaid, through contraception, by an objectively contradictory language, namely, that of not giving oneself totally to the other. This leads not only to a positive refusal to be open to life but also to a falsification of the inner truth of conjugal love" (*Familiaris Consortio*, 32).

Perhaps the best thing you can do to prepare for a faithful marriage later is to learn to be faithful to the language of your body now. St. Paul tells us that **fornication** (having sex outside of marriage) and adultery (a married person having sex with someone who is not his or her spouse) are very serious sins (see 1 Cor 6:10). Learning to speak the language of the body truthfully is a sure way to avoid a great deal of heartache.

In the United States, immigrants from all over the world speak different languages, but our common language is English. On a deeper level, the common language of all people is that of love. While we are called to love everyone, we are not called to love everyone in the same way. The language of the body as expressed in the sexual act can only be spoken honestly to one's spouse. To say it another way, the language of sexual love can only be fully spoken and understood in the "country" of marriage!

When this language of love is spoken between a man and a woman, the two become participants in the **one-flesh union**. At times, this union results in the creation of new life, making the two co-creators with God in His own work of creation.

In the beginning, the "Spirit of God was moving over the face of the waters" (Gn 1:2), signifying that the Holy Spirit was present with God the Father in the work of creation. This is why we say in the **Nicene Creed**, "I believe in the Holy Spirit, the Lord and Giver of life." This same Holy Spirit is the creative author and the invisible, yet essential, dimension of sexual intercourse. Therefore, in order for the language of the body to be true, it must be open to the Holy Spirit's creative presence. Not inviting the Holy Spirit into the marital act is like not inviting your Mom to your family's Mother's Day celebration; without her, the party can never be what it was meant to be.

The Language of Contraception

Some examples of the language of the body are clearly "true" or clearly "a lie." Others take more thought and consideration. This is especially true when two people truly appear to be loving each other well in a marriage. So what about the issue of contraception? What is a couple saying when they introduce contraception into the marital act? Surely, spouses who love each other are at least attempting to say in the sexual union, "I am all yours." As we discussed earlier, the giving of oneself in the sexual act is a profound thing. You are saying with your body, "I am totally committed to you—so much so, that I am willing to give you my very person in this most intimate of ways." But in reality, when a couple introduces **contraception** into their sexual union, they are saying with their bodies, "I refuse to give you all of myself. I won't give you my fertility. I refuse to receive all of you. I won't receive your fertility." Instead of becoming one flesh, they bring a barrier into the act of sex—a barrier between their full love and gift of self.

Couples often turn to contraception because of the fear of having a child. By

"Finally, brethren, whatever is true, whatever is honorable, whatever is just, whatever is pure, whatever is lovely, whatever is gracious, if there is any excellence, if there is anything worthy of praise, think about these things."
(Phil 4:8)

his or her existence, a child who is conceived says, "I'm permanent, so you two should be as well!" But the couple often knows that they're not ready for the total giving and commitment that their act is saying, so they deny the natural process of life-giving love. In a sense, they see their fertility as something that needs to be fixed. In a sense, they treat pregnancy as a disease against which they must be protected or vaccinated. They do not see the gift of fertility as something to be received with joy.

You might wonder, "If I can't use a condom, then how am I supposed to protect myself?" Let's think about this—does it really sound like love if you are trying to protect yourself somehow from your beloved and his or her fertility? We protect ourselves from enemies, not our spouses' fertility or the child that may come from a union of love. We are called to receive our beloved without reserve. If you are not married and ready to receive that person fully, it's not time to give that person your body. God did not design us to give ourselves away in pieces.

Today, we see this problem in **pornography**, where the body is separated from the person. Pornography presents a clear example of people lying with their bodies. If you step back and analyze pornography honestly, the people in the magazines or movies aren't giving themselves to anyone. They do what they do for money. One of the biggest lies of Internet pornography is that there are people on the other end of the computer that want to please you. Pornography is really a counterfeit of love because there are no "real" people, and no real unions involved. That's not to say that porn stars are not "real" people, but they intentionally take on fictitious roles that blur the lines between reality and fiction.

A body by itself without a soul is not a person; instead, it is an object. When pornography places all of the focus on the body, then the spectator's view is no longer really focused on persons (body and soul), but merely on their bodies. John Paul II said that when the naked body is uprooted from its proper place within an interpersonal relationship through the media, the body "becomes an object, and what is more, in a way, an anonymous object."[2] An anonymous object is not the same as a person. Persons are meant to be loved, never used. This is why pornography degrades everyone involved. John Paul II also said that love is, "the unification of persons."[3] With pornography, you are entering a fantasy play of lust, where every single character, including the spectator, is a selfish one. There is no real relationship, no mutual exchange of self between persons. There is no true gift of self and no real union, only self-centered counterfeits.

After considering many lies in the language of the body (fornication, contraception, pornography, etc.), consider the true language of Christ's body. Beaten. Bruised. Bloodied. Broken for you. As He stretched out His arms to all of humanity from the Cross, He allowed himself to be crucified so that we could have victory over sin and freedom to live with Him forever. The words of Christ from the Cross are less memorable than the act of total self-donation that He made for us. So powerful was His non-verbal promise of love made to us through the language of His body that it has become the standard visual aid in the Catholic Church. The crucifix is the pre-eminent symbol of love. The

Did you know?

Should a married couple have a serious reason to delay pregnancy for a period of time, they can use what is called Natural Family Planning (NFP). Many people confuse NFP with the "rhythm" or "calendar" methods, which are only moderately effective methods used by couples in the past century. According to the British Medical Journal and other highly respected entities, NFP is highly effective, reaching 98 and 99 percent effectiveness in several independent studies. For example, in the British Medical Journal Study, nearly 20,000 impoverished women in India [using NFP] had a pregnancy rate approaching zero.[iii] The point is not to find a "Catholic" way to avoid children. But if serious reasons to postpone pregnancy arise in married life, there is a moral alternative to contraception.

language of Christ's body on the Cross was so powerful that we now also use it at the start and end of every prayer.

What will your sign be? What will you say with your body today, tomorrow, and for the rest of your life? You could imitate Christ and learn to speak a beautiful language of love with your body by living sacrificially for others. In this life of self-donating love, you will find what it means to be fully human.

COMPREHENSION & DISCUSSION QUESTIONS

1. If a physically beautiful person is rude, selfish, and deceitful with the language of his or her body, does this make that person seem more or less attractive to you? Why?

2. Name three lies of the body that are non-sexual.

3. Name three sexual lies in the language of the body.

4. What does the "one-flesh" union mean?

5. Who are the three involved in creation when, from the marital act, a new life is conceived?

DIGGING DEEPER:
The Pornographic ~~Life~~ Lie

"[There is] a reciprocal circuit which takes place between the image and the seeing, between the ethos of the image and the ethos of seeing. The creation of the image, in the broad and differentiated sense of the term, imposes on the author, artist, or reproducer, obligations not only of an aesthetic, but also of an ethical nature. In the same way, 'looking,' is understood according to the same broad analogy, imposes obligations on the one who is the recipient of the work."[4]

The body "expresses precisely 'the element' of the gift"[5] This means that as an "element," the naked body is an agent of sorts through which a person gives himself or herself to another in a communion of persons. The body always carries its own dignity, and this means that it is possible to represent the naked body in art without objectifying the person. John Paul II offers two points that must be analyzed. He calls them the **"ethos of the image"** and the **"ethos of seeing,"** which refers to the fact that any artistic expression of the body holds within itself an ethical character through both the way it is represented and the way it is viewed. This means that both the creators and the viewers of art that portrays the human body have real moral responsibilities.

notes

If the artists (painters, photographers, actors, filmmakers, etc.) intend to arouse lust in the viewers of their art, they have violated the ethos of the image. On the other hand, the act of physically viewing art that portrays the human body carries with it a responsibility for the one who looks—the responsibility to look with purity at the person as a subject to be loved, rather than an object to be used. Looking at tasteful art with purity of heart is sometimes difficult, especially in our cultural climate. But it is possible to see the human body rightly if we allow Christ to begin redeeming us and our desires.

Pornography violates the ethos of the image and the ethos of seeing because there is one fundamental intention of this type of body "art"—to arouse lust and make the person an "object of enjoyment, intended for the satisfaction of concupiscence itself."[6]

In the first case, those who participate in the creation of pornography take an intimate view of the body, which rightfully belongs in an interpersonal relationship, and turn it into an object of "public property." Once this violation happens, the body, detached from its true purpose, becomes an "object" to be used without limits. This deeply offends the true purpose of the body as a representation of the personal gift of self to another.

Pornography is a particularly difficult temptation for guys because they respond more readily to visual stimuli. In addition, some guys who are exposed to porn at a young age soon form an addiction to it. Though many girls have learned to cope with men and their pornography by laughing at it or ignoring it, it should never be tolerated in a relationship. Pornography is largely responsible for the way many guys habitually **objectify** women, treating them as objects of pleasure rather than as persons with dignity.

Girls, if you want to be respected, demand respect from the guys with whom you hang out. Do not tolerate pornography or anything else that degrades you as a woman. Guys, if you want to be a real man, turn to Christ and allow Him to purify your desires. Ask Him for the grace to see women with respect. Learn how to love, and the girls around you will respect and appreciate you all the more for it.

MOVIE CLIP/SONG SUGGESTIONS

MOVIE CLIPS:

1. *Glory:* Show the segment that falls between 45:34 and 50:20. This segment shows the whipping of Denzel Washington's character, Private Trip, for "deserting" the Army, when in reality he was merely looking for some shoes. Private Trip does nothing verbally to respond, but his body language screams volumes. He takes the beating silently and stares with tears in his eyes at the man who ordered the punishment for something that was not a crime. Ask your students what they think he was saying with his body in this scene. Among other possibilities, he seemed to be saying, "You can't break me. I'm right. You better reconsider the way you look at all of us."

2. *Life is Beautiful:* Show the segment that falls between 41:27 and 47:35. This segment shows the moment when Roberto Benigni's character, Guido, discovers the woman he loves (Dora) is getting engaged to another man. This woman's body language also says that she loves him (Guido), and his body language is dramatically fixated completely on her. Prior to showing the clip, have your students watch for each character's body language and then discuss it afterward.

3. *The Passion of the Christ:* A) The Crucifixion. Show the segment that falls between 1:35:06 and 1:43:13. *[NOTE: Before showing this clip to students, we strongly recommend that you get written parental permission. This is a very violent scene.]* The visual depiction of Christ on the Cross, making the ultimate sign of love with His body. **B)** Jesus's Betrayal. Show the segment that falls between 9:14 and 11:14. This is the scene where Judas betrays Jesus through using one of the most recognized signs of love: a kiss. **C)** Jesus Falls. Show the segment between 1:14:50 and 1:19:19. This is the scene in which Mary has the flashback of Jesus falling down as a boy. Without words, we see her run to Him, pick Him up and hold Him. The language of the body here is one of profound love of a mother for her son.

4. *The Incredibles:* First, show the segment that falls between 15:39 and 16:15. This is the scene in which Violet acts self-consciously, hides herself in her hair and then makes her head disappear when a guy looks at her. Then show the segment that falls between 1:14:50 and 1:15:40, where Violet has progressed in confidence, symbolized by wearing her hair half-way across her face, but still hiding part of herself. Finally, show the segment that falls between 1:45:33 and 1:46:22 where, after achieving success as part of a family and team effort, Violet–who always looked down and slumped her shoulders in depression and discomfort–finally expresses herself differently with confidence. She shows a new openness to life with her hair pulled away from her face and then confidently plans a date with the guy she earlier avoided.

5. *Romero:* Show the segment that falls between 1:01:26 and 1:07:21. This is mostly a silent scene in which Archbishop Romero and the whole town come together to stand in defiance and take back their church from the Communists.

SONGS:

1. *Sometimes Love* — Chris Rice *(Deep Enough to Dream)*

This song is all about sacrificial love and how it is necessary to give of ourselves for another, modeled after Jesus' example. Features the words, "Sometimes love has to drive a nail into its own hand." Folk/Acoustic Ballad.

2. *Barlow Girls* — Superchic[k] *(Karaoke Superstars)*

This song tells the story of three sisters who have chosen to wait to have sexual relations until marriage. Pop.

3. *Stay True* — Stacie Orrico *(Genuine)*

There are many pressures in the world, but God calls us to stay true to His word. Pop.

SCIENCE AND THE THEOLOGY OF
THE BODY: The Medial Pre-Optic Nucleus

"Nobody's getting hurt … right?" Many high school guys have repeated these words to themselves whenever their consciences would bug them about their habit of looking at porn. Years later, they wish they had been right. Although the images only took seconds to see, they would take years to forget.

One reason for this is the Medial Pre-Optic Nucleus (MPN), which is the pleasure center of the brain. The MPN is easily trained, so when sexual arousal accompanies a sexual image, the brain learns to associate sexual excitement with whatever you are experiencing. This is one reason why there are perfume samples in men's porn magazines. The marketers of the fragrances want the men to associate those scents with sexual arousal, thus making them more likely to purchase the products.

So what do you imagine will happen to a man who trains his brain to associate sexual excitement with porn? Research shows that people who looked at porn were more likely to be less satisfied with their intimate partner's affection, physical appearance, sexual curiosity, and sexual performance. They had conditioned their minds to look for arousal in hundreds of forbidden, trashy fantasies.

But no matter how perfect the model is, the man usually flips the page after five seconds. While his standard of physical beauty becomes that of impossible perfection, he experiences arousal followed by boredom and dissatisfaction. But if the most seductive supermodels fail to keep his interest for more than a few moments, what will happen to his bride? How is she expected to captivate him?

Some men think that it's their right to be aroused by fantasies. By the time they get married, they think that marriage is going to be the fulfillment of porn. They may assume, "If my wife isn't flawless, that's kind of her fault." Needless to say, the marriage suffers because the man's ability to love is warped. As author Christopher West has said, "A man who develops a porn or masturbation lifestyle at a young age will, more often than not, carry those habits into marriage and cause untold suffering to his wife."[7] Man has been created to make a gift of himself to his spouse, but porn teaches him a lifestyle of indulgence that only knows how to take. He must realize that it's not his bride's fault that she's not Miss September, but his fault that he allowed porn to make himself a user instead of an authentic lover.

APPLICATION

Option #1: Break your students into groups of three to four and have them work as teams to solve the Chapter #6 Word Search (found in the appendix of their student workbooks) as fast as they can. Doing this activity reinforces the words used in this chapter, helping them to become more familiar with the terms and to more quickly memorize their meanings. And, of course, it's just fun to do a puzzle.

Option #2: Sign Language

If you know sign language, know someone who does, or if you can learn a little of it, teach your students a short prayer (or a few words) in sign language. If you want to, use a John Paul II quote and teach them how to "speak" the truth by literally making the sign language movements with their hands. If possible, have the students "say" the closing prayer in silence, without words of their mouths, but with words of their bodies that they choose (kneeling, arms lifted, bowing, etc.), along with the words of their hearts.

Option #3: Language of the Body at Mass

Have someone stand in front of the class and "mime" (or if they cannot mime it, describe) the following actions performed during the Holy Mass (the explanations are given below).

- The *Epiclesis*
- Kiss of peace
- *Orans* posture
- Fraction Rite
- Sign of the Cross
- Signing before the Gospel proclamation

Have your students guess which part of the Mass is being imitated and have them try to name the action. Then, explain the significance of each of these "languages of the body." Below are quick summary explanations you can offer:

The *Epiclesis*

During the Eucharistic prayer, the priest brings his hands down over the bread and wine in sort of a sweeping motion. This "movement" is called the *epiclesis*. *Epiclesis* is a Greek word meaning "to call down upon." At that moment in Mass, we believe that the priest is, in a special way, invoking the Holy Spirit, who "comes down" and transforms (or transubstantiates) the bread and wine into the body and blood of Jesus Christ.

This bodily action mimics that of the high priests of ancient times when offering the sacrificial lamb or goat in the Temple area. Back then, the priest moved his arms as an outward expression of gathering all of the sins of the people assembled there and then placed the sins on the goat or sheep they were about to sacrifice (see Lv 16:7-9). When the animal was killed, it was believed that the sins the animal had "taken on" were forgiven.

Likewise, it is through the sacrifice of the Lamb of God (see Jn 1:29), our Lord Jesus Christ, that we are set free from our sins.

The Kiss of Peace

You are all aware of that moment during Mass when it's time for "the sign of peace." The history and evolution of the sign of peace or, as it used to be known, the kiss of peace, is fairly extensive.

To give you an overview, for centuries it remained a private prayer for the priest. The General Instruction of the Roman Missal (GIRM) is the document that gives theological explanations and liturgical directives concerning the Holy Mass. This document tells us that the manner of giving the sign of peace is to be determined locally and should take into account the character and customs of the people. In the United States, the embrace or the kiss on the cheek were never widespread customs, but the handshake has served in a similar function; while it can be a simple formality, it is also capable of expressing the warmth and closeness of friendship. This is something that should be remembered, since gestures are more expressive than words alone.

(Continued on next leader's page)

Many people who want to be pure have become so entrenched in lustful habits that breaking free seems impossible. If you share this fear, do not give in to discouragement. Rather, set reachable goals for yourself. For example, "I'm not going to look at pornography today (or for a week or some period of time that you know you can reach)." You will gain confidence in your ability to be pure if you focus on the next twenty-four hours instead of the next ten years. God only asks that you try to be pure one day at a time.

To persevere in your desire to lead a pure life, practice the following steps:

1. **Remove the temptation.** If you struggle with looking at online porn, get a filter for your computer (go to www.filterreview.com for suggestions) or take advantage of an accountability site, such as www.covenanteyes.com. If you struggle with remaining pure in relationships, avoid dating people who will only bring out the worst in you. Instead, only date a person with high standards, whom you can see yourself marrying. Also, pay close attention to the dating tips suggested in Chapter Eleven. No matter what your weakness may be, you have much more control over the situation than you may like to admit.

2. **Frequent the sacraments.** Jesus said, "Apart from me you can do nothing" (Jn 15:5). Therefore, if we pull away from confession and the Mass, it will only be a matter of time before we fall back into our old habits. Some people may say, "I've been to Mass and to confession, but I still mess up." We must realize the sacraments do not remove our sexual desires or the causes of temptation; rather, they are like medicine that helps to heal our selfish desire to lust. But like any virtue, purity is not developed overnight. We must persevere.

Also, it is important that we not approach the sacraments looking to be entertained or focusing on what we're "getting out of it." Our relationship with God is a lot like our human relationships. If you're in it only to take, the relationship will not last. We must learn to give of ourselves. When we do this, the sac-raments will have a much greater effect in our lives. So if you have an adoration chapel at your church or a chapel at your school, spend time there, and be generous with your time. Considering that the average American will spend about a decade of his or her life watching TV, it's safe to say that we can all make a little more time for God.

3. **Keep busy.** St. John Bosco warned, "The principal trap that the devil sets for young people is idleness. This is a fatal source of all evil." It is important that we keep busy and not get bored and feel sorry for ourselves. So practice a sport. Start taking guitar lessons. Go out with friends. Serve the Church. Just do something. As St. Francis said, "Always be doing something worthwhile; then the devil will always find you busy."

4. **Pray for the redemption of your desires.** While it is good to stay active, it is even more important to be still in the presence of God through prayer. If you want to truly overcome lust, you will need to do more than just avoid temptation. A true change of heart is necessary to become free from lust and free for love. Spending quiet time with God will allow Him to gently rehabilitate the desires of your heart—molding them into true, good, and beautiful desires that are ordered toward Him and a life of purity. Consider praying the following prayer below on a daily basis: *Lord, You are the giver of all good gifts, and I thank You for the gift of my sexual desires. I give You all of my desires, both holy and impure. Please "untwist" the lustful desires in me that sin has twisted, and help me to grow in purity of heart, mind, soul, and body. Help me to experience good sexual desires that will help me to love as You intend for me to love. Amen.*[8]

(Cont.)

Orans Posture

This is a form of prayer in which the arms are lifted with hands open and palms up. During the anamnesis prayer, the celebrant holds his hands in the orans gesture. He also does so during the Lord's Prayer when praying, "Deliver us, Lord, from every evil …".

The ancient prayer position of arms lifted and hands open signifies many things. The arms lifted are a sign of thanks and praise. The open hands serve to demonstrate our trust in God and eternal openness to His will. When it all comes together, it is a receptive action, allowing the Lord to give us whatever He wants to give us. The action of this prayer symbolizes the intention of the "pray-er," who is demonstrating surrender, openness, trust, etc.

Fraction Rite

During Mass, after the Sign of Peace (kiss of peace), the priest breaks the host and drops a sliver of it into the chalice of consecrated wine. Today, this is considered to be a symbol of the reunion of Jesus' body and blood after His Resurrection (rather than the shedding or "separation" of His body and blood as the sacrificial lamb). Historically, however, this tradition is traced back to the early Church. In those days, the bishop was generally the celebrant of Mass. A runner would take a host from the bishop's Mass and deliver it to the local Masses celebrated by priests. These priests would then drop the host into the chalice prior to Communion. This served to symbolize the unity between the bishop's Mass and all the local Masses. As the Church grew, this custom was no longer practical. Today, the fraction rite remains as a symbol of the unity of all the Masses celebrated in the Catholic Church.

Sign of the Cross

The Sign of the Cross is one of the many ways Catholics externalize their faith. Not only does it serve as a means of blessing, but it also symbolizes core Catholic beliefs. When Catholics touch their right hand to their forehead, chest, left shoulder and then right shoulder, while saying, "In the name of the Father, and of the Son, and of the Holy Spirit," they demonstrate their belief in the Trinity. This gesture also symbolizes the Catholic belief in the salvific power of Christ through His death on the Cross. By signing ourselves with the cross of Christ, we outwardly deny everything worldly and signify an embrace of the Catholic faith. The words used in the blessing are taken from Matthew's gospel: "Go therefore and make disciples of all nations, baptizing them in the name of the Father, and of the Son, and of the Holy Spirit" (Mt 28:19).

Prayer before Gospel

Before the Gospel is read at Mass, Catholics customarily use their right thumb to make the Sign of the Cross on their forehead, lips, and heart. This bodily action symbolizes the petition to God that He may bless our thoughts, words, and actions. It acts as a blessing and as a silent prayer during which we prepare ourselves for the Gospel reading by asking God to be on our mind, tongue, and heart. Moreover, this action demonstrates that the Good News is the source of the Catholic faith–the Gospel is not just "another text being read publicly" but that it demands a response; the Gospel is meant to be proclaimed and received, spoken and actualized. This ritual draws Catholics into the Gospel and then calls on them to proclaim what they have heard. By performing this gesture and saying this prayer before the Gospel reading, Catholics prepare themselves to hear the Gospel and to live it thereafter.

Notes & Nuggets: In the closing prayer today, we pray through the intercession of St. Maximilian Kolbe. St. Maximilian was a priest who was imprisoned in the Auschwitz death camp during World War II. He gave his life for another man—a husband and father—who was about to be executed. As a selfless martyr and a faithful man who knew the meaning of speaking the truth with his body (love), we ask him to help us live and die purely and selflessly.

WORK IT OUT

Assignment #1: Search through your own music collection and find a song that speaks of telling the truth with the body. Find another that speaks a lie. Compare and contrast them in a short essay.

Assignment #2: Examine the following Scripture about King David (2 Sam 11:1-27) and explain how this story reveals lies of the body. Write a short essay summarizing your findings.

Assignment #3: Write an essay analyzing the suffering and death of Jesus, applying your new knowledge of the language of the body. What signs and symbolism do you see in the things Christ said with His body throughout His life? Conclude your essay with your analysis of Jesus' death upon the Cross.

Assignment #4: (The following is an assignment that should be done only with parental consent.) Watch one hour of television and catalog the following into a data sheet: the number of sexual jokes, verbal references, and innuendos; sexual scenes; and immodestly dressed characters. As you go along, have a separate column at the end where all entries fall into either category: language of the body (true) language of the body (false). Be sure to catalog commercials on your data sheet as well. Then, create a short summary of your findings, especially noting any patterns that you found (i.e, most of the references were funny, most were said by men, etc.).

Project #1: Pornography and the Human Body in Art. Dig deeper into the primary source by reading Pope John Paul II's thoughts on the human body in art and pornography, and the ethics involved. Relevant insights can be found in his audiences of April 22, April 29, and May 6, 1981. Write an in-depth paper explaining what he means by the "ethos of the image" and the "ethos of seeing."

Project #2: Corporal Work of Mercy. The word "corporal" means "bodily." What better way to live the Theology of the Body out than through the corporal works of mercy? There are seven corporal works of mercy:

- feeding the hungry
- sheltering the homeless
- clothing the naked
- visiting the sick
- visiting the imprisoned
- giving drink to the thirsty
- burying the dead

Consult your teacher for your options of possible organizations or people whom you can serve; then choose one of the works listed above and see it through to completion. When you are finished, write an essay that summarizes your experience, particularly highlighting the response of others to your generosity. Note the body language of others as you use your own body to minister to them. Finally, reflect on the use of your own body and how it affected your own spiritual journey (and that of others) as you ministered to others by giving of yourself.

CLOSING PRAYER

Leader: In the name of the Father, and of the Son, and of the Holy Spirit. **Amen.**

All: St. Maximilian Kolbe, please pray with me that I, like you, would offer my very body in an effort to love others sacrificially. **Amen.**

IN HIS OWN WORDS

• **On the Language of the Body:** "[Man] has already been constituted in such a way from the beginning, in such wise that the most profound words of the spirit–words of love, of giving, of fidelity–demand an adequate language of the body. Without that they cannot be fully expressed" (January 12, 1983).

• "The language of the body reread in truth keeps pace with the discovery of the interior inviolability of the person" (May 30, 1984).

• "… the most profound words of the spirit–words of love, of giving, of fidelity–demand an adequate language of the body. Without that they cannot be expressed" (January 12, 1983).

• "Man is precisely a person because he is master of himself and has self-control. Indeed, insofar as he is master of himself he can give himself to the other. This dimension–the dimension of the liberty of the gift–becomes essential and decisive for that language of the body, in which man and woman reciprocally express themselves in the conjugal union" (August 22, 1984).

• **On the Language of the Body and Marriage:** "The sacramental sign of marriage is constituted by the fact that the words spoken by the newlyweds use again the same language of the body as at the "beginning," and in any case they give a concrete and unique expression to it. They give it an intentional expression on the level of intellect and will, of consciousness and of the heart. The words 'I take you as my wife or as my husband' imply precisely that perennial, unique, and unrepeatable language of the body" (January 5, 1983).

• "We can then say that the essential element for marriage as a sacrament is the language of the body in its aspects of truth" (January 12, 1983).

• **On Conjugal Chastity:** "Conjugal chastity (and chastity in general) is manifested at first as the capacity to resist the concupiscence of the flesh. It later gradually reveals itself as a singular capacity to perceive, love, and practice those meanings of the language of the body which remain altogether unknown to concupiscence itself" (October 24, 1984).

Glossary
of Key Terms

Contraception: Every action before, during, or after sexual intercourse that deliberately attempts to impede its procreative potential. These acts are intrinsically evil and always morally unacceptable (CCC 2370).

Ethos of the image: The responsibility that every artist has to represent persons with dignity, especially through the depiction of the human body in artistic form.

Ethos of seeing: The responsibility of all viewers of the human body portrayed in art, to see humans as persons with dignity, not objects to be lustfully desired.

Fornication: Having sex outside of marriage.

Language of the body: The capability of the body to speak its own language and to communicate without words.

Language of love: Generally speaking, the words that speak truth and compassion. Specifically regarding the body, the truth and totality of self communicated through the body in sexual intercourse.

Nicene Creed: The most widely-accepted statement of Christian faith, the Nicene Creed was first adopted at the Council of Nicaea in A.D. 325.

Objectify: To treat someone as a thing rather than as a person through actions that disregard his or her inherent dignity as a human being.

One-flesh union: The loving embrace of a married couple through sexual intercourse, in which they become "one flesh" (see Gn 2:24). The Scriptures teach that this union prefigures the total communion we will have with God in heaven (see Eph 5:31-32).

Pornography: The sexually-explicit depiction of persons, in words or images, created in order to cause the arousal of lust on the part of the observer.

OBJECTIVES At the end of this lesson, the student should know and be able to:

- Differentiate between sex that is self-seeking and love that is self-giving.
- Demonstrate that reception of God's love is the prerequisite for truly loving self and others.
- Recognize Mary as the perfect model of receiving God's love.
- Recognize that marriage is an absolute prerequisite for sex to be free, total, faithful, and fruitful.
- Explain free, total, faithful, and fruitful love as they are found in the life of Christ.
- Apply the free, total, faithful, and fruitful characteristics of Christ's love to the love spouses should display for each other in marriage.
- Analyze the love of Christ for the Church in Ephesians 5:21-33 as being free, total, faithful, and fruitful.
- Compare the sacrifice of Christ for His Church to the love of a husband toward his wife in marriage.
- Compare the Church's relationship with Christ to the role of a wife with her husband.
- Compare the ideas of free, total, faithful, and fruitful love with the commitments made at the altar between spouses.
- Recognize that homosexual acts cannot image divine love and are contrary to both the divine and natural laws.

Notes & Nuggets: Pray today that your students would allow God to cultivate in them a spirit of generosity–one that seeks to do more for others rather than less.

TWO MINUTE DRILL — VERBAL REVIEW:

1. What is "the language of the body"?
Answer: The way that the body speaks a language all its own, without words.

2. How can teens begin now to train themselves for faithfulness in their future marriage?
Answer: By speaking the truth with their bodies now, through purity and self-control.

3. Name two ways that someone can tell the truth with the language of the body.
Answer: For example, smiling, hugging, shaking hands, holding hands, and, between spouses, sexual intercourse. These gestures are true when their outward goodness is matched by pure intentions. In other words, the actions are only as true as the honesty of the person who performs them. All of the above gestures can also be used as lies, if their generally good meanings are contradicted by dishonesty in the heart of the person who performs them. For example, smiling at someone is universally used and understood as a positive sign to show happiness or contentment. But smiling at someone while thinking evil thoughts about that person and later gossiping about him or her would be lying with the language of the body.

4. How is pornography a lie of the body?
Answer: Pornography is based on the lie that the body is truly being given as a gift. The body is the gift of the person, not a means for a person. Pornography casts every participant in the selfish role of taking, using the body merely as a means to pleasure rather than as an expression of true love. Instead of acknowledging the dignity of the person with love, pornography reduces the person to body parts to be used. Pornography "changes" the subject of a person into an object.

5. How is contraception a lie of the body?
Answer: God designed us for authentic love, wherein both persons give of themselves to each other completely. The act of intercourse says, "I give you all that I have and all that I am." Contraception disorders the sexual act by saying, "I'll give you some of me, but not my fertility." This is a contradiction of the very essence and meaning of human sexuality and, thus, turns the sexual act into a lie.

Chapter Seven

Free, Total, Faithful, Fruitful

Jesus demonstrated for us, as a man, how to be fully human by giving all of Himself for us. Meanwhile, the Blessed Virgin Mary acts as the perfect model (the greatest "supermodel"!) of what it means to receive God's love and then to share it with the world. Both Jesus' and Mary's love flowed from an abundance of grace, which gave vibrant life to all they touched. Now, while "What Would Jesus Do?" is a good start for making moral decisions, "How Would Jesus Love?" is a good start when it comes to trying to build a loving, lasting communion with others.

The first thing to remember is that Jesus loved as His Father desired Him to love, and this relationship involved both receiving and giving. Being open to receive God's love enables us to enter relationships of giving and receiving with others. Loving relationships that are giving and receiving have at least four marks by which they can be identified. In this chapter, you'll see that Jesus' love is free, total, faithful, and fruitful, and you will discover what that means for us as we try to imitate His example of perfect love.

ICEBREAKER (optional): Total Lap-Sit

This is a classic icebreaker with a creative theological explanation.

STEP #1: Have the students stand in a tight circle, shoulder to shoulder.

STEP #2: Have the students all turn to face one direction (right or left). Now, everyone should be facing the back of the person in front of them. Have the students shuffle closer toward the center of the circle until they are all standing in a tight, closed-in circle.

STEP #3: Have each student hold on to the shoulders of the person in front of him or her.

STEP #4: Explain to the students that on your signal, everyone will sit down. This will take faith, but if all are pressed tightly enough pressed together, as they all sit onto the knees of the person behind them, a virtual chair will be established and all will be sitting in mid-air.

STEP #5: Tell the students that they are dependent on each other. If anyone loses faith and pulls out, the entire group will fall.

Note: To make it a competition, set two groups against each other to see who can do the lap sit the longest without falling down.

Tell your group that you will explain the meaning of the game in the middle of the lesson.

OPENING PRAYER

Leader: In the name of the Father, and of the Son, and of the Holy Spirit. **Amen.**

(Option #1)

Leader or Reader #1: Read Ephesians 5:21-33
"Be subject to one another out of reverence for Christ. Wives, be subject to your husbands, as to the Lord. For the husband is the head of the wife as Christ is the head of the church, his body, and is himself its Savior. As the church is subject to Christ, so let wives also be subject in everything to their husbands. Husbands, love your wives as Christ loved the church and gave himself up for her, that he might sanctify her, having cleansed her by the washing of water with the word, that he might present the church to himself in splendor, without spot or wrinkle or any such thing, that she might be holy and without blemish. Even so husbands should love their wives as their own bodies. He who loves his wife loves himself. For no man ever hates his own flesh, but nourishes and cherishes it, as Christ does the church, because we are members of his body. 'For this reason a man shall leave his father and mother and be joined to his wife, and the two shall become one.' This is a great mystery, and I mean in reference to Christ and the church; however, let each one of you love his wife as himself, and let the wife see that she respects her husband."

Leader or Reader #2: Jesus, help us to learn to love as You love humanity. Help us, even now, to train ourselves so that we may give of ourselves to others in the way that You desire. **Amen.**

(Option #2)
Leader or Reader #1: Read Galatians 2:20
"I have been crucified with Christ; it is no longer I who live, but Christ who lives in me; and the life I now live in the flesh I live by faith in the son of God, who loved me and gave himself for me."

Leader or Reader #2: Lord, we ask that You would help us to believe that happy, holy marriages are both possible and real, in and through Your love. Help us to learn to offer ourselves to others in unconditional love so that we can train ourselves for a future of happiness and authentic love. **Amen.**

Need a Review of Lesson 6?

Verbal Review of Lesson 6

1. What is "the language of the body"?

2. How can teens begin now to train themselves for faithfulness in their future marriage?

3. Name two ways that someone can tell the truth with the language of the body.

4. How is pornography a lie of the body?

5. How is contraception a lie of the body?

STORY STARTER: Following Tobit

I stood at the altar and could see her silhouette behind the stained glass doors at the back of the church. The musical notes of a violin floated through the church, and everyone stood up to honor the bride. As I attempted to look calm in front of all my groomsmen, I was biting the inside of my lip with anticipation. Blurred behind the window, I noticed the wedding assistants frantically making sure that my fiancée's veil was perfect and her hair flawless.

At last, the doors swung open, and there she was. I'm not one for visions, and I can't say that I had one that day, but I had this overwhelming sense of God the Father's hands behind my bride, saying to me, "Here she is. I give her to you." She walked down the aisle, and we both wiped away tears as her veil was lifted and she was given to me.

Years before meeting her, I remember coming across the story of Tobit in the Old Testament. In the story, the archangel Raphael heard the cry of two young people in search of love and brought their petition to the throne of God. By God's providence, Tobias (Tobit's son) and Sarah found each other and fell in love. On the night of their wedding, they turned their hearts to God in gratitude and petition, and the young man prayed to God, saying out loud that he was taking his wife not because of lust, but for a good purpose. Then, he asked for God to send down mercy upon them both, allowing them to live together to a happy old age. Together, they said "Amen" and went to bed for the night (see Tob 8:7-9).

Before reading this, I knew that men in the Old Testament generally got married at about eighteen. This shocked me: Here was a young man saying to God that he married his bride not because of lust but for a noble purpose. At that moment, I decided that I wanted to offer the same prayer on my wedding night. So, as my own wedding and honeymoon approached, I memorized the prayer and tried to make my heart (and relationship) as pure as that of Tobias.

When we stood at the altar that Saturday morning, we made several promises before God and the Church. We vowed that we came to the sacrament freely. We came to make a total gift to each other and to be faithful "until death do us part." Lastly, we promised to welcome children into our marriage.

The night came, and together we knelt on the glass floor of our honeymoon bungalow, which stood over the darkened, turquoise waters of an island near Tahiti. After leading her in the prayer of Tobias, we renewed our wedding vows without words.

The consummation of our marriage on our wedding night was a renewal of the exact vows we had taken earlier that morning. Our physical union was a free gift that we gave each other, and like our marriage, was not pressured or driven by lust. We made a total and faithful gift of our bodies, just as we had promised to do so at the altar. Lastly, our physical union was open to the gift of life, just as we had promised during the wedding Mass. Our vows were spoken with our bodies.

– Jason Evert

Did you know?

Jesus said that a husband and wife become "one flesh." Did you know that hormones from the man can be detected in a woman's bloodstream within hours of intercourse?[i]

COMPREHENSION & DISCUSSION QUESTIONS

1. How does it make you feel when you read a story that depicts a young man approaching sex in such a respectful way?

2. How would you feel if your spouse wanted to pray the prayer of Tobias with you on your wedding night?

3. Why would you feel this way?

4. What can you do today to make wedding vows more meaningful if you one day profess them to someone?

5. How is it that vows can be made both verbally and bodily?

6. Do you think wedding vows are generally viewed differently today than they were fifty or a hundred years ago in our culture? If so, how and why?

BRIDGING THE GAP

As teenagers, you have a unique opportunity similar to that of Adam and Eve. In the book of Genesis, we read how they "woke up" to find each other and discover the meaning of their existence—and the roles that their bodies played in that existence. In your pre-teen and early teen years, you experience something similar. Suddenly, the meaning of your body takes on a new dimension in your mind.[1] After learning the basics of your identity as a person created in the image and likeness of God, meant for love, you are now ready to learn more about the specifics of that love you are meant to express.

You're still "waking" to the meaning of your body and the importance of the ways you can use it to express yourself in your life. Hopefully, you will see that you determine a large part of your future with your body and whether it is used as an outward expression of the inward mystery of love, of God's life and love within you. But your future largely depends on your openness toward and understanding of God's will for your life. As you head toward studies in a seminary or convent, or toward the vocation of marriage, consider the fact that unless you learn to receive the love of God, you will be unable to give love to another person in the awesome ways that Christ gave Himself for us. You cannot give what you do not have. Once you have actually received His love, you're ready to step out and live it freely, totally, faithfully, and fruitfully.

Christianity has always greatly esteemed marriage. Christ himself restored the full stature of marriage as a sacrament, that is, a sacred and effective sign of divine love in the world. At Catholic wedding ceremonies, you will witness the couple answering three "Questions of Intention to Marry" and then stating the actual wedding vows.

Questions of Intention to Marry

1. Have you come here freely and without reservation to give yourselves to each other in marriage? (Bride and groom respond, "I have.")

2. Will you love and honor each other as man and wife for the rest of your lives? (Bride and groom respond, "I will.")

3. Will you accept children lovingly from God, and bring them up according to the law of Christ and his Church? (Bride and groom respond, "I will.")

Notes & Nuggets: To drill these points home, you may want to generally define them for your students:

- **Free:** No person and no desire is controlling you. No one is forcing or pressuring you to love. You do it freely.

- **Total:** You do not hold anything back. You give all of yourself.

- **Faithful:** You are committed to your spouse and that commitment guides your other actions. You keep your promises once you have made them, no matter how your feelings may change. You stay committed to that one person until death separates you.

- **Fruitful:** Your love is life-giving, because it is free, total, and faithful. It is open to to the possibility of new life (if it's God's will) in the physical realm and is life-giving in the spiritual and emotional realm as well.

TO THE CORE

In the story that opened this chapter, we discussed the four parts of the wedding vows—free, total, faithful, and fruitful. Now, consider what happens when you take these vows as they apply to sex—and then flip them upside down:

- Instead of sex being free, it is pressured at the end of a date, forced in sexual abuse, paid for in prostitution, and not freely given by the person dominated by lust.

- Instead of a total gift of self, we have one-night stands, supposedly "safe" sex, and a contracepting husband and wife witholding their fertility.

- Instead of promoting chastity and fidelity, we have TV shows such as *Desperate Housewives* and *Sex in the City* dominating the culture.

- Instead of being fruitful, the act of sex is sterilized with contraception and is not open to new life.

Do these ideas sound familiar? Unfortunately, most of these points describe the world's approach to sex. If you remove one leg from a chair, it will collapse. In the same way, if you remove any one of the four parts of the wedding vows from the gift of sex, it will no longer be a true gift. As a result, those having sexual encounters outside of marriage find themselves unfulfilled. Knowing that people are searching for answers, "experts" from *Cosmopolitan* and *Maxim* seem to offer them a dozen new sexual techniques with each new monthly issue. But no matter what they try, the readers of these magazines cannot change the fact that they have been created for total self-donation. Anything less will never satisfy them.

This vision of human sexuality is not a list of four rules the Church forces us to follow. These are the demands of love already written on our hearts and stamped into our bodies. And if we live out this call to love through a sincere gift of self, we become a visible image of Christ's love for the Church.

Many people assume that the Church is down on sex. This could not be further from the truth. Here's just one small example of the thousands that exist. Did you know that the canopy (baldacchino) often built over the altar in Catholic churches represents the canopy over a marriage bed? The symbolism reminds us that on the altar during Mass, the Bridegroom (Christ) gives His body (the Eucharist) to His bride (the Church), so that we may have eternal life. Likewise, as a husband and wife renew their love and wedding vows through their **one-flesh union** on their marriage bed—the altar of sacrifice in their home—we renew our love and our union with Christ when we pronounce "Amen" and receive His body. St. Paul spoke of this deep symbolism when he wrote, "'For this reason a man shall leave his father and mother and be joined to his wife, and the two shall become one.' This is a great mystery, and I mean in reference to Christ and the church" (Eph 5:31-32).

Vows/Consent of the Couple

The bridegroom says: I, (name) take you, (name), to be my wife. I promise to be true to you in good times and in bad, in sickness and in health. I will love you and honor you all the days of my life.

The bride says: I, (name) take you, (name) to be my husband. I promise to be true to you in good times and in bad, in sickness and in health. I will love you and honor you all the days of my life.

Or: "I, _____, take you _____, for my lawful wife/husband, to have and to hold, from this day forward, for better, for worse, for richer, for poorer, in sickness and in health, until death do us part."

After the rings are exchanged, *each says:*

(Name), take this ring as a sign of my love and fidelity. In the name of the Father, and of the Son, and of the Holy Spirit.

COMPREHENSION & DISCUSSION QUESTIONS

1. Name one real-life example for each: free, total, faithful, and fruitful love.

2. Do you think people intend to be unfaithful when they take their wedding vows?

3. Why do you think it is so hard for spouses to stay faithful to each other today?

4. What does a canopy (baldacchino) above an altar in a church symbolize?

5. A husband and wife renew their wedding vows through their _____.

Baldacchino

When a man and woman get married, they do not simply receive a sacrament, as they did in Baptism or Confirmation. They *become* a sacrament. They become a sign and instrument of God's love for the other person. The only other time a person becomes a sacrament is in the Eucharist (Jesus), and, to a certain extent, in Holy Orders, when a priest becomes a representative of Jesus (and His love). Clearly, there must be something very important the Lord wishes to teach us here.

At the Last Supper (the first Mass), Christ said of the Eucharist "This is my body, which is given for you" (Lk 22:19). It is precisely through His total gift of self that He shows His love for the Church. We, as the faithful, are given an incredible invitation to respond to Christ's sacrifice at each and every Mass. When the priest, standing ***in persona Christi*** ("in the person of Christ"), utters these words of Christ, we have the opportunity to offer the totality of our bodies back to God, as if to say "And this is my body; I give it to You."

Pope John Paul II said a young heart feels, "a desire for greater generosity, more commitment, greater love. This desire for more is a characteristic of youth; a heart that is in love does not calculate, does not begrudge, it wants to give of itself without measure[2] ... There is no place for selfishness—and no place for fear! Do not be afraid, then, when love makes demands. Do not be afraid when love requires sacrifice[3]... Real love is demanding. I would fail in my mission if I did not tell you so. Love demands a personal commitment to the will of God."[4]

In a similar way, a husband and wife express their love for each other through their free, total, faithful, and fruitful gift of themselves. So this call to love is not only stamped into our bodies but into the Body of Christ in the Eucharist! This is not sexualizing the Eucharist. This is realizing the sacredness of sex.

From the beginning of the Bible to the end, there is one comparison or analogy that God uses above all others to express His love for us: the love between a husband and wife. The story of God's love in the Bible begins in Genesis with the marriage of Adam and Eve and concludes with the book of Revelation in which we read about the marriage of the Lamb—the union of Christ and the Church in heaven. The reality is that when the love of a bride and groom is a

Notes & Nuggets: Be prepared for students to ask questions on the topics covered here in the text.

Masturbation: Through our collective experiences in teaching and ministry with teenagers over the years, the authors of this program agree that masturbation is a key problem for many teenagers today. Many are addicted to pornography, and, in turn, are often addicted to masturbation. We encourage you to review the *Catechism* (CCC 2352) and charitably point out the selfish nature of the act of masturbation. Masturbation trains the person to be selfish with their sexuality (and, most likely, in many areas of life). Such selfishness is the direct antithesis of the mutual, self-giving purpose of our sexuality.

It may be a helpful exercise to write the three examples in the last paragraph on the board (pornography, masturbation, contraception) and ask your students to point out their similarities. Selfishness and a lack of self-gift should quickly come into the discussion, at which point you can again show your students that generous people do not buy gifts for others and then use them for themselves. Gifts are meant to be given to another. Our sexuality is a gift from God.

Homosexuality: To go deeper in exploration of homosexuality, you may want to have your students read the "Digging Deeper" section in this chapter before fielding questions or launching into discussion.

To start, it is important that your students understand the difference between homosexual acts and "deep seated homosexual tendencies" (CCC 2358). The Church defines homosexual acts as "acts of grave depravity" that are "intrinsically disordered" (CCC 2357) and are always unacceptable. But the Church acknowledges that homosexual tendencies are not freely chosen, and though they are disordered desires, they are not sinful in and of themselves. It is imperative that, as a catechist, you stress our call to love those who struggle with homosexual desires, not condemn them. In a society that is often split between the "anything is acceptable" and "homosexuals are disgusting people who are going to hell" schools of thought, we Catholics are called to speak the truth in love, acknowledging that persons with same-sex attractions are called to chastity–as all people are–but also are welcome in our Church.

The Theology of the Body offers us an anthropology (a general study of humanity) that is founded upon the idea that a man's body does not make sense without a woman's body, and vice versa. Moving from this simple recognition to the realization of marriage as a sign of the communion between God and man—between Christ and the Church—should help us see why "homosexual marriage" is simply not possible. The one-flesh union between man and woman is the defining act of marriage. Two men or two women engaging in some form of sexual activity are simply not capable of engaging in the marital act because of the design of their bodies. Your students are likely to have questions in this area, and we encourage you to respond to these difficult questions.

Contraception: Please note that we will cover contraception in detail in the next chapter. To read more about it and prepare yourself for a discussion in this chapter, read the "Digging Deeper" section of Chapter Eight.

notes

total gift, it makes God's love visible to the world. So the real question to ask when it comes to sexual morality is this: Am I expressing God's love in a free, total, faithful, and fruitful way through my body?

Apply this standard to any issue relating to sexuality, and you quickly can spot the counterfeit of lust. For example, pornography is not a total gift of self—nor is it life-giving, faithful, or even free. Likewise, **masturbation** is not a total gift of self at all, nor is it life-giving or faithful. Many times it is not even free because it becomes an addiction that can be very hard to resist. While some may argue that **homosexual acts** can be freely exchanged between committed people, these acts clearly cannot be fruitful or a total gift of self, and they are not faithful to God and His plan for love. **Contraception** actually breaks all four of these marks of love (more on this in Chapter Eight). None of these acts reflect the love of God. They all fall short of the very purpose of sex. For this reason, the famous painter Salvador Dali once said, "The only way to make love is as a sacrament."

COMPREHENSION & DISCUSSION QUESTIONS

1. How does marriage preeminently show us Christ's free, total, faithful, and fruitful love through the gift of His body?

2. Which symbol or analogy is used more than any other throughout Scripture to describe God's love for us? Why do you think this analogy is used so often?

3. What is the one question that can help you to judge the morality of a sexual act?

4. Why does *pornography* not reflect the love of God? What about *masturbation*, *homosexual acts*, and *contraception*?

Notes & Nuggets: If you did the icebreaker for this chapter, now is the time to explain the meaning of the Total Lap-Sit game. It could be said that the group members displayed actions similar to love that is free, total, faithful, and fruitful. You could make the comparison for them using an explanation like this:

- **FREE:** No one made you participate. You chose to take the risk and to sit on the person's knees behind you, whom you could not see. This free act to participate took faith.

- **TOTAL:** There was no middle ground for playing the game. Either you did it all the way, or you would ruin the experiment. If you did not hold back–even though you feared you would fall–the gift of yourself to the group was total.

- **FAITHFUL:** Once you sat down, hopefully you did not bail out and leave the group to fall apart. If you stayed in the group until the exercise was over–even though you may have been uncomfortable, nervous, fearful, or physically tired–then your participation was faithful.

- **FRUITFUL:** If you gave of yourself freely, totally, and faithfully, and if those around you did the same, then your participation was fruitful in that the group benefited from your gift; you succeeded as a group in creating a Total Lap-Sit. Even if the group fell apart, your gift was open to fruitfulness and gave life to the effort of trying to do a successful lap sit.

In a sense, the students' participation in the exercise resembles the wedding vows of a couple at the altar, as they will learn more fully through the next exercise "Spousal Vows of Love" versus "Christ's Example of This Love" in their workbooks.

If it serves you and your lecture/teaching/discussion period better, skip down to the following exercise as a visual part of (rather than the conclusion of) the content of this lesson.

Has there ever been a more perfect sign of bodily love than Jesus' gift of Himself to us upon the Cross? Consider the crucifixion of Jesus:

- Jesus modeled for us, through His passion and death, what **free** love really means. He could have escaped the pain of giving Himself in sacrifice, but He freely chose to obey Our Father and freely gave all He had.

- As Jesus gave all that He had, stretching out His arms upon the Cross to embrace you and all of humanity, He showed us what **total** love really looks like "[he] emptied himself. … And being found in human form, he humbled himself and became obedient unto death, even death on a cross" (Phil 2:7-8).

- Jesus was **faithful** to His Father's will and faithful to each one of us. As He embraced His Cross, He faithfully chose to love you each step of His painful journey. He thought of you and was faithful to you by giving all He had.

- There was never a more **fruitful** life and death than that of Jesus Christ. His life brought heaven to earth as God took the form of a human, and His death brought life to you and opened the gates of heaven to all of humanity, bridging the gap between God and man created by Adam and Eve at the Fall. Adam's life brought us death. Christ's death brought us life again.

God communicated His love for us by giving His body for us. This is why the Church has obeyed Jesus for thousands of years, repeating His words daily during the sacrifice of love we call the Mass, "This is my body, which will be given up for you." Meanwhile, Mary's "yes" in her *Fiat*: "Let it be done unto me according to your word" (Lk 1:38, NAB) also encourages us to humbly receive God's love and then offer our hearts to Him through the gift of our bodies.

The words and examples of Jesus and Mary can forever remind us of their free, total, faithful, and fruitful love that moved from conception in the womb to culmination upon the Cross. In this way, both Mary and Jesus provide us with extraordinary examples of free, total, faithful, and fruitful love. As teens called to chastity, Jesus and Mary can be your models for living and loving well.

notes

COMPREHENSION & DISCUSSION QUESTIONS

1. Do you see yourself as a gift worthy of someone else's sacrifice? Why or why not?

2. The truth is that you are worthy of love and sacrifice. What can you do to better accept and live this truth?

3. What gift is proper enough to give to a spouse?

4. What does the word picture of the "reservoir" teach us?

5. How was Jesus' love in the crucifixion free, total, faithful, and fruitful?

6. How was Mary's love free, total, faithful, and fruitful?

7. How can you, as a teenager, offer yourself freely, totally, faithfully, and fruitfully as God desires?

8. Compare and contrast your abilities and opportunities to love with those of a married person. What are the similarities and differences?

DIGGING DEEPER: Homosexuality

To understand the Church's teaching on homosexuality, one could read the Bible, browse the *Catechism*, or study Church history. However, we can also simply look at the human body. Its design is not an accident but rather was created by God with an order and purpose.

By observing our body parts, their purposes become evident. For example, the ear is obviously made for hearing, not for scratching the itch on your lower back. Our eyes are made for seeing the beauty of roses, not for smelling them. These truths arise from nature itself—just like gravity and other truths of science—and are called laws of nature, which apply to all of creation (including our entire bodies). Laws of nature deal with how things function from a scientific standpoint.

There is another law, the **natural law**, that specifically governs the behavior of man (who is the only rational creature on earth) and is written into the very nature of every person. Natural law is the set of moral norms that we discover when we look at how we are created physically, psychologically, and spiritually. These are things that, by design, we need as a whole person to achieve God's plan of happiness for us. The acts that bring us closer to the goal of happiness are morally good, while those that do not are evil. The natural law tells us which is which. Ultimately, the purpose of natural law is for our happiness, and happiness is something that we all desire.

We can look at the body and see that it is created for certain functions. These functions should operate in accord with what is good and what fulfills the natural law. We do not always, however, order our desires in a way that fulfills this law. Here's an example: Imagine there was a man who desired to eat dirt instead of food. Though it would be easy to tell him that eating dirt is not good for him—and will, therefore, not really make him happy—he may rationalize that he has a real desire to eat dirt. He then proceeds to dump a handful of dirt in his mouth and eat it. It is easy to conclude that his body is not created for this. The initial evidence is that he will likely get sick. Rather, his body was created

to digest real food, giving energy and nutrients for him to live. Now, the man may argue that eating dirt is perfectly fine and even good. Clearly, though, his subjective desire is not in line with the objective order of his body. He is circumventing the purpose for which his mouth and digestive system were made.

Just because this man has free will does not mean that every desire of his psyche is actually good for him and will bring him happiness. The natural law of his own body calls him to choose that which is objectively good, such as eating nutritious food instead of dirt. Natural law concerns what we *should* do—that which will make us happy—not merely what we *can* do.[6] This is a key distinction.

With this in mind, here is a quick analysis of **homosexuality**, looking through the lens of God's design for the human body as well as the gift of sex.

Have you ever thought about the fact that a man's body really doesn't make sense without a woman's body with which to compare it? This is probably such an obvious question that we have, in fact, never really thought about it. It's true though. If the world was made up of nothing but males, the men would surely wonder why they were created this way. They wouldn't see the purpose of their design. The same goes for females. A woman's body is created to receive a man's body, not another woman's. The two complement each other on every level. Even the man's sperm and the woman's egg serve no purpose in isolation from each other. In fact, everyone exists because of the union of the two.

Even on a microscopic level, men and women have been made for each other. For example, the immune system of a woman is designed to fight off any foreign substances that enter her reproductive system. To do this, the woman's body uses lymphocytes to destroy foreign matter in order to keep the womb healthy. However, there's a substance in a man's sperm cells and semen that tell the woman's immune system to relax. Thus, it is considered an immunosuppressant, because it suppresses her immune system. It tells her body to accept the foreign substance, almost as if it were her own body. This allows the sperm to travel safely to the egg in order to fertilize it. It also helps her body accept a newly conceived baby.

Our sexual organs do not have the same clear purpose when matched up with a person of the same sex. In fact, using them in this way can sometimes be physically damaging (similar to the actions of the "dirt eater" mentioned earlier). To intentionally use (abuse) the body in such a way that radically goes against its purpose is to treat it as merely something to be used in whatever way one subjectively desires. This approach disregards the integrity of the body and ultimately separates it from the whole person—body and soul. In this way, the body becomes a slave to the will rather than an integral element that shows forth the person. Abusing the body or treating it as an object to be used goes against natural law and the natural design that God gave to our bodies.

This natural design is built into every man and woman, and so it can be said that everyone's body, both from a law of nature and natural law standpoint, is oriented toward the opposite sex. However, not everyone's attractions are oriented

in this way. So, while these biological facts may be interesting, they do not make life any easier for the people who struggle with same-sex attractions. In fact, it may make them feel like they're "trapped" in the wrong body.

Sadly, the world tells these people that they have two options: hide in the closet in fear; or come out, embrace their "identity," and make their own rules when it comes to sexual decisions. Acknowledging their attractions and living a pure life isn't even proposed as a realistic choice. The world assumes that sexual activity equals love, and most people would agree that no one should have to live without "love."

There is a viable third option, though—one that brings great freedom and peace—not oppression or isolation, as the world might have you believe. It is the choice to live a celibate life of purity, aiming to love God above all else. There are numerous Catholics with same-sex attractions who choose to live a celibate life of abstinence and chastity.

If you think about it, their chaste lifestyles are not much different than those of St. John, St. Paul, Blessed Pier Giorgio Frassatti, Blessed (Mother) Teresa of Calcutta, Pope John Paul II, and countless others who have conformed their wills to that of Jesus Christ. While these individuals may not have struggled with same-sex attractions, neither did they repress their sexuality. Instead of getting married, they offered their bodies as living sacrifices to God. And by making a gift of themselves to Him, they brought life to others.

If you struggle with same-sex attractions, realize that you are not alone. God loves you and has a plan for your life. Also, the Church has a network for those who carry the same cross and choose to glorify God with their bodies (see www.CourageRC.net). Through fellowship in groups like Courage, some people have come to realize that their temptations were not permanent. Others learn the origin of their sexual desires (e.g., often due to broken family relationships or abuse in early childhood, particularly with their fathers) and find healing of these deep wounds or abuse.[7] Even if the source of their attractions remains a mystery and the desires do not subside, such persons are offered an environment in which they can be accepted, loved, and challenged to live godly lives.

Whether or not you struggle with same-sex attractions, as a Christian, it is your duty to respect and love those who do. Just because their struggles are different than yours does not mean that they deserve to be looked down upon. Remember the "personalistic norm" discussed in Chapter Two: all persons deserve nothing less than love. If you live as Christ calls us to live, you will not only treat them with dignity, you will encourage them to be pure as you would encourage other friends to be pure. The Church has canonized saints who have struggled with every temptation imaginable. While we cannot be sure of any who struggled with same-sex attractions, we should look forward to the day we have saints who have chastely carried this cross as well.

Notes & Nuggets: You may want to encourage your teens to take this "Four-Day Challenge" *together* so, at the end of the fourth day, they can compare notes with their friends to see what they experienced and what they learned. This may also give them some motivation to stick to the project, even when it is not easy for them. The other neat thing that may come of this is that if a number of students are doing "the challenge" during the same set of days, others will find out about this radical choice and will ask them about it. Tell your students this and encourage them to use it as an opportunity to share their faith with others. It will also be a good witness to other teachers and staff members in your school or parish community.

APPLICATION

OPTION #1: Holy Mass or Adoration of the Blessed Sacrament

At this point in the overall program, your students have heard a lot about love and a lot about their bodies as agents of love and communion. By the end of this lesson, they will also have a good opportunity at viewing Jesus as the perfect example of free, total, faithful, and fruitful love. If at all possible, we encourage you to arrange for a priest to come and say a Mass for your class so that they can receive Christ in an intimate communion. This Mass will tangibly reflect the beauty they have been studying somewhat abstractly. If Mass is not possible, try to arrange for Eucharistic Adoration.

OPTION #2: Reach Out In Selfless Service

There are plenty of other books written on empowering teens to serve others. Once you have decided how much time can be devoted to a particular outreach project, either propose a few options to your class or guide them in a brainstorm session that surveys the needs of your school, church, and community.

If you have limited time, settle for a "small" project such as packing up gift bags or grocery bags for the poor, writing letters or making rosaries for the troops overseas, sending care packages to a third-world mission, or cleaning a certain room or area on the school campus or church property.

The idea here is to get into the habit of serving others and giving of self more freely, more totally, more faithfully and more fruitfully, so as to bring life to those in your community. If you choose to take on a larger service project, plan it well; if needed, get someone to underwrite your costs. Have students analyze and reflect upon their experiences.

OPTION #3: Service Field Trip

To apply this teaching of loving freely, totally, faithfully, and fruitfully in a real way, consider (possibly in a brainstorm session with your class) the possibility of doing a class service project in the form of a "field trip." One of the simplest ways you can do this is by going to visit the elderly in a nursing home, visiting terminally ill children at a hospital, or some similar "visitation" venue. Being physically and bodily present to someone else makes all the difference in the world, and these are good applications of the Theology of the Body. If you choose this route, take some time beforehand to encourage your students to share their gifts with those they visit. This can be done through playing music, reading stories, doing a skit or a puppet show, or just talking and listening to those they visit. Another option that takes minimal preparation is to have your group serve food at a soup kitchen in your area or work for a few hours at a local food bank.

Have you ever gotten so annoyed with your computer that you wanted to throw it out a window? Maybe the troubles were caused by a virus that ended up in your inbox because of a "forward-happy" friend. Maybe it was because your computer had less memory than you do when your parents question you about breaking curfew. Whatever the case, at some point you have probably felt frustrated because your computer just "doesn't function like it did" when it was new.

And neither do you. That's what sin does. Selfishness slows us down, clogs our communication with God, and keeps us from living as peacefully and purely as we are called to live.

Living this concept of "free, total, faithful, and fruitful" is possible. Millions are doing it and are inspired by this call to live as the saints did. No matter where you are in your life right now, you can begin to really live like a saint. But before you can "download" God's grace to live the challenge, you might need to "deprogram" yourself a little bit or maybe even reload your entire operating system.

Take the Four-Day Challenge:

Day One

First, "FTFF" is more than a call to selflessness. It is the shunning of all things selfish in your life. The world programs us to be selfish. So, in order to "deprogram" that selfish influence in your life, you must first "unplug" from the world, disconnecting from any worldly influences that would put you at risk.

So, spend an entire day free of all technology. "What, are you crazy?!" you might wonder. No, not crazy—focused. Remember, before God can reprogram you, you might need to be deprogrammed.

Don't turn on the television for an entire day. Don't log on to the computer. That's right, no email, no surfing, no IMing. Next, turn off your cell phone and don't answer it. Not even text messaging. You can do it. Finally, no music—not even spiritual or uplifting tunes. See if you can do it for one full day. Challenge yourself. What you will probably find is that the silence drives you crazy … at first. But you will grow to love it the more you silence your world.

Day Two

After you've spent a day without media, try something even harder. Deny your desires for an entire day. Let your little brother or sister choose the channels on TV. When your Mom or Dad ask you to do something, jump right up and do it, regardless of what you're doing. (Be prepared: they might go into shock if you do this.) Ask your friends or boyfriend or girlfriend where *they* want to go that night. Let your parents control the music in the car. Don't even ask what is for dinner. Whatever is put in front of you, be thankful you have it and eat with gratitude.

Day Three

On the third day you are only going to do things that serve others. There won't be any hanging out or zoning out in front of a screen. It'll be cleaning, washing, folding, vacuuming, playing with younger siblings, and helping others. That's it. There won't be any activities just for you. You will live for everyone else in your household. If your household is small, get over to your church—there's always a closet or room that needs cleaning out. Be careful when you offer: the parish staff might be so thankful that they'll even pray for you!

Day Four

Head to your church and spend time in adoration of our Lord. It's OK if the Eucharist is not "exposed;" Jesus is still there: body, blood, soul, and divinity in the Blessed Sacrament. Sit in adoration for at least thirty minutes (an hour would be even better). Write the following verses on a piece of paper and take it with you, or highlight these verses in your Bible. Prayerfully read and meditate on them before Jesus and ask Him to reveal to you, deep within your heart, what they mean to your life right now.

- "…it is no longer I who live but Christ who lives in me; and the life I now live in the flesh I live by faith in the Son of God, who loved me and gave himself for me."   – Galatians 2:20

- "…by the mercies of God, present your bodies as a living sacrifice, holy and acceptable to God, which is your spiritual worship. Do not conform yourselves to this world but be transformed by the renewal of your mind, that you may prove what is the will of God, what is good and acceptable and perfect."
        – Romans 12:1-2

(Continued on next page)

MOVIE CLIP/SONG SUGGESTIONS

MOVIE CLIPS:

1. *Shrek:* Show the segment that falls between 1:14:49 and 1:22:47. This is the scene when Shrek, the ogre, talks to Fiona, the beautiful princess, to discourage her from marrying Lord Farquaad, because they don't really love each other.

2. *Ever After:* Show the segment that falls between 1:40:55 and 1:43:35. The prince releases the princess he's about to marry from the obligation to marry him, because they are both in love with other people.

3. *Ever After:* Show the segment that falls between 1:46:16 and 1:49:10. A good depiction of free, total, and faithful love is offered to Danielle, a commoner, by the prince, who is willing to marry her despite who she is and despite her dishonesty.

4. *The Princess Bride:* Show the segment that falls between 48:06 and 49:48. This is the scene where Buttercup gives herself up for Wesley in order that he may be saved and set free.

5. *The Last of the Mohicans:* Show the segment that falls between 1:33:09 and 1:40:40. A British soldier offers his life in the place of the woman he loves and the man who has been his rival. A clear example of FTFF love. (Note: There are subtitles in this scene.)

SONGS:

1. *Sex is Easier than Love* — Switchfoot (*Nothing is Sound*)

Clearly points out the truth about sex being a commodity in our society and that having sex is much easier than actually loving another. Modern Rock.

2. *Testify to Love* — Avalon (*A Maze of Grace*)

A song of witness, proclaiming that "for as long as I shall live" I will be a living testament to love. Adult Contemporary.

3. *Someday* — Larue (self-titled)

The story of expectations of authentic love. Pop/Ballad.

4. *No Greater Love* — Steven Curtis Chapman (*Declaration*)

There is no greater love than to give one's life so another may live. This is a powerful song that tells the true story of five American martyrs killed by Waodani tribesmen in Ecuador in the 1950s. The tribal chant at the end of the song is the voice an old man–one of the actual tribal murderers who later converted to Christianity and now "walks God's trail." Contemporary/Rock. (For more information on the whole story, check: http://www.beyondthegatesthemovie.com)

LIVE IT OUT *(cont.)*

Later on in the day, before you go to bed, journal about the three days prior. Ask yourself what you learned, what elements of your Four-Day Challenge were most difficult and which came easy. Reflect on how your activity somehow mirrored FTFF. And try to commit these two verses to memory.

If you follow these spiritual "exercises" for four days, you will be surprised at how tangibly different you look at the call to be "free, total, faithful, and fruitful," and you will have taken a significant step in your spiritual maturity. You'll be one step (or maybe four steps) closer to loving like Jesus.

 WORK IT OUT:

Assignment #1: Read Tobit 8:1-9. Using Tobias' prayer as inspiration, write your own prayer for purity that you could use on your wedding night, should you ever be married.

Assignment #2: Read the encyclical of Pope Paul VI, **Humanae Vitae** ("Of Human Life") and write an essay connecting the four pillars of this chapter (free, total, faithful, and fruitful) to the different areas of this landmark Church document.

Assignment #3: Break down the text of the "questions of intention to marry" and the marriage vows included in this chapter (pp. 98-99) as you see them lived out by a couple that you admire. Write an essay analyzing their relationship as defined by the four areas of Christ's love that we have focused on: free, total, faithful, and fruitful. If you have time, call or visit the couple when you complete the assignment and read them your observations so that you can encourage them in their vocation to love in marriage.

Assignment #4: Read Romans 12:1-21. Select your favorite three verses and write a paragraph on each of them.

❖

Project #1: This project is a slightly modified version of Assignment #2 (above). In the seventeenth section of his encyclical *Humanae Vitae*, Pope Paul VI made numerous predictions about the effects that widespread contraception would have on our culture. Read this section of the encyclical and create a PowerPoint presentation (or some other multimedia presentation) connecting his predictions in 1968 to life as you see it in our society today.

Notes & Nuggets: In this closing prayer, we intercede through Blessed Teresa of Calcutta (Mother Teresa), a modern-day example of Christ's unfailing love. Blessed Teresa completely gave of herself to the poorest of the poor and is widely recognized as one of the most influential persons of the 20th century. Her love was humble. In her simplicity, she loved freely, totally, faithfully, and fruitfully as a servant of the poor, a public voice for the unborn, and a leader of a religious order, the Missionaries of Charity, which she began in 1950. Mother Teresa died in 1997 and was beatified by Pope John Paul II in 2003.

Project #2: Read the *Catechism* (CCC 2351-2359) and write an essay or create a PowerPoint presentation detailing how and why masturbation, pornography, fornication, prostitution, rape, and homosexuality are never free, total, faithful, and fruitful expressions of love. In your conclusion, using what you learned in this chapter and in the *Catechism*, make a list of your own top three recommendations as to how these disordered sexual acts can be overcome by those who may be struggling with them.

CLOSING PRAYER

Leader: In the name of the Father, and of the Son, and of the Holy Spirit. **Amen.**

All: Blessed Mother Teresa, please pray with me that I, like you, can learn to give my complete self, each day, to the promotion of life and living the love of the Gospel. **Amen.**

IN HIS OWN WORDS

- **On Contraception and Abortion:** "It is frequently asserted that contraception, if made safe and available to all, is the most effective remedy against abortion. The Catholic Church is then accused of actually promoting abortion, because she obstinately continues to teach the moral unlawfulness of contraception. When looked at carefully, this objection is clearly unfounded. It may be that many people use contraception with a view to excluding the subsequent temptation of abortion. But the negative values inherent in the 'contraceptive mentality'–which is very different from responsible parenthood, lived in respect for the full truth of the conjugal act–are such that they in fact strengthen this temptation when an unwanted life is conceived" (*Evangelium Vitae*, 13).

- **On the Language of the Body Expressing Wedding Vows:** "In the reflections on the sacramental sign, it has already been said several times that it is based on the language of the body reread in truth. It concerns a truth once affirmed at the beginning of the marriage, when the newlyweds, promising each other 'to be always faithful … and to love and honor each other all the days of their life,' become ministers of marriage as a sacrament of the Church. … In fact, the man and the woman, living in the marriage 'until death,' repropose uninterruptedly, in a certain sense, that sign that they made on their wedding day, through the liturgy of the sacrament" (July 11, 1984).

Glossary
of Key Terms

Anthropology: The overall study of man and what it means to be a human person.

Contraception: Every action before, during, or after sexual intercourse that deliberately attempts to impede its procreative potential. These acts are intrinsically evil and are always morally unacceptable (CCC 2370).

"Faithful" love: Love that is committed. That commitment guides all other actions. You keep your promises once you have made them, no matter how your feelings may change.

"Free" love: Love that is not controlled or manipulated by another person or by a disordered desire. No one is forcing you to love. You love freely because you want to.

"Fruitful" love: Love that is life-giving, because it is free, total, and faithful. It is open to procreation in the physical realm and is life-giving in the spiritual and emotional realm as well.

Homosexual acts: Actions of genital stimulation with a person of the same sex. According to the *Catechism*, "homosexual acts are 'intrinsically disordered' and 'contrary to the natural law … Under no circumstances can they be approved" (CCC 2357).

Homosexuality: The attraction that a man or woman has to a member of the same sex. The homosexual inclination is disordered but not sinful in and of itself, since it is not freely chosen.

Humanae Vitae: Pope Paul VI's 1968 encyclical on human life. It is most famous for its clear and definitive teaching on why contraception is immoral and sinful, explaining that it separates the sexual act from one of its intrinsic purposes: procreation.

In persona Christi: A Latin phrase meaning "in the person of Christ"; describes the identity and actions of a priest, particularly when he celebrates the sacraments and preaches the Word of God.

Mary's Fiat: The Blessed Virgin Mary's "yes" to the Lord, which demonstrated her faithful obedience to God's will.

Masturbation: The "deliberate stimulation of the genital organs in order to derive sexual pleasure … Masturbation is an intrinsically and gravely disordered action" (CCC 2352). Instead of training a person in faithfulness in order to make a gift of oneself, masturbation trains a person in selfishness.

Natural Law: The law or purpose that God has "written" naturally into the hearts, minds, and bodies of men and women.

One-flesh union: The loving embrace of a married couple through sexual intercourse, in which they become "one flesh," (see Gn 2:24). The Scriptures teach that this union prefigures the total communion we will have with God in heaven (see Eph 5:31-32).

"Total" love: Love without strings attached that holds nothing back. In total love, you make a gift of yourself to another—total self-donation.

OBJECTIVES At the end of this lesson, the student should know and be able to:

- Analyze the roles of husband and wife as complementary, a union that expresses the love of God in a tangible way.
- Recognize God as the one who established marriage and is the source of its holiness.
- Recognize the love of the husband for his wife as similar to the love of Christ for the Church.
- Demonstrate the true meaning of "submission" in marriage, and distinguish it from its distortions.
- Recognize the sacrament of marriage as an earthly foreshadowing of the perfect marriage between Christ and the Church in heaven.
- Defend marriage as the building block upon which civilization is built.
- Recognize Christ as the center of Christian marriage and the source of grace, which allows us to love like God.
- Recognize marriage as the primordial (or original) sacrament in which grace comes through Christ.

Notes & Nuggets: Pray today that your students will see the grace of God as something powerful and effective in their lives as they learn how to love. Pray also for their families, especially those broken by divorce and infidelity. Pray for a healing of their parents' hearts and the realization that they, too, can have a life of faithful love.

TWO MINUTE DRILL — VERBAL REVIEW:

1. Name the four parts of self-donating love.
Answer: Free, total, faithful, and fruitful.

2. How do a husband and wife continually renew their wedding vows?
Answer: Through all of married life lived in true service, but especially through their one-flesh union, the marital act of sexual relations.

3. How is the sacrament of marriage different from baptism or confirmation?
Answer: The couple doesn't just receive the sacrament, as in baptism or confirmation; they become the sacrament.

4. How can you prepare to give yourself as a gift to another?
Answer: We can fill ourselves with God's love, receiving all He wants to give us.

5. How did Jesus and Mary both image the free, total, faithful, and fruitful love of God?
Answer: They offered their bodies to God and said "Yes" to His will in every moment of their lives. Jesus' death on the Cross was free because no one made Him do it; it was total because He gave everything; it was faithful in that He stayed the course until the end; and it was fruitful because it brought us life, reversing the death sentence resulting from original sin. Mary's life–offering her body to God to become the Mother of God–was free because no one made her say "Yes"; it was total because she gave all she had to give; it was faithful because she never abandoned her Son, even when He was on the Cross; and it was fruitful because her "Yes" brought God to earth, cooperating with the Savior in His work of life-giving salvation.

Chapter
Eight

Marriage

God created marriage to be a beautiful sacrament in which a man and woman give themselves completely to each other, and the two become one flesh. God created marriage to be the building block of civilization. Unfortunately, history has shown that the plan is not as simple as it sounds.

Instead of men and women experiencing the love of God and "a taste of heaven on earth," marriage is sometimes seen as a risk not worth taking. However, in Christ we find redemption, a renewal of marriage, and a foreshadowing of the joy to be found in heaven. In Christ's sacrificial love for the Church, not only do we see God's love for us, but we see a model of love for married couples.

The Theology of the Body also highlights the woman's ability to image the Church and the man's ability to image Christ as the initiator of the gift—one who loves and serves generously. The sacrament of marriage between a man and woman serves as a tangible and resounding image of God's love for all of us. As we learn more about marriage, we learn how to live out our purpose (to love) selflessly in a culture that does not value marriage as it once did.

ICEBREAKER (optional): All Tied Up*

Divide your students into pairs. Give each pair of students two pieces of rope that are each two to three feet long. Tell the students that you are going to have a race to see who can braid the rope together the best in under thirty seconds. When the time is up, the students will naturally be frustrated because it is impossible to truly braid two pieces of rope together. A third rope is neccessary.

Next, give each pair a third piece of rope, and have a real race to see which group can braid it and knot each end the quickest to make a strong piece of rope.

After the race is over, make the connection to marriage. God is the central piece around which strong marriages are braided. Without Him, a couple is left weak, loose, and easily breakable. In fact, just as two pieces of string wrapped around each other do not qualify as a piece of rope, neither does two people living together qualify to as a marriage.

---

* This activity is based upon the common observation of marriage being the joining of two strands (people) around a central strand (God's love). The activity is adapted from the example as employed in chapter one of *The Marriage Manual*, an online book by Rev. Michael P. Clark, found at: www.unionpc.org/clark/Marriage%20Manual/Chapter%20One.htm This chapter takes a look at marriage through the lens of Ecclesiastes 4:12, "A threefold cord is not quickly broken."

OPENING PRAYER

Leader: In the name of the Father, and of the Son, and of the Holy Spirit. **Amen.**

(Option #1)

Leader or Reader #1: Read 1 John 4:7-8

"Beloved, let us love one another; for love is of God, and he who loves is born of God and knows God. He who does not love does not know God; for God is love."

Leader or Reader #2: Lord, we know that You have created us for love. Help us to learn to love well so that we can fulfill our future vocations. Please also bless the relationships of the married couples in our lives, especially the marriages of our parents. Bring peace and healing to those marriages that need it most. **Amen.**

(Option #2)

Leader or Reader #1: Read Jeremiah 29:11-14a (NAB)

"For I know well the plans I have in mind for you, plans for your welfare, not for woe! Plans to give you a future full of hope. When you call me, when you go to pray to me, I will listen to you. When you look for me, you will find me. Yes, when you seek me with all your heart, you will find me with you, and I will change your lot."

Leader or Reader #2: Lord, help us to live with hope and to seek You with all our hearts. Help us to trust the plan that You have for our lives, and if You call us to marriage, we pray for those who may one day be our future spouses. Help us to live and love in communion with You and with those around us. **Amen.**

Need a Review of Lesson 7?

STORY STARTER: Love Conquers All

Dave Roever was a normal high school kid from Texas who liked to work on cars. He had a good Christian family and was raised to believe in being faithful to God, family, and country. The girl he liked in high school, Brenda, felt he was a bit over-zealous when he told her in the hallway at school one day that he loved her. She slapped him across the face, telling Dave never to say it again, unless he really meant it.

A few years later, after spending more time with her—dating with purity and showing that he really cared—Dave asked Brenda to marry him. She said yes, and shortly after, they were married. Then one day, the news came in the form of a draft letter: Dave was ordered to serve in the military during the Vietnam War. Not wanting to dodge the draft and not wanting to die, he chose the Navy, thinking it would give him a safe ride out on the water, instead of intense combat in the jungle. He soon found that he was selected to serve as a member of the Brown Water Black Beret, a unit trained for special warfare by the Navy. After a rigorous term of river patrol training, Dave was given a ten-day break to go home. Dave cherished the time with Brenda, and on the day of his departure

Verbal Review of Lesson 7

1. Name the four parts of self-donating love.

2. How do a husband and wife continually renew their wedding vows?

3. How is the sacrament of marriage different from baptism or confirmation?

4. How can you prepare to give yourself as a gift to another?

5. How did Jesus and Mary both image the free, total, faithful, and fruitful love of God?

for his service in Vietnam, he kissed her and promised her, "Baby, I'll be back without a scar."[1] However, the word "scar" would soon take on an entirely new meaning for Dave Roever.

He flew to Sa Dec, south of Saigon, where he joined River Division 573 and served on the front lines against the Vietcong. In the eight months that followed, Dave held on to his faith. He had been trained to be faithful to the men with whom he served and also to his wife, Brenda. While many guys gave in to the shallow escape of drugs, pornography, or prostitutes, Dave stayed true to his vows. He was in love, and he was saving all of his military payment certificates to present to Brenda as a gift—a bundle of money that he had saved for her rather than spending it on frivolous acts of self-satisfaction.

Dave was just a week away from a military paid trip to Hawaii where he planned to meet Brenda for a five-day second honeymoon. But the enemy was close at hand and, during an intense firefight on July 25, 1969, Dave's unit was ambushed. His riverboat team survived the attack, but something (a bullet or shrapnel) ripped a small hole in his cheek. Dave got it stitched up without a problem and was grateful to be alive. But this was a small scar. It was the *next* day that would change his life forever.

It was July 26, 1969 at Thu Thua, near the border of Cambodia, that Dave's unit moved upriver to do surveillance of the same area where they had the intense firefight the day before. As the boat slowed and headed toward the bank, all was still. Dave suddenly sensed something was wrong. He reached down and grabbed a white phosphorus grenade, pulled the pin and cocked his arm to throw it, intending to create a smokescreen for his boat to make a getaway.

A light flashed and the world seemed to explode. A sniper had shot Dave through the back of his hand and into the grenade, which was just inches from his face. The grenade, which burned at 5,000 degrees, was ignited.

In an instant, Dave's body was on fire; the right side of his face was blown off. He jumped into the water and managed to swim to shore, where he collapsed, still on fire. He was rushed out by helicopter where the medic thought he was dead. Dave resisted the dog tag being shoved into his mouth and whispered "medic," at which point the medic nearly jumped out of the helicopter. They flew him to Japan and after some recuperation, sent him back to San Antonio.

The soldier in the bed next to his was skinless, burned from head to toe. Dave heard the man's wife come in and toss her wedding ring down at his feet. She said she could never walk down the street with him again. She walked out. As Dave waited for Brenda to see him, he feared the worst. How could he, a "half-headed freak," even spend time with a beautiful girl like Brenda, much less remain the love of her life?

There he was—a mangled shell of the man who had kissed Brenda goodbye eight months earlier. All he could do was wait in fear. Finally, Brenda arrived. Not able to identify Dave by appearance, she approached his bed and checked

Notes & Nuggets: Before launching into the questions in the student manual, ask your students the following questions:

- If you were married, how many of you would want your spouse to love you as Brenda or Dave loved each other?

- What is it about their love that makes you want to be like them?

the name on his chart and the tag on his arm to be sure it was him. Then, she bent down and kissed him … on the face. "I want you to know that I love you," she said as she looked him in his one good eye. "Welcome home, Davey."[2]

Brenda stayed as long as they allowed her that day, and through her love, hope rose in Dave's heart.

Dave began to experience love in a way he never imagined back when he had said "I do" on July 15, 1967. Brenda's "I do" became a daily commitment. She had meant her vows, and she kept them. Dave's body remained disfigured, and Brenda remained completely faithful. God was faithful to them both, and now, thirty-nine years later, Brenda and Dave still share an amazing love with two kids and a number of grandchildren, the enduring fruit of their faithful marriage.

Theirs is a marriage made in heaven, strengthened in war, and forever etched in the faithful vows of a love that burns deeper than any grenade and speaks louder than any scars.

You Decide

Consider these two different views of sex and the human person:

Bloodhound Gang, "The Bad Touch"

"You and me baby ain't nothin' but mammals, so let's do it like they do on the Discovery Channel."

vs.

Cardinal Carlo Martini

"In the Bible, the man-woman couple is not meant to be simply a preservation of the species, as is the case for the other animals. Insofar as it was called to become the image and likeness of God, it expresses in a bodily, tangible way the face of God, which is Love."

COMPREHENSION & DISCUSSION QUESTIONS

1. How do you think Brenda was able to love Dave, even though he had become physically unattractive?

2. How was Brenda's love both heroic and simple at the same time?

3. What do you think you would do if you were in a situation like Dave's?

4. How did Dave and Brenda both will the good of the other?

5. What language of the body can you recall from the story?

6. How did the bodies express the persons in the story?

7. How do you think Dave was able to make a gift of himself, even in his brokenness?

8. What percentage of teenage relationships do you think are so based on mere physical attraction that they could never survive such a test?

BRIDGING THE GAP

It's easy to look around today, see a bunch of broken marriages, and say "I'll never end up like that!" This is a noble statement but, unfortunately, many people realize this goal by choosing to avoid marriage. Instead of operating out of fear and looking at the many marriages that fail, we can look to God's intentions for marriage and see a beautiful plan. Jesus told the Pharisees, "For your hard-

ness of heart Moses allowed you to divorce your wives, but in the beginning it was not so" (Mt 19:8). Jesus is letting everyone know that something has gone terribly wrong—to have such hardness of heart—and that in the beginning, marriage was beautiful.

As we studied in earlier chapters, the marriage of Adam and Eve was perfect in the beginning. After original sin, just as man and woman became harder to distinguish as sons and daughters of God, marriage itself lost the "likeness" of divinity that it once held. But Jesus did not come to condemn our world; He came to liberate it. And so, He teaches us how to imitate Him, so we can live as whole people with redeemed bodies, hearts, minds, and souls.

The love of Christ is what enables couples to be faithful like Brenda and Dave Roever, even when wedding vows seem impossible to keep. This redemption that Christ brings is the hope that we have for living out the vocation to marriage with peace and fidelity the way that God intended it.

 TO THE CORE

In the first chapter, we discussed how God is a communion of persons (Father, Son, and Holy Spirit) united in love, and that we are made in His image and likeness. When we live out our vocation to love, we become a reflection of God Himself.

This sounds like a nice, holy concept, but what does it really mean? Pope John Paul II taught us that marriage (and family life) is a school of love. In the words of St. Francis De Sales, marriage is a "perpetual exercise of mortification," adding that "occasions for suffering are more frequent in this state than in any other." Some people would complain that this makes marriage look like death. In a way, they're right. Marriage is the best place on earth to learn how to sacrifice for the sake of the other while often denying one's own desires for the greater good of the marriage. At the core of this training is learning to *die to one's self*. It is precisely in this offering—in the death of one's own desires—that true love comes to life.

The Spousal Analogy

Love to the point of death is what Jesus taught us so clearly through His passion. It is this theme that St. Paul speaks of in Ephesians 5, when he outlines the roles of husbands and wives in marriage. He does this through an analogy of marriage as expressed through Christ's deep love for the Church. In fact, Pope John Paul II insisted that this **spousal analogy** of Christ's love for the Church is "the only key to understanding the sacramentality of marriage."[3]

The spousal analogy of God's love for His people is not new. As noted previously, marriage is the analogy used most often throughout the writings of the prophets

when teaching about the faithfulness of God to Israel, His spouse. When Israel turns away from God in the Old Testament, prophets such as Hosea and Ezekiel further the analogy and speak of Israel as an unfaithful wife, even a prostitute who gives herself to anyone but her Husband, the Lord. John Paul II describes Ephesians 5 as the crowning of the biblical analogy of spousal love. It teaches us about two things: the nature of the love relationship between Christ and the Church, and the loving "essence of marriage to which Christians are called."[4]

The analogy in Ephesians is a bit like one of those hidden 3D pictures. The instructions tell you to stare at a dot on the center of the image. You see nothing for twenty seconds or so ... and then bam: the image jumps out at you and makes you wonder, "Why didn't I see that before?" More than anything else, the spousal analogy in Ephesians 5 of Christ and the Church helps us to see marriage as a union between two persons who "become one flesh" (Eph 5:31; see Gn 2:24).

We should note that the following verses are probably some of the most widely misunderstood in the entire Bible, yet they contain profound truth about marriage: "Wives be subject to your husbands as to the Lord. For the husband is the head of the wife, as Christ is the head of the church, his body" (Eph 5:22-23). The problem arises with these verses when we look at them in isolation, outside of the context of the verses immediately before and after them.

Submission in Love

In verse 21, before he speaks to wives, St. Paul speaks of mutual **submission** of husbands and wives "out of reverence for Christ." A moment later, he puts the pressure on the men, saying, "Husbands, love your wives, as Christ loved the church and gave himself up for her" (Eph 5:25). The question we must ask is: How did Christ love the Church? The clear answer within the text is that He "gave himself up for her." He died for her. Christ gave all that He had for the Church, loving her and serving her until the very end. He symbolized this offering of Himself most concretely in the gift of His naked body upon the cross, as the bridegroom who gives Himself totally to His bride.

The word "submission" can be broken down like this: *sub* means "under" and "mission" refers to a special assignment or purpose. In this case, the husband's mission is to love his wife as Christ loved the Church—even to the point of death. If husbands were living out this mission of love everywhere, would women have any problem placing themselves "under" this mission? What wives wouldn't want their husbands to love them and serve them in a radical way? What girl doesn't dream about a brave young man who will honor her and be willing to risk his own life to love her? Pope John Paul II points out that the woman's submission to her husband, if understood in the context of the whole passage, "signifies above all the 'experiencing of love.'"[5]

On the other hand, if women loved and served their husbands the way that the Church gives herself to Christ, would men have any complaints about their

wives? Marriage is an amazing opportunity for spouses to image ***agape*** love (God's unconditional love) for each other through mutual respect and total self-donation. Throughout the sacrament, the body is the means and visible sign of this love.

COMPREHENSION & DISCUSSION QUESTIONS

1. What does John Paul II refer to as a "school of love"? Why do you think he says this?

2. Why do you think Ephesians 5:22-23 are some of the most misunderstood verses of the Bible?

3. How does St. Paul say that husbands should love their wives?

4. How can submission in marriage be a good thing for each spouse?

5. Do you think that most women want men who will serve them rather than boss them around? Why is this so?

The Primordial Sacrament

With the high rate of divorce, it is easy to think that marriage is nothing more than a contract on a piece of paper, but this is not the case. Marriage was and is God's idea. He created it. John Paul II called marriage the **primordial sacrament** (the original sacrament), which "transmits effectively in the visible world the invisible mystery hidden in God."[6] Simply put, God reveals Himself to our world through marriage. Civilizations throughout history have been built upon this primordial sacrament—upon marriages and the families that grow from them. Marriage is the basic building block upon which society is built because, starting with Adam and Eve, God made it this way: "For this reason, a man leaves his father and mother and cleaves to his wife" (Gn 2:24).

God wants us to choose to love, which will bring us deep joy within a life of virtue and holiness. After all, holiness makes us whole, and we are only whole when our hearts are filled with God Himself. While God wants us to be happy, and while it is also true that marriage is filled, at times, with romance and bliss, God never promised that marriage would always make us feel good.

Marriage is a rollercoaster ride filled with joy and sacrifice, with peace and pain. But what separates a rollercoaster from a kiddy ride? Total surrender. In the rollercoaster of marriage, a husband and wife get into the first car, throw their arms in the air, and through all the twists and turns, are held in only by the safety bar of God's love. Sometimes, such a ride is a rude awakening for young married couples whose unwillingness to surrender is better suited to the

Notes & Nuggets

Pay attention to "Comprehension and Discussion" questions 4 through 6. These questions can bring to light some interesting differences between a teen's view of marriage, in general, and the same teen's view of his or her own future marriages, in particular. After hearing some of their answers, you may want to follow up with questions and points such the following:

- Isn't it interesting that when asked about ourselves we look positively on the future, but when asked about others, we suddenly get pessimistic?

- Why do you think this is?

- We think we are far more "marry-able" than the others in the room. We think we are more capable and that others seem to lack the commitment to be fully committed to marriage.

- We think we are capable of total self-donation but doubt the ability of others to give of themselves and stay committed.

- How can we build greater trust in our own hearts and the hearts of others concerning our futures?

controlled cycle of a merry-go-round. Why do you think the majority of divorces happen within the first few years of marriage? Reality hits. When the **infatuation** fades and some stress or suffering comes along, you are left with the real person you have chosen to marry. At this point, love is tested, and its value comes to light.

Pope John Paul II tells us that at this point, "If their love is a true gift of self, so that they belong to the other, it will not only survive but grow stronger, and sink deeper roots."[7] But if the two people do not see the value of sacrificial love and rely on superficial benefits and emotions, they often quickly run from the challenges.

Family of Giving and Forgiving

If you think about who knows your faults the best, it's probably your family. They live with you day and night, seeing you at your best and at your worst. The same is true for marriage, where faults that are often unknown in the dating days come to the surface. The couple must learn how to live with these newly-discovered faults and still love and forgive. Successful marriages are not based upon finding the perfect person but upon loving the imperfect person that you have chosen to marry.

It is through this total and sincere self-giving that a married couple makes visible the life-giving love of God. The concept of Jesus loving the Holy Spirit or the Holy Spirit loving the Father is not something we think of often, but the perfect communion of love within the Godhead is the most foundational and important of all Christian mysteries (see CCC 234).

If you want to image this love on earth and prepare for a solid marriage, the best way to do this is to practice loving your own family members. In fact, pick the member of your family you find most annoying, and conquer your annoyance through love. If you are able to do this, you will begin to see the sacrificial approach to relationships needed for marriage

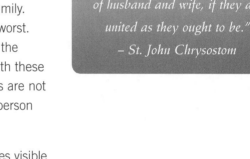

"There is no relationship between human beings so close as that of husband and wife, if they are united as they ought to be."
– St. John Chrysostom

COMPREHENSION & DISCUSSION QUESTIONS

1. What is the basic building block of society?

2. Why did John Paul II call marriage the *primordial sacrament*?

3. How do you think the primordial sacrament leads us to the other sacraments of the Church?

4. How many people here plan on getting a divorce?

5. How many people think that someone else in this room will get a divorce?

6. Why do you think there is such a difference between the responses to these two questions.

7. Successful marriages are not built on marrying the perfect person, but upon what?

8. When is love tested in marriage? When is its value brought to light?

9. How does a married couple make visible the life-giving love of God?

notes

From Fear to Faithfulness

Perhaps you have no desire to get married or you are afraid of a divorce. This is pretty common today, considering the low standard of marriage found in our culture, and perhaps in our own families. But do you remember the story of Tobias and Sarah in the last chapter? As they were praying together on their wedding night, guess what Sarah's father was up to? He was digging a grave for her new husband! Sarah had been married seven times before, and every single groom died on the wedding night. (Think about the faith of Tobias, knowing that seven men before him had died on their wedding night with Sarah.) So, to be on the safe side, Sarah's dad figured that he'd save some time and start digging a hole for Tobias.

Thankfully, God protected Tobias and gave him a long life with his bride. But just as Sarah's previous marriages all ended in death, perhaps many of the marriages in and around your family have been broken in one way or another. This need not be the case with your marriage.

While it's OK never to be married, and wonderful to live a life of service and celibacy instead, look at your intentions. Each vocation is a calling, and each requires courage, love, and sacrifice. God may call you to the married life and ask you to trust Him despite all the failed marriages you have seen. If there has been a rash of broken marriages in your family, perhaps God plans on using you to turn the tide for the future generations in your family. There's no reason why you need to follow in your parents' footsteps (if they are divorced or have a struggling marriage) when you can make the decision to love so that your kids will want to follow in yours.

So, if we want a great marriage, we need to start building love's foundation now. If you consider that the average couple spends 200 hours getting ready for their wedding, and half of those relationships end in divorce, it makes you wonder how much time is being spent preparing for the *marriage*. If we start educating and disciplining ourselves now, we'll have a firm foundation on which to build a lifelong love.

Notes & Nuggets: At the end of the exercise, have your students volunteer some of their answers and make a list of the top qualities on the board.

Then, ask them, "By the way you are living today, do you deserve such a person?" Also ask, "Are you yourself living these virtues or characteristics?" Use this exercise to explain how the decisions we make now will not only influence where we will be in ten years but who will want to be with us. Make sure that you offer your students hope, stressing that no one is unlovable because of mistakes made in the past.

(Physical attraction should be on the list — it's not a bad thing to list at all! Our attraction to beauty is a very good thing. God made us this way! In a sense, this attraction is rooted in our innate attraction to the beauty of God we will experience in the Beatific Vision. But we must also be aware of how our culture has warped our understanding of beauty.)

Finally, encourage the teens to pick one quality to work on in order to become a better potential spouse.

COMPREHENSION & DISCUSSION QUESTIONS

1. What did Sarah's father do while Tobias and Sarah were praying on their wedding night? Why did he do this?

2. What is the first thing you can do to avoid having a broken marriage in the future?

   Exercise: What characteristics would you want in a marriage or a spouse? (For example, honesty, faithfulness, respect, etc.) List 15 of them in the spaces below:

   1. _____   9. _____
   2. _____   10. _____
   3. _____   11. _____
   4. _____   12. _____
   5. _____   13. _____
   6. _____   14. _____
   7. _____   15. _____
   8. _____

DIGGING DEEPER:
The History of Contraception

Most people seem to think that **birth control** was invented in the 1950s. While it's true that the birth control pill was invented around then (the FDA approved the first birth control pill product in 1960), history records people using various methods of contraception 4,000 years ago. Ancient people would swallow potions to cause temporary sterility; they would use linens, wool, or animal skins as barrier methods; they would fumigate the uterus with poison to keep it from bearing life. Some cultures even inserted crocodile dung into the woman in order to keep her from conceiving!

At the time of Christ, **contraception** was practiced among the Roman people. However, the early Christians would not conform to the culture and refused to use contraception. Much later, the Protestant reformers unanimously rejected the practice of contraception. In fact, until 1930, all Christian denominations agreed that contraception was immoral.

The Southern Baptists at that time said, "The dissemination of information concerning contraceptives and birth control … would prove seriously detrimental to the morals of our nation."[8] Lutherans agreed, saying that the use of contraceptives "is one of the most repugnant of modern aberrations, representing a 20th-century renewal of pagan bankruptcy."[9] The Methodist Episcopal church added, "The whole disgusting [birth control] movement rests

on the assumption of man's sameness with the brutes."[10]

Drastic changes occurred in the 1930s, when leaders in the Anglican Church decided to allow contraception in some circumstances. They soon caved in completely, and before long, all the major Protestant denominations followed suit. Many people in the secular world were shocked by the widespread acceptance of contraception within Christianity. In 1931, the *Washington Post* wrote that this "would sound the death knell of marriage as a holy institution by establishing degrading practices."[11]

Even leaders from other religions were opposed to the idea. For example, (Mahatma) Gandhi said, "Man has sufficiently degraded women for his lust, and contraception, no matter how well-meaning the advocates may be, will still further degrade her."[12] He added, "Self indulgence with contraceptives may prevent the coming of children but will sap the vitality of both men and women, perhaps more of men than of women."[13] His attitude toward the issue was very similar to the early feminist leaders of the 19th century, such as Elizabeth Cady Stanton, Victoria Woodhull, and Dr. Elizabeth Blackwell, who were well aware of the negative consequences contraception would have on the dignity and treatment of women.

Despite the widespread use of contraception, the Catholic Church holds firmly to the teaching of historic Christianity and the natural law. In 1968, Pope Paul VI issued an **encyclical** letter to the Church called *Humanae Vitae*. While explaining the Church's teaching on procreation and the meaning and purpose of the sexual gift, he offered reasons for the immorality of contraception and predicted what would take place if it were to become common in society. Among other things, he warned that there would be an increase of marital infidelity (because pregnancy has always been the main deterrent to committing adultery). He also predicted a general lowering of morality, especially among the youth. He said men would grow accustomed to the practice of separating sex from the gift of life and would begin to see women as a mere instrument of enjoyment. Men would lose respect for their beloved companions. Unfortunately, his predictions have been realized.

In an age when many in our society are obsessed with "natural living" (from natural foods to hybrid automobiles), it's shocking how easily our culture accepts such an unnatural way to thwart our natural fertility. What if there was a completely natural way to plan a family, without taking pills or injecting anything into the woman's body? What if by a study of the signs of a woman's body we could know when a woman was fertile and infertile? The good news is that this is not an imaginary solution—it exists! It is called **Natural Family Planning (NFP)**, and there have been numerous studies substantiating NFP's high level of effectiveness.[14] At the same time, when NFP is practiced with the proper motivations, it is an aide to authentic marital love, not a hindrance like contraception.

The beauty of NFP is that it acknowledges that our bodies are beautifully and wonderfully made, according to the divine design of God Almighty.

notes

122-L

SCIENCE AND THE THEOLOGY OF THE BODY: Oxytocin = Human Superglue

In the January 2006 issue of *Discover* magazine, a summary of the top 100 scientific stories of 2005 was published. Number 83 was entitled "Inhaled 'Cuddle' Hormone Promotes Trust." The article was referring to **oxytocin**, a neuro-peptide (hormone) that is released by the pituitary gland of the brain during childbirth, breastfeeding, and intercourse, working as human "superglue."

It has long been known that oxytocin causes emotional bonding and impairs critical thinking ability and memory. New research shows that it also increases trust.

This trust factor was discovered when scientists had several people inhale the hormone prior to testing them in a financial investment game. The subjects who had taken a whiff of oxytocin were "substantially more willing to trust strangers with their money." In fact, they were more than twice as likely to give all they owned toward a foolish investment. The article concluded that when it comes to relationships, "Oxytocin may affect the extent of these negative evaluations, causing us to say, 'Oh, this won't be too bad.'"

How does this all apply to sexual relationships? Since oxytocin is released during intercourse, sexually-active couples experience emotional bonding, decreased critical thinking abilities, impaired memories of negative experiences, and increased trust. In marriage, this is ideal. But when it comes to sexually-active teenagers, it can be disastrous.

For example, have you ever had a friend who was in a dead-end relationship where he or she was getting used, and no matter what you tried to say to the person or how bad things got, he or she just couldn't seem to see the problems? Or, the person couldn't muster up the will to break off the relationship. This is partly because oxytocin *blinds* us and *binds* us. Not only does this prolong bad dating relationships, it often impairs a couple from making a smart marriage decision. They feel so close because of the sexual intimacy that they are unable to see the real value of the relationship. In other words, they're more likely to make a bad decision and enter into marriage that could end in divorce.

Since estrogen enhances the oxytocin response, women are capable of more intense bonding than men and usually suffer more from broken bonds.[15] According to Drs. Diggs and Keroack, "People who have misused their sexual faculty and become bonded to multiple persons will diminish the power of oxytocin to maintain a permanent bond with an individual."[16] Can you imagine the ramifications of this in a culture that openly embraces unbridled sexual relationships? People who damage the ability to bond—due to too many past, intimate relationships—will have a harder time bonding with their future spouse.

God created us to become one flesh with our spouses, but when we disregard His laws, we disregard the design of our own bodies.

APPLICATION

Option #1: Write Your Own Wedding Vows. Have students write up wedding vows, in modern language, to which they would want a future spouse to agree. To get insight from the Church to aid their understanding regarding marriage and the demands of love within this sacrament, have students consult the *Catechism of the Catholic Church*, paragraphs 1601-1666.

Option #2: What Will You Give? Ask students to reflect on how exactly they plan to use their gifts and talents to communicate their vows on a daily basis if they are called to an earthly marriage. Divide your students into groups of four or five people and allow them to create "mini skits" that run sixty seconds or less through which they can creatively demonstrate ways they can express marital vows on a daily basis.

Option #3: Word Search. Have your students use the word search on page 193 of their book to become better acquainted with the terms in this chapter and to better understand their meanings.

MOVIE CLIP/SONG SUGGESTIONS

MOVIE CLIPS:

1. *Good Will Hunting:* Show the segment that falls between 45:59 and 49:24. A psychiatrist played by Robin Williams talks to his patient, played by Matt Damon, about his wife and true love.

2. *Shrek:* Show the segment that falls between 1:14:49 and 1:22:47. This is the marriage scene when Shrek, the ogre, talks to Fiona, the beautiful princess, discouraging her from marrying Lord Farquaad, because they don't really love each other. Shrek and Fiona go on to marry after she realizes that he loves her despite her outer appearance. He loves her for who she is.

3. *Spanglish:* Show the segment that falls between 1:39:10 and 1:52:36. This is a scene that picks up just after Adam Sandler's character finds out that his wife has been unfaithful. He then spends time with his maid, to whom he is attracted; she is unmarried and has fallen in love with him. They spend time together and fight the temptation to commit adultery. They resist and love wins victorious.

4. *Braveheart:* Show the segment that falls between 34:13 and 37:35. This scene shows the proposal and the clandestine, yet sacramental marriage of William Wallace and his bride in the woods. [Note: Be sure to cut off this scene when the marriage ceremony is over because there is a sexual scene (their consummation of the marriage) that follows shortly after it.]

SONGS:

1. *I Will Be Here* — Steven Curtis Chapman (Greatest Hits)

Unconditional love will take you through ups and downs. Acoustic/Piano Ballad.

2. *Try* — Bebo Norman (*Try*)

When you meet the right person, he or she will build you up in all that you do and make you want to try. Acoustic.

3. *Go There With You* — Steven Curtis Chapman (*The Great Adventure*)

A song of faithfulness to wedding vows and a commitment to love even in the midst of trials, pain, and uncertainty. Adult Contemporary.

In high school, I remember going over to a friend's house, seeing both of her parents and asking her, "Isn't it weird having your dad around?" She just gave me a confused look and said, "Uh ... no. It's not."

My parents got a divorce when I was two. Out of my six aunts and uncles, five were divorced, and most of my best friends lived in single-parent homes. In my eyes, relationships weren't meant to last. So, by the time I began dating, I had no concept of what a healthy relationship was supposed to look like.

The drama of my dating relationships usually took this path: you flirt and "fall in love," and then you go too far physically. This is followed by disrespect, abuse, infidelity, sarcasm, and dishonesty. Then you break up (usually a few times), and then you repeat the process with someone new. I know it sounds pretty depressing, but since all my friends were in similar situations, this was reality for me.

After a few years of this life, you can imagine that I didn't have much of a desire to get married. In fact, I looked down upon people who viewed marriage as a goal in life. I'd think: "How naive could they be? They're just setting themselves up for disappointment." I never wanted a divorce, and I knew just how to avoid it: don't get married.

But eventually it struck me: If none of us want a divorce, why do we all live like we're practicing for one? Instead of training ourselves in faithfulness, we have this "if it feels good, do it" mentality. Instead of teaching others how to respect us, we let them use us, and then we dish it back. But how far will these habits take us in marriage? Nowhere, because it's all about me.

Since I didn't really know how I was supposed to be treated, changing my lifestyle did not happen overnight. I'd relapse from time to time, but I would always think to myself, "If I'm going to give my kids the family I never had, I need to quit acting like a victim." It's easy to give up, despair, and admit defeat, just like it's easy to get a divorce.

What's not easy is making yourself vulnerable, practicing self-restraint, staying out of dead-end-relationships, and having the courage to hope that love still exists. But it seems like the only people who find real love do exactly this. The idea of becoming a husband or wife may seem distant, but the virtues or vices you practice today will shape who you will become and how you will allow yourself to be treated in the future.

– Crystalina Evert

"If two pieces of wood are carefully glued together, their union will be so close that it is easier to break them in some fresh place than where they were joined; and God so unites man and wife, that it is easier to sever soul and body than those two."
– St. Francis De Sales

Notes & Nuggets: In this closing prayer, we ask the intercession of St. Thomas More. St. Thomas spent a good amount of time discerning whether he was called to the priesthood before answering God's call to marriage. He married in 1505 and had four children before his young wife died. He then married again (a widow this time), and though his second wife never seemed to appreciate his jokes, they enjoyed a happy marriage. St. Thomas More was executed by King Henry VIII for refusing to recognize Henry's attempts to divorce his wife in order to marry another woman. St. Thomas More's death came about because he defended the sacredness of marriage.

WORK IT OUT:

Assignment #1: Analyze the lyrics of your favorite love song, using what you've learned so far about marriage. Summarize your analysis in an essay, separating the positive and negative messages that may be present in the song.

Assignment #2: Make a collage using magazine or newspaper clippings with half of the poster showing the world's view of marriage and the other half the truth about marriage. Write a short summary explaining the difference.

Assignment #3: Write a song or poem, or draw a picture depicting the beauty of mutual submission in marriage as described by St. Paul in Ephesians 5.

Assignment #4: Interview your parents or another married couple that has been married at least ten years. First, read them the story from this chapter about Dave Roever. Next, ask them to put themselves in the place of Dave or his wife, Brenda, explaining what they would have done and why. Ask them to describe the most difficult time in their marriage and explain how they survived. Then, ask them to describe the best time in their marriage. Compile your interview into an essay and conclude with your own thoughts on marriage.

Assignment #5: Write an essay entitled "What our culture would look like if Ephesians 5 was understood and lived in every marriage." In the essay, analyze how things would be better or worse on multiple levels of society if married couples truly understood and lived marital love as God intended. You may want to consider some of these issues of society: education, poverty, divorce, parenting, child abuse, abortion, adoption, mental health, politics, etc.

❖

Project #1: Research Natural Family Planning (possibly through calling your diocesan Family Life Office), and write a persuasive paper you would give to a Catholic couple who is considering using contraception to avoid getting pregnant.

Project #2: Interview one couple or several couples to find examples of the free, total, faithful, and fruitful components present in their marriage. Create a fun video or PowerPoint presentation that presents these couples in contrast to the opposite world view using movie or TV clips. Make sure all clips are appropriate for a class video.

notes

CLOSING PRAYER

Leader: In the name of the Father, and of the Son, and of the Holy Spirit. **Amen.**

All: **St. Thomas More**, please pray with me that I, like you, would make intentional and prayerful discernment concerning my vocation. Then, if marriage is my call, pray again that I, like you, may be a model of holiness within marriage, and a warrior to defend it when it is threatened. **Amen.**

IN HIS OWN WORDS

- **On the Body as a Gift of Love:** "This is the body–a witness to creation as a fundamental gift, and so a witness to Love as the source from which this same giving springs. Masculinity and femininity–namely, sex–is the original sign of a creative donation and an awareness on the part of man, male-female, of a gift lived in an original way. Such is the meaning with which sex enters the theology of the body" (January 9, 1980).

- "Man appears in the visible world as the highest expression of the divine gift, because he bears within him the interior dimension of the gift" (February 20, 1980).

- "At the same time, however, the concept of 'giving' cannot refer to a nothingness. It indicates the one who gives and the one who receives the gift, and also the relationship that is established between them" (January 2, 1980).

- **On Marriage as the Primordial Sacrament:** "A reflection of this likeness is also the primordial awareness of the spousal meaning of the body, pervaded by the mystery of original innocence. Thus, in this dimension, a primordial sacrament is constituted, understood as a sign that transmits effectively in the visible world the invisible mystery hidden in God from time immemorial. This is the mystery of truth and love, the mystery of divine life, in which man really participates" (February 20, 1980).

- **On the Nuptial Meaning of the Body:** "The revelation, and at the same time the original discovery of the spousal meaning of the body, consists in this: it presents man, male and female, in the whole reality and truth of his body and sex ('they were naked') and at the same time in full freedom from any constraint of the body and of sex … It includes right from the beginning the nuptial attribute, that is, the capacity of expressing love, that love in which the person becomes a gift and–by means of this gift–fulfills the very meaning of his being and existence" (January 16, 1980).

- **On Adultery in the Heart:** "Adultery in the heart is committed not only because man looks in this way at a woman who is not his wife, but precisely because he looks at a woman in this way. Even if he looked in this way at the woman who is his wife, he could likewise commit adultery in his heart" (October 8, 1980).

- **On Conjugal Intercourse as an Affirmation of Vows:** "Indeed the very words, 'I take you as my wife–my husband' refer not only to a determinate reality, but they can be fulfilled only by means of conjugal intercourse. This reality (conjugal intercourse) has moreover been determined from the very beginning by the institution of the Creator: 'Therefore, a man leaves his father and his mother and cleaves to his wife, and they become one flesh'" (January 5, 1983).

- "Both of them, as man and woman, being the ministers of the sacrament in the moment of contracting marriage, constitute at the same time the full and real visible sign of the sacrament itself" (January 5, 1983).

- "Respect for the work of God contributes to seeing that the conjugal act does not become diminished and deprived of the interior meaning of married life as a whole, that it does not become a habit. It sees that it expresses a sufficient fullness of personal and ethical content, and also of religious content, that is, veneration for the majesty of the Creator, the only and the ultimate depository of the source of life, and for the spousal love of the Redeemer" (November 21, 1984).

Glossary
of Key Terms

Agape: The Greek term for unconditional and sacrificial love; the type of love with which God loves us.

Birth control: Normally refers to the general method of preventing pregnancy through various ways of altering or changing the body's natural state of fertility into a state of infertility.

Contraception: Every action before, during, or after sexual intercourse that attempts to prevent it from being procreative. These acts are intrinsically evil and may never be approved (CCC 2370).

Encyclical: A letter written by the pope, normally addressed to the bishops of the world (and sometimes to a wider audience of all the faithful), usually intended to teach or clarify a doctrine of the Faith.

Infatuation: Strong feelings of curiosity or attraction often rooted in the physical appearance and apparent mystery of another person. When one truly gets to know someone, infatuation can grow into love or disappear altogether.

Natural Family Planning (NFP): The term referring to various effective, natural, and moral methods for achieving or postponing pregnancy.

Oxytocin: A hormone released by the pituitary gland of the brain during childbirth, breastfeeding, and intercourse, causing emotional bonding between persons in whom it is released.

Primordial sacrament: The sacrament of Marriage as it was in the beginning—the original revelation of God's love in the world.

Spousal analogy: The scriptural imagery using the earthly understanding of marriage to convey the power and fidelity of God's love for humans and Christ's love for the Church.

Submission: Placing oneself "under the mission" (*sub-mission*) of another, surrendering to someone. In the case of marriage, this means deferring to each other in love. For the wife, it means allowing her husband to love her as Christ loved the Church—to the point of death. In the case of the husband, it means serving his wife and loving her at all costs.

OBJECTIVES At the end of this lesson, the student should know and be able to:

- Understand that celibacy is an exceptional calling from God.
- Understand that celibacy, just like marriage, is a vocation–a call from God, not merely a "choice" by an individual.
- Connect celibacy with the nuptial meaning of the body.
- Demonstrate that celibacy is more than a foregoing of sex and earthly marriage; it is embracing a life that is a sign of the heavenly marriage to come between Christ and the Church.
- Explain the reasons why the ministerial priesthood is reserved only for men.
- Describe the essence and value of spiritual fatherhood and motherhood.

Notes & Nuggets: As you head into the last four sessions of this curriculum, your students will be challenged to listen for God's voice in their lives. Today, ask the Lord in prayer to give your students the grace to be open to His will, no matter what that may be-even if they are called to a life of celibacy. Ask your friends and prayer supporters to ask the Lord to help your teens see celibacy as a gift and a privilege, rather than merely as a renunciation of sex and earthly marriage. We suggest praying an Our Father for your teens today.

TWO MINUTE DRILL — VERBAL REVIEW:

1. What is the spousal analogy?
   Answer: It is an analogy that looks to marriage as an image of Christ's profound love for the Church.
2. Explain the mutual submission St. Paul speaks of in Ephesians 5.
   Answer: Spouses are to donate themselves (submit) to each other in imitation of Christ's union with the Church. The husband symbolizes Christ and the wife symbolizes the Church.
3. What is agape love?
   Answer: It is unconditional love, like the love God has for us.
4. What is the primordial sacrament?
   Answer: Marriage, the original sacrament through which God reveals Himself to the world.

Chapter Nine

Celibacy and Religious Life

Celibacy is a special vocation ("divine calling") to which God calls some people to live as their way to holiness. "Celibacy for the kingdom" is much more than simply not having sexual relations. It is a call to live as a gift, uniting oneself completely to God in a way that foreshadows the heavenly marriage to come between Christ and the Church. While earthly marriage points us toward the reality of this heavenly marriage in a sacramental way, the celibate life does so in a way that is even more revealing. Celibacy for the kingdom is all about total self-donation to God and neighbor, showing the world what it means to love God with all your heart, mind, soul, and strength. Celibacy reveals that the fulfillment of all human longing is the marriage of heaven, not only the marriage of earth.

ICEBREAKER (optional): Bet You Didn't Know

Have your students turn to page 199 in the activity appendix, entitled "Bet You Didn't Know." Ask them to write their name in the space provided, and upon your signal, move around the room as quickly as they can, trying to find people who "fit" the 30 descriptions. When they find a person who matches the description on the page, they must write down that person's name on the activity sheet. To make it slightly more time-consuming, make them get the person's signature in the properly designated place. Finally, the students may not use anyone's name for more than three slots on the sheet.

You can either set a time limit (e.g., three minutes) and see who comes up with the most signatures, or see who is the first one to fill at least 10 (or 12, 15, 18, etc.) slots.

Closing Point: Hold the students in suspense and tell them you will talk later with them about the point of this game (unless you feel it will work better now). If you can, wait until the middle of your lecture to make the following simple point:

There are many things that we do not know about each other. By talking and listening to each other, we find out things we never would have known otherwise. In the game, you may have been surprised to find out certain things about certain people.

God knows how He wants each of us to live, as married or as celibate people. But don't assume that you know what His plan is for you. If you talk to Him, you may discover that His desire for you is greater than you expected.

OPENING PRAYER

Leader: In the name of the Father, and of the Son, and of the Holy Spirit. **Amen.**

(Option #1)

Leader or Reader #1: Read Romans 12:1-12

"I appeal to you therefore, brethren, by the mercies of God, to present your bodies as a living sacrifice, holy and acceptable to God, which is your spiritual worship. Do not be conformed to this world, but be transformed by the renewal of your mind, that you may prove what is the will of God, what is good and acceptable and perfect. For by the grace given to me, I bid every one among you not to think of himself more highly than he ought to think, but to think with sober judgment, each according to the measure of faith which God has assigned him. For as in one body we have many members, and all the members do not have the same function, so we though many are one body in Christ, and individually members one of another. Having gifts that differ according to the grace given to us, let us use them: if prophecy, in proportion to our faith; if service, in our serving; he who teaches, in his teaching; he who exhorts, in his exhortation; he who contributes, in liberality; he who gives aid, with zeal; he who does acts of mercy, with cheerfulness. Let love be genuine; hate what is evil, hold fast to what is good; love one another with brotherly affection; outdo one another in showing honor. Never flag in zeal, be aglow with the Spirit, serve the Lord. Rejoice in your hope, be patient in tribulation, be constant in prayer."

Leader or Reader #2: Lord, help us to recognize that You are the one that calls each of us to live a life of faithfulness to You. No matter who we are, You have promised that all parts of the body of Christ have valuable and necessary functions. Help us to be open to Your still, small voice within us that nudges us to seek the higher things of life. Help us also to learn today about more ways that we can serve You and the Church. **Amen.**

(Option #2)

Leader or Reader #1: Read Revelation 21:1-4

"Then I saw a new heaven and a new earth; for the first heaven and the first earth had passed away, and the sea was no more. And I saw the holy city, new Jerusalem, coming down out of heaven from God, prepared as a bride adorned for her husband; and I heard a great voice from the throne saying, 'Behold the dwelling of God is with men. He will dwell with them and they shall be his people, and God himself will be with them and he will wipe away every tear from their eyes, and death shall be no more, neither shall there be mourning nor crying nor pain any more, for the former things have passed away.'"

Leader or Reader #2: Heavenly Father, we know that You desire for us to join You one day in heaven. We know You want to make all things new in our lives through Your Son, Jesus. Help us to apply what we learn today so that we can live and love like You. Help us call upon our Mother Mary to intercede for us and to draw us closer to Your Son, Jesus. **Amen.**

Need a Review of Lesson 8? Look to next page.

STORY STARTER: A Waste or a Gift?

At his Catholic high school in Detroit, Brian Walsh enjoyed the popularity that came with being the captain of the basketball team. Although he would go to Mass with his family on Sunday morning, there was no telling where he'd been the night before. Like many of the other students at his school, Brian would always be at parties and would often get drunk. He also slept with his girlfriend, liked looking at porn, and didn't use the cleanest language.*

Needless to say, it was quite a surprise for his friends when he announced at the end of his senior year that he was going to enter the seminary! He was pretty much the last guy on campus that anyone could see becoming a priest. But he responded to a quiet call he felt deep under the noise and excitement of his social life. Since he came from a wealthy family, he wasn't quite prepared for the austere seminary room he was given: bare floors, no air conditioning, etc. So, he quickly remedied the situation and brought in wall-to-wall carpeting, a television set, his stereo, as well as his favorite whiskey, a few porn magazines, and an air conditioner. He would often invite the other seminary guys to his room for a party. They soon agreed he wouldn't last long.

However, toward the end of his first year in seminary, he attended a silent retreat with the rest of the young men. In the time he spent in recollection, he heard the call of Christ again. He responded. He realized he had been living a double life and no longer wanted to settle for mediocrity. He quit cursing, gave away all his luxuries, and trashed the porn and whiskey. What possessions he had left he gave to the poor, including his car.

When his second year of seminary began, he was assigned to a poor parish in St. Louis. Living at the rectory, he would often meet the poor people who would show up at his doorstep looking for help. Initially, he would offer them some donated food or clothing, but then he began giving away his own clothes. When he ran low, he'd go into the closets of the priests and give away their clothes! He would strip the blankets off their beds, toss in their pillows, and even donate the food they were all supposed to eat for dinner.

It didn't take long before the priests sat Brian down for a chat. They appreciated his charity but said that if he kept this up, that they would have nothing left to give the poor. They suggested that perhaps he was called to live a more radical form of Christian poverty. He took their advice and began working in India with Mother Teresa. After some time with her, she sent him to do missionary work in Vietnam and Cambodia. While in Cambodia, the Communists violently persecuted the Church and told all missionaries to get out of the country. In a letter to his seminarian friends back in the United States, Brian wrote, "If I am asked to leave, I will stay, because I feel called to mix my blood with the blood of Christ for the salvation of these people's souls."

* Note: The habits of viewing pornography and being sexually active outside of marriage could both be serious obstacles to a priestly vocation. Discernment with an experienced spiritual director is needed to determine if a young man in this situation could still have a viable vocation to the priesthood.

Verbal Review of Lesson 8

1. What is the spousal analogy?
2. Explain the mutual submission St. Paul speaks of in Ephesians 5.
3. What is *agape* love?
4. What is the primordial sacrament?

"Some are incapable of marriage because they were born so; some, because they were made so by others; some, because they have renounced marriage for the sake of the kingdom of heaven. Whoever can accept this ought to accept it."

(Mt 19:12)

Sure enough, Brian's calling was fulfilled. Each day at 4:00 a.m., he would sneak in the darkness to Mass, but on one particular morning, he was followed by Communist soldiers who arrested him during Mass, pulled him out of the cathedral, and beheaded him outside of the church. He was twenty-three years old.

Some people will look at this young man's martyrdom and think, "What a waste." Others will see his witness and example and say, "What a gift."

COMPREHENSION & DISCUSSION QUESTIONS

1. How are you inspired by people who live their call in such a radical way?

2. How does Brian's life show you that priesthood and religious life are calls to *ministry* rather than just *careers*?

3. What are the similarities and differences between Brian Walsh and your friends?

4. What do you think is the greatest misunderstanding about people like Brian?

5. If God called you to live this way, would you be ready to accept His invitation? Why or why not?

6. If Brian had not said "Yes" to God's call, how might the lives of those he touched have been different?

BRIDGING THE GAP

"Young people know that their life has meaning to the extent that it becomes a gift for others."
– Pope John Paul II

There was once a man who walked a tightrope across Niagara Falls, to the amazement of a cheering crowd. Then, the daredevil went a step further, pushing a wheelbarrow across the great expanse. The crowd went crazy with awe and admiration. Then, he asked the crowd if they thought that he could make it across the falls with someone *sitting in* the wheelbarrow. They cheered even louder as they affirmed his amazing gift of balance, encouraging him to do the stunt with someone in the wheelbarrow. As the applause died down, the man asked for a volunteer to get in the wheelbarrow. Suddenly, the crowd went silent. Their admiration for the daredevil's ability was real, but their faith in him was not great enough to join him in his efforts.[1]

After reading a story like the one about Brian Walsh, you may be amazed, but think, "I could never do that." And you are right. Your strength alone is not enough. But what if God *called* you to do it? Do you have great enough faith

Notes & Nuggets: Since this chapter deals with celibacy, and the next chapter is on "Finding Your Vocation", we encourage you to arrange for a guest speaker for the class who will serve as an attractive witness to the vocations discussed (celibacy and religious life). For example, invite a joyful religious sister who is sincere in her call and fun to be around. Invite a monk who normally joyfully prays his days away at a monastery. Invite a priest who constantly finds himself by giving himself away in heartfelt service to his parish or community. It's important to arrange for a priest or religious who is happy in his or her vocation.

You may ask your guest to answer questions on celibacy, or even invite him or her to teach this lesson (chapter 9), if willing (but be sure to provide it well in advance). Or, consider asking the guest to come in toward the end of this lesson on celibacy, acting as a link between this lesson and the next lesson regarding vocational discernment. Though it may take more time, invite your guest to tell the story of how God called them to their vocation. If you are worried they will go "too long," invite them to come for the last part of your class. This way, you will have a definitive end time for their sharing.

in the One who ordered the universe and can order your life? Wanting what is ultimately best for us, God would never ask us to do more than we are capable of doing. If we doubt that we can accomplish what God is asking, we doubt God Himself. As we move forward with the rest of this chapter on celibacy, remember that God has a special call for you, and it is possible that your call is to the celibate life. Take comfort in God's promise: We "can do all things" in Christ who strengthens us (Phil 4:13) … even if it means martyrdom, or foregoing an earthly spouse to more fully embrace our Heavenly One. Remember that Jesus tells us, "Everyone who has left houses or brothers or sisters or father or mother or children or lands, for my name's sake, will receive a hundredfold" (Mt 19:29).

 TO THE CORE

Everyone on earth is called to marriage. This may seem like a strange way to begin a chapter on celibacy and the religious life, but it's true. When a priest is ordained, he chooses to marry the Church as his bride. When a woman enters the consecrated life, she is being espoused by Christ Himself. Like a bride, she wears a veil as a visible sign of her marital union with Jesus. Among other things, these expressions of the celibate vocation are reminders that heaven will be an eternal wedding celebration between God and His bride, the Church.

Here on earth, married couples are a sacramental sign that points to this eternal reality. As we mentioned in Chapter Four, when a sign on the road says, "Florida: 500 Miles," what will happen in 500 miles? You will have arrived at the destination and the sign will have fulfilled its purpose. The sign of marriage on earth is fulfilled only in heaven: our total union with God. So, when a person chooses to be celibate for the sake of the kingdom instead of the sacrament of Marriage, he or she is basically skipping the sacrament (the sign), and, in a very real way, living the eternal reality to which the sacrament pointed: undivided union with God.

Who Are We? How Do We Live?

In the first half of the Theology of the Body, Pope John Paul II answers the question, "Who are we?" We learned that we are sons and daughters of God made in His image and likeness. This image is inscribed upon the very bodies of Adam and Eve (and therefore, upon our bodies also) to love and image the communion of love in the Holy Trinity.

The second half of the Theology of the Body answers the question, "How do we live?" The first way to live, covered in Chapter Eight, is a way of loving communion through the **vocation** of marriage to a human spouse. The second way is marriage to Christ and the Church through **celibacy**. As John Paul II stressed, celibacy must be freely chosen if it is to correspond to Christ's invitation. Celibacy is a free choice to renounce marital communion with a

"In the first place I say this: you must never think that you are alone in deciding your future! And second: when deciding your future, you must not decide for yourself alone!"
– Pope John Paul II

Notes & Nuggets: To get a richer perspective on the spousal meaning of celibacy, remind your students that the nuptial meaning of the body means that all persons are created to be a "gift" for another. At this point, we suggest reading Matthew 19:10-12 aloud with your students. Challenge them to unpack what Jesus is saying, and help them to see that He is explaining celibacy as a calling and a choice that is only for some people. John Paul II taught that Christ's own words about celibacy (Mt 19:11-12), "consequently show that this gift 'for,' present from the beginning at the basis of marriage, can also be at the basis of continence 'for' the kingdom of heaven!" Just as a person is free to become "one flesh" with a spouse through the conjugal act, so also is that person "capable of freely renouncing such a giving of himself to another person, so that, choosing continence for the sake of the kingdom of heaven, he can give himself totally to Christ" (April 28, 1982).

spouse in order to serve God and the Church more fully. The Church forces no one to be celibate. In the case of priesthood, the Church chooses her priests from among those men who have discerned and freely chosen celibacy as their life's vocation (see CCC 1579).

COMPREHENSION & DISCUSSION QUESTIONS

1. What does the veil of a consecrated religious woman signify?

2. What two main questions does the Theology of the Body answer?

3. What are the two main ways that the Theology of the Body teaches us to live?

4. What is *celibacy*?

5. Does the Church force people to be celibate?

Celibacy Does Not Reject Sexuality

notes

All too often, people think of celibacy as something a person is *not* doing with their sexuality. This view misses the point of celibacy. Those who enter the religious life as priests, brothers, sisters, etc., are a foreshadowing of how all of us will live in the heavenly kingdom. In heaven, being in the presence of God will far exceed any earthly joy. Celibacy is a witness to the fact that there is a greater joy—heaven—than the joys of this world. Celibates do not reject their sexuality. They're showing us the ultimate purpose and meaning of sexuality, the giving of ourselves to God. In their decision to renounce marriage on earth, celibates embrace their sexuality and channel that energy toward full communion with God, reflecting in a unique way the meaning of sexuality and self-donation.

Addressing the youth of the world, Pope John Paul II wrote

> You perceive it in the depths of your heart: all that is good on earth, all professional success, even the human love that you dream of, can never fully satisfy your deepest and most intimate desires. Only an encounter with Jesus can give full meaning to your lives: "for you made us for yourself, and our heart finds no peace until it rests in you" (St. Augustine, *Confessions*, book 1, chapter 1). Do not let yourselves be distracted from this search. Persevere in it because it is your fulfillment and your joy that is at stake.[2]

Notes & Nuggets: At this point, if you used the icebreaker at the beginning of this lesson, this would be a good time to explain to your students the point of that game. Refer back to the instructor's page next to page 135. Remind them that, although their desires for marriage and family are excellent desires, those desires do not disqualify them from a possible call to celibacy and spiritual fatherhood or motherhood. The only way they will know God's will is if they open their spiritual and physical eyes, pay attention to God's "smoke signals" through prayer and counsel, and ask Him to reveal His call while they live out their faith in a radical way! It is a good idea to make an inventory of one's gifts, but it is not God's desire for us to *decide* our vocation. Though we may know many things about ourselves, only He knows the vocation He wills for us. Our job is to constantly seek to know His desire for our lives. Remind your students that the only way they learned more about each other in the "Bet You Didn't Know" game was by asking and then listening. In the same way, as we ask God what He wants for our lives, He will continue to lead us and to teach us things about ourselves that we did not previously know or understand. Prayer and counsel are keys to learning more about God, about ourselves, and about God's will for our lives.

COMPREHENSION & DISCUSSION QUESTIONS

1. How do those who live the call to celibacy foreshadow the heavenly kingdom for us?

2. What did Pope John Paul II point out as the only thing that can give full meaning to our lives?

3. What do you think John Paul II meant when he noted that our "joy … is at stake"?

4. Which saint wrote, "Our heart finds no peace until it rests in you"? What do you think about this statement?

5. Do you know anyone whose life changed for the better when that person allowed his or her heart to "rest" in God? Explain.

Celibacy Points to Heaven

Through their total dedication to Christ, men and women in the religious life point us to the ultimate purpose of our lives: union with God. They also show us how to get there by making a sincere gift of ourselves in love. In Chapter Three, we discussed the **nuptial meaning of the body**. We learned that our bodies reveal our calling to make a total gift of ourselves in love. It's obvious how a married couple makes a gift of themselves, but what about a celibate man or woman? When a person enters the religious life, he or she does exactly this. They totally dedicate their lives to the service of God and humanity and offer themselves at our service. They teach us God's word and His love through the corporal works of mercy, through the sacraments, and through spiritual works of mercy.

If you have ever thought "I must not be called to the religious life because I want to be a spouse and a parent," know that we are all called to be these things. All men are called to be a husband and father in some way, and every woman is called in some way to be a wife and mother. These desires do not exclude people or give them a reason to disqualify themselves from a religious calling. These desires are stamped into us for a reason. There is a reason that priests are called "Father." There is a reason why the little nun from Calcutta was called "Mother." Both of them begot (generated) many spiritual children by their union with Christ and the Church. So, the real question is: How is God calling you to live out these desires?

" … people should cultivate chastity in the way that is suited to their state of life. Some profess virginity or consecrated celibacy which enables them to give themselves to God alone with an undivided heart in a remarkable manner."
(CCC 2349).

134-L

Celibacy Is Not Repression

Some people are turned off from the idea of the religious life because they think, "I just can't imagine not having sex." If we think of marriage as an outlet for lust or sexual tension, we're bound to think of the religious life as sexual repression. We should realize, though, that both the married person and the celibate person must have dominion over his or her lust. When people are in control of their sexuality, only then are they capable of making a gift of themselves. This gift can be given to a spouse, or it can be offered as a sacrifice through celibacy.

If you continue to struggle with the idea of not having sex, consider praying to St. Joseph or the Blessed Virgin Mary for spiritual assistance. St. Joseph is more than a mere model of chastity but an archetype of celibacy; he lived out celibacy every day. He was so enraptured by the love of God that no earthly love could possibly compare. St. Joseph's chastity allowed him to more perfectly give himself to God, the same way celibacy frees modern men and women to serve Christ and the Church in totality of mind, body, and spirit. Do not doubt that if God calls you to a life of celibacy, your communion with Him can be just as awesome as an earthly marital relationship—in fact, as John Paul II indicates, it can be even *more* awesome.

COMPREHENSION & DISCUSSION QUESTIONS

1. What is the *nuptial meaning of the body*?

2. If you desire to be married, does this mean you are not called to celibacy? Why or why not?

3. Knowing what you know about the Theology of the Body and marriage, why is it improper to view marriage as an outlet for lust or even sexual tension?

4. How should the above answer affect our view of celibacy?

notes

Isn't celibacy abnormal?

If you mean "abnormal" as in "weird" or "wrong," then no, celibacy is not abnormal. But it is abnormal in the sense that it is "not the norm." It is true that most people in the world marry. Marriage is a noble way of life and remains the calling for most people on earth. However, we cannot separate Genesis (in which there is a general mandate from God for humans to marry) from the rest of Scripture. If we look forward to Jesus' words in the Gospels, as well as the teaching of St. Paul, we see celibacy as "an exceptional vocation,"[3] as John Paul II puts it, to which only a few are called to respond. However,

don't hide in the statistics! The Church needs consecrated, celibate men and women, and when we think celibacy is too hard, we must remember that every vocation will require sacrifices.

Priesthood in the Catholic Church is a special call for many reasons. First and foremost, without the priesthood, we would not have the Eucharist, the greatest gift that priests offer their bride, the Church, who "draws her life from the Eucharist."[4] The Eucharist is only brought about through a priest who, in the name of his local bishop, holds **apostolic succession**, the line of priestly power and grace that links directly back to Christ. The priests you see today were ordained by a bishop who was ordained by a bishop who was ordained by a bishop … all the way back to the twelve apostles, who were ordained by Christ!

So why is the priesthood reserved only to men?

Questions about why the Catholic Church has a male-only priesthood are natural in this day and age. A general awareness about the role of women has been a big topic of discussion for the past hundred years, and especially during the last forty years or so. Today, we see women performing all sorts of functions that were traditionally reserved to men, and so we naturally question why the institution of the priesthood is reserved to men alone.

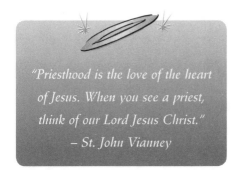

"Priesthood is the love of the heart of Jesus. When you see a priest, think of our Lord Jesus Christ."
– *St. John Vianney*

To begin, the reason has nothing to do with any kind of mean-spirited or sexist discrimination. Even in the natural order, we see obvious differences between the sexes that result in only one of the sexes being able to participate: only women have the God-given ability to give birth. Likewise, in the supernatural order, there are also unchangeable realities. This is what St. Paul talks about when he speaks about there being many parts, but only one body of Christ. He says, "If the foot should say, 'Because I am not a head I do not belong to the body,' that would not make it any less a body part...God arranged the organs of the body, each one of them, as he chose. If all were a single organ, where would the body be?...The eye cannot say to the hand, 'I have no need of you,' nor again the head to the feet, 'I have no need of you'" (1 Cor 12:15, 18-19, 21). Obviously there are many parts—many members of the Body of Christ with different functions—and *all* are valuable.

For you girls who would like to see how amazing and wonderful you are in your femininity, read John Paul II's apostolic letter on the dignity and vocation of women, *Mulieris Dignitatem*. This document speaks of the extraordinary giftedness of women and how the world would be utterly deprived without the feminine gifts.

But to answer the question specifically about the male priesthood, priests act *in persona Christi* ("in the person of Christ"), as they provide us with the Sacraments and other ecclesial services (CCC 1548). As we read in Scripture, the Church is the Bride of Christ (Eph 5:23-32). Since God created marriage to be a union between a man and a woman, only a man can act in the person of Christ—as a groom—meant to marry His bride, the Church. There would be an

Notes & Nuggets: Some women see the all male priesthood as a "power-trip" for men in the Church, but remind your students that power should never be a reason for a man to join the priesthood. Rather, the priesthood is about being a servant like Jesus, who said "the Son of man came not to be served but to serve, and to give his life as a ransom for many" (Mt 20:28). For more in-depth discussion on reasons for the all-male priesthood, read John Paul II's apostolic letter, *Ordinatio Sacerdotalis.*

ontological (in one's very essence) problem with a woman standing *in persona Christi* because Christ was a man. He was married to the Church, to whom we refer in feminine terms. You simply can't have a female standing as Christ, a male, and saying the Mass (at which the consummation of the marriage between Christ and the Church takes place).

As well, Jesus purposely chose twelve men (the apostles) and no women, not even the Virgin Mary, to be His first priests. This is not due to the cultural customs of His time, which Jesus did not hesitate to break on several occasions. In fact, there were other religions at that time that had priestesses. It is due, instead, to the inherent differences between men and women. As much as a man cannot be a mother, a woman cannot be a father. the priesthood is spiritual fatherhood.

Lastly, many people do not realize that, even if the pope or bishops *wanted* to change this teaching, the Church does not have the authority to change it. The Catholic Church is not the pope's church, or your church, or our church. It's God's church. Therefore, we do not have the right to change a defined teaching simply because our culture is demanding it. The male-only priesthood is a part of the divine law instituted by Christ. It is an infallible teaching of the Church that priesthood is to be reserved for men (see CCC 1577). This teaching of the Church was beautifully explained by John Paul II in his apostolic letter ***Ordinatio Sacerdotalis***.

Why can't religious sisters be allowed to do more than just pray and help the poor?

Religious sisters are a beautiful testament to the profound gifts that women have to offer the Church. They usually live in convents and dedicate themselves to active ministry wherever there is a need. Across the globe, you will find women in various religious orders and communities doing everything imaginable to serve the body of Christ, including education, counseling, mass media production, and caring for the sick. They are amazing models of love who inspire and touch souls across the globe for the greater glory of their spouse, Jesus Christ. Then there are **nuns**. Though often used interchangeably with the term "religious sisters," nuns are, by definition, **contemplative** women celibates who live in monasteries, dedicated to a life of **contemplative prayer** for the Church. In this day and age, we certainly need dedicated and humble people who are willing to make prayer their full-time mission. Prayer remains the backbone of every active effort to serve humanity and convert the world.

Why can't priests be married?

Catholic priests have been married in the past (the mention of St. Peter's mother-in-law in Matthew 8:14 shows us that St. Peter was married), but in the Latin rite of the Church, priests have been chosen from among celibate men for more than 1,000 years. Unlike the male-only priesthood issue, which is rooted

notes

_____

_____

_____

_____

_____

_____

_____

_____

_____

_____

_____

_____

_____

_____

_____

_____

_____

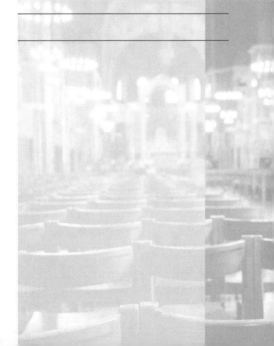

Notes & Nuggets: Remind your students over and over that priesthood and religious life are not just renunciations of sex and marriage. In fact, in the same way that a proper understanding of marriage allows a man to be free to love his wife (rather than cramped because he can't date other women) so also does a priest become totally free to be a gift to others. The freedom to give of oneself in the priesthood has been powerfully demonstrated by many priests throughout the history of the Church. The stories of the lives of countless saints and missionaries attest to this freedom. The story of St. Maximilian Kolbe's life—a priest who freely chose to die in the place of a married man at Auschwitz during WWII—would be a great one to share with your teens to illustrate this point. Another option is to assign your students to research St. Maximilian's life. Check our "Project 3" in the "Work It Out" section of this chapter.

in unchangeable doctrine, the Church could change its norm on married clergy, although such a change is unlikely. Such a practice is referred to as a **Church discipline**.

As we have seen, there are many beautiful theological reasons that the Theology of the Body offers in support of priestly celibacy. One of the main reasons is that if a priest acts *in persona Christi* and marries the Bride of Christ, the Church, he should give himself completely to her.

Recall the concept of *total self-donation*, and remember that the Church is a bride to whom one gives himself! If a priest were married to a woman while married to the Church, it would be a great challenge for him to be completely dedicated to the Church. St. Paul encourages celibacy for this very reason (see 1 Cor 7:32-35). While some say that allowing married men to be ordained would fill more seminaries with willing applicants, even other churches—such as the Eastern Catholic and Orthodox Churches, which ordain married men—are not experiencing a surge in vocations. One also has to wonder if it would make sense for the Church to change its practices in order to make this vocational call "easier" for men to answer. The Church has always taught that celibacy is an objectively "higher" calling than marriage, because it more directly reflects the heavenly marriage of the Church and the Lamb of God (see Rev 21:2).

Subjectively speaking, however, the better vocation for you is the one to which God is calling you. This obviously means you need to discern prayerfully what gift God has for you.

Wouldn't celibate men and women be happier if they could marry?

Look at the life of John Paul II and Blessed Teresa of Calcutta. Did they seem less happy from giving themselves totally to Christ? Although they were filled with joy, their lives were not without sacrifices. In fact, the celibate person "freely chooses to remain in the 'ache' of solitude in this life in order to devote all of his longings to the union that alone can satisfy."[5] This is what led John Paul II to say, "Earthly **continence** [celibacy] for the kingdom of heaven is undoubtedly a sign … that the body, whose end is not the grave, is directed to glorification."[6] While celibacy may be lonely at times, that is not *always* a bad thing. Celibacy is both a great gift to offer God, as well as a powerful reminder that we were not created to live on earth forever but destined to be with God forever in heaven. As well, think of the "aches" that can come with married life: the care of children, the struggle to love the spouse's extended family, and the sacrifice of many personal preferences for the common good of the family. In short, each of the two primary vocations—when lived as they are supposed to be lived—involve sacrifice. However, with these "little deaths" comes resurrection.

"*Religious orders are not formed for the purpose of gathering together perfect people, but those who have the courage to aim at perfection.*"
– *St. Francis de Sales*

COMPREHENSION & DISCUSSION QUESTIONS

1. How is celibacy an "exceptional" calling?

2. Why is the priesthood reserved for men alone?

3. What does it mean when we say a priest acts *in persona Christi*?

4. What is the main role of a religious who is a *contemplative*?

5. What does the term *Church discipline* mean?

DIGGING DEEPER: Celibacy as an Eschatological Sign

If you read more about the Theology of the Body on your own, you might come across phrases describing celibacy as is "an expression of heaven on earth" or "celibacy is an eschatological sign." Those are lofty phrases, but keep reading for the not-so-tricky explanation. The word *eschatology* comes from the Greek word *eschatos*, which means "last." Eschatology is simply the study of "last things," the part of theology concerned with death, judgment, and the final destiny of our lives.

Celibacy is considered an **eschatological sign** because it foreshadows what heaven will be like. In heaven, we will be totally enraptured by the love of God. Human love, no matter how grand on earth, is finite and pales in comparison to God's love. Sacramental married love communicates the love found in the Trinity, but the exchange between God and man and between Creator and His creation finds its perfection, not in earthly marriage, but in the marriage of the Lamb: that is, in heaven.

In heaven, we will all have hearts perfected and directed toward God and the **communion of saints**. We will be undivided and will not have a desire for earthly marriage because we will be fulfilled by God's love of the Trinity and the love of all the men and women who have responded to God's "marriage proposal." From this perspective, we can see that celibacy in no way devalues marriage. Rather, it complements it. While marriage is a sacrament of heaven on earth, celibacy is in a more direct sense "heaven on earth," as it anticipates the eschatological reality of total fulfillment in God.

Celibate people are living testaments to selflessness and, by their sacrifice, are blessed through a union with God that can bring a taste of the divine, a glimpse of the sheer ecstasy awaiting us in heaven. In a world that often equates ecstasy with sexual pleasure, this idea of divine union may be hard to grasp. Contemplate how total union with God supersedes a mere human union. It is a

notes

_____

_____

_____

_____

_____

_____

_____

_____

_____

_____

_____

_____

_____

_____

_____

_____

APPLICATION

Option #1: Small Group Discussion

Divide your students into groups of four to five and have them discuss the following questions:

1. Do you know any priests or religious? (In your family or parish, or among your friends?)

2. What do you think they like most about their vocation?

3. What have you learned from them (even from just witnessing their life) about their call to celibacy?

4. Have you been to an ordination or a ceremony where religious made their vows? What was is like? What were the different symbols of the ceremony?

Then have the students come back into a large group and share the answers from their small group discussion.

Option #2: Eschatological Sign Construction

Pair up your students, and have them create "Eschatological Signs" with markers, poster board, glue, construction paper, etc. Ask them to be creative as they construct actual signs with words and drawings that point toward "heaven," which may resemble some type of road signs along the highway. For example, the sign may be created like a "one way" sign, but could say, "One Way to Heaven." Then have the group members explain their eschatological signs and what they mean. If you have room, let the students put their signs up around your classroom or meeting room as a good reminder throughout the rest of the class year.

Option #3: Have your students do the Chapter #9 Word Search, using the terms at the end of this chapter (see page 193)

Option #4: Field Trip

Take your students on a field trip to a nearby seminary, monastery, convent, motherhouse, or even a parish. Contact the superior and plan to be there at a time when your class can possibly join the community in its time of prayer or work. Set up a tour of the facility where students can get a first-hand impression of what this particular life of a celibate entails. Allow your students to ask questions, and have them write some type of reflection paper or summary of their experience.

concept, for sure, that is difficult to grasp and calls for some serious reflection and prayer.

These topics may seem foreign to you. Maybe you've never considered the celibate life before. Maybe you've just always assumed you'd get married one day. Start praying a prayer of openness today, that you might consider the celibate life as an option if God should call you to it. Rest assured, celibacy is "an exceptional calling," not a lesser one. It's not for the socially inept or for people who can't get a date, but for those who want to give themselves to God in a radical way.

Pray and reflect on Proverbs 3:5-6: "Trust in the Lord with all your heart, and do not rely on your own insight. In all your ways acknowledge him, and he will make straight your paths."

Would you be willing to give your life to Jesus through celibacy if He asks? Ask God to help you trust Him more. Then, make a stop at an adoration chapel and ask God to remove any fear you may have related to your call. On your knees, offer your body to God. Also, don't get nervous that this effort will somehow "talk God into calling you to the priesthood or religious life." Before time even began, God has had a plan for your life, including your particular vocation. This spiritual exercise of offering yourself to God will just give you the reflective time you need to discern which vocation you are to live.

Remember that religious life is not just your gift to God, but His gift to you.

LIVE IT OUT: The Happy Celibate

Celibacy is certainly a livable vocation. It is possible to live without having sex. The thing to remember is this: *celibacy does not equal isolation.*

God calls us to communion with Him, and that communion is mirrored in our communion with others. So, while a celibate priest is not called to be a physical father, he is called to be a *spiritual* father. Among other things, a good father spends time with his family. While religious brothers or sisters are called to celibacy, they are also called to communion.

Celibates who break their vow of chastity almost always have at least one thing in common. Maybe you have seen shows about predators on Animal Planet or the Discovery Channel. How do lions make a kill from among the herd of 100 water buffaloes? They separate one from the herd, and if it is a runt (the smallest animal of the herd) or already injured, it makes the chase even easier. Similarly, priests and religious are most likely to be tempted to be unfaithful to their vows when they are disconnected from friends and family, and living somewhat isolated lives. In this capacity, the devil tries to divide and conquer.

So, if God calls you to celibacy, how can you say "Yes" and be happy and faithful?

Just as a husband's love for his wife is tested when an attractive woman looks his way, so will a celibate man's

MOVIE CLIP/SONG SUGGESTIONS

MOVIE CLIPS:

1. Sister Act: Show the segment that falls between 37:52 and 40:27. Sister Mary Clarence, played by Whoopi Goldberg, is disguised as a nun for her protection from the Mafia. She encourages one of the nuns who shares about struggling with her call.

2. Spiderman: Show the segment that falls between 1:50:26 and 1:55:13. Mary Jane tells Peter (Spiderman) that she loves him, and although he loves her, too, he tells her he cannot be with her because of his vocation to be Spiderman and the focused commitment this will take. This scene contains the line, "With great power, comes great responsibility."

3. Keeping the Faith: Show the segment that falls between 32:09 and 35:50. Fr. Brian Finn, played by Ed Norton, is a priest in the movie who talks to his lifelong female friend about celibacy. Although he does struggle later in the movie with this commitment, he stays true to his call to the priesthood.

4. Keeping the Faith: Show the segment that falls between 1:35:39 and 1:37:58. Fr. Brian Finn, played by Ed Norton, a main character and priest in the movie, talks with his pastor about his recent struggles with his commitment to his vocation, specifically regarding his celibacy.

5. In America: Show the segment that falls between 59:40 and 1:01:16. This movie depicts a single man (the visitor) displaying his love for his host's entire family. "No, I love you ... and I love your woman ... and I love your kids ... " It can be compared, in a certain way, to the ache of a celibate for his own family. It shows his ability to love them in his own sacrificial way.

[NOTE: Be sure to watch this clip before showing it to your class. There is a subtle but offensive expletive near this clip. Be sure that the time code on your tape or DVD is cued up correctly and that you know exactly when to start and stop this clip.]

6. Therese: Ordinary Girl. Extraordinary Soul. Show the segment that falls between 1:04:55 and 1:07:53. This is the scene of Therese dancing with the Lord–her Spouse–in her mind. She is totally wrapped in her love with Him. Foregoing things of the world for simple charity, she serves an annoying sister by helping her to walk.

7. With God in Russia: This is the story of Fr. Walter Ciscek, S.J., a missionary priest held captive in Siberia for twenty-four years. It is a powerful story of total gift of self in celibacy. (30 mins, Ignatius Press)

8. Fishers of Men: This fast-paced video may be the best short film on priestly vocations ever created. Short testimonies interspersed with dramatic presentations of heroic priests in action will grab the attention of any young person and surely spark quality discussion after the credits roll. Available through the USCCB website: www.usccb.org/vocations

SONGS:

1. Getting into You — Relient K (*Two Lefts Don't Make a Right ... But Three Do*)

Making the switch to live for God and not for ourselves will make us see things in a different perspective. Punk/Ballad.

2. My Will — DC Talk (*Exodus*)

God's will and our will are often different, but once we surrender God's plan becomes clearer. Pop.

3. Be Not Afraid — Janelle (single — *Be Not Afraid*)

An uplifting song about the life of John Paul II. Pop.

4. The Great One — Fr. Stan Fortuna and Righteous B (single — *The Great One*)

A rap about the life and witness of John Paul "the Great." Rap/Hip-Hop.

LIVE IT OUT: *(Cont.)*

commitment be tested. Just as faithfulness is a choice for a married woman, so also is celibacy a daily choice for a nun or religious sister who has answered this call.

If celibacy is your call, God will give you the grace to live it out. Every day, you will need to choose again to take the road less traveled—the road to the Cross. It is there that your lust can be crucified, and Christ can redeem your desires. Choose happiness over simply "feeling good." Choose authentic love over simple sexual pleasure. Choose eternity over the "passionate" moment. Choose—and sometimes create—community over living in isolation. Choose good over evil.

The good choices seem clear enough when you are not in the midst of temptation, but it is at these times that the degree of your commitment is tested.

While the media often shows people "the day after" having sex as being super-charged and almost giddy, in real life this is obviously not always the case. In fact, real joy is found in those who love, not in those who are merely having sex. So, the next time you see Sister Mary Joyful beaming after Mass, remember her reason: she is deeply in love with Jesus Christ, her Spouse. Conversely, when you meet celibates who seem depressed and unhappy, the problem is not that they are *not* having sex. The problem is likely that they are not united with the spouse (Christ or the Church) that they have chosen. Something is standing in the way of their experiencing powerful love. In this case, pray for them, and offer your own support and love in whatever ways you can.

Here are our Top Ten ways that you, as a teenager right now, can help celibates be happy and faithful to their vocations:

1. Ask your parents to invite a priest or religious over for a family dinner, or invite him or her to your game, recital, concert, etc.

2. Ask them about their lives and listen long enough to hear their answers.

3. Pray for them daily, and let them know that they are in your prayers.

4. Thank them for their witness to love and for their commitment to their vocation.

5. Find a funny or meaningful song that reminds you of them, and let them hear it. Tell them it's their theme song.

6. Write them a good old-fashioned letter, or e-mail them, thanking them for their spiritual fatherhood or motherhood.

7. Give them a gift on Father's Day or Mother's Day.

8. Find out the anniversary date of their ordination or vows and send them a card.

9. Call on them in your time of need, allowing them to serve you and minister to you on behalf of Christ and the Church.

10. Smile often and share your life and energy with them.

If you are called to be celibate (remember, this means devoting yourself to the heavenly marriage *now*), you are called to be happy *through* this vocation, not in spite of it.

Notes & Nuggets: In the closing prayer, we ask for the intercession of St. Augustine and St. Frances Cabrini. St. Augustine, born in the year 354 in North Africa, had a pagan for a father and a saint for a mother (St. Monica). Monica prayed for Augustine for decades while he lived an immoral life, including roughly fifteen years with a concubine who bore him a son (Adeodatus). Yet, Augustine always sought the truth, sampling many philosophies and even rigorously defending Manichaenism, a heresy that posited that matter (the body) was evil and spirit was good. But once he found the truth in Christ and the Catholic Church, he dramatically changed his life and eventually became the Bishop of Hippo, where he served the Church for thirty-four years in dedicated celibacy.

Later, Maria Francesca Cabrini, born in Italy in 1850, was one of thirteen children. At the age of twelve, she vowed herself to virginity, and in 1887 she took formal vows as a religious sister and soon desired to do missionary work in Africa. But she obeyed her bishop and Pope Leo XIII when they asked her to work in the United States with poor Italian immigrants. She and the members of the new order she founded, the Roman Catholic Missionary Sisters of the Sacred Heart, did amazing service for the poor through nearly thirty years of work in the United States as they founded hospitals, schools, convents, and orphanages there and in other countries throughout the world. Through her celibacy, her life was one of complete dedication of her mind, body, and soul to the work of Christ and the Church. In 1946, she was canonized and became the first American citizen to become an official saint of the Church.

IN HIS OWN WORDS

- **On Celibacy for the Kingdom:** "Subsequently, the motivation influences the choice of continence, accepted after having understood its significance for the kingdom of heaven. In the second part of his statement, Christ declared then that a man makes himself a eunuch when he chooses continence for the kingdom of heaven and makes it the fundamental situation or state of his whole earthly life" (March 31, 1982).

- "Based on the same disposition of the personal subject, thanks to which man fully rediscovers himself through a sincere gift of himself (see GS 24), man [male and female] is capable of choosing the personal gift of his very self ... He is also capable of freely renouncing such a giving of himself to another person, so that, choosing continence for the sake of the kingdom of heaven, he can give himself totally to Christ" (April 28, 1982).

- **On Celibacy and the Nuptial Giving of Self:** "In this way, continence for the sake of the kingdom of heaven, the choice of virginity or celibacy for one's whole life, has become in the experience of Christ's disciples and followers the act of a particular response of love for the Divine Spouse. Therefore it has acquired the significance of an act of nuptial love, that is, a nuptial giving of oneself for the purpose of reciprocating in a particular way the nuptial love of the Redeemer. It is a giving of oneself understood as renunciation, but made above all out of love" (April 28, 1982).

(Continued on next teacher's page)

WORK IT OUT

Assignment #1: Interview a consecrated religious person who is living a celibate life. Consult your teacher as to whether you will follow option A or option B.

(Option A) If your teacher approves, write your own list of ten questions to ask this person about his or her life, with at least half of these questions specifically dealing with celibacy. Record this person's answers, and write a summary paragraph of what you learned.

(Option B) Ask him or her to share with you examples of how his or her commitment to Christ and the Church is a foreshadowing of our union with God in heaven. Write a short essay explaining what you learned from this conversation.

Assignment #2: Interview a priest and ask him to share with you the moment in his life, as a priest, when he has felt the most profound realization of acting *in persona Christi*. Paraphrase his answer in a short essay, and if time allows, share his story with the class when you turn in your assignment.

Assignment #3: Instead of Assignment #2 above, if you *know* a priest who profoundly touched your own life through his acting *in persona Christi*, write an essay on *your own* experience with this priest, and if time allows, share it with your class.

Assignment #4: Research the actual rite of ordination, and make a log sheet of all the bodily signs and symbols found in the ceremony. Pay particular attention to body posture as well as the details of anointing contained in the rite. Apply your learning from Chapter Six, Language of the Body.

Project #1: Read the document *Ordinatio Sacerdotalis*, and write a summary of what you learn regarding Pope John Paul II's reasons for reaffirming that the priesthood as a vocation proper to men.

Project #2: Do a research project on the priesthood, detailing the difference between the Church discipline of the celibate priesthood and the divine law of an all-male priesthood.

Project #3: Select a particular religious order and do a research project on its founder, the way the order originated, and the details of the order's particular *charism*.

Project #4: Do a research project on a saint who lived a life of celibacy. Some interesting ones to consider are St. Ignatius of Loyola, St. Augustine, St. Therese, St. Catherine of Siena, St. Teresa of Avila, St. Maximilian Kolbe, St. Francis of Assisi, and St. Pio (Padre Pio). Reflect on how their lives were particularly exceptional because of their celibate call, and the way they made a free gift of their lives for God and the Church.

CLOSING PRAYER

Leader: In the name of the Father, and of the Son, and of the Holy Spirit. **Amen.**

All: Sts. Augustine and Frances Cabrini, please pray with me that I, like you, would have the presence of mind to choose God's will over my own and His plan in all things. Help me to offer my body, as you both did, as a living sacrifice for the building of God's Kingdom here on earth. **Amen.**

(In His Own Words continued)

- **On Celibacy Affirming Marriage:** "The renunciation is possible only when one admits an authentic knowledge of that value that is constituted by the nuptial disposition of masculinity and femininity to marriage. In order for man to be fully aware of what he is choosing [continence for the sake of the kingdom], he must also be fully aware of what he is renouncing. ... But a renunciation made with full awareness of the above mentioned value is not enough. In the light of Christ's words, and also in the light of the whole authentic Christian Tradition, it is possible to deduce that this renunciation is at the same time a particular form of affirming that value from which the unmarried person consistently abstains, following the evangelical counsel ... So continence for the sake of the kingdom of heaven [virginity, celibacy] orients the life of persons who freely choose it toward the exclusion of the common way of conjugal and family life. ... In no way can one see in this a denial of the essential value of marriage. On the contrary, continence serves indirectly to highlight what is most lasting and most profoundly personal in the vocation to marriage" (May 5,1982).

- **On Marriage and Celibacy as Complementary Vocations:** "These two dimensions of the human vocation are not opposed to each other, but are complementary. Both furnish a full answer to one of man's fundamental questions, the question about the significance of 'being a body,' that is, about the significance of masculinity and femininity, of being 'in the body' a man or a woman" (July 14, 1982).

- **On the Freedom of the Gift of Continence:** "At the basis of Christ's call to continence there is not only the sexual instinct, which is in the category, I would say, of a naturalistic necessity. But there is also the consciousness of the freedom of the gift. This is organically connected with the profound and mature knowledge of the nuptial meaning of the body, in the total makeup of the personal subjectivity of the man and woman" (April 28,1982).

- **On Fruitfulness of the Spirit:** "Only Mary and Joseph, who had lived the mystery of his conception and birth, became the first witnesses of a fruitfulness different from that of the flesh, that is, a fruitfulness of the Spirit: 'That which is conceived in her is of the Holy Spirit.'(Mt 1:20)" (March 24, 1982).

- **On Cloistered Nuns:** John Paul II described the vocation and mission of cloistered nuns as "a sign of the exclusive union of the Church as Bride with her Lord, whom she loves above all things." (Post-Synodal Apostolic Exhortation on the Consecrated Life and its Mission in the Church and the World, *Vita Consecrata* [25 March 1996], 59.)

- "As the Apostles, gathered in prayer with Mary and the other women in the Upper Room, were filled with the Holy Spirit (see Acts 1:14), so the community of the faithful hopes today to be able to experience, thanks also to your prayer, a renewed Pentecost for a more effective Gospel testimony on the threshold of the Third Millennium." (Address to Cloistered Nuns, Loreto [10 September 1995], 4.)

- **On the All-Male Priesthood:** "Furthermore, the fact that the Blessed Virgin Mary, Mother of God and Mother of the Church, received neither the mission proper to the Apostles nor the ministerial priesthood clearly shows that the non-admission of women to priestly ordination cannot mean that women are of lesser dignity, nor can it be construed as discrimination against them. Rather, it is to be seen as the faithful observance of a plan to be ascribed to the wisdom of the Lord of the universe" (*Ordinatio Sacerdotalis*, 3).

- "Wherefore, in order that all doubt may be removed regarding a matter of great importance, a matter which pertains to the Church's divine constitution itself, in virtue of my ministry of confirming the brethren (see Lk 22:32) I declare that the Church has no authority whatsoever to confer priestly ordination on women and that this judgment is to be definitively held by all the Church's faithful" (*Ordinatio Sacerdotalis*, 4).

Glossary
of Key Terms

Apostolic succession: A line of priestly power and authority originating from Christ and handed down from the apostles to the present through their successors, the bishops.

Celibacy (for the kingdom): It is a choice to "skip" the marriage of earth to devote oneself entirely to the marriage of heaven.

Church discipline: A practice or norm created by the Church that is firm and should be followed, but could be changed by the Church in the future. Examples are abstaining from meat on Fridays during Lent, needing to be sixteen years old to be a confirmation sponsor, and priestly celibacy. This is different than Church doctrine (teaching), which is unchanging.

Communion of saints: We already enjoy this communion here on earth with each other (the Church Militant). In spirit, we are connected with those who have died and are still being purified in purgatory (the Church Suffering). In prayer, we have communion with the saints in heaven (the Church Triumphant), who intercede for us before God (Rev 5:8). In the Resurrection, we will experience a fullness of communion as human members of the Church, sharing eternity together as persons perfectly integrated in bodies and souls.

Contemplative: A person who chooses a life that focuses on an interior life of prayer and intercession for the benefit of the Church.

Contemplative prayer: "A gaze of faith, fixed on Jesus" and the mysteries of His life (CCC 2715). It is placing oneself in God's presence and resting there in His love.

Continence: Maintaining control of one's desires, appetites, and passions rather than being controlled by them. Furthermore, continence lived as a virtue involves directing one's passions toward the true, good, and beautiful.

Eschatological sign: A sign that points toward the final stage of humanity (*eschaton* = end times) in the total fulfillment of heaven.

in persona Christi: A Latin phrase meaning "in the person of Christ"; it describes the identity and actions of a priest, particularly when he celebrates the sacraments and preaches the Word of God.

Nuns: Contemplative women celibates who live in monasteries, dedicated to a life of prayer for the Church.

Nuptial Meaning of the Body: This is the call that God has stamped into our bodies as male and female to love as He loves, through a sincere and total gift of self.

Ontological: Concerning the very essence or nature of a being. One of the ontological realities about humans is our sexuality. Being a male or female is an essential part of human nature.

Ordinatio Sacerdotalis: An apostolic letter written by John Paul II in 1994 regarding the reservation of the priesthood to men alone.

Religious sisters: Women celibates who generally live in convents and dedicate themselves to active ministry wherever there is a need.

Vocation: A call from God to live a life of holiness in a particular manner and state of life.

OBJECTIVES At the end of this lesson, the student should know and be able to:

- Explain that God has a unique plan for the life of every person.
- Demonstrate an understanding of every human life as being the fruit of a loving act of a generous God.
- Recognize and explain that our purpose in life is to know, love and serve God in a particular vocation: marriage or celibacy.
- Recognize that everyone has a vocation to love and to holiness.
- Recognize that man will only find his life when he learns to give it away in love (GS 24).
- Recognize that living a sacramental life is a key element of knowing God's will and being able to follow it with commitment.
- Recognize and practice various styles of silent and vocal prayer as a way to hear God's voice in our lives
- Recognize biblical characters who heeded God's voice and cite scripture passages that demonstrate examples of these (Moses, Jeremiah, Mary, Peter, Paul, etc)
- Recognize the gifts God has given to us and be able to offer them back to Our Lord as we live out our vocation.
- Demonstrate an understanding of and simple application of five principles for vocational discernment.

Notes & Nuggets: Clarifying the Word 'Vocation' Today, pray for your students as they seek out their vocations. Pray that they will be able to approach God and honestly say in faith, "Here I am Lord, I come to do your will." As you teach today, renew your own commitment to God with the same prayer of surrender. We suggest preparing yourself for this lesson by saying a Glory Be, reminding yourself that your own teaching vocation is all for the greater glory of the Father, Son, and Holy Sprit.

TWO MINUTE DRILL — VERBAL REVIEW:

1. Explain how everyone on earth is called in one way or another to marriage.
   Answer: The ultimate fulfillment of every longing for love is the marriage of Christ and the Church, and everyone–without exception–is invited to this marriage.

2. Define celibacy for the kingdom.
   Answer: Celibacy is a choice to serve God and the Church more fully while choosing to give up earthly marriage in anticipation of the heavenly marriage to come.

3. How does the celibate life foreshadow the Heavenly kingdom for all of us?
   Answer: It points us to the ultimate purpose of our lives: union with God in heaven.

4. Explain why the teaching that only men can be priests is one that, unlike a mere custom, discipline, or tradition, can never change.
   Answer: The Church cannot change the reality that only a man can be a priest just as the Church cannot change the reality that only a woman can become pregnant.
   This reality is due to the very nature of sexual difference.

Finding Your Vocation

In this chapter, you will see that God has a unique plan for your life. You will learn that God not only has a general plan for humanity, but He also has a special invitation—a special calling—to issue to you personally. This calling is your *vocation*, which can be understood on many levels. We will focus on helping you to listen for God's voice, recognize His call, and respond to this call. Prayer is the primary way one discerns a vocation. This lesson will help you realize that God still speaks to each of us today; He did not stop calling people to do His will when the Bible was completed. If you are unsure of what you are to do with the rest of your life, then it's a great day for you. As you stand on the edge of the unknown, this chapter will help you "learn to discern" in which state of life God is calling you to live out your vocation: marriage or celibacy.

ICEBREAKER (optional): "Trust Walk"

[Note: While this activity is commonly used, the experience is a good one that will allow you to make solid foundational points from which to continue your teaching.]

STEP 1: Pair each teen with another person. Have one person from each pair blindfolded ("walkers"). Direct the ones who are not blindfolded ("guides") to follow a preset path that you have mapped out. The teen who is blindfolded cannot grab or touch the person who is their "guide."

STEP 2: The guide is not allowed to physically touch the walker either. The only communication allowed between them can be made through verbal commands, questions and responses. If possible, have your students walk out of the room, out of the building, and around the parking lot, etc., and finally, have them return to the starting location. Be sure to allow enough time for the partners to switch so that each teen can experience both roles.

EXPLANATION: Our fear of trusting another is one of the biggest obstacles stopping us from living in authentic freedom. Often, we lack trust in God and try to do our own thing, hoping that it will make us happy and free. If we are to reach heaven–the home our hearts long for–we must allow God to lead us there.

The following are a few questions that will generate a good discussion about the reason for this activity:

- In this game, did you doubt the ability of the other person to lead you in the correct way?

- How easy would it have been to just sit down or crawl to protect yourself rather than to trust your guide?

- Did you fear the person leading you might play a trick on you?

- Did these or any other fears and emotions prevent you from being led?

- What role do your emotions play in your life? Why is basing decisions primarily on emotions not a wise idea? (We have to guide our emotions and direct our passions, because if we do not, they control us and we lose our freedom.)

CONCLUSION: Part of our study here is trusting God's revelation to us. Jesus said that He is the "way, the truth, and the life." He knows the way and what is true, because He is the Way and He is the Truth. When we are open to His voice and His truth, it is then we learn what it means to be truly free in following God's will. But how will your students know God's voice? The rest of the chapter will help them learn this skill.

Notes & Nuggets: You'll notice in this chapter that we insist everyone has a vocation–a personal call from God. For a long time in the Church, ninety-five percent of the time when someone used the word "vocation" it meant a call to the priesthood or religious life, and there are still pockets in the Church that unfortunately reserve the word "vocation" for clergy alone. But with the fuller understanding of the role of the laity in the Church brought about by the Second Vatican Council, many are growing into a broader understanding and a richer sense of the word "vocation," as we are using it in this curriculum. It cannot be overstated how important it is to help your students understand that everyone has a vocation. But this idea of vocation has at least two specific senses that need to be understood in order to see how it is that we are all called to marriage or celibacy.

The Christian vocation, for everyone, begins with the universal call (vocation) to holiness and the fundamental call to love as God loves. This first sense of the word "vocation," is described succinctly in the following quotes from the Catechism of the Catholic Church:

"God who created man out of love also calls him to love." Love, therefore, is "the fundamental and innate vocation of every human being. For man is created in the image and likeness of God who is himself love" (CCC 1604).

(Continued on next leader's page)

OPENING PRAYER

Leader: In the name of the Father, and of the Son, and of the Holy Spirit. **Amen.**

(Option #1)

Leader or Reader #1: Read Jeremiah 1:5-8

"'Before I formed you in the womb I knew you, and before you were born I consecrated you; I appointed you a prophet to the nations.' Then I said, 'Ah, Lord God! Behold, I do not know how to speak, for I am only a youth.' But the Lord said to me, 'Do not say I am only a youth; for to all to whom I send you you shall go, and whatever I command you you shall speak. Be not afraid of them, or I am with you to deliver you, says the Lord.'"

Leader or Reader #2: Heavenly Father, we thank you for calling each of us by name to love and serve You and our neighbor through the Church family You have given us. Help us to recognize our gifts and to be open to Your will in our lives, no matter what that may be. Help us to hear Your voice of truth so that we can be guiding lights that help others to know and love you. We ask this in the name of your Son, Jesus. **Amen.**

(Option #2)

Leader or Reader #1: Read 1 Samuel 3:1-10 (NAB)

"During the time young Samuel was minister to the LORD under Eli, a revelation of the LORD was uncommon and vision infrequent. One day Eli was asleep in his usual place. His eyes had lately grown so weak that he could not see. The lamp of God was not yet extinguished, and Samuel was sleeping in the temple of the LORD where the ark of God was. The LORD called to Samuel, who answered, 'Here I am.' He ran to Eli and said, 'Here I am. You called me.' 'I did not call you,' Eli said. 'Go back to sleep.' So he went back to sleep. Again the LORD called Samuel, who rose and went to Eli. 'Here I am,' he said. 'You called me.' But he answered, 'I did not call you, my son. Go back to sleep.' At that time Samuel was not familiar with the LORD, because the LORD had not revealed anything to him as yet. The LORD called Samuel again, for the third time. Getting up and going to Eli, he said, 'Here I am. You called me.' Then Eli understood that the LORD was calling the youth. So he said to Samuel, 'Go to sleep, and if you are called, reply, "Speak, LORD, for your servant is listening."' When Samuel went to sleep in his place, the LORD came and revealed his presence, calling out as before, 'Samuel, Samuel!' Samuel answered, 'Speak, for your servant is listening.'"

Leader or Reader #2: Holy Spirit, help us to recognize your voice, whether it is through Scripture, a person, the small voice deep in our heart, or some other way. Help us, like Samuel to be persistent in our efforts to answer Your call. We ask this in the name of Jesus, Our Lord. **Amen.**

Need a Review of Lesson 9? Look to next page.

STORY STARTER:
Shepherds and Lullabies

It was a summer evening, and a young priest friend of mine was spending a few weeks working on an archaeological dig in Israel. Daylight didn't give

"The vocation of humanity is to show forth the image of God and to be transformed into the image of the Father's only Son" (CCC 1877).

"All men are called to the same end: God himself" (CCC 1878).

The "common vocation of all Christ's disciples" is the "vocation to holiness and to the mission of evangelizing the world" (CCC 1533).

As mentioned in Chapter Nine, the word "vocation" comes from the Latin word *vocare*, "to call." Vocation, then, refers to a person's calling in this life and the next. So, in this first and general sense of the word, every human being has the same vocation—to love as God loves so as to live in union with God forever.

Obviously, this universal call is lived out uniquely in each person's life. God, of course, is the One who calls us, inviting us to respond with faith. So, the second sense (the more specific one) of the word "vocation" refers to the free, irrevocable gift of one's whole life either in marriage or in celibacy for the kingdom. Some may wonder how single life fits into this picture of marriage and celibacy. The words "free," "irrevocable," and "whole life" are important here. If one makes a free, irrevocable gift of oneself for the whole of life to remain single (not in the consecrated religious sense) but just to devote him or herself to worthy causes, then we are very close to the word "vocation" in its more specific sense. But if one is single by circumstance and not by choice, and if one would readily abandon being single if the right person came along, this is not a "vocation" but more a "state in life."

In 1981, in the midst of his lectures on the Theology of the Body, Pope John Paul II issued *Familiaris Consortio*, an apostolic exhortation on the role of the Christian family in the modern world. The following selection is a particularly important quote in the conversation regarding single life as a vocation. It is carefully worded, as each word counts:

"Christian revelation recognizes two specific ways of realizing the vocation of the human person, in its entirety, to love: marriage and virginity or celibacy. Either one is in its own proper form an actuation of the most profound truth about man, of his being 'created in the image of God'" (FC, 11).

In the end, "Christian revelation"—what we have in Scripture and Tradition, as interpreted by the Magisterium—recognizes marriage and celibacy as "vocations" in the strict sense of the word.

One of the recurring themes of John Paul II in the Theology of the Body is that we are called to communion and to loving self-donation. Whether the single life is lived in selfish isolation or as a generous, intentional commitment to service and community in the Church is a telling sign of whether it bears a resemblance to the aforementioned "specific way" of life as celibacy for the kingdom. It should be stated that the Church values single life and recognizes the unique contribution that singles can make to the life of the Church. Here are a few more pertinent quotes from the Catechism of the Catholic Church:

(Continued on next leader's page)

to the dark of night until between nine and ten o'clock in the evening. Being unable to sleep well in the sticky heat, Father Harry decided to take a walk. He wandered across the foothills of the mountains within miles of the very spots where God had called Moses, Jeremiah and others in the Old Testament to be leaders and prophets for the Lord.

As he topped a hill, he looked down into a small valley where many shepherds were herding their sheep into a large pen, a plain, rectangular holding area for the animals. As the hundreds of sheep made their way from different areas of the hills into one mass of wool between the walls, Father Harry could not help but wonder how the shepherds would know which sheep belonged to which shepherd. As the shepherds locked the gate and headed off to their homes, Father Harry mentally wrestled to figure out the dilemma. He went back to his own tent to sweat in silence for a few hours before dawn. Still curious, he resolved to return early in the morning to watch the shepherding drama unfold.

The sun had barely risen above the horizon when Father Harry found his perch on the hillside above the sheepfold, waiting with anticipation as the shepherds gathered in front of the main gate to the pen. Suddenly, the gate was opened, and each shepherd began to simultaneously sing and walk away from the pen. The sheep flooded out of the gate and made their way in five or six different directions, forming lines as they followed their respective shepherds. *How did the sheep know which shepherd to follow?*, he thought.

As the sun rose higher into the sky, the answer dawned on him in a profound way. The little balls of wool with feet were trotting after their masters because they *recognized their voices*. In reality, the shepherds had been singing all throughout the day to their sheep, loving them, guiding them, and keeping them familiar with their voices. Father Harry couldn't help but hear Jesus' words echoing in his mind in a new way, "The sheep hear his voice as he calls his own by name and leads them out…the sheep follow him because they recognize his voice…I am the Good Shepherd. I know my sheep and my sheep know me" (Jn 10:3, 4, 14).

– Brian Butler

Verbal Review of Lesson 9

1. Explain how everyone on earth is called in one way or another to marriage.

2. Define celibacy for the kingdom.

3. How does the celibate life foreshadow the heavenly kingdom for all of us?

4. Explain why the teaching that only men can be priests is one that, unlike a mere custom, discipline, or tradition, can never change.

"For I know well the plans I have in mind for you, says the LORD, plans for your welfare, not for woe! plans to give you a future full of hope. When you call me, when you go to pray to me, I will listen to you. When you look for me, you will find me. Yes, when you seek me with all your heart, you will find me with you, says the LORD, and I will change your lot."
(Jer 29:11-14, NAB)

COMPREHENSION & DISCUSSION QUESTIONS

1. How many shepherds can one sheep follow?

2. What happens if we try to follow more than one voice?

3. What can the sheep pen symbolize in our lives?

4. How can we be sure we are following the Good Shepherd, instead of one who may want to hurt us or lead us astray?

Notes & Nuggets (Cont.)

"We must also remember the great number of single persons who, because of the particular circumstances in which they have to live—often not of their choosing—are especially close to Jesus' heart" (CCC 1658).

"Some forego marriage in order to care for their parents or brothers and sisters, to give themselves more completely to a profession, or to serve other honorable ends. They can contribute greatly to the good of the human family" (CCC 2231).

BRIDGING THE GAP

Vocation discernment. These are not two words most teens are "Googling" and Instant Messaging about late at night. Some of you may even think they are intimidating words. But remember what you have learned so far: We are all called to "love and holiness," and this means that we all have a vocation. The word **vocation** comes from the Latin *vocare*, meaning "to call." If we all have a call (which we all do), then we all must figure out what that call from God is.

Palm reading and fortune tellers are not the way to figure out your future. Intense prayer and living a radical life of faith are. (Actually, because of free will and our ability to "change the future" through our choices, it is impossible for a fortune teller to really know anyone's future. No creature, not even the devil himself, knows the future of any human or created being.) Keep reading in order to learn how to hear the voice of The Good Shepherd.

TO THE CORE

In the last two chapters, we discussed the different vocations to which God may call you in order to make a gift of yourself. But how do you know which path God is calling you to follow?

The first step is to learn how to listen to God. We make this normally simple action pretty difficult through our own choices. Here are five reasons it's so hard to hear His voice:

1. **Too Noisy:** We wake up to music, watch television over breakfast, listen to the radio in the car, talk all day, and then go home to the internet, the phone, and more television. None of these things are bad in themselves, but if we could just turn off some of the noise, we would find it easier to be still and quiet in prayer. In the words of Pope John Paul II, "Above all, create silence in your interior. Let that ardent desire to see God arise from the depth of your hearts, a desire that at times is suffocated by the noise of the world and the seduction of pleasures."[1]

2. **Really Busy:** We wait until we have the time to pray, and that time never comes. Like any good relationship, our friendship with God will deepen according to how much effort we put into it. So set a daily prayer time, and stick to it. Morning and night prayers are a good place to start. Set your alarm clock ten minutes early each day, and reserve that time to say some morning prayers, read the Bible and talk with God.

3. **Scared Stiff:** We don't trust God, and we're afraid to hear what He has to say. Maybe He's asking us to let go of something or do something that's really hard—and we don't want to listen.

"When it's God who is speaking... the proper way to behave is to imitate someone who has an irresistible curiosity and who listens at keyholes. You must listen to everything God says at the keyhole of your heart."
– St. John Vianney

4. **Don't Care:** Perhaps we simply don't care what God has to say. A large number of teenagers simply do not think much or care about God for a whole host of reasons. Some are being raised in homes where faith plays little role. Others have been entertained to death with the toys of the world. And others have lived lives of such comfort that they have not felt the need to rely on God.

5. **Blurry Vision:** Our sins make it hard for us to see clearly. When we sin, it's almost as if we place a dirty window between ourselves and God. Each time we turn from Him, we add to the dirt. Before long, we can barely see through it. And very little light comes in to us from the other side. Then, we complain that we don't see God in our lives. Especially when we commit sexual sins, the mind seems to fill up with such worldly thoughts that we are unable to recognize the voice of God. But the Sacrament of Reconciliation serves as a potent cleanser to wash away the dirt and make the panes of the window clear for us to see God.

If we begin to create silence in our lives, make time to pray, trust God, and avoid sin, it will be much easier to listen to what God has to say. Through prayer, we come to know and trust Him. And only if we trust Him will we pay attention enough to know His plan for our lives.

During this time of discernment, it's smart to find a holy priest who can act as your spiritual director. If you're feeling a tug towards the priestly or religious life, don't be afraid to talk to those who have chosen this vocation and ask them how they experienced a call. You could also go on a discernment retreat. By calling your local diocesan vocations office, you should be able to find a good director and retreat.

Doing these things does not mean that you're going to be a priest or nun. It simply means you're open to seeing where God is calling you. After all, you'll have much more peace in a vocation if you have a confident sense that you sincerely explored both primary vocations and finally chose the one that was God's calling for you. In this way, answering your vocation is not like answering a multiple-choice question. Rather than using a "process of elimination" technique, you take knowledge of the different vocations and choose the one that you feel God calling you towards.

As mentioned in Chapter Nine, the normal calling for most people is marriage to an earthly spouse. But how can you know for sure? The answer to this question is a very important as it is connected to another very common question, "How do you know if this person is the *one*?" It is important to remember that you must be called to marriage *before* you are called to marry a *certain person*.

Here is one practical reason for first discerning whether you are called to marriage or celibacy: If you are entertaining marriage to a certain person and that person disappoints you or the relationship does not work out, you may think this is a sign that you were not meant for marriage at all. While there have surely been times that God has worked through breakups to show some-

notes

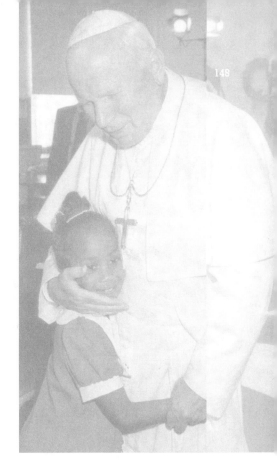

one a call to celibacy, this is not the norm. Thus, praying for God's will as you spend time with people of the opposite sex is the best way to discern marriage. Obviously, spending time around good married couples is also an invaluable way to assist in your discernment. As you get older, spending a weekend with a young couple and their energetic kids is a great way to explore whether you are called to be married. This is sort of like the equivalent to a "come and see" experience for potential seminarians or religious.

Some people do not see themselves in the married or celibate life because they've made some bad choices in the past. But as the saying goes, "God does not call the qualified; he qualifies the called." He can easily make up for our defects. For example, did you know that Moses had a speech impediment? How would you feel if you had that fault, and God said he wanted you to be a prophet? Or, consider St. Paul, who persecuted the followers of Jesus, but was then called by God to be a witness of his love? You may be reluctant, but so were many of the saints. When God asked Jonah to preach in Nineveh (located in modern-day Iraq), Jonah hid himself on a boat and headed towards Spain, hundreds of miles in the opposite direction! We can run all we want, but only in listening and responding to God's voice will we find peace.

The hardest decision is deciding between "two goods" (you know, like deciding between chocolate or vanilla, fries, or onion rings). If you find yourself trying to decide between something good and something evil, this is not the same type of discernment we have discussed thus far. Rather, it is a clear choice for God or against Him. **Moral discernment** and **discernment of God's plan** for our lives are not the same thing. Moral discernment is judging an action, deeming whether or not it is right or wrong. Technically speaking, this process can be an easy one if you want to follow Christ, know what the Church teaches, and have a well-formed conscience.

But when it comes to discerning God's plan for our lives, the process can be quite involved. One main reason is because there are many more decisions (e.g., which college to choose, which friends to hang out with, which doctor to see when one is sick, etc.) to be made than which of the vocations one should pursue. So, how do you know what to do? Here are five steps that can help you to discern God's will in a particular instance:

1. Pray.

It's hard to keep a good friend if you never talk to him or her. Imagine if you kept emailing or text messaging your friend every day and in return that person called you only on Sundays. It wouldn't take long for the relationship to break down. The more time you spend getting to know God through prayer (sacraments, rosary, personal prayer time, etc.), the better you'll be at recognizing His voice in your life.

"The search and discovery of God's will for you is a deep and fascinating endeavor. Every vocation, every path to which Christ calls us, ultimately leads to fulfillment and happiness, because it leads to God, to sharing in God's own life."
– Pope John Paul II

2. Ask yourself if this decision is in line with God's teaching.

God promised that his Church would be "the pillar and foundation of truth" (1 Tim 3:15), and that whoever heard it, would be hearing him (Lk 10:16). Even if there are scandals and hypocrites in the Church, God still promised that He would be faithful in preserving it. So, if our decision goes against what the Catholic Church teaches, either explicitly in Tradition or in the Bible, we can rest assured that it is not God's will. God can and does bring good out of evil. But this never means we should choose evil so that good results.

3. Get advice.

If you're struggling with a decision, ask your spiritual director, priest, or some other people who are strong in the faith for advice. Ask them what they think about a decision you are facing. Ask them to pray that God would make His will clearly known to you. You could also ask the saints to intercede for you. Consider going straight to Jesus in Eucharistic Adoration a few minutes each day or each week until a peaceful decision is reached.

4. Go to reconciliation.

It may sound odd, but the sacrament of Reconciliation (a.k.a. confession) can improve your hearing. When we sin, it's like bringing a bunch of static into a phone conversation, making it very difficult to hear the voice of God. Making an act of humility and contrition not only cleanses our souls, but our spiritual hearing as well.

5. Listen to your heart.

God often speaks to us through our conscience and our intuition. If we have peace about one choice and great anxiety about another, it may be an indication of which decision should be made. If you are really confused, do not make any big decisions until the confusion clears up. Remember not to base serious decisions on feelings. "Feelings" or emotions are different from "listening to your heart." Feelings are often fleeting whereas one's gut instinct is more rooted in one's conscience. That said, we recommend you join this type of discernment (one's own gut instinct) with one or more of the other recommendations above.

Thankfully, there are times when God's will is obvious. For example, you applied to two different colleges. You received an acceptance letter from one and were not accepted to the other school. Or maybe you were discerning whether or not to break up with your boyfriend, and he broke up with you first. It's much more likely that it is God's will that you go to the college that accepted you and you not continue to pursue the person who just broke up with you. In most cases, God works through the everyday people and events of life.

"Confidently open your most intimate aspirations to the love of Christ who waits for you in the Eucharist. You will receive the answer to all your worries and you will see with joy that the consistency of your life which he asks of you is the door to fulfill the noblest dreams of your youth."
– Pope John Paul II

During a time of discernment, remember to be patient. At times, God does not want you to know His will as it relates to your future. That may sound strange, but we often best grow in faith and trust in those times when He seems silent. His will is your holiness, and trusting in Him during times of uncertainty may be all He is calling you to do right now. Meanwhile, start now by praying one Hail Mary each day for the discernment of your vocation. In the words of Pope John Paul II, "My desire is for the young people of the entire world to come closer to Mary. She is the bearer of an indelible youthfulness and beauty that never wanes. May young people have increasing confidence in her and may they entrust the life just opening before them to her."[2]

No matter what one's vocation is, we are all called to a life of holiness. Your life is not an accident. God has created you for a reason. The ultimate reason for His creating you is to share his own eternal bliss with you in heaven, but there are plenty of things He has in mind for you in the meantime. He simply waits for you to say yes. He waited for the Blessed Virgin Mary to say yes to Him, just as He waited for Pope John Paul II's response. Even Christ Himself had to say yes. It's hard to imagine the world today if any of them had said no. When we say "yes" to God, it begins the chain of events that leads to God's perfect plan unfolding in our lives. If you doubt that such a hopeful future awaits you, take a moment to read the words of Sirach, "Study the generations long past and understand; has anyone hoped in the Lord and been disappointed?" (Sir 2:10).

DIGGING DEEPER:
Testimonies from the Front Lines

One Religious Sister's Vocational Discernment Testimony

I never wanted to be a sister. I am not a sister because I thought it was a good idea or something I would be particularly good at, or because I just couldn't wait to pray or go to Church or serve the poor. I am a sister for one reason only, because God invited me to be His bride.

Growing up, I wanted to do a million things, all of them big. I wanted to be a dancer, an actor, a doctor, an astronaut; you name it. And I wanted to do everything in a grand manner. Being a religious sister or nun was not on my list. I also really wanted to be married and have children and love them as much as I could. So what happened? God showed up.

In college, I made the most important decision of my life. I decided to take a risk on God. I dared to hope in God. I dared to believe that God was real, that He loved me and that He had a plan for me to be the greatest person I could be. More than anything else in the world, I wanted to be loved and cherished by someone and to love that someone with my whole heart. I decided to see if

"A discovery of the importance of silence is one of the secrets of practicing contemplation and meditation. One drawback of a society dominated by technology and the mass media is the fact that silence becomes increasingly difficult to achieve."
– Pope John Paul II[1]

God could be the subject of my exclusive love. When I first felt God asking me to be His bride by becoming a religious sister, I was afraid that life would be boring and dull. I even cried at the prospect of being called to this life.

I soon realized I was acting like a fool. I had just spent several years discovering how awesome God is. He was bigger than I ever imagined. And there I was wondering if the God of the universe would fall short of my expectations (and at the same time thinking some regular guy would meet those same expectations). So, with all my courage I said "Yes" to God's invitation to be His bride. It's not always fun and glamorous, but it is truly an awesome life.

– **Sister Chiara Land** *(Franciscan Sisters, T.O.R. of Penance of the Sorrowful Mother)*

One Seminarian's Journey

No flash of light. No heavenly vision. No booming voice. God's call came to me gently and quietly. In fact, the way He "spoke" was really quite ordinary. He spoke through simple thoughts that peacefully slipped into my mind. I might have just dismissed them as coming from myself but somehow I knew they weren't from me. I can't explain exactly how I knew. I just knew.

It happened when I was a sophomore in college. For about a year I had been thinking about the priesthood *and* about getting married. There were times when the priesthood was an attractive idea, but then one of the beauties on campus would walk by, I'd say to myself, "Priesthood? What was I thinking?!"

One day during these times of indecision, I went into the campus chapel to pray. As usual, it was quiet. I looked up at the big crucifix above the altar; Jesus seemed sad. Gazing on Him, I began to feel especially loved by Him. Then, very gently, some thoughts came.

Although what I'm about to describe may seem extraordinary, it didn't seem so at the time. In fact, if I hadn't reflected on the experience afterwards, I might have forgotten it altogether. I know it sounds weird, but over and over this has been my experience of prayer.

The gentle thoughts went something like this: "Michael, I'd like you to make a choice. You are free to get married. And if you choose that path, you will be happy. I will still love you. But I want you to be a priest. *Will you quench my thirst for souls?*"

After these thoughts, the memory of so many blessings in my life flooded into my mind. I said to myself, "I can't say no! How can I say no when he's given me so much?" It was a "no brainer." I was at peace. I would choose the priesthood.

Shortly after this peaceful time of prayer, I became distressed. The priesthood

began to appear as such a miserable life. So many sacrifices. Such stark loneliness. Such daunting responsibility. But something called me back to the memory of the Lord's gentleness and especially of his thirst for souls. While reflecting on that thirst, a few thoughts gently slipped into my mind.

The thoughts made me understand that Jesus' plea, *"Will you quench my thirst for souls?"* was not primarily about vast multitudes of people. Rather, it was about me: "Michael, will you quench my thirst for souls…by giving me your soul?" He wasn't just looking for another worker; he was thirsting for a friend. That's when it all made sense: he thirsting for me, me thirsting for him, then together thirsting and laboring for souls. The priesthood began to appear as a beautiful, intimate, joyful life.

Some time later, I was in St. Peter's Basilica for the Easter Vigil Mass. Although I was far from the front of the Church, I had an aisle seat. The lights were dimmed. Then, Pope John Paul II came walking in from the back of the Basilica. He paused every ten yards or so to pray and then would continue walking. One of his stops was right in front of me. From my heart, I "spoke" to him interiorly: "Holy Father, I want to be a priest like you. I want to pour myself out completely."

As soon as I finished, he lifted his bowed head and opened his eyes. He looked right at me. His look seemed to say (pretty clearly): "This is serious, Michael. You have to be quite serious about it." This look took me by surprise, but I gathered myself and, as the Pope was bowing his head again and closing his eyes, I firmly repeated what I had "spoken" before. As soon as I finished, the Pope opened his eyes, raised his head, and again looked directly at me. This time his look seemed to say, "Alright, then."

– **Michael Gaitley** *(Seminarian)*

Called to Marriage

You may have heard this story told before. One day at a store, amidst a pile of trinkets, a little girl named Anne saw the most beautiful thing she had ever seen and snatched it up. In her hand, she tightly clenched a plastic box containing a white "pearl" necklace made of plastic. "Mom, can I please buy this?" she pleaded. "You don't need that," replied her mother, "you have plenty of dress ups." But Anne was persistent. After much debate, her mother struck a deal. "Save your money, and I will bring you back to buy it yourself." Anne agreed.

Anne saved every penny she could. She begged for change from her Dad's pockets, searched under pillows and cushions and did small favors for her Mom. Finally, she had enough money for the necklace. At the store, right before the final purchase, her mother asked, "Are you sure you don't want to wait and save for a real pearl necklace?" Anne laughed and replied, "What's the difference, Mom? They look the same, and I can have this one now!"

Anne wore her necklace everywhere. She slept in it, showered in it, and played in it. One evening, when visiting her father, he tucked her into bed and asked, "Anne, do you love me?"

"Yes, Daddy, you know that I love you!" she replied.

"Can I have your necklace?" he asked.

Shocked, she replied, "Daddy, I love you very much, and I would do anything for you, but please, don't ask for my necklace. It is my favorite thing in the whole world!"

"Very well," her father replied, "I love you." And with that he kissed her and said goodnight.

Weeks passed and Anne's father repeated his question, as he tucked her into bed. Frustrated, she replied "Daddy, I told you that I can't do that. I do love you but this necklace is too important to me because I saved so much for it!"

"Very well," her father replied. "Good night. I love you."

Again, weeks went by, and it was time for Anne to be with her father. He came into her room to tuck her into bed and was surprised to see Anne crying with her necklace in her hands.

"Anne, what's wrong?" he asked.

Anne sniffled and said, "Daddy, I love this necklace so much, but I love you more than anything. I want you to have it."

Anne's hands trembled as she gave the necklace to her Father. He embraced her with a smile, saying "Thank you so much." Then, he reached into his pocket and pulled out a black velvet box and opened it. Inside was a beautiful, real pearl necklace. "I have been waiting to give this to you. But I couldn't give it to you until you were ready to give the fake necklace up." Anne cried but this time tears of joy. She never knew someone could love her so much!

In my dating experience, I was a lot like Anne. I was so influenced by the world's cheap idea of love that I became impatient. I dated to feel loved, to fill the emptiness that was left from hurt, and I hoped to find a fairytale life. Yet when I dated, I had a difficult time letting God be in charge. How could I trust him? I had witnessed too much pain in broken relationships.

In high school, I traded my values and morals away with the consolation that, as I gave myself away piece by piece, I would gain a lasting love that would never fail. My plan failed every time, since people can't give one another all the love they truly need; only God can. But the world is so focused on getting a bargain. Rather than wait for my pearl necklace, I settled for the plastic version for many years. I saved up plenty for this necklace, but then quickly traded it for the emptiness of a worthless object that appeared to be so much more than it really was.

notes

_____

_____

_____

_____

_____

_____

_____

_____

_____

_____

_____

_____

_____

_____

_____

_____

_____

After years of living in the world of plastic pearls, I found myself longing to escape. So I left everything I knew to live in a new place. I also prayed a new prayer to God. Rather than striking a bargain with Him, I said, "Lord, I am yours; do with me as you will. I am tired of trying to make love work. Please fill me and lead me, heal me and teach me. Jesus, I trust in you." As I prayed that prayer, it hurt to know that I could no longer cling to my plastic pearls. But I surrendered to the Lord and waited for the real thing.

Soon after, I met a wonderful young man who was seeking the Lord as I was. We became good friends and discerned that the Lord was calling us to date. This relationship was very different from the ones of my past. We were committed to keeping God as our center. We lifted one another up to God, instead of trying to fill one another with ourselves. Time flew by, and before you knew it, I was standing in my mother's living room all dressed in white. I truly felt like a new creation.

As I waited to go to the church where I would become one in marriage with this man God had hand-picked for me, my mother approached me with a black velvet box. I opened it and inside was a beautiful *real pearl* necklace. As she placed the necklace around my neck, I cried and so did she. This was more than just a pearl necklace. It was the fulfillment of God's promise. The necklace represented the true love that God was giving to me and my husband to share in our life together. As I reflect on my marriage, I am filled with the joy of knowing that every person's love story (and discernment of it) is in good hands with God. Let the Creator of the pearl present you with the true "pearl of great price."

Kelley Brown

– Kelley Brown *(Wife and Mother)*

notes

_____

_____

_____

_____

_____

_____

_____

_____

_____

_____

_____

_____

_____

APPLICATION

Go to Eucharistic Adoration

Take your students to an Adoration chapel at your school or a nearby church. First, set the mood: Dim the lights, and if possible, light a few candles. If you are a musician, play quiet worship music. If not, consider using an instrumental worship CD. Many students may never have been to Eucharistic Adoration before and most will be uncomfortable with the complete silence. Interspersing silence with music is a good way to get them accustomed to the new atmosphere of prayer.

Teens may have trouble sitting still if they are too close together, so have them spread out while remaining as close to the front of the chapel as possible. Guide them by making suggestions for silent prayer or reflection. Before you even enter the chapel, remind them of the proper protocol in the chapel (silence, genuflecting, etc.). Remind them that Jesus is truly present in the Eucharist. Tell them to be real with Jesus, to dialog with Him, and even to bring to Him any doubts or fears they may have. Begin the Adoration time with a prayer encouraging them to be open, so they might hear God's voice. At the end of the designated time, close with a prayer thanking Jesus for His presence in the Eucharist and for the work He began today in the hearts within the chapel.

MOVIE CLIP/SONG SUGGESTIONS

MOVIE CLIPS:

1. *The Return of the King:* Show the segment that falls between 1:39:29 and 1:42:24. [Note: This time code is from the extended version.] This is the scene with Aragorn, the heir to the throne of Gondor. Lord Elronde says to him, "Become who you were born to be."

2. *Spiderman:* Show the segment that falls between 1:50:26 and 1:55:13. We see Spiderman sacrificing for his vocation. This scene contains the famous line, "With great power, comes great responsibility."

3. *Keeping the Faith:* Show the segment that falls between 8:15 and 13:40. This scene depicts two childhood friends, one who grows up to be a priest and the other, a rabbi. It portrays how each of their calls was different, yet important.

4. *Batman Begins:* Show the segment that falls between 3:40 and 5:49, 32:09 to 35:50, and then 35:58 to 38:44. Each of these segments show Bruce Wayne searching and discerning his call.

5. *Rounders:* Show the segment that falls between 46:14 and 51:38. Martin Landau, who plays a judge, talks to Matt Damon, who plays a law student, about rejecting his parent's idea that he should become a rabbi.

6. *Therese:* Show the segment that falls between 31:20 and 36:43. Therese learns she has a great desire to reach souls for God and a calling to pray for sinners. Her intercessory prayer helps convert a murderer before his execution.

SONGS:

1. *My Desire* — Jeremy Camp *(Restored)*

This is the prayer of someone desiring to be holy again, returning to do God's will. It is an anthem of commitment, of allowing the Lord to use us as he sees fit. The song's style and volume move from acoustic and reflective to a strong, full-throated sound that resembles the total commitment of the lyrics. Contemporary Praise & Worship.

2. *By Name I Call You* — John Angotti *(Common Ground)*

God has not set us upon earth without a mission and without a clue; He has a call for each of us—a personal call. He calls each of us intimately by name. Piano/Ballad.

3. *Open My Eyes* — Jesse Manibusan *(Power of Peace)*

A gentle request for the Lord to help us see, hear and love like Him. Acoustic Worship.

4. *I Turn Everything Over* — Switchfoot *(New Way to Be Human)*

Once we turn our lives over to God we often wonder about the plan He gives us. Pop/Rock.

5. *Take Me* — Hawk Nelson *(Letters to the President: Expanded Version)*

God takes us under His wing and He will guide us in the lost times. Punk/Ballad.

6. *Run* — Kutless *(self-titled)*

Why do you run? Why do you hide? He just wants to be with you. Rock/Ballad.

"Applying to seminary doesn't mean you will become a priest any more than applying for medical school means you'll become a doctor. And *going* to seminary is just like dating. Of course, there are fewer girls and you won't spend nearly as much money."

My priest uttered these words to me and my friend, Pete, during my junior year in high school. He was trying to reassure us that discerning priesthood did not automatically mean that we would be ordained priests. Discernment is not about "you *choosing* God." It's about figuring out if God is choosing *you* for a specific vocation. The priest's words to us were true and today, several years later, I call my friend, Father Pete. Father Pete, in turn, baptized my wife's and my second child.

God already has a vocation in mind for you. The rest is a question of whether or not you will seek his plan and make it your own. Most of you can't go off to seminary or a convent tomorrow because of your state in life—you have to finish high school, for example. In fact, you're not even necessarily called to decide today what vocation God is calling you to. You *can*, however, be more authentic with yourself in regards to your talents and passions. You can also begin taking daily steps to put yourself in a better position, an environment more conducive to really *hearing* the call of your Creator. In addition to the points made in the main part of the chapter, here are a *few* more concrete tips to help you discern God's will:

1. **Make a list.** Take out a piece of paper and make a list of your talents and your passions. Put "Talents" on one side of the page, draw a line and write "Passions" on the other side (or use the worksheet on p. 198). Why the distinction? Because there might be things that you are passionate about that you don't necessarily think you are good at (i.e. painting, music, writing, speaking) but that God can and will use. Additionally, there might be things you are good at (i.e. math, science, speaking) that you don't always like to do, but that God can and will use to build the Kingdom. If your list of passions is twice as long as your talent list, you're probably being too hard on yourself or not looking deeply enough for your talents. God has graced you with talents; it's time to unearth them. Ask others for their thoughts on what your talents include. You might be surprised that people see things in you, put there by God, that you fail to see yourself.

2. **Spend time with priests and religious.** Nothing will open your eyes to "the real world" like seeing what a parish priest or a religious sister actually *does* when they're not at Mass or working at a church or school. You'll be amazed at how *full* their lives really are and how beautiful a life of service in this way can be. It will go a long way in dismantling any misconceptions you might have about Holy Orders and/or religious life.

3. **Dream big.** This might not sound practical, but it can be. Take another sheet of paper and dream of all the ways you could "bless God" or "lead others to Him" if money were not a problem and if others were to join you in working to achieve your goal. Dream of things that might seem totally crazy at first. God gave you your imagination. Give it back to Him. You will be amazed at how creative you will be when your imagination is directed back to God. Remember, money and the support of others should not be obstacles to your thinking. If God wants it, it will happen because "all things are possible with God" (Lk 1:37).

4. **Spend time with holy married couples (other than your parents).** Find a couple or two who really exemplify a holy marriage. If they have children, spend time watching how they interact with each other. You will see the reality of married life and this will go a long way in helping you in your discernment.

– **Mark Hart**

Notes & Nuggets: As an example of project #2, here is a very short version of a possible story:

Amy's Life: "Amy was the best violinist at her high school and she went on scholarship to Notre Dame. Once there, she met Mark her junior year and they dated for a while. But then she felt a call to become a religious sister, so she talked with Mark about it. After praying for another month, Amy decided not to continue the relationship until she could better discern if she should enter the convent.

Amy went to Mass every Sunday and sometimes on Friday as well. Upon graduation, she was offered to play first chair violin for the Boston Pops Orchestra, but a tug on her heart led her to make a retreat with the Sisters of the Holy Family. After discussing with her parents and praying hard and often, she developed a real sense of peace about the call to the religious life. Instead of putting down her violin, she took it with her, where she became a novice with the sisters and a teacher of music at their local elementary school......"

—OR—

"After her retreat, she was still feeling uneasy and missed Mark terribly. She spoke with one of the sisters who told her that God would give her peace if she was to become a nun. But no peace came. She got frustrated and went late night to an Adoration chapel she rarely visited, asking God to make His will for her clear. Just then, Mark walked into the same chapel, and Amy's heart was filled with peace and love. She finally knew she was called to marriage..."

Notes & Nuggets: For Project #3, using "Amy's Life" as an example, the student would take pictures of Amy wearing a Notre Dame hat, playing violin, walking hand in hand with Mark, praying at the convent, etc. This is how one could visually tell the story.

Notes and Nuggets: In the closing prayer, we ask the intercession of St. John Vianney. Vianney was born in 1786 in France. Once hearing his call to the priesthood, he entered the seminary and struggled greatly through his studies, so much so that his formation directors and even his bishop were unsure that he would be a good priest. Still, he persisted in answering the call to the priesthood. Finally, he became a priest in 1815. His bishop assigned him to the small town of Ars in an effort to keep him out of the way. But Vianney would soon have great crowds coming to see him. He was a simple man with extraordinary holiness, touching his parishioners in many ways, always giving of himself to those in spiritual need. He often heard confessions all day long as people came from all over the world to see him. Many people said that Vianney could read their souls, often making their own sins known to them. In the end, St. John Vianney became widely known as a great spiritual mystic. Today, he is also known as the patron saint of parish priests.

WORK IT OUT

Assignment #1: Create a Top Ten list of common myths about the religious life. After you are finished, call or visit a priest or nun and show them the list. Let this person give his or her opinion of the accuracy of your list. Summarize his or her comments in a short paper.

Assignment #2: Write out the article that you would want to appear in the newspaper on the day that you die. Although this sounds a bit morbid at first, it can actually be an eye-opening exercise. Write an "article" that basically describes your life, the kind of person you were, the kind of life you led, and the lives that you touched. If you are honest, it will go a long way in revealing to you what you believe is most important in life and what treasures (see Mt 6:21) direct your discernment, prayer, and future.

Assignment #3: Write a letter to God about your call to your vocation. Ask Him any questions you have. Discuss with Him what you think He may be calling you to and why. Finish with a prayer asking God to help you be open to whatever His call for you may be.

Assignment #4: Write an essay about discernment of some situation in your life that is now in the past. Now that you know more about the discernment process, revisit that situation and analyze whether or not you made a good discernment. If you made good discernment, point out the specific reasons why this was the case. Conversely, if you did not make good discernment, point out specific ways in which you could have arrived at a better decision.

Project #1: Make a short promotional video or other multimedia presentation (PowerPoint, etc.). Promote marriage, priesthood, or religious life. Make your video appealing to teenagers and incorporate interviews with married couples, priests, or religious in your area, including their own views on their respective callings.

Project #2: Write a short story or a skit of discernment. Use your creativity to create a modern day story that shows the difficulty, joys and humor of the discernment process.

Project #3: Create a visual story of discernment. To do this, you could create a presentation (possibly a PowerPoint, Flash presentation, video, or slide show), perhaps complimented by an appropriate song that you could use as the "soundtrack." Create a fictional story of someone making mature discernment by simply using visual images and maybe a few captions. Take photos, create computer images, or draw a number of pictures. Create a presentation that clearly shows your main character at peace after completing a good discernment process. You could create a flip chart, comic strip, or some other art form of choice to tell the story.

CLOSING PRAYER

Leader: In the name of the Father, and of the Son, and of the Holy Spirit. **Amen.**

All: **St. John Vianney**, please pray with me that I, like you, would have the courage to take an honest look at God's plan for my life, opening myself up to all that God wants to do within me and through me. **Amen.**

IN HIS OWN WORDS

- **On Vocation to Love:** "Love is the fundamental and innate vocation of every human being" (*Familiaris Consortio*, 11).

- **On Vocation to Purity:** "According to the evangelical doctrine, developed in such a stupendous way in Paul's letters, purity is not just temperance or abstention from unchastity (see 1 Thess 4:3). At the same time, it also opens the way to a more and more perfect discovery of the dignity of the human body"(April 1, 1981).

- **On Vocation to Service:** "Dear young people, I hope you can know how to listen to the voice of God calling you to service. This is the road that opens up to so many forms of ministry for the benefit of the community: from the ordained ministry to various other instituted and recognized ministries, such as Catechesis, liturgical animation, education of young people and the various expressions of charity (see *Novo millennio ineunte*, 46). At the conclusion of the Great Jubilee, I reminded you that this is 'the time for a new "creativity" in charity' (ibidem, 50). Young people, in a special way it is up to you to ensure that charity finds expression, in all its spiritual and apostolic richness."(Message for 40th World Day of Prayer for Vocations, May 11, 2003)

- **On Why He Became a Priest:**"I am often asked, especially by young people, why I became a priest....at a certain point in my life, I become convinced that Christ was saying to me what he had said to thousands before me: 'Come, follow me!' There was a clear sense that what I heard in my heart was no human voice, nor was it just an idea of my own. Christ was calling me to serve him as a priest. And you can probably tell that I am deeply grateful to God for my vocation to the priesthood. Nothing means more to me or gives me greater joy than to celebrate Mass each day and to serve God's people in the Church. That has been true ever since the day of my ordination as a priest. Nothing has ever changed this, not even becoming Pope!" (Los Angeles, USA, September 14, 1987, as quoted in *The Meaning of Vocation*, p. 29)

Glossary
of Key Terms

Church discipline: A practice or norm instituted by the Church that should be followed but which could be changed by the Church in the future. Examples include abstaining from meat on Fridays, needing to be 16 years old to be a Confirmation sponsor, and priestly celibacy.

Discernment of God's plan: Listening for the voice of God through prayer and the counsel of others in an effort to discover His desire for our lives.

Moral discernment: Judging whether an action is right or wrong, based upon the truths that God has revealed to us.

Vocation: From the Latin *vocare* (to call), this is the call that God speaks to each of us, asking us to live for Him and love Him in a particular way in a particular state of life (e.g., a man who is called to marry, become a doctor, and to write in medical journals about the truth and sacredness of life at conception.)

OBJECTIVES At the end of this lesson, the student should know and be able to:

- Define the purpose of dating.
- Explain the value of building dating relationships on authentic friendship and seeing others as brothers and sisters in Christ.
- Point out why the modern dating "norm" hurts, rather than helps, one's chances of entering a happy and faithful marriage.
- Differentiate between healthy and unhealthy dating.
- Differentiate between dating and courting.
- List a number of ways to avoid getting into situations that would compromise a life of purity.
- Demonstrate that the gift of sex is valuable and worth protecting.
- Explain the difference between being prudent and being prudish with sexuality.
- List practical ways of staying pure while living a radical life for Christ and discerning a vocation to marriage or celibacy.

Notes & Nuggets: Pray for purity for your students today. Ask that Christ would redeem their minds and hearts, and that they would be transformed through His grace to desire more from their relationships—to desire faithful and lasting love.

Chapter Eleven

Dating with Purpose and Purity

In order to date with *purpose* and *purity* you must understand yourself and your desires—not only how to control them, but how to direct them toward the true, good, and beautiful. Dating may be fun, but its purpose is much deeper: to find a spouse. Granted, this is not what you think of when you give out your phone number, but without a clear dating plan that has purpose and boundaries, your dating life will likely result in serious heartbreaks and possibly more. With God at the center of your life, you can channel your desire for love into positive choices that respect yourself and members of the opposite sex.

Finding happiness through purity is not about merely saying "No" to sexual activity, but rather saying "Yes" to love and to the responsibility that comes with spending quality time with others. It's about loving each other as a brother and sister in Christ before getting into a serious dating relationship. Through a life of chastity and authentic love, not only can you enjoy good relationships that are pure, but also set yourself up for a future of happiness and romance without regret.

Notes & Nuggets: For "Prayer Option #2" below, you can make this a community prayer effort by asking the teens to read it as a group, with each student solemnly speaking just one word of the verse as they "read and pray" it as a community. This exercise works best if they sit in a circle or in rows. There are twenty-seven words in the verse in this version from the New American Bible. Adjust this procedure if you have significantly more than twenty-seven students.

ICEBREAKER (OPTIONAL): "Two Truths and a Lie"

The object is for the students (or a few selected students, if you are pressed for time) to share two truths and a lie about themselves. Start the fun off by sharing two truths and a lie about yourself. Make sure your example is a good one, where you really try to fake out the teens. After a given person shares his or her three "facts," others in the class should try to guess which statement is the lie. Upon finishing with the last student, ask the class to share some common denominators that surfaced throughout the process of watching others tell truths and lies. What things did many have in common as they told the truth? What about when they lied?

CONCLUSION: Make the point that unless we are honest in our dating relationships—about our intentions, our motivations, our beliefs, etc.—we are setting up ourselves and others for disappointment and failure. You can also make the point that a huge portion of relationships revolve around communication. Explain that if we don't practice telling the truth and listening to the truth, then we may end up unable to spot a lie when we see one. This inability to recognize lies could land us in dead-end relationships that, instead of helping us learn to love, become stumbling blocks on our path of purity and bad experiences that haunt us later in life.

Note: Be sure to tell your teens that this is not intended as an opportunity to share deep or dark secrets about themselves, especially if you are working with a large group. It is better that they use simple but unusual facts about themselves as the material for this activity.

OPENING PRAYER

Leader: In the name of the Father, and of the Son, and of the Holy Spirit. **Amen.**

(Option #1)

Leader or Reader #1: Sirach 2:1–6, 10, 11

"…if you come forward to serve the Lord, prepare yourself for temptation. Set your heart right and be steadfast, and do not be hasty in time of calamity. Cleave to him and do not depart, that you may be honored at the end of your life. Accept whatever is brought upon you, and in changes that humble you be patient. For gold is tested in the fire, and acceptable men in the furnace of humiliation. Trust in him, and he will help you; make your ways straight, and hope in him. . . . Consider the ancient generations and see: who ever trusted in the Lord and was put to shame? . . . For the Lord is compassionate and merciful."

Leader or Reader #2: Mother Mary, as we rise to the challenge to live purely, we ask you to lead us to your Son Jesus and pray that we may live purely like you. As your children seeking guidance and strength, we together pray the words of the *Memorare*: Remember, O most gracious Virgin Mary, that never was it known that any one who fled to your protection, implored your help, or sought your intercession was left unaided. Inspired by this confidence, I fly unto you, O Virgin of virgins, my Mother; to you I come, before you I stand, sinful and sorrowful; O Mother of the Word Incarnate, despise not my petitions, but in your mercy hear and answer me. **Amen.**

(Option #2)

Leader or Reader #1: Read John 3:16

"For God so loved the world that he gave his only Son, so that everyone who believes in him might not perish but might have eternal life" (Jn 3:16, NAB).

Leader or Reader #2: Lord, help us to listen to Your Word and to learn to love like You. Together as brothers and sisters in the family of God, let us pray in the way Jesus taught us to address our Heavenly Father:

Our Father, who art in heaven, hallowed be Thy name. Thy kingdom come. Thy will be done, on earth as it is in heaven. Give us this day our daily bread, and forgive us our trespasses, as we forgive those who trespass against us. And lead us not into temptation, but deliver us from evil. **Amen.**

Need a Review of Lesson 10? Look to next page.

TWO MINUTE DRILL — VERBAL REVIEW:

1. Name five problems that may keep us from hearing God.
Answer: It's too noisy; we're really busy; we're scared; we have blurry vision because of sin; or we just don't care.

2. "God does not call the qualified; He qualifies the called." Name two people from the Bible who exemplify this statement.
Answer: Jonah, St. Paul, Moses, and Peter, among others

3. What is moral discernment? How does it differ from discernment of God's plan for one's life?
Answer: Moral discernment is judging an action as to whether it is right or wrong. Discerning God's plan involves listening for the voice of God through prayer and the counsel of others in an effort to discover His desire for our lives.

4. Explain why the teaching that only men can be priests is a teaching that can never change.
Answer: The Church cannot change this teaching because it is a divine law instituted by Christ.

STORY STARTER:
Friends and Bodyguards

"Mom, where are the towels?!" I screamed. I was a little kid, standing naked in the front doorway of our house. I couldn't find a towel after taking a bath in the afternoon. Why I was taking a bath in the afternoon I cannot remember, but what I will *never* forget was hearing shrieks of laughter as I stood drip-drying in the doorway. I snapped my head around toward the neighbor's house and there, fifty feet away on our swing-set, was my best friend, Kimberly, along with her little sister and two of my guy friends from down the street. I froze, looked at myself, and spun around back into the safety of the house, slamming the door and shutting out the continuous laughter in my back yard.

There I had stood, naked, vulnerable (in all my seven-year-old glory), and totally embarrassed. I tried to forget about it. The next day, the same group of peers was together, and my sarcastic friend, Andy (who was two years older than I) immediately teased me, "So, uh, Brian … did you ever find a towel?" he laughed. "I mean, you must have been cold, huh?!" Kimberly blushed and looked at the ground. I shot Andy a look that I didn't know I had in me. I stepped forward a bit and narrowed my eyes. He heard me loud and clear. No one ever brought up that day again, including me.

Kimberly was the cute girl-next-door whose bright smile, blonde pig-tails, soft blue eyes, and adventuresome spirit made her very easy to like. Kimberly and I had a special friendship that was different than all others. I had other healthy friendships with guys, but this was different. We shared something special and unique until we were ten years old. That's when her dad announced that their family was moving out of state. I was crushed.

I prayed hard that I would not lose her friendship, and though we wrote letters for a few years, things just weren't the same. That's until *my* family moved on my thirteenth birthday to the same city where she lived!

When we arrived and Kimberly and I reunited, things were different. We were both going through puberty, but she being taller than I was only one of numerous differences. (We guys can't stand that girls often hit their growth spurts first.) In the next year, I quickly discovered that I was attracted to Kimberly as never before.

The beauty of the relationship was that we talked about anything and everything, knowing that we were safe in our friendship. She was blossoming into a beautiful young woman, and while she trusted me completely, the line was clear to her that we were only friends. That line was getting blurry for me, however.

As we moved into ninth grade, our friendship grew stronger and richer, and I knew we had to have *the talk*. One night, as we sat on the sidewalk beneath a lamppost outside her house, I asked her out. She raised her eyebrows. "You mean, like girlfriend-boyfriend stuff?"

Verbal Review
of Lesson 10

1. Name five problems that may keep us from hearing God.

2. "God does not call the qualified; He qualifies the called." Name two people from the Bible who exemplify this statement.

3. What is moral discernment? How does it differ from discernment of God's plan for one's life?

4. Explain why the teaching that only men can be priests is a teaching that can never change.

162

"Yeah, I mean, we're such awesome friends" I explained, "Wouldn't that be cool?" Kimberly blushed and looked at the ground, fidgeting with a stick or something in silence.

This is good, I thought. *At least she's not running away screaming*. I got up and shuffled around with hands in my pockets, awaiting her answer. Finally, after what felt like hours, she gave her thoughtful response.

"I don't want to lose our friendship," she told me as she turned her soft blue eyes upward toward mine. I huffed in response and sat down to listen. She flashed her smile (which stole my heart) and explained that she cared for me more than that. In her mind, boyfriends came and went, but friends were forever. I wasn't ready to let it go that quickly, so we argued about it for a while. I gave her plenty of reasons it could work, but she held her ground, all the while subtly teaching me how to respect a woman: Be her friend, treasure her, respect her, protect her, love her like a sister.

So, I honored her wishes and became the best friend that I could. I spent plenty of time with her, and we loved each other as friends. She tuned into what was important to me and often asked me about those things. I did chores around her house with her and helped her family members with their paper route each week. We played board games, went to the movies, and even went to Mass together sometimes. She played the piano for me and I played the guitar for her. We helped each other with homework and other school projects, and hung out with our friends together and separately as our friendship grew and matured. Though it did feel odd at times when we dated other people, it was a friendship that brought us both security and freedom as we learned how to love.

Now some people believe that guys and girls can't stay *only* friends, but that's just not true. Kimberly and I remained friends throughout high school and college, hurting together when the other was hurt and celebrating our victories together as well. I learned more about girls from her than from anyone else, and I taught her a lot about guys, too. We both got married to wonderful spouses, and we both now have children of our own.

Today, I am so grateful that Kimberly had the wisdom to see into the future. I treasure her friendship and all that I learned from her over the years. I am also grateful that she cared for me in two of my most vulnerable moments: when I was stark naked before her in the doorway as a boy, and emotionally naked before her as a young teen. She quietly loved me more than any girlfriend of mine did, and I quietly and respectfully loved her more than any boyfriend of hers did. We were bodyguards for each other!

Our spouses now can only look at that friendship and thank God that we acted in this way. How would you like it if someone were guarding your future spouse this way? Then do the same for others.

– Brian Butler

notes

"'Purity?' they ask. And they smile. They are the ones who go on to marriage with worn-out bodies and disillusioned souls."
– St. Josemaria Escriva

Notes & Nuggets: Normalizing Chastity

Remember that along with teaching your students the basics of the Theology of the Body, your greater aim is to **_normalize_** the idea of purity and instill virtue of chastity in your teenagers. Recognizing chastity as a counter-cultural message can be used to your advantage. Promote this virtue by appealing to a teen's desire to be unique and different. Remember that if you can get athletes and other leaders in your school or group to embrace this message, you will quickly find others jumping onto the bandwagon of purity. This is peer pressure at its best!

Pray for your student leaders and look for ways to evangelize them–perhaps by taking them on a retreat, etc. Asking your administration team to bring a quality chastity speaker to your school is a great idea, among many others. Starting a Pure Love Club or integrating chastity in a visible way into your overall campus ministry program is also a great way to rally students for purity and give them an outlet to support each other. For more info on helping your students start such a club, see: www.PureLoveClub.com

Even though living a life of chastity may remain countercultural, if you can succeed in immersing your students in a flood of purity messages that normalize this virtue, you can create an environment where chastity is respected and admired as the popular lifestyle. Although this will take faith, effort, prayer, and teamwork, achieving this will be a major victory and create a vital support system for your teens as they attempt to live grace-filled lives of virtue and self-mastery. This chapter is about equipping your teens to live such lives with purity and with purpose.

COMPREHENSION & DISCUSSION QUESTIONS

1. Share an experience or relationship with the opposite sex when you felt affirmed, protected, and respected. How did this relationship affect you?

2. What did Kimberly do that was so pivotal to keeping a good relationship with the author of the story?

3. What benefits do you see from remaining close friends with someone of the opposite sex?

4. What potential problems can arise from having such close friendships?

5. Name one thing you can do to enable yourself to see others (and for them to see you) as a brother or sister in Christ.

6. Do you think that it is necessary to date in order to learn about the opposite sex?

Did You Know?

Some people assume that there's no reason not to date in high school. But eighty-four percent of boys and eighty-two percent of girls who do not date until they are sixteen graduate high school as virgins.
If they began dating when they were in seventh grade, only twenty-nine percent of boys and ten percent of girls were still virgins by the time they graduated high school.[i]

BRIDGING THE GAP

It's not that you can never date. But you must first learn to see the other as a sister or brother in Christ instead of allowing attraction and infatuation to cloud your decision-making. Seeing other teens this way helps push lust out of the picture. What person would lust after his or her sister or brother?

The reality is that if you pray and spend quality time in good friendships, you'll learn a ton about the opposite sex. You will learn how to become a person who "wills the good of the other." Think of it as a "school of love" that will train you in virtue as you prepare for your vocation. As Pope John Paul II said, "Only the chaste man and the chaste woman are capable of true love."[1]

TO THE CORE

Some kids start dating these days at a very young age. (The authors of this program were in "committed" dating relationships as early as fifth grade.) You remember sixth grade, right? That's the year that relationships get *serious*. The note passing gets more intense, the boxes to check ("Do you like me? Yes or No?") get more legible, and friends sometimes fight over who will get to go out with whom.

The story of many young couples goes like this: "You're cute. You're fun. Let's date … OK … You're annoying. Let's break up." What's the point of this type

of dating relationship? Furthermore, what is the whole point of dating anyhow? What is our driving motive or desire to date at such young ages? And, once you start dating, the question soon follows: "How do you know how far is too far?" And if you're not supposed to get married for another ten years, how are you supposed to stay pure in the meantime? The purpose of this chapter is to give solid answers to these good questions.

What's the point of dating?

The modern practice of dating is really less than 100 years old. Before the car was around, a man would "court" a woman in the presence of her family, with the hope of marrying her. Once the car was invented, the family was cut out of the dating scene, because a guy usually could just pick up a girl at her house and leave. With the family largely out of the picture, dating with the goal of marriage soon fell out of sight. And before long, dating became something to do for recreation.

With this "recreational" approach to relationships, a person ends up breaking up with each person he or she dates … except for the one who becomes that person's spouse. Think about it. Does this sound like good preparation for a lifelong marriage? A common response might be, "Yes, because you get to see what type of person you like and can, therefore, make a better choice someday." Perhaps, but the downsides to this approach far outweigh this possible benefit. Here's why: For one, the ultimate purpose of dating is to find a spouse. If you date for recreation, you're just training yourself in the habit of failed relationships. So, do not date anyone whom you cannot see yourself marrying, and never date a person expecting that he or she will change.

Secondly, casual dating—versus the more purposeful concept of courting—creates a much higher probability that the relationship will involve sexual activity. As you have seen throughout this program, this comes with a whole host of spiritual, emotional, and psychological problems. In short, sexually active relationships are recipes for disaster.

The Relationship Pyramid

Imagine a pyramid—let's call it a "Relationship Pyramid." At the base of the pyramid is friendship, the most basic of human relationships. As you move higher in the pyramid, the different levels (in order) include: Getting to Know the Person Better; Getting to Know the Person's Family Better; Exclusive Relationship; Engagement; and Marriage. At the top of the pyramid is the intimacy of sex. Now, what would happen if you built a pyramid upside down, trying to balance it on the point of the pyramid? It would collapse from all the weight at the top. At the very least, it would fall over and get damaged. The same happens when you begin a relationship with sexual activity, in hopes that friendship and love will follow. It doesn't work. It is contrary to God's plan for life and love, and, in almost all cases, the relationship ends up collapsing or really hurting the persons involved.

The Courtship Alternative

Should you date only the person you marry? Should you hang out with his or her family on your dates? Oh, boy, that sounds like fun! Actually, there are practical and fun ways you can apply the principles of old-fashioned courtship to help you find real love.

But before we get into those details, we should really address two obvious questions: "Why should I be thinking about marriage when I'm just a teenager?" and "How do you know if a person is marriage material?"

We've addressed the first question in detail in Chapter Eight, but here's a quick refresher: God has a special calling for every person on earth. Each person is called to some form of marriage—either to an earthly spouse or to the mystical marriage of Christ and the Church as a celibate. We should be discerning which vocation we are called to even at a young age. When a person is in high school, this discernment should grow and become more focused because he or she is getting closer to some major life decisions (college, seminary, convent, marriage, job, etc.). Our teen years should not be dominated only with school and fun. These are serious, formative years. This is why questions related to dating and marriage should begin to be addressed by teenagers.

So how can you discern if a particular person is someone you might want to marry? The short answer is that you make smart choices that will help you discover as much "data" as possible while keeping your head clear.

Courting (versus dating) teaches you to first be friends with a particular person for a good period of time before jumping into a romantic relationship. That way, you'll know that person's family, friends, level of faith, etc. When we skip this process and jump right into dating, we often end up in unhealthy relationships. Our desire to find love is so intense that it makes us impatient. It's usually true that healthy relationships bring us closer to those who love us: God, family, friends, etc. On the other hand, unhealthy relationships alienate us from those who love us.

Chill Out—You Won't Become Weird

Many teens think that something is wrong with them because they don't have a boyfriend or girlfriend. But as much as they might miss having a date on Friday night, they're actually better off in the long run. When they finish high school, they won't feel like they've been through a teenage soap-opera and three emotional divorces. Granted, not all high school relationships end with a bitter breakup, and a few even end in happy marriages. But for the most part, those teens who hold off on serious dating relationships give themselves more of an opportunity to discover their identity. As a result, their independence helps them to have more successful relationships, discovering their dreams and goals.

COMPREHENSION & DISCUSSION QUESTIONS

1. How old is the common practice of dating for recreation?

2. What is the real purpose of dating?

3. Give an example of a type of relationship that does not fulfill the real purpose of dating.

4. What is one of the sure signs of a healthy relationship?

5. How does a relationship building on friendship help stabilize things?

How do you know "How far is too far?"

When it comes to this question, most people have two sets of standards: one that applies to themselves and one that applies to others. For example, if a person were to walk up to you and say, "I know whom you are going to marry … but I'm going to date that person first. So I wanted to ask you, 'How far is too far?'" Or, what if this person asked how far he or she could go with your sister or brother? In both cases, you would have a very clear set of boundaries for their actions.

Why, then, do the standards change when it comes to setting boundaries for our own actions? Often, we come up with all kinds of reasons or excuses why those standards do not apply to us. We say to ourselves, "I really love him, and I can see myself marrying him" or "Why is it that bad? She's willing to do it."

Why do we feel a sense of protection for our future spouses or our siblings, but when it comes to guarding our own dignity and innocence, we are sometimes casual or downright reckless?

In the Bible's love poem, the Song of Songs, the man says to his beloved, "You have ravished my heart, my sister, my bride" (Song 4:9). The same is true for the story of Tobias and Sarah in the book of Tobit. Young Tobias referred to his new wife as "this sister of mine" (Tob 8:7) when he prayed with her on their wedding night, asking God to bless their marriage. Before anything else, these two young men saw each of their brides as a sister in humanity—as a sister under one heavenly Father. As a result, neither woman was an object of lust to be conquered. Each was a treasure to be cherished. If we can see each other first as brothers and sisters—as persons to be cared for—it is easier to move past the temptation of lust into the triumph of love.

The purpose of purity in dating is not to repress all our desires, but to be free to fall in love for all the right reasons. One university football player said, "I know God has a deeper love for us to find. … It's like if I haven't messed around in a couple of days I start to … feel this unbelievable love that God has for us." He

knew in the depths of his heart that the fingerprint of God on a relationship is purity and peace. He knew, even as he struggled to live in purity, that sacrificing for the good of the other brings a couple closer than any pleasure on earth.

So, if you really want to know "How far is too far?" realize that you're asking the wrong question. What we should be asking is, "God, how do You want me to live and love so I can find the happiness for which I really long?" If we approach God with this type of sincere faith and trust, He will bless us beyond our hopes. Instead of asking how far you can go *away* from purity, perhaps it's time to start asking how far you can go *toward* it.

You will soon realize that the more pure you are, the easier it is to be pure. St. Paul writes, "To the pure, all things are pure" (Ti 1:15). What makes it hard to be pure is when we try to be "sort of" pure while allowing ourselves to get sexually revved-up with things like foreplay, pornography, and masturbation. When we compromise our purity like this, our appetite for sexual union only increases and makes us feel like purity is impossible. But purity *is* possible for the one who truly seeks it.

Unfortunately, many people think that purity is equal to being a prude. It is not. A prudish person thinks sex is somehow bad or "dirty." A person who possesses the virtue of chastity, however, is someone who respects, protects, and saves sex precisely because it's so valuable, beautiful, and wonderful.

COMPREHENSION & DISCUSSION QUESTIONS

1. Why is "How far is too far?" the wrong question to ask?

2. How did the young men in Tobit and Song of Songs refer to their brides? Why do you think they did this?

3. What do you think it means to say, "To the pure, all things are pure?"

4. What is the difference between *purity* and bring a *prude*?

5. Why is being a prude not consistent with the teaching you have learned so far from John Paul II in The Theology of the Body?

notes

_____
_____
_____
_____
_____
_____
_____
_____
_____
_____
_____
_____
_____
_____
_____
_____
_____
_____
_____
_____

If you're not supposed to get married for another ten years or so, how are you supposed to stay pure in the meantime?

It's reasonable to wonder why God would give teenagers such a powerful sexual drive when marriage is so far away. Possessing a desire during times when it is not appropriate to act on that desire gives us the opportunity to train ourselves in faithfulness and self mastery. Through the self-denial required in living chastely, we learn the skills that will help to make marriage last: patience, sacrifice, honesty, restraint, self-discipline, etc.

When we resist certain desires, we grow in virtue. We literally become stronger morally, psychologically, and spiritually. We learn self-mastery. Once a person has this sort of self-control, he or she possesses the freedom to make a gift of himself or herself. If a person does not have self-control and cannot even say "No" to sex, then such a person's "Yes" becomes meaningless. That person is like a slave—a slave to his or her passions. Such a person's "Yes" is meaningless because he or she always say "Yes" to impulses of the moment.

If you want to experience the freedom that comes with self-mastery, here are Ten Tips to help you stay pure:

1. Pray for purity every morning. Don't repress sexual desires, but pray for their redemption. Three Hail Marys are a great way to do this.

2. Avoid impure relationships before they begin.

3. Once you're in a relationship, avoid places and situations in which you're likely to fall into sin.

4. Know your boundaries before you're tempted, and make sure your date knows them before you even date the person. This may mean you need to have a specific discussion about it.

5. Choose friends who will help you grow in purity.

6. Double date or group date with friends who have high standards.

7. Get rid of impure music, magazines, and TV shows. If you want to be trashy, just look at and think about trash. But if you want to be good, look at and think about good things. St. Paul tells us, "If there is any excellence and if there is anything worthy of praise, think about these things" (Phil 4:8, NAB).

8. Listen to the advice of your wisest friends and family members who are committed Christians.

9. Try to go to confession at least once a month.

10. Lastly, if things are going too far, do not be afraid to say "No."

Undoubtedly, at some point in a relationship, your conscience will pull you in

> *"The sign of the cross is the most terrible weapon against the devil. Thus the Church wishes not only that we should have it continually in front of our minds to recall to us just what our souls are worth and what they cost Jesus Christ, but also that we should make it at every juncture ourselves; when we go to bed, when we awaken during the night, when we get up, when we begin any action, and above all, when we are tempted."*
> – St. John Vianney

Notes & Nuggets: Remind your teens that while temptations will always be there on some level, we do cause most of our temptations ourselves by compromising our faith and values. We choose which parties to go to, which music to listen to, which TV shows to watch, and which movies to see. The more we can avoid temptation through wise choices, the better our chances will be to live purely as we should.

Notes & Nuggets: At this point, it is probable that many of your teens are thinking about how they will be pure, and some of them are contemplating if they will remain pure. Remind your teens not to compare themselves with people who are in worse relationships than theirs. You may want to say something like: "If you compare yourself with those who are far from God, you will become more like them. Instead, compare yourself with the saints who will inspire you to grow in purity and virtue."

Notes & Nuggets: To adults, it can sometimes seem elementary or overly simplistic to train teens in "refusal skills," but actually it can be quite helpful to those teens who really need direction. At this point, you may want to do some role playing with refusal skills. The teens may get a bit silly during this role play, but that's OK as long as they are respectful and are getting comfortable with the idea of saying "No" to those things they should refuse in real-life situations. Even helping teens to politely but firmly refuse a date can be very empowering, especially for young girls. Help them to refuse *tactfully, firmly,* and *truthfully* so they can do so *confidently.* This will also help the guys from being "led on" because of an unclear message. Considering that girls are more sexually aggressive today than ever before, guys can certainly use some support in their efforts to make good choices. They need encouragement to say "No" to sexual advances and avoid moments of sexual opportunity, rather than taking advantage of them.

one direction while your hormones tug you in another. This is part of our fallen nature. But remember, your conscience is a "smoke alarm," letting you know that danger is just around the corner. So, the more you inform your conscience, like you're doing here with this program, the more capable you will become in maintaining pure relationships.

COMPREHENSION & DISCUSSION QUESTIONS

1. How does self-denial through chastity help train us for better marriages?

2. Which of the Ten Tips on the previous page is the most difficult for you? Why?

3. Add two or three of your own tips that could help you and your friends stay pure.

But if you do find yourself in a bad situation, what do you do?

First, say a quick prayer for strength and then immediately act. You could say:

- "If you love me, you won't pressure me."

- "I respect you too much to do this with you."

- "I really like you, but I want to fall in love for the right reasons."

- "I can't do this. My parents would kill me."

- "We need to stop."

Or, don't say anything and just stop. If the person gives you a difficult time about it, then you have all the more proof for yourself that he or she is trying to *get* something from you versus *loving* you as you deserved to be loved.

Temptations will come, but it is important to realize that purity—like love and faithfulness—is an act of the will, not an absence of desire. For example, a couple may be tempted to engage in sexual activity, but they choose to abstain from acting out their sexual desires. Attractions, temptations, and desires will always be there, but their presence does not make us impure. Our purity is determined by what we choose.

And as we said earlier, a person does not become pure by suppressing his or her passions. We become pure by a life of intimacy with Christ, allowing Him to love others through us. In the words of Pope John Paul II, "Love ... is victorious because it prays."[2]

You Decide

The Offspring, "Self Esteem"

"Now I know, I'm being used. That's OK, man, cause I like the abuse. I know she's playing with me. That's OK, cause I got no self-esteem."

vs.

Pope John Paul II

"Deep within yourself, listen to your conscience which calls you to be pure . . . a home is not warmed by the fire of pleasure which burns quickly like a pile of withered grass. Passing encounters are only a caricature of love; they injure hearts and mock God's plan."

COMPREHENSION & DISCUSSION QUESTIONS

1. What are some other things you could say to get out of a sexual situation?

2. To whom should you compare yourself if you want to grow in purity?

3. Our purity is determined by what?

4. How did John Paul II say that love is victorious?

How do you know when to end a relationship?

Here is a list for girls of sixteen behaviors, any one of which, if exhibited by a particular guy you like or are dating, is enough to end a relationship—or, at the very least, place serious doubt in your heart about continuing the relationship.

The "dump him" list for girls, adapted from the book *Pure Womanhood*:

1. You've had to tell him more than once to stop.

2. You feel the need to "fix" him.

3. He looks at pornography.

4. He hits you, pushes you, or does anything to frighten you.

5. He has a drinking or drug problem.

6. He doesn't care if you lie to your family.

7. He leads you away from God.

8. He puts you down—even if he then says he's "just kidding."

9. He cheats on you.

10. He lies to you.

11. He flirts with other girls.

12. He uses guilt to get you to do what he wants.

13. He resents time you spend with your friends and family.

14. He behaves badly and then blames it on other people or on things that happen to him.

15. He can't stand on his own two feet without you; he's emotionally unable to function by himself.

16. You can't stay with him and remain pure.[3]

171-L

These are not minor faults but are signs of major issues than can be disastrous to a future marriage. If any *one* of these applies to him, we strongly recommend you end the relationship now. Remember, girls—you are young and have so much to offer a young man when the time is right. Why settle for someone who doesn't honor himself and you? Dump him.

And now a list for the guys. If any of these behaviors are exhibited by a girl you like or are courting or dating, move on. We cannot overstate how important it is to be prudent in your dating choices because, again, dating or courting often leads to marriage. And, making a wrong choice in marriage can cause tremendous heartache. Choose well when it comes to dating and marriage.

1. She cheats on you or flirts with other guys.

2. She is materialistic and only seems to like you when you buy things for her.

3. She pushes herself on you sexually or teases you with her sexuality.

4. She is emotionally dependent on you; she really can't live without you.

5. She has a drinking or drug problem.

6. She lies to you or to her own family.

7. She leads you away from God.

8. She is superficial, caring about things that do not matter and ignoring the things that do.

9. She constantly gossips or puts others down.

10. She manipulates you by threatening to break up with you.

11. She is completely unmotivated and apathetic; she doesn't care about anything.

12. Your relationship is based only on attraction; the two of you have nothing in common.

13. You can't see yourself marrying her.

14. You feel that you need to change or "fix" her.

15. She demands that you spend your time with her, rather than with your friends and family.

16. Your family members and best friends can't stand her and do not think she is good for you.

DIGGING DEEPER: Keeping Dignity and Chasing Purity through Grace

"In the Sermon on the Mount, Christ gave his own interpretation of the commandment, 'You shall not commit adultery.' This interpretation constitutes a new ethos. … he assigned as a duty to every man the dignity of every woman. Simultaneously, he also assigned to every woman the dignity of every man. Finally, he assigned to everyone—both to man and woman—their own dignity, in a certain sense, the sacrum [sacredness] of the person."[4]

The morality section of the *Catechism of the Catholic Church* begins with a challenge: "Christian, recognize your dignity" (CCC 1691). *Dignity* is your inherent, God-given worth. Therefore, dignity is something intrinsic to self, something irrevocable, indisputable, and indivisible from your created being. It is something that is uniquely yours and can never be taken away, only given away.

After seeing how atrocities of the Holocaust attacked the dignity of millions of people, governments around the world in 1948, through the United Nations, emphasized the dignity of every human being in the document, *Universal Declaration of Human Rights*. This declaration did not give you your dignity; it merely recognized the dignity you already have.

When it comes to dating and living a life of purity, how can you set yourself apart in a culture that does not recognize or understand the dignity of every person? How can you honor the *sacrum* (or the *sacredness*) of yourself and every person? How can you live by this new *ethos*, this fundamental disposition of the heart that honors the dignity of those you date? Honestly, you can't—if you rely on your own efforts, that is. With God, however, you can do all things (Phil 4:13). The only way you can proclaim "life" and overcome concupiscence (the tendency to sin) in a fallen world is through God's grace.

Sacred Scripture tells us that "grace and truth came through Jesus Christ" (Jn 1:17). The Church teaches us that "the sacraments confer the grace that they signify"[6] and that "by the grace of God we acquire holiness."[7] What does all this mean? What is grace? Put simply, **grace** is God's life within us.

Here's an analogy to consider the gift of God's grace in our lives. Imagine that it is Christmas morning and Grandpa Joe gives you a gift. The gift is important not because of what is in the box, but because Grandpa Joe gave it to you. If you were to open the box, take the gift, and walk away without thanking Grandpa Joe, in a sense, you would be accepting the gift but rejecting the giver. Likewise, if we want to accept God's grace, but are not willing to do His will, we are saying that the gift of grace is more important than the Giver (God).

Through Scripture, Sacred Tradition, and the teaching authority of the Church (the Magisterium), God reveals to us that all grace comes from Him, through

Regarding Mary, "She is the one whom every man loves when he loves a woman—whether he knows it or not. She is what every woman wants to be when she looks at herself. She is the woman whom every man marries in ideal when he takes a spouse; she is the secret desire every woman has to be honored and fostered; she is the way every woman wants to command respect and love because of the beauty of her goodness of body and soul."[5]
– Archbishop Fulton Sheen

APPLICATION

Option #1: Dating "Game Theory"

In economics, there is something known as game theory, which is a method of making a smart decision in a time of uncertainty. In it, you plot out your potential decisions with their potential consequences. Then, you compare the results, and see which choice makes the most sense.

The same approach can be used for relationships. Here's how it works. To the left of the table below, students have the choice between an unchaste relationship and a chaste one. Above the table are the possible outcomes of the relationship. Since nobody knows the outcome of a relationship, what's the best decision in the midst of that uncertainty?

	The relationship continues and you get married	The relationship does not work out and you break up
Chaste (pure) relationship	**A** Pros:_____ Cons:_____	**B** Pros:_____ Cons:_____
Unchaste (Sexually active) relationship	**C** Pros:_____ Cons:_____	**D** Pros:_____ Cons:_____

To find out, draw the table on the board and explain this concept to your students. Through class discussion, have the students fill in the blanks with pros and cons of each scenario. Or, use the worksheet on page page #201 and hand it out to students in groups of three or four. Have them fill out the sheets in small groups and then come back to a large group setting to discuss their answers.

Here are some possible answers that could be added to the class discussion. Freely allow the students to add as many answers as possible. The point is to weigh all the consequences:

A.
Pros:
- No fear of pregnancy
- Wedding night is more special
- Don't have to hide the truth from your family
- Can focus on relationship and friendship
- Avoid gossip
- More likely to have successful marriage
- No guilt
- Train yourselves in faithfulness, self-denial, and love
- Peace of conscience
- Living in God's will

Cons:
- Less physical pleasure before marriage
- Possible mockery from "friends"

B.
Pros:
- Easier breakup
- Friendship more easily maintained after the relationship ends
- No risk of unwanted pregnancy or leaving with an STD
- Grew in purity during the relationship
- No regrets or scars that could affect future relationships
- In short, less suffering

Cons:
- Missed opportunity of pleasure
- Possible mockery from "friends"

C.
Pros:
- Pleasure
- Feeling of closeness
- Fun

Cons:
- Higher divorce rate (more likely to have married because of passion, lust, or infatuation)
- Higher rates of infidelity within marriage
- More likely to cause tension in family
- Pregnancy might precede the wedding

D.
Pros:
- Pleasure
- Feeling of intimacy (although temporary)
- Feeling of being wanted and desired
- Fun

(Continued on next leader's page)

Jesus Christ. This grace comes most specifically through the Sacraments, outward signs instituted by Christ to give us grace.

When Christ became man, the dignity of all humanity was, in a sense, raised to an entirely new level—we became partakers of the divine nature. Furthermore, through the Eucharist, Christ's true presence, heaven touches earth over and over again. The human body becomes an earthly **tabernacle** for the heavenly—the divine Lord. As St. Paul explicitly affirmed, "Your body is a temple of the Holy Spirit" (1 Cor 6:19), *literally*.

Your designation as a walking tabernacle, a tabernacle filled with extraordinary dignity, demands something great from you: your whole self. A sinful body is not a worthy dwelling place for the sinless God. And so you're faced with a decision: to follow Him and to honor your and others' God-given dignity or to reject His truth and disrespect both the gift and the Giver.

Choose wisely each day until God calls you home. Tap into the power of the Sacraments. By living a life of grace, you will better recognize and honor the dignity that has been given to you and all those you are called to love.

"To be pure, to remain pure, can only come at a price, the price of knowing God and loving Him enough to do His will. He will always give us the strength we need to keep purity as something beautiful for Him."
– Blessed Teresa of Calcutta

"Devotion to the Blessed Sacrament and devotion to the Blessed Virgin are not simply the best way, but in fact the only way to keep purity. At the age of twenty, nothing but Communion can keep one's heart pure ... Chastity is not possible without the Eucharist."
– St. Philip Neri

Cons:
- Harder breakup (feels more like an emotional divorce)
- STD risk
- In the case of pregnancy, you may be left as a single parent (child suffers)
- Feeling of being used
- Gossip
- Regrets
- Lowered self-worth
- Feeling of alienation from God

CONCLUSION: Explain to your students that, when you add it all up, the chaste life is the smartest choice. They are protected against uncertainty, reduce the risk of suffering, and ultimately make the most loving decision for themselves and others. In the words of one young woman, Jamie, who was about to tell her boyfriend that they needed to stop having sex, "I hate hurting him, but if we continue what we're doing I know we'll just be hurting ourselves in the long run."

Option #2: Clock Appointments

This classic "get to know you" activity can serve as a fun way to orient guys and girls to the world of dating with purity and purpose. Have your students use the "clock" found on page 200 as their "appointment sheet." This activity can work well even if you teach an all-guy or all-girl class, though the nature of the appointments will be different.

The idea is for students to create "appointments" with those they know the least about in their class. Best friends should avoid each other in this activity to get the most out of the exercise. Have the students move around to quickly fill their appointment schedule with the names of others whom they know the least. (If you have a small class or a very intimate group, have them at least fill in their appointments so as to meet with those they know the least well *first*.) For example, Billy asks Annie "Do you have a 1:00 p.m. open?" If Annie is available, she writes Billy's name on her 1:00 p.m. line and Billy writes Annie's name down for his 1:00 p.m. line. The students proceed in this manner until their clocks are full.

If you have an odd number of students, you should end up with one student being left out for each "appointment." If you so choose, meet with that student yourself

at the appointed time. If this is the case, use your own clock provided on page 200 to fill in the names of your students. Once their clocks are filled, give them the following instructions:

Use the following questions for a short interview period with those appointments you will have in a few moments.

1. **Music and Movies:** What kind of music do you like? What is your favorite band? What is your all-time favorite movie?

2. **Hobbies:** Are you involved with any extracurricular activities at school? What are your hobbies and things you like to do on the weekends?

3. **God:** What is your relationship with God like? What is the coolest thing you have learned in this program so far? Do you have a favorite Bible verse?

4. **Growing Up:** What ideas do you have for college? What do you think God wants you to do as a career? What do you want to do?

5. **Family:** How many siblings do you have? Are your parents together? Do you want to get married? If so, how many kids do you think you would want to have?

6. **Biggest Fear:** What is your biggest fear?

7. **Travel:** If you could go anywhere in the world, where would it be? Who would you take with you?

Depending on how much time you want to devote to this activity, designate an amount of time for each appointment. For each appointment, it is crucial that the teens face each other, sit in the same position, and do not focus on anyone else in the room. Remind them to look each other in the eye, be active listeners, and not dominate the conversation.

If teens focus on this activity, they can likely cover most of the above questions in five or six minutes. Give a one-minute warning before the time is up. Clap or ring a bell to end the session and have students quickly move to their next appointment. At this pace, you can likely get three appointments done in fifteen minutes. Allow the students to interview as many other students as time allows. Also have them save their clocks for possible use on another day or challenge them to finish their clock appointments outside of class (at lunch, in the parking lot, etc.).

(Continued on next leader's page)

SCIENCE AND THE THEOLOGY OF
THE BODY: The Chemistry of Attraction

Remember the first time you fell "head over heels" for someone? Your heart raced, your stomach was in knots, and you felt nervous jitters. Have you ever wondered why your body had such a physical reaction to your emotional feelings? One reason is because of the chemical known as phenylethylamine (PEA). It is a natural amphetamine in your brain that triggers a release of dopamine, giving you a blissful feeling. Meanwhile, another chemical known as norepinephrine kicks up the level of adrenaline in your body, making your blood pressure increase.

In all, this makes for an intense experience. However, it's believed by some scientists that the body develops a tolerance for these intense chemicals and, in time, they wear off. Somewhere between eighteen months and four years into the relationship, they lose a significant amount of their effect on the brain. For teenagers, the duration seems to be even shorter, between three months to four months. As a result, people who rely too heavily on the "feelings" of love often bail out of relationships when this feel dissipates. The infatuation fades, and so do they.

Sound familiar? Odds are, you know people who seem to flutter from one relationship to the next, and never seem to be able to make things last. This is why Pope John Paul II wrote the following in his book *Love and Responsibility*:

> The essential reason for choosing a person must be personal, not merely sexual. Life will determine the value of a choice and the value and true magnitude of love. It is put to the test most severely when the sensual and emotional reactions themselves grow weaker, and sexual values as such lose their effect. Nothing then remains except the value of the person, and the inner truth about the love of those connected comes to light. If their love is a true gift of self, so that they belong to the other, it will not only survive but grow stronger, and sink deeper roots. Whereas if it was never more than a synchronization of sensual and emotional experiences it will lose its [reason for existence] and the persons involved in it will suddenly find themselves in a vacuum. We must never forget that only when love between human beings is put to the test can its true value be seen.[8]

The fading of our emotions is a real test of love. But when we pass through this desert, a deeper and more powerful love will take its place. As one expert puts it, "Young love is a flame; very pretty, very hot, and fierce, but still only light and flickering. The love of the older and disciplined heart is as coals, deep-burning and unquenchable."[9]

If time allows, follow up the appointments with a short discussion of what your students experienced in their conversations. Help them realize how much they learned about the other person in the span of just five or six minutes. Sometimes, because of shallow conversation and poor teenage dating choices, people can go months without knowing as much information about their girlfriend or boyfriend as they received in these five-minute interviews. Encourage your teens to relate on this level with their friends and dates sooner rather than later. The answers to these and other questions can tell us a lot about someone else, and give us a great sense on how fruitful a given dating relationship will be.

MOVIE CLIP/SONG SUGGESTIONS

MOVIE CLIPS:

1. *A Walk to Remember:* Show the segment that falls between 1:04:19 and 1:09:12. Jamie, the preacher's daughter, demands that her boyfriend, Landon, respects her wish to stay pure.

2. *Spanglish:* Show the segment that falls between 1:39:10 and 1:52:36. This is a scene that picks up just after John (Adam Sandler) finds out that his wife has been unfaithful. He then spends time with his maid to whom he is attracted; she is unmarried and has fallen in love with him. They spend time together and fight the temptation to commit adultery. They resist and love emerges victorious.

3. *The Last Samurai:* Show the segment that falls between 1:48:17 and 1:50:45. As Nathan (Tom Cruise) prepares for battle, the widow to whom he is attracted honors him by dressing him in his armor. The scene is tender and carries great dignity in the way the characters treat the body. With tears in her eyes, the widow places her head on Nathan's shoulder, knowing that he will probably die that day. There is no nudity or sexual activity, yet there is pure love and sexual expression.

4. *The Jeweller's Shop:* This video version does not do justice to the play by Karol Wojtyla and is recognized by many as a sub-par effort, but there are a few monologues from which to choose that could make for good conversation regarding purity in relationships. (95 mins.)

SONGS:

1. *Wait for Me* — Rebecca St. James (*Wait for Me: The Best of Rebecca St. James*)

A song imploring a possible future spouse to stay pure until they meet someday. Pop.

2. *Peace* — Michael McGlinn (*Virtues*)

A song about the peace that comes from waiting for the love of a lifetime. Acoustic/Ballad.

✓3. *Beautiful Soul* — Jesse McCartney (*Beautiful Soul*)

Pretty faces and fun times are great–but what about the soul? The singer wants deep love, a love that reaches the heart and soul in faithfulness. Pop/Ballad.

4. *Fly Away* — Paul Wright (*Fly Away*)

You have dreams and you have standards, God calls us to be men and women of high standards who wait for the right one with whom to fly away. Acoustic.

Girls:

Have you ever asked yourself: "When will guys grow up? All they think about is sex. Why can't they just be respectful and treat us like ladies?" Well, the solution to this dilemma is closer than we ladies would like to believe. We have a lot of say about the way guys treat us. Throughout history, women have been the gatekeepers of their own dignity. If we speak like ladies, dress like ladies, and dance like ladies, we are far more likely to be treated like ladies.

We can complain all we want that "Guys should respect us however we dress." While that's true, it's not likely to happen anytime in the near future because, in so many ways, we women are not setting high enough standards—for ourselves and for those we date. It's like guys saying, "Women should respect us, no matter how we act."

The fact is, no matter how you dress, you have power in your body and the way that you use it. But how will you use that power? I once heard it said that "Men are lost through women and they are saved by women. By their vanity, they will make a man fall; by their modesty, they will save him."

So if we want the boys in our lives to be gentlemen, we'll need to do our part. Ask yourself, "Why do I sometimes resent guys?" Odds are it's because many of them would rather satisfy their sexual desires than do what is best for us. But aren't we doing the same thing when we dress seductively? I used to have all the little outfits. I knew exactly what I was doing. Instead of doing what was best for guys, I preferred the fleeting satisfaction of feeling desirable. But if we are ever going to get out of this mess, guys and girls alike will have to make some sacrifices for each other.

When picking clothing, if you find yourself asking, "Is this too tight or too short?" you have likely answered your question. We have to step back and begin to ask our-selves: Does this outfit teach men my dignity, or distract them from it?

Because we live in a culture that glorifies meaningless sex, it's easy to become desensitized. It takes prayer and better formation of our consciences to develop the skills of discernment. Most of the time, though, we ladies know instantly in our hearts and minds the right choices. We just need the courage to stand up for ourselves and set a higher standard than perhaps we've done in the past.

– **Crystalina Evert**

Guys:

Do your conversations sound like you're reading from the wall of a bathroom stall? If so, I can relate. I know what it's like to have a trash mouth, because that's what got me booted out of Catholic grade school!

As little boys, we weren't "mature" enough to know bad words. But once we got exposed to the world, we thought we were all grown up because we sounded like Howard Stern. Sadly, many guys never move beyond this stage. They cling to their eighth grade locker-room vocabulary and quiet their consciences with the slogan "Boys will be boys." Indeed, they will. But men will also be men. In the words of the book of Sirach: "A man who has the habit of abusive language will never mature in character for as long as he lives" (Sir 23:15).

At some point, we learn, as the author of Sirach went on to say, that "His conversation is the test of a man" (Sir 27:5). It is not his athletic ability, his intelligence, or his success. More than anything, his speech reveals the quality of his character. In the words of St. Josemaria Escriva, "Don't say, 'That's the way I am—it's my character.' It's your lack of character. *Esto vir!*—Be a man!"[10]

– **Jason Evert**

Notes & Nuggets: If the students get into this project and create really good skits, select a few of the best ones to be performed in class, or even in front of some other classes in your school.

Notes & Nuggets: Tips for Underground Theatre

This play has seven characters in it. To really get into the spirit of John Paul II, create an "underground dinner theatre" experience for students to perform the play by candlelight one evening. Since the play was originally written during a time of Nazi oppression in Poland, everything should be done simply and compactly. For example, there are no costumes, props, or even a set design. While dramatizing the play well is not easy, the simple set-up is ideal and unique. You could even turn the event into a fundraiser for your campus ministry program, inviting faculty, parents, alumni, local youth groups, and the community at large. The students who are not cast or serving as support crew for the play could serve food and beverages for the event. Collaborating with the drama director at your school would likely make this an even more professional experience.

The nature of the play lends itself to discussion afterward. Getting students and adults to dialogue on such a play and the underlying moral principles in it could be a very valuable experience for all involved.

Catholic Culture in Your School: A different idea would be to get permission from your principal to perform the play as a special assembly for the entire student body (or at least for the upper grade levels). This would be a great incentive for your students who would love to perform in front of their peers, as well as being a great witness to the school and other faculty members. You may not be in a Communist country like John Paul II when he wrote the play, but you would be doing your part to preserve culture–Catholic culture–in your own community!

Notes & Nuggets: In this closing prayer, we ask the intercession of Sts. Perpetua and Felicity, two martyrs of the third century. Both were threatened repeatedly by Roman officials (and Perpetua, by her own family members) to deny the Christian faith or suffer greatly. They refused to acknowledge the divinity of the emperor Septimus Severus, and though Perpetua was only twenty-two and the mother of an infant, she was still sentenced to death for her steadfastness to Christ. Both women responded consistently with pure faith and ultimately were thrown, with a few others, to wild beasts in an amphitheatre before a large crowd. After being wounded by the animals, they were finally killed by swordsmen. Through the entire process, they never strayed from the Faith, nor stopped proclaiming it to others around them. The lives of these two heroic women can be models for our young people to hold fast to Christ and to purity, no matter what others say or do–even when family members hurt, rather than help, their cause of purity.

WORK IT OUT

Assignment #1: Get creative and write your own "Top Ten Cool Down List," a blend of serious and humorous things to say that would freeze a hot and passionate physical situation.

Assignment #2: Search the Bible to make a list of ten Scripture passages you can read regularly to support your commitment to chastity in a world that is overly focused on sexual pleasure.

Assignment #3: Write a persuasive essay (or give a persuasive speech or multimedia presentation) on the benefits of living a life of purity and purpose as a teenager. Include at least two Scripture passages and two quotes from John Paul II.

Assignment #4: Dig deeper into the primary source by reading John Paul II's address from May 30, 1984. Write an essay that analyzes the use of the image of the "sister bride," considering what is meant by saying that woman is the "master of her own mystery." In the second part of your essay, practically apply your analysis of this idea specifically to the issues of modesty and chastity in every day life.

❖

Project #1: Go back to the beginning of this program and read the Introduction again. Taking a similar theme, write a skit about one teen (or one teenage couple) struggling to live a life of chastity. Make it a short journey through drama and comic relief. You may get really creative and have one character somehow meet John Paul II and share his or her struggle with him. As part of the Pope's response, have him exit the skit with the line, "Love … is victorious because it prays."

Project #2: Find and read (or watch on video) the play, *The Jeweller's Shop* written in 1960 by Karol Wojtyla (later Pope John Paul II). Write a summary, similar to a book report, on the plot of the play, which revolves around the lives of three married couples. Be sure to include your own analysis of the deeper significance, "reading between the lines" of the play.

Project #3: Put together groups of students to create a cast to practice, discuss, and perform (or do a dramatic reading of) the play mentioned above, *The Jeweller's Shop*. Give extra points to the students if they can convince the drama director to help them out.

CLOSING PRAYER

Leader: In the name of the Father, and of the Son, and of the Holy Spirit. **Amen.**

All: Sts. Perpetua and Felicity, please pray with me that I, like you both, would have the courage to safeguard my purity, especially when others are willing to jeopardize my salvation in the process. **Amen.**

IN HIS OWN WORDS

- **On Purity and Truth:** "Purity is a requirement of love. It is the dimension of its interior truth in man's heart" (December 3, 1980).

- **On Dignity and Purity:** "In the Sermon on the Mount, Christ gave his own interpretation of the commandment, 'You shall not commit adultery.' This interpretation constitutes a new ethos. With the same lapidary words he assigned as a duty to every man the dignity of every woman. Simultaneously, he also assigned to every woman the dignity of every man. Finally he assigned to everyone–both to man and woman–their own dignity, in a certain sense, the *sacrum* of the person" (November 24, 1982).

- **On Purity and the Body:** "Purity is the glory of the human body before God. It is God's glory in the human body, through which masculinity and femininity are manifested" (March 18, 1981).

- **On the Greatness of the Body:** "For the Manichean mentality, the body and sexuality constitute an 'anti-value.' For Christianity, on the contrary, they always remain a value not sufficiently appreciated" (October 22, 1980).

Glossary
of Key Terms

Courtship (courting): A time of relating with another, getting to know the person—and his or her friends and family—through friendship before moving into a dating relationship. This low-risk, balanced approach to pursuing relationships creates a firm foundation upon which love can be built.

Grace: God's life within us, which is a gift from God that helps us grow more like Him.

Tabernacle: A portable sanctuary containing the Ark of the Covenant (and God's presence) that the Jews carried with them on their travels in the Old Testament before they had a permanent temple for worship. In the Catholic Church, it is the place in which the Church reserves the Eucharist, Christ's body in the form of bread. When we speak of the body as a temple of the Holy Spirit, we mean that it is a dwelling place for God—a tabernacle of His presence.

OBJECTIVES At the end of this lesson, the student should know and be able to:

- Integrate the Theology of the Body into a life of authentic love and radical holiness.
- Explain the purpose of the body as discovered through the Theology of the Body.
- Defend the body and sexuality as good gifts given to us by God.
- Connect the meaning of the original experiences of Adam and Eve to modern humanity and daily life.
- Apply an understanding of the Theology of the Body to an active life of service and evangelization.

Notes & Nuggets: Pray that your students will have the grace to say "Yes," as the Blessed Mother did, to live a life of purity, love, and holiness. We suggest saying a "Memorare" today, ending this curriculum through the intercession of Mary. You may also want to ask John Paul II to help you to deliver this message of hope in a way that is faithful to his spirit of evangelization.

Chapter Twelve

Living the Good (and Free!) Life

The Theology of the Body gives us a new lens through which we can view ourselves, our world, and eternity. In this new, rich understanding of some of the most important questions in life, we discover compelling truth—truth that sets us free. We will likely also come to see that a personal response to these truths on our part is necessary. Then, with the grace of Christ in our relationships, we can have great hope that our God-given desires can be purified, honoring our Creator and ourselves in the process. Such a transformation is challenging, to be sure. And it takes commitment. But it can happen.

Now it is time to apply the truths we have learned in this curriculum to a life that reflects God's purpose for our bodies and our very lives. Now is the time to pray for the redemption of our hearts, minds, and bodies. Now is the time to be honest with ourselves and to choose a path to authentic love. Now is the time to become free, to experience the joy that comes from a life of purity, a life that will culminate with our union with God in heaven.

ICEBREAKER (optional): LET THE SCALES FALL

Get five or six volunteers from the class. Tell them they will be participants in a contest to decide who can "see" the best without their eyes. Before moving further, remove the participants from the room (or to another part of the room) so they cannot see the preparation for the game as it occurs. Blindfold the contestants.

Hand out Play-Doh® to the rest of the class and instruct certain groups to sculpt specific types of figures so you have five or six different types (categories) of figures. In each category, have five or six different figures created so that, when all the figures are completed, there are five or six different figures allotted to each of the contestants.

For example, the categories could be something like this:

1. **Animals:** bear, horse, dog, alligator, rhinoceros, giraffe, etc.

2. **Food:** apple, pie, hamburger, pizza, piece of cantaloupe, etc.

3. **Hobbies:** water skiing (skis), skateboarding (skateboard), fishing, playing piano (piano), surfing (surfboard), reading (a book), etc.

4. **Heroes:** Batman, Spiderman, policeman, soldier, fireman, doctor, the Pope, etc.

5. **College Mascots:** Jayhawks, Green Wave, Nittany Lions, Spartans, Crimson Tide, Fighting Irish, Boilermakers, Buffaloes, etc. (Some of these will be nearly impossible!)

Step 1: Bring the blind-folded contestants to the front of the class and line them up.

Step 2: Arrange so that they each have five figures in front of them, one from each category.

Step 3: Announce the first category (e.g., animals) and hand them each a figure from that category. Give them thirty seconds to gently "see" it with their hands, by holding them and touching them. Then have the contestants guess what the figure is. DO NOT let them mangle the figures; keeping them intact will help make a point at the end of the game.

Step 4: Record their guesses but do not tell them whether they are right.

Step 5: Repeat the process through the five categories to see which person can guess the most figures correctly.

Step 6: Take their blindfolds off and let them look at the figures they have just held.

Make the Connection: The perspective changes completely once the blindfolds have been taken off. Their perceptions of the figures in their hands take on new depth and meaning when they look with clear vision. Such it is with our views of the body, sexuality, and God. Once the "scales" have been lifted from our eyes and we allow the truth of the Theology of the Body to sink in, we will never view reality or our connection to it the same way again.

TWO MINUTE DRILL — VERBAL REVIEW:

1. What is the ultimate purpose of dating?
   Answer: To find a spouse.

2. Why is "how far is too far" the wrong question to ask?
   Answer: Because it asks how far away from purity–toward sin–we can go, instead of asking how much toward purity and holiness we can go. The question also implies that we want to take something from someone and "get away with" as much as possible.

3. Name three reasons a girl should dump a guy.
   Answer: Among other things: he looks at pornography; he lies; he uses guilt to get what he wants.

4. Name three reasons a guy should dump a girl.
   Answer: Among other things: she lies; she manipulates to get what she wants; she is only happy when the guy is buying things for her.

5. Name three things you can practically do to practice self-mastery and find happiness through chastity.
   Answer: Among other things: pray for purity (the redemption of desires, not repression!) every morning; avoid impure relationships before they begin; and know your boundaries before you are tempted.

OPENING PRAYER

Leader: In the name of the Father, and of the Son, and of the Holy Spirit. **Amen.**

(Option #1)

Leader or Reader #1: Read John 1:35-39a

"The next day again John was standing with two of his disciples; and he looked at Jesus as he walked and said, 'Behold, the Lamb of God.' The two disciples heard him say this and they followed Jesus. Jesus turned and saw them following, and said to them, 'What do you seek?' And they said to him, 'Rabbi' (which means Teacher), 'where are you staying?' He said to them, 'Come and see.'"

Leader or Reader #2: Lord, help us to have deep within our hearts today the desire to be ready when You ask us what we seek. Give us the grace to be able to say that it is You whom we want. Help us to say "Yes" to Your invitation to follow You as true disciples. **Amen.**

(Option #2)

Leader or Reader #1: Read Matthew 4:18-20

"As he walked by the Sea of Galilee, he saw two brothers, Simon who is called Peter and Andrew, his brother, casting a net into the sea; for they were fishermen. And he said to them, 'Follow me and I will make you fishers of men.' Immediately they left their nets and followed him."

Leader or Reader #2: Jesus, Your call to follow You is the greatest invitation we will ever receive. Your call to serve You and Your Church through the vocation to marriage or celibacy is a challenge for which we need grace to respond in love. Help us not to respond in fear, in anxiety, or in guilt, but solely out of love for You, trusting in the perfect plan that You have for our lives. **Amen.**

Need a Review of Lesson 11?

STORY STARTER: What Do You Want?

Jeff was a normal seventeen-year-old guy. He liked girls and football, but he never gave much thought to the deeper things of life. He lived for himself. Though most people would have said, "Jeff is a good guy," in reality he was fairly selfish and did whatever felt good to him. Most of Jeff's friends were Catholic, but he knew that did not mean much. He saw their lives. They went to church but lived just like he did, doing whatever they wanted most of the time. They were hypocrites, and he couldn't stand that. Jeff wasn't sure he believed in God and, frankly, didn't really care whether God existed.

But that changed when he met Rachel. She was gorgeous. Beyond her physical beauty, Jeff noticed that Rachel was *different*. Something about her radiated peace and joy, even though their two-minute conversations each day between Trigonometry and Chemistry were never very deep. Jeff started talking with his friends about Rachel. They all felt the same about her. Yes, she was beautiful, but her beauty also ran *deep*.

Verbal Review of Lesson 11

1. What is the ultimate purpose of dating?

2. Why is "how far is too far" the wrong question to ask?

3. Name three reasons a girl should dump a guy.

4. Name three reasons a guy should dump a girl.

5. Name three things you can do to practice self-mastery and find happiness through chastity.

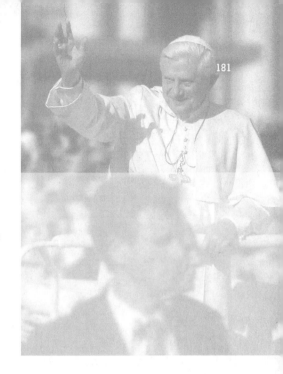

181

Finding out that she was a religious person, Jeff was intrigued. He was still an agnostic and didn't know what to believe about God. He asked Rachel about her beliefs and suddenly their conversations plunged deeper as she revealed that Jesus was her source of joy and strength. Living for Him, she said, made all the difference in the world. Jeff began reading and studying up on Rachel's Catholic faith. Though his own mom was Catholic and he had actually been baptized, he didn't know anything about the Bible or the Church. The only time he heard Jesus' name was when his dad was using it as a curse word. Soon, Jeff began going to Mass and his faith began to grow. Within a month or two, he was even willing to say out loud that he was a Christian, a Catholic who believed.

Though Jeff's beliefs changed, his life didn't. He still did whatever he wanted, drinking until he couldn't see straight, getting into fights, and still being pretty selfish. He knew Rachel was "out of his league," so eventually he began dating a girl named Lacy. She was a lot of fun but didn't have a very good reputation. Just a few weeks into the relationship, Jeff slept with Lacy for the first time. And for the first time in his life, he wondered if that was a good thing to do. He quickly decided that it was, but he went home that night and had a strange experience.

Jeff had begun carrying a plastic rosary ring in his pocket, which had ten peg-like beads that protruded from it. As he emptied his pockets that night, he noticed that one of the beads had broken off and was *gone. That's odd,* he thought, but went straight to bed. The next weekend he slept with Lacy again and upon arriving home and emptying his pockets he found that another ball was now missing from the rosary ring. *I wonder if this is some kind of sign,* he thought. He quickly concluded that it couldn't be, and to be sure, he stuffed the rosary ring in his drawer and never wore it again. But God *was* calling.

A few weeks later, Jeff and Lacy started kissing and proceeded toward having sex again. Suddenly, Jeff's scapular—a small wool necklace dedicated to the Blessed Virgin Mary—fell out of his shirt and dangled between him and Lacy. The light struck the gold cross on the wool rectangle and stunned Jeff into a motionless stare. It hung there between them, begging Jeff to be real and to *do something* about his newfound "faith." As he quietly mumbled "No … No," Lacy's hand flashed upward and ripped the scapular from his neck. She hurled it across the room onto the floor and angrily pushed him away.

"What do you want?!" she screamed into his face. "I am so sick and tired of you being a hypocrite!" She paused for only a moment before raging on with an ultimatum, "Do you want to do *this* and be normal … or do you want to do your Jesus freak little things with your Jesus freak little friends? What … do … you … want?!"

Jeff was stunned and reeled backward toward the door. Even when Lacy calmed down and began to say she was sorry, Jeff didn't move a muscle closer to her. He walked across the room, picked up his tattered scapular and went home. Confused and angry, he burst into his house and slammed the door to

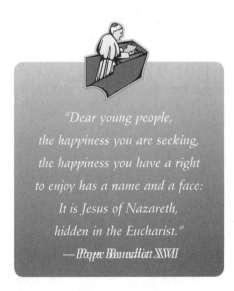

"Dear young people, the happiness you are seeking, the happiness you have a right to enjoy has a name and a face: It is Jesus of Nazareth, hidden in the Eucharist."
—Pope Benedict XVI

his room shut. It was 12:30 a.m., but he didn't care if his parents heard him. In a rage, he cursed and threw things around his room. Then he looked above his door at his crucifix, pointed to Jesus and growled, "Dude … before the sun comes up, I will either be an atheist and do whatever I want, living as I please … or I will be a real Catholic and will follow You wherever You lead me. But if You're there then you gotta' help me because I don't know what I want."

Jeff huffed, sobbed, yelled, and tossed and turned all night. At 5:30 a.m., he finally dropped to his knees. As the sun came up through his window, he surrendered completely to Jesus Christ, and fell peacefully asleep.

The next day, he still had the same desires and temptations, but one thing was different: he had made a decision to love rightly. In that one reality, everything changed forever. Although he still fell into sin, he slowly grew out of his vices as he began praying daily, going to confession, attending Mass regularly, and dating with purity. Twelve years later, God brought him a magnificent wife and four amazing children. And though he is still not perfect, the grace of Christ is perfecting him every day. As he awaits the full redemption of his body, he walks with confidence knowing that if God could redeem him and help him to be pure, then anything is possible.

Jeff still says that he believes there will come the time in everyone's life when he or she must choose for Christ or against Him. Jesus will come to us in some way, look each person in the eye and ask the daring question, "What do you want? Do you want me, or do you want something else?"

When your moment comes, what will be your answer?

COMPREHENSION & DISCUSSION QUESTIONS

1. Why do you think so many people use the hypocrisy of others as an excuse to live as they like?

2. Why is hypocrisy not a valid reason for not practicing one's faith?

3. Have you ever had a moment of clear choice (maybe not so dramatic as the one in the story) in which God asked you a question?

4. What are the things in your life that keep you from choosing Jesus completely?

5. If you died today and were to stand before Him in judgment, how do you think you would feel?

6. What can you do to share the good news of Jesus and the freedom He brings with your friends and family that may not know Him yet?

"Brothers and Sisters! Do not be afraid to welcome Christ, and to accept his power! Help the Pope and all who want to serve Christ and, with the power of Christ, to serve the human person and all of humanity! Do not be afraid! Open, in fact, break down the doors for Christ!"
– The first homily of Pope John Paul II, October 22, 1978

BRIDGING THE GAP

There are times in everyone's life when we must make choices for good or for evil. We live this experience on a daily basis because, within all of us, there is a tug-of-war, a battle raging between love and lust. The battle involves both life-saving and faith-rattling messages from our peers, parents, church, the media, etc. The battle will continue, but we do not need to fight it alone. Embracing Pope John Paul II's teaching found in the Theology of the Body (and finding others who will embrace it with you) can lessen the intensity of the battle, especially if you submit your desires *daily* to Christ. It is in prayer that you will gain the interior strength to turn the tide from impurity to purity, from selfishness to generosity, from lust to love.

TO THE CORE

All too often, doctrines taught in religion class stay in the classroom. A teen-ager might get an A+ on a religion test but may not see any practical way that the material affects his or her daily life. One of the awesome realities of the Theology of the Body is its ability to transform our lives if we grasp and apply what is being taught.

What we are taught in the Theology of the Body is simple, yet unbelievably profound. What we learn with Pope John Paul II's unpacking of *original man* (i.e., man as he was created in the beginning before the Fall), is that God created us for love. We find this truth—that we were created for love—stamped in our very own bodies. We discover in our own bodies that "man was not meant to be alone" but, rather, that we were called to give ourselves to another in love. This is what is meant by the phrase *nuptial* or *marital* meaning of our bodies. Our bodies also point us to our destiny: our eternal communion with God.

The teaching on *historical man* reveals that man suffers from concupiscence. As a result, we must struggle to love each other with truth and integrity. Even still, purity is possible. Because of the grace won for us on the Cross through Christ's death and resurrection, we can overcome vice and fulfill our call to love. Christ does not condemn us for our past. Instead, He heals us and gives us strength to overcome temptation and to live a life of grace, to overcome shame, and find the freedom that comes through purity of heart.

In John Paul II's explanation of *eschatological man* we discover that we have been created for a glorious destiny—heaven. Heaven is the destination and ultimate fulfillment of everything for which we have been created. In heaven we will experience the joy that comes from giving the total gift of ourselves and a radical reception of God's very life. Through this experience, we will be con-sumed in the perfect heavenly marriage between Christ and the Church. We will be fulfilled beyond all human expectation.

"With all the strength of my soul I urge you young people to approach the Communion table as often as you can. Feed on this bread of angels whence you will draw all the energy you need to fight inner battles. Because true happiness, dear friends, does not consist in the pleasures of the world or in earthly things, but in peace of conscience, which we only have if we are pure in heart and mind."
– Blessed Pier Giorgio Frassati

"When you decide firmly to lead a clean life, chastity will not be a burden on you: it will be a crown of triumph."
– St. Josemaria Escriva

Understanding the knowledge of our past (original man), present (historical man), and future (eschatological man) is not merely an academic exercise. Once we understand these realities we can look to Christ and allow Him to redeem our desires. As a result, we have the *hope of every day* that comes with His grace, helping us to rise from confusion to clarity and from lust to love.

"Virtue can only come from spiritual strength."
– Pope John Paul II

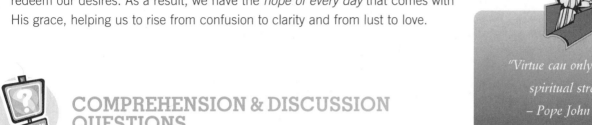

COMPREHENSION & DISCUSSION QUESTIONS

1. What does the teaching on *original man* show us?

2. What does the teaching on *historical man* show us?

3. What does the teaching on *eschatological man* show us?

4. In which era of the three do we live?

5. What does love have to do with our creation and purpose?

Realizing there is a specific *language of the body* that we speak helps us to pay attention to the "words" we speak, words that even deaf people can "hear." The task of our lives is to learn to speak the language of the body as God intended: freely, totally, faithfully, and fruitfully. It is a challenge, to be sure, but also provides us with the opportunity to be schooled in the art of love. Living this life of virtue will not only lead us to happiness, but to holiness.

When we learn to live faithfully and to love rightly, we will have peace as we discern the path that God is asking us to walk. We will know that our joy comes from giving ourselves completely to God, regardless of the vocation to which we're called.

If we love with all we've got, and live for Jesus Christ in every area of our lives, we will have the peace and happiness we desire. We will be fulfilling the purpose for which we were created! We will be living according to the truth of who we are—a truth that will set us free (see Jn 8:32). And you can count on this being an adventurous journey.

"Holy purity is granted by God when it is asked for with humility."
– St. Josemaria Escriva

Being made in God's image and likeness is the starting point. Receiving God's love and loving others through self-giving is the path. And union with God in heaven is the destination. If we allow these truths to sink in, it will transform the way we view life itself.

But life is not simply *viewed*. Life is *lived*. While the need to "give of yourself" may not be hard to understand, putting this truth into practice is another matter. One way to do this is through the **corporal works of mercy**. This makes sense when you consider that the word "corporal" means "bodily." Living the

Theology of the Body involves using our bodies to help others.

There are seven corporal works of mercy: feeding the hungry, sheltering the homeless, clothing the naked, visiting the sick, visiting the imprisoned, giving drink to the thirsty, and burying the dead. There are people all over this country who fit these descriptions, giving you plenty of opportunities to love and serve like Jesus. This is where the call to love collides with daily life.

As you share your time and energy with others, be ready to share your faith not only with your body, but with your words as well. As you engage others with the liberating truths you have learned, you will be joining an effort of **evangelization**. Evangelization is sharing the Christian faith with others. The word "evangelist" comes from a Greek word that means "bringer of good news." Evangelization is not the same as **proselytism**, which is *forcing* your belief on others and restricting their freedom by "beating them over the head" with the truth. Instead of this approach, John Paul II constantly encouraged us to take up the **New Evangelization**, which is an active effort to share Christ with the modern world. This new evangelization recognizes that in our times there is a special need to take share the Gospel with new enthusiasm, new methods, and new expressions.

notes

COMPREHENSION & DISCUSSION QUESTIONS:

1. How is the *language of the body* connected to free, total, faithful, and fruitful love?

2. What are the *corporal works of mercy*?

3. How are they connected to the Theology of the Body?

4. What is the difference between *evangelization* and *proselytism*?

5. Can you think of some ways we can be sure we are evangelizing and not proselytizing?

6. What is the *New Evangelization*?

7. Can you give some examples of the *New Evangelization* in action?

A simple step to joining the New Evangelization is to learn how to give your **testimony**. Your testimony is *your personal story* of hope and redemption. If God has touched your heart and transformed your faith, others need to know this! So practice telling your story and then begin to share it. Be able, at a moment's notice, to articulate why you are living out the call to chastity and purity in your life—something that is so countercultural. There are people who will be blessed

by what you share and who will make changes in their lives, embracing the Theology of the Body as you have. God will put people in your path who need to hear what you have to say about His plan for our bodies. Never underestimate the power of your testimony.

Even more important than your verbal testimony is the life you actually live, which will speak more eloquently than words ever could. With this in mind, if our lives are not consistent with what we preach, we will be considered hypocrites and will give scandal to the Faith. Remember, our actions often speak louder than words.

If you cannot express your faith and love through giving of your time and energy to serve others with your body, you are like an adult who chooses to stay in the kiddy pool while all the others are swimming in the ocean. If you recognize the beauty of John Paul II's teaching in your mind, but do not put it into practice or share it with others, is the teaching really worth anything? Faith is meant to be lived, but also meant to be given away.

If you want to go deeper into the ocean of God's grace and truth, then you need to be willing to dive into the deep waters. This is why St. James wrote that "Faith without works is dead" (Jas 2:20), and St. Peter wrote, "Always be ready to give an explanation to anyone who asks you for a reason for your hope" (1 Pet 3:15-16, NAB). We are called to give away what has been given to us (see Mt 10:8).

"Preach the gospel at all times, and when necessary, use words."
– St. Francis of Assisi

Though this dive may feel like a major leap of faith, realize that you will be joining millions of others around the world who are committing themselves to this teaching and putting it into practice. The dive is more than worth it! The excitement and freedom you will experience through living a life of purpose, in accord with your dignity, is far beyond any pleasures the world offers you.

You may have heard the phrase, "If it looks too good to be true, it probably is." Although this is generally true, it is not the case when it comes to the Theology of the Body. It's the real deal. When lived, it delivers what it promises: peace, truth, confidence, joy, and countless other natural and supernatural gifts.

If your dating relationships are not as satisfying as you believe you deserve, God has something extraordinary to offer you. Or maybe you have despaired that life seems void of meaning. Take heart in knowing that God is here and He's ready to help. In fact, He is actually calling you to join Him in an awesome, personal relationship—a love like no other, and the fulfillment of all your heart's deepest desires. Are you ready to give your "Yes"?

"Show now that you are truly converted; call others to repentance. The graces I have bestowed on you are not meant for you alone."
– St. Margaret of Cortona (words spoken to her by Jesus)

Notes & Nuggets:

Finish the course by asking the teens to come to class the next day or next session with comments regarding their thoughts on the whole curriculum. Ask them about their experience of learning this teaching. What did they like? With what did they struggle? What confused them? What challenged them? What got them excited?

At Ascension Press, we are committed to bringing you the greatest resources that help you share the Catholic faith, and we know that means sometimes revising things to make them better. Please feel free to share the comments of your students with us, as well as your own comments about what you enjoyed about this curriculum. If there is something not in these pages that you think would have helped you, please share that with us, too.

Write to us at: Ascension Press, P. O. Box 1990, West Chester, PA 19380, or email us at: TOBforTeens@AscensionPress.com

COMPREHENSION & DISCUSSION QUESTIONS

1. What is a *testimony*?

2. What other ways can you think of to apply the teaching of the Theology of the Body in your daily life?

3. What do you foresee as some great opportunities for sharing this message with others who are really hurting or may still be lost in concupiscence?

4. What do you think will be some of the challenges of sharing this message of hope with others?

DIGGING DEEPER: Mary, Joseph, and the Theology of the Body

Imagine being an unmarried teenage girl, living in a small town of about 500 people ... and being pregnant. Odds are, the Blessed Virgin Mary can relate to the pain of high school gossip more than you ever realized. Imagine the looks she may have received and the comments she might have heard behind her back as she walked through town. The same goes for St. Joseph, her fiancé. Everyone would have assumed the worst about him, too.

In a similar way, our modern culture often looks down upon young people, assuming the worst. For this reason, we can look to Joseph and Mary as examples of how to rise above any person or culture that may look down upon you. They were two people who did not allow the opinions of others to determine their calling and their sense of worth. They knew their value in God's eyes. Instead of growing bitter through their sufferings and drifting from God, they grew in wisdom and turned to Him in times of uncertainty.

The foundation of their courage could very well have been due their knowledge of their worth. St. Joseph knew that he was a son of God, and he also surely knew the tremendous dignity found in Mary. Being a just and righteous man, Joseph also knew about the inherent dignity of her body. Therefore, he would have guarded her innocence. The resulting fact is that the Catholic Church honors him with the title "Guardian of the Virgin."

As for Mary, in her human relationships she teaches us that through purity of heart, one becomes free to love another with the greatest love possible—the love of God. Her love for God and her husband was so great that the more Joseph came to know her, the closer he would get to God. Mary is a model of how to be married in true love.

"Love Our Lady. And she will obtain for you abundant grace to conquer in your daily struggle."
– St. Josemaria Escriva

APPLICATION

Option #1: "Is Sex Good or Bad? The Great Debate"

Designate twenty-five to thirty minutes of class to stage a debate. Use this opportunity to challenge your students to really articulate the truths of the Theology of the Body through a role-play debate. If possible, invite another teacher (or a priest or chaplain) to come in and play the role of someone who is from a deserted island and has never heard of John Paul II or the Theology of the Body. Have the visitor act as if he or she thinks the body and sex are bad. Position yourself in the center of your students so you can quietly give them suggestions to win the debate together, convincing the visitor of the truths of the body, sexuality, and the purpose of our lives as revealed in the Theology of the Body.

If you cannot have a visitor to play the role of debater, then play the role yourself. Debate with your students, but if you are "winning" the debate, be sure to leave enough time at the end of class to revisit the arguments and clarify the best answers to the objections which you had pretended to espouse in the debate. It is an "unforgivable" classroom mistake to somehow not allow enough time for this clarification.

Option #2: Meditation/Journal: Christ Has No Body Here On Earth Now But Yours

Use the song by John Michael Talbot, "St. Teresa's Prayer" [available on the albums *Quiet Reflections* (1987) and *Master Collection* (1989)] as a meditation and primer for a closing prayer journal for the curriculum. The song is a call to be Christ to all that we meet and to not only represent Him with our spirits but with our bodies–eyes, hands, feet, etc.

Option #3: Prayer Reflection: Conversion to Clarity, Saul to Paul"

Have the students read and reflect in silence upon Saul's conversion, including the time of his "sending out" when the scales fell from his eyes, and his sight was restored through the prayer of Ananias (see Acts 9:1-19). During the reflection time, you may want to play some soft, meditative music to help the students focus and remain in a state of prayer. Ask the students to reflect on the following:

1. Do you see any similarities between Saul's life and your own? If so, what are they?

2. Who is someone in your life who could act as your modern day "Ananias," praying for you (and with you) to help you stay close to God when you are tempted to drift away?

3. St. Paul encouraged us to boast of our weaknesses (see 2 Cor 11:30). Think of someone you trust, with whom you can share your weaknesses, and ask him or her to keep you accountable. Remember that Scripture says, "As iron sharpens iron, so man sharpens his fellow man" (Prov 27:17 NAB). Consider asking this trusted friend to be "iron" in your life, helping you to become all that God wants you to be.

4. How clearly do you see the purpose of your life right now?

5. The Lord tells us, through Scripture, "My grace is sufficient for you, for power is made perfect in weakness" (2 Cor 12:9, NAB). Pray for the ability to be humble and to receive God's perfect grace, which will help you to be free to live the good life of purity and authentic love.

Furthermore, by her relationship with God, she's a model of the religious life for us. She shows us that we first must understand spousal love before we can understand the true meaning of virginity. For example, a woman does not become a nun because she wants to avoid relationships. Nor does a man choose celibacy because he cannot find a date. They choose their vocations because they want to give life to others by making a gift of themselves to God. Without understanding the spousal meaning of virginity, the religious life simply looks like the absence of sex. By understanding Mary and her calling to virginity, we can understand the rich meaning of the celibate life. But no matter what vocation one chooses, married or the celibate life, Mary is the model. She makes the Theology of the Body come to life.

You have learned throughout this curriculum that because you are made in the image and likeness of God, you are created to exist for others, to be a gift for them. With this in mind, we can see why Mary is the perfect example of what it means to be human. She made a total gift of herself to God. By doing so, she not only brought life into the world, she brought *eternal* life into the world by giving birth to the Savior! She proves how fruitful a life can become when it is lived for others.

Look to Our Lady as you strive to live the teachings of the Theology of the Body. She's not abnormal because she's so close to God; instead, she is the model of what we are created to be. We often have the impression of Mary as a hyper-pious and even prudish person. Mary, rather, lived the truth of her body to the full. Because God spared her from sin, she was able to live and understand the true meaning of her sexuality without any confusion. This is why we should turn to her seeking help to live the Theology of the Body.

notes

LIVE IT OUT: Living the Free Life

So *how* does one live these teachings out in a practical way and on a daily basis? Here's a twelve step plan, one that follows the theme of each chapter.

1. **Build up your family.** You are created for *love and communion*. The members of your family may or may not exemplify these words, but they are still your family. Your initial reaction to this suggestion may be one

of hesitation, but ask yourself this: Am I going to be part of the problem or part of the solution? Blessed Pier Giorgio Frassati once said, "I cannot build one family on the ruins of another."[1] If you can learn how to love your family, you will be training yourself to be able to love anybody.

2. **Be willing to sacrifice.** Never underestimate the power and grace that comes our way when we make

MOVIE CLIP/SONG SUGGESTIONS

MOVIE CLIPS:

1. *Bruce Almighty:* Show the segment that falls between 1:15:29 and 1:21:21. Bruce, the main character played by Jim Carrey, leaves his job because he knows God has other plans for him. This decision comes after a brief time when he has actually played God, disastrously.

2. *Finding Nemo:* Show the segment that falls between 1:04:59 and 1:13:37. Dory, the fish with short-term memory loss, encourages her friend Marlin to let go of his fear so he can live free.

3. *Coach Carter:* Show the segment that falls between 2:04:33 and 2:11:28. The main character, Coach Carter, gives a speech to his team which has just lost the state championship. He encourages them telling them that they achieved more than a win with a victory within. (NOTE: In this movie, one of the main characters has an abortion and the movie portrays this as a responsible decision, rather than the grave moral evil that it is.)

4. *The Shawshank Redemption:* Show the segment that falls between 1:51:38 and 2:00:27. This is the scene when the main character, Andy, (Timothy Robbins) breaks out from the tunnel into the field and the water. This imagery could be seen as symbolizing baptism, freedom, redemption, and new life.

SONGS:

1. *St. Theresa's Prayer* — John Michael Talbot (*Quiet Reflections*)

A quiet, meditative song about being Christ to others in everyday life, and doing so in particular with our bodies. Acoustic/Meditative.

2. *I Will Choose Christ* — Tom Booth (*Find us Ready*)

A clear song of commitment, where we're called to say "Yes" to Christ and the demands of love. This is a good one to sing at a closing prayer service or liturgy with your teens. Contemporary/Worship.

3. *More Than Fine* — Switchfoot (*The Beautiful Letdown*)

A call to not settle for a life of mediocrity but to go beyond just getting by–to where one lives for more than this moment. Alternative Rock.

4. *It's All About to Change* — Tree 63 (*The Life and Times of Absolute Truth*)

Now that you know the truth, it's all about to change. Pop/Rock.

5. *Free* — Shawn McDonald (*Ripen*)

The song challenges us to believe that if we don't lose sight of the truth, the truth will set us free. Acoustic/Folk.

6. *Take My Life* — Scott Underwood (*Winds of Worship*)

A song of commitment. Sometimes people substitute the word "purity" and sing a spontaneous fourth verse with this one. Worship.

7. *Getting into You* — Relient K (*Two Lefts Don't Make a Right, But Three Do*)

Making the switch to live for God and not for ourselves will make us see things in a different perspective. Punk/Ballad.

LIVE IT OUT: *(Cont.)*

sacrifices. Fasting is a great way to offer your body back to the Lord. When you are in the car, turn off the radio once in a while and spend time in silence or in prayer. Tune into the needs of those around you and practice sacrificing for them as you learn to will the good of another. The more you learn to "go without," the more you will be going "with" God over yourself.

3. **Expose your *inner* beauty.** Do your family and friends know the authentic you? Instead of avoiding your parents, try spending some time with them … just you, no siblings. Make time in your schedule just to "waste time" with your youth minister or priest from church. Giving of your heart through rich conversations with others will help you grow in interpersonal relationships. This will be a step toward the advice of St. Catherine of Siena, who said "If you are what you should be, you will set the whole world ablaze!"

4. **Don't ever forget how *good* you are.** God sees you and says, "Behold, you are very good!" He loves you more than you can imagine, no matter what you've done in the past. If it's sexual sin, addiction, self-hatred, or any other sin that binds you, admit it and reconcile it. You are beautiful in His sight. Remember the words of John Paul II: "We are not the sum of our weaknesses and failures; we are the sum of the Father's love for us and our real capacity to become the image of His Son."² Jesus offers you hope, healing, and a new life of redemption. Say "Yes" to His love!

5. **Increase in knowledge.** The more truth you know, the more you can share it with others and help them find freedom. Actually, the more you know, the more God can share through you. Let this curriculum act as a beginning of your new world of faith learning. Get some CDs or books on the Theology of the Body and make the subject your own. Read the Bible for a few minutes each day. Got questions? The *Catechism of the Catholic Church* has your answers. Open your mind and soul up to a whole new world of truth that will set you free.

6. **Practice the power of silence.** The language of your body must correspond to the language of your mouth.

If gossip is a habit of yours, ask a friend to help you to stop. Reflect on the wisdom of Scripture: *"For one who hates gossip, evil is lessened. Never repeat a conversation and you will lose nothing at all. With friend or foe do not report it, and unless it would be a sin for you, do not disclose it"* (Sir 19:6-8). The language of your mouth and body will flow from the language of your heart. Pray for the grace not to judge the hearts of others.

7. **Learn to give.** Reach out in selfless service to be a servant; imitate Jesus' love by giving of yourself. Don't give until you feel better; give until it *hurts*. After all, you are trying to imitate the free, total, faithful, and fruitful love of Christ, which was not fulfilled in the comfort of a hammock. The height of love was demonstrated on the Cross. Ask the Lord to give you a generous heart so you can make a gift of yourself to others.

8. **Train yourself in faithfulness.** Be faithful to every promise that you make, large and small, in *all* of your relationships—even with the people you would rather ignore. Practice may not make you perfect, but it will make you prepared for a life of fidelity to one person, should God call you to marriage.

9. **Pray for priests and religious.** Make a habit of offering daily prayers for celibates, whether they live in your city or across the globe. Take the time to ask your parish priest, religious sisters, or priests or brothers in your school about their own prayer requests. Remember the power of intercessory prayer. And, as you pray for those who are already celibate, pray also for all those teens who are studying the Theology of the Body curriculum. Pray that they—and you— would be open to answering the call to celibacy if God calls you.

10. **Find some heroes and spend time with them.** Hopefully you have people in your life who live out their call to holiness in a bold way. Seek them out and spend time with them. In addition, spend time with the heroes in heaven, such as the Blessed Mother and St. Joseph—models of marriage and celibacy, as well as humility and love. While you're at it, ask John Paul

Notes & Nuggets: S.M.A.R.T. Plan Project (found in appendix). This is an intense project but, if done diligently and neatly, it can be a really powerful souvenir with which to leave the class. The project will help students to remain intent on really living out the Theology of the Body in a well-rounded way. The lives of teenagers can generally be divided into the five S.M.A.R.T. areas noted in the example below. "S.M.A.R.T" is an **acronym** for Specific Measurable Attainable Result-Oriented Timebound. Teens struggle to make their goals specific, measurable, and time-bound. These will probably be the areas in which you need to help them most.

On pages 199-201 of the appendix is an example of how a student would go about doing this project. Notice the deadlines and action plans beneath each item. Remind your teens that if it is important enough to prioritize, then it should be important enough to write down and plan clearly.

LIVE IT OUT: *(Cont.)*

II to pray for you, too. It was his "Yes" to God that allowed the Spirit to prompt and instruct him in the concepts that would become the Theology of the Body.

11. **Tell the truth with your body.** Reject the counterfeits of lust and fleeting pleasure and build your relationships on the truth you have discovered. Remember these wise words of John Paul II: "Deep within yourself, listen to your conscience which calls you to be pure. ... A home is not warmed by the fire of pleasure which burns quickly like a pile of withered grass. Passing encounters are only a caricature of love; they injure hearts and mock God's plan."[3] Don't settle for meaningless hook-ups. Don't cheapen yourself by being a "friend" who offers "benefits." Practice purity and reap the benefits of authentic love.

12. **Rise and fall with prayer.** Blessed (Mother) Teresa of Calcutta said, "Purity is the fruit of prayer." So, pray before you get out of bed in the morning and before you close your eyes at night. Be intentional about your prayer. Don't just pray quickly in the morning, but wake up earlier so that you have ample time to start your day with God. Do the same thing at night, spend time talking *and* listening to Him. Do more than just offer a prayer as you fall asleep. Before you count sheep, have a good talk with the Good Shepherd.

"Remember: Christ is calling you; the Church needs you; the Pope believes in you and he expects great things of you!"[4]

WORK IT OUT:

Assignment #1: If you have ever had a conversion experience—a clear moment when you chose Christ and said "Yes" to God's will—write the details of it into a short autobiographical story. If you are comfortable, share the story with your class. If it turns out well and you want to really evangelize, put it into email form and blast it out as a special message to everyone on your email list. You never know when your story of grace and redemption will touch someone else's heart and help him or her to choose Christ as well.

Assignment #2: If you have not clearly made a commitment to Jesus Christ, be honest about it. Are there questions about Jesus or the Catholic faith that are unanswered? Are you afraid to change? Do you not believe God's love can change your life? Put your thoughts into your journal and get serious with God. Wrestle with Him and pray yourself through a long "dialogue" with Him on paper. If you wish, when you are finished, write a prayer asking for His help.

Assignment #3: Rewrite the lyrics to a popular song (for example, "Good Riddance" ["Time of Your Life"] by Green Day or Aretha Franklin's classic "Respect"). Use the song as a tool to express your new knowledge of the Theology of the Body and to commit to proclaim these truths with conviction. If you are allowed to work on this assignment with a friend or a group, practice the song and sing it for the rest of the class.

Notes & Nuggets: The following projects work well as group projects and can serve as a review before taking an exam on this material, or as a type of summary assignment that integrates all their learning into one synthetic project.

Notes & Nuggets: In the closing prayer, we ask the intercession of St. Catherine of Siena. Born in Italy in the year 1347, Catherine had her first vision when she was only six years old and became a Dominican sister when she was only fifteen. She dedicated herself to helping the poor and the sick. Because of her boldness and wisdom, Pope Urban VI asked her to work with politicians, royalty, and members of the Church to settle disputes and find peace. Her deep faith and the profound insights in her writings earned her the title "Doctor of the Church" in 1970. She was a fearless and charitable ambassador of the truth.

Assignment #4: Choose a corporal work of mercy and invite your family (or friends) to join you in serving the physical needs of someone else. Write a short essay summarizing your experience.

Project #1: Create a Theology of the Body Trivia Game. Use the Jeopardy format, or create your own. Use all of the material you have learned in this curriculum to create a comprehensive game you can play in your class. Create the game on paper, in PowerPoint, or some other format of your choice. Be neat, and be sure to include information from every chapter. Make four, six, or eight categories (ask your teacher) with at least five questions each (and if it is Jeopardy format, a "final Jeopardy" question). Use the game as a review for your test, if you have one.

Project #2: Create a Comprehensive "Goal Sheet" (see appendix, pp. 199–201). In this project, you will put your thoughts and commitments into a comprehensive action plan regarding the purpose and goals of your life. Create your own goals beneath these five overarching categories: Spiritual, Social, Academic, Physical, and Personal. Consult your teacher for directions and help in making your goals into S.M.A.R.T. ones: Specific, Measurable, Attainable, Results-oriented, and Time-bound. Be sure to have a detailed action plan for each goal on your goal sheet. For example, if your goal is to "learn to play the guitar" it must be followed up with a step-by-step plan as to how you will achieve that goal by the desired date, including earlier dates that will serve as markers as you progress along your route. When your sheet is complete, type it out neatly and try to laminate it. Put a copy of it in your locker at school and one at home to be daily reminders of the purposes and goals in your life.

Project #3: Write a one-act play called "Pure Sexual Revolution." This will work best as a group project, but only with mature students who can take this opportunity seriously. Using the list of four resources below, write a one-act play using only two to six characters who poetically reflect the truths that you have learned in this curriculum. Consider addressing the following topics: God, love, lust, chastity, sex, procreation, vocation, marriage, fidelity, unfaithfulness, total self-donation, celibacy, the personalistic norm, happiness, suffering, purpose, good, evil, heaven, hell, eternity, etc. Get creative and set your play in whatever period of time you desire, including one or two characters (if you wish) such as Jesus, Mary, Joseph, John Paul II, or other saints or famous persons from history.

Resource list for Project #3:

- Scripture, particularly spousal imagery (as found in Ezekiel, Hosea, Song of Songs, Ephesians, etc.)
- The Theology of the Body
- Quotes from John Paul II
- Pope Benedict XVI's encyclical, *Deus Caritas Est* ("God is Love")

CLOSING PRAYER

Leader: In the name of the Father, and of the Son, and of the Holy Spirit. **Amen.**

All: St. Catherine of Siena, please pray with me that I, like you, would have the conviction to live and proclaim the truth to a world desperately in need of it, both to those within the Church and to those far away from her. **Amen.**

IN HIS OWN WORDS

- **On Sharing the Good News:** "Gratitude and joy at the incomparable dignity of man impel us to share this message with everyone: "that which we have seen and heard we proclaim also to you, so that you may have fellowship with us" (1 Jn 1:3). We need to bring the Gospel of life to the heart of every man and woman and to make it penetrate every part of society" (*Evangelium Vitae*, 80).

- **On Evangelization Bringing Hope and Freedom:** "It is the proclamation of a living God who is close to us, who calls us to profound communion with himself and awakens in us the certain hope of eternal life. It is the affirmation of the inseparable connection between the person, his life and his bodiliness. It is the presentation of human life as a life of relationship, a gift of God, the fruit and sign of his love. It is the proclamation that Jesus has a unique relationship with every person, which enables us to see in every human face the face of Christ. It is the call for a 'sincere gift of self' as the fullest way to realize our personal freedom" (*Evangelium Vitae*, 81).

- **On Evangelization as being Christocentric:** "We are certainly not seduced by the naive expectation that, faced with the great challenges of our time, we shall find some magic formula. No, we shall not be saved by a formula but by a Person, and the assurance which he gives us: I am with you!" (*Novo Millenio Inuente*, 29).

- **On New Evangelization:** The "new evangelization [involves] a vital effort to come to a deeper understanding of the mysteries of faith and to meaningful language with which to convince our contemporaries that they are called to newness of life through God's love" (Springtime of Evangelization, p. 55 [The 1998 *ad limina* addresses of John Paul II to the Bishops of the United States]).

"It is not therefore a matter of inventing a 'new program.' The program already exists: it is the plan found in the Gospel and in the living Tradition; it is the same as ever. Ultimately, it has its centre in Christ himself, who is to be known, loved and imitated, so that in him we may live the life of the Trinity, and with him transform history until its fulfillment in the heavenly Jerusalem. This is a program which does not change with shifts of times and cultures, even though it takes account of time and culture for the sake of true dialogue and effective communication" (*Novo Millenio Ineunte*, 29).

- **On Service:** "Dear young people, service is a completely natural vocation, because human beings are by nature servants, not being masters of their own lives and being, in their turn, in need of the service of others. Service shows that we are free from the intrusiveness of our ego. It shows that we have a responsibility to other people. And service is possible for everyone, through gestures that seem small, but which are, in reality, great if they are animated by a sincere love. True servants are humble and know how to be 'useless' (see Lk 17:10). They do not seek egoistic benefits, but expend themselves for others, experiencing in the gift of themselves the joy of working for free" (Message for 40th World Day of Prayer for Vocations, May 11, 2003).

Glossary
of Key Terms

Corporal works of mercy: These are actions of love that meet the physical needs of others. The seven works include feeding the hungry, sheltering the homeless, clothing the naked, visiting the sick, visiting the imprisoned, giving drink to the thirsty, and burying the dead. The word "corporal" comes from the Latin word for body.

Evangelization: It is sharing the Christian faith with others. The word "evangelist" comes from a Greek word that means "bringer of good news."

New Evangelization: A term referring to the special need to share the Gospel with new enthusiasm, new methods, and new expressions. The new evangelization is not a new Gospel, but it recognizes that as the world changes, the methods for sharing the Good News need to change if they are to be effective.

Proselytism: The *forcing* of one's beliefs on others instead of *sharing* them charitably. It is restricting the freedom of others by pressuring them with the truth, instead of allowing God to work in their hearts. We must remember that ultimately God is the One who converts others, not us.

Testimony: Your *personal story* of hope and redemption in Jesus Christ that you share with others.

Word Searches

Chapter #6 Word Search
(From the terms in Chapter 6)

Word bank:

Adultery	Language
Body	Love
Contraception	Objectify
Fornication	Pornography
Interpersonal	Relationship

```
Y N L L N B J B V Y P V U R L
D O E A B O I X R J G W E F A
O I F O N T I E U M C L E S N
B T P I C O T T E Q A E Z T G
K P Q Q U L S K A T K E X L U
K E X Q U I P R I C A R T G A
S C W D M G J O E A I X V N G
J A A Q H D N V Q P I N E E E
D R J Q N S J C H D R D R O H
K T R A H Q E C R A F E R O B
W N A I L O V E O Z T T T S F
T O P O B J E C T I F Y V N N
H C Y H P A R G O N R O P M I
W C T S E I Z M X L X E U F V
E U K W J I R T B M L O E S J
```

Chapter #8 Work Search
(From the terms in Chapter 8)

It's game time again. This time find the key words highlighted in Chapter 8. Compete with other teams in your class or youth group—seeing who can find all the words first.

Word bank:

Agape	Oxytocin
Encyclical	Spousal analogy
Infatuation	Submissi
NFP	

```
D P N F P K M B C P R H G A A
Y E W I J F A X R J I L M S C
V B R L Q P O K J R D   P U G
D J J Y P L O I I T D O B B N
Q L K M Z X A E N P U S S M I
S F B V F E T P F S K F O I D
H S U B E Q P G A A H W V S K
A T R Q W V E L T R V X I S M
Y I E P A G A Y U K D H T I B
I A W Z P N K S A A B E Y O B
O T L I A D M C T Z I K F N E
T I S L W V B N I C O T Y X O
F O O B E N C Y C L I C A L E
J G T I S K V T N L M D Y P Q
Y R J W E H Q A U D L I S P L
```

Chapter #9 Word Search
(From the terms in Chapter 9)

Word bank:

Celibacy	Nuns
Contemplative	Ontological
Continence	Vocation
Eschatological	

```
S T W U H K E D Q I R D O Y K
V C A C O N T I N E N C E S Y
O O G W Q D I U J R D U P S G
S N J Y O F C S I T P A N U U
U T G M Z N D R N P U X V S J
M E S C H A T O L O G I C A L
W M U B E Q P O A A L W V S L
Q P B R Q F J E L T A V X A S
J L S N O I T A C O V H G O E
D A P Y P N K P A A G E Y S G
I T L I A E J A D Z P I A N T
T I I A W I B T Q C O T C X E
R V O B P N F W G Y U R A A H
C E L I B A C Y T C J T K Y P L
L I C I J E S E I R S J S D G
```

Media Analysis

(The following assignment should be done only with parental consent.)

Watch one hour of television and catalog the following into the data sheet below:

- Number of sexual jokes

- Verbal references to sex and innuendoes

- Sexual scenes

- Immodestly-dressed characters

As you are viewing, ask yourself if the "language of the body" message being communicated is "true" or "false." Use the chart to the right to keep track of your analysis. Be sure to catalog the commercials on your data sheet as well. Then create a short summary of your findings, especially noting any patterns that you found (i.e., most of the references were made under the guise of humor, most were said by men, etc.)

	Language of the Body TRUE	Language of the Body FALSE
Number of sexual jokes		
Verbal references to sex and innuendoes		
Sexual scenes		
Immodestly-dressed characters		

Summary

_____

_____

_____

_____

_____

_____

_____

_____

_____

_____

_____

_____

Bet You Didn't Know

Name : _____ Date: _____

Find someone who:

1. Was born in another state: _____

2. Has had more than one surgery on their body: _____

3. Has officially broken a bone in their body: _____

4. Is the youngest child in their family: _____

5. Is one of five or more children: _____

6. Knows how to play a musical instrument: _____

7. Knows how to build or fix a computer: _____

8. Has caught a fish larger than two pounds: _____

9. Has a grandparent who is more than eighty years old: _____

10. Is double-jointed: _____

11. Can make "cracking sounds" with their knuckles, ankles, or necks: _____

12. Can run the forty-yard dash in less than 4.8 seconds: _____

13. Is an honor roll student: _____

14. Is a twin or a triplet: _____

15. Has not been absent for even one day of school this year: _____

16. Likes cottage cheese: _____

17. Has eaten shark, alligator, snake, or sushi: _____

18. Has been to a foreign country: _____

19. Knows how to speak another language fluently: _____

20. Has a pet: _____

21. Has a parent who is or was in the military: _____

22. Has more than twenty email addresses in their address book: _____

23. Has a quarter in his/her pocket or purse: _____

24. Still sleeps with a teddy bear or some other stuffed animal: _____

25. Is scared of heights or scared of the dark: _____

26. Can sing or draw well: _____

27. Can text message as fast as they can write with a pencil: _____

28. Has seen a Japanese "anime" film: _____

29. Thinks Elvis is still alive: _____

30. Can sing (or recite the lyrics) of the theme song for *Barney*: _____

Clock Appointments

Use this clock to make an "appointment" with students or fellow youth group members whom you know the least. If you're good friends with someone, you should avoid each other in this activity, unless you have a small class and have remaining spots on your clock. We still encourage you, though, to first fill up the spots with those whom you know the least.

Move around the room quickly to fill up your appointments. For example, Billy asks Annie "Do you have 1:00 p.m. open?" If Annie is available, she writes Billy's name on her 1:00 p.m. line and Billy writes Annie's name down for his 1:00 p.m. line. You should proceed in this manner until your clock is full.

Once your clock is filled, conduct a short interview, asking the following questions:

1. Music and Movies: What kind of music do you like? What is your favorite band? What is your all-time favorite movie?

2. Hobbies: Are you involved with any extracurricular activities at school? What are your hobbies and things you like to do on the weekends?

3. God: What is your relationship with God like? What is the coolest thing you have learned in this program so far? Do you have a favorite Bible verse or Bible story?

4. Growing Up: What ideas do you have for college? What do you think God wants you to do for your vocation? What do you want to do? What about a career?

5. Family: How many siblings do you have? Are your parents together? Do you want to get married? If so, how many kids do you think you would want to have?

6. Biggest Fear: What is your biggest fear?

7. Travel: If you could go anywhere in the world, where would it be? Who would you take with you?

It is very important that you focus on each other, facing each other and not looking at anyone else in the room. Try to avoid having one person dominate the conversation.

Dating "Game Theory"

In economics, there is something known as *game theory*, which is a method of making a smart decision in a time of uncertainty. In it, you plot out your potential decisions, along with their potential consequences. Then you compare the results and see which choice makes the most sense.

The same approach can be used for relationships. Here's how it works. To the left of the table below, try to make the choice between an unchaste relationship and a chaste one. Above the table are the possible outcomes of a given relationship. Since nobody knows the outcome of a relationship, you should ask yourself, "What's the best decision in the midst of that uncertainty?" You should fill in the blanks with pros and cons of each scenario.

	The relationship continues and you get married	The relationship does not work out and you break up
Chaste (pure) relationship	**A** Pros: _____ Cons: _____	**B** Pros: _____ Cons: _____
Unchaste (Sexually active) relationship	**C** Pros: _____ Cons: _____	**D** Pros: _____ Cons: _____

Make a List

This exercise is intended to be used with 'Live It Out' in Chapter 10.

Talents	Passions
_____	_____
_____	_____
_____	_____
_____	_____
_____	_____
_____	_____
_____	_____
_____	_____
_____	_____
_____	_____
_____	_____

The S.M.A.R.T Life Action Plan

In this project, you will put your thoughts and commitments into a comprehensive action plan regarding the purpose and goals of your life. Create your own goals beneath the following five overarching categories: *Spiritual*, *Physical*, *Social, Academic*, and *Personal*. Consult your teacher for directions and help in turning your goals into S.M.A.R.T. ones: Specific, Measurable, Attainable, Results-oriented, and Time-bound.

Be sure to have a detailed action plan for each goal on your goal sheet. For example, if your goal is to "learn to play the guitar" it must be followed up with a step-by-step plan as to how you will achieve that goal by the desired date, including earlier dates that will serve as markers as you progress along your route. When your sheet is complete, type it out neatly and try to laminate it. Put a copy of it in your locker at school and one at home to be daily reminders of the purposes and goals in your life.

This project certainly requires work but the end result will be worth it: you will have an excellent action plan on how you can live out the Theology of the Body.

Here is an example of a detailed S.M.A.R.T. plan. Feel free to use some of the items listed below in your list. Notice the deadlines and action plans beneath each item.

1. SPIRITUAL (Taking care of my spirit; drawing closer to Jesus)

  a. Go to Mass every Sunday with family

    i. Be in bed no later than midnight on Saturday, or on Saturday evening (before going out), discuss sleeping late Sunday morning and going to Sunday evening Mass with Mom & Dad

    ii. Listen better to the readings; read the gospel again on Sunday night before bed (check readings at: www.usccb.org/nab)

  b. Go to confession once a month

    i. Invite *(fill in a friend's name)* to go with me

    ii. If I can't make it Saturday afternoon, make an appointment with Fr. *(fill in a priest's name)* on Tuesday night after practice

  c. Pray daily

    i. Quietly pray a decade of the rosary on the way to school

    ii. Try to talk to God mentally between classes

    iii. Read at least five minutes of the Bible before bed

    iv. Listen to Christian music while doing homework instead of secular music

  d. Go to Youth Group every Wednesday/Sunday night

    i. Do homework right after school on Wednesday so I can go

    ii. If invited somewhere else by other friends, invite them to youth group instead

  e. Only put good information into my mind

    i. Use the family room computer at night instead of your computer in your bedroom, laptop, etc. when temptations may arise

    ii. Don't go to any movies that compromise the purity of my mind

    iii. Ask *(name)* to help me sift through my music; throw out bad stuff by January 1

    iv. Read daily online devotional at *(name)* website

2. PHYSICAL (Taking care of my body; using it well)

  a. Lose five pounds by May 1

    i. No eating between meals

    ii. Fast from food one day every other week

    iii. Only eat fast-food once every other week

  b. Bench twenty pounds more by May 1

    i. Work out three times per week with *(name)* (Monday/Wednesday/Friday)

    ii. Bench ten pounds more by Christmas

  c. Sleep eight hours a night

    i. Do homework before using computer or TV

    ii. Turn off cell phone at 9:30 p.m.

    iii. Start reading Bible/prayers at 9:45 p.m.

    iv. Lights out at 10:00 p.m.

v. Get up at 6:00 a.m.

d. Make the starting line-up for (*list sport*)

   i. Stick hard to work out schedule

   ii. Stay after practice to do extra sprints on Tuesday/ Thursday

   iii. Never miss practice unless deathly sick

   iv. Listen to coach and give 100 percent on every play

   v. Stick tight to diet, drink three waters a day, go to bed on time

3. **SOCIAL** (Building and maintaining good family, friend and dating relationships)

a. Make two new friends by Christmas

   i. Go to youth group every week

   ii. Invite (*name*) and (*name*) to come camping with the family at Thanksgiving

   iii. Go to all home basketball games this year

b. Spend time each week with Mom/Dad

   i. Help Dad wash his car on Saturday

   ii. Talk to Mom on the way home from school

   iii. Call if my plans change when I am out

   iv. Go with Mom shopping once a month

c. Stay close with Grandma

   i. Visit her every other Sunday

   ii. Call her on the weeks I don't visit

d. Keep good relationship with (*name*)

   i. Call him/her at least twice a week

   ii. Do something thoughtful for him/her on weekends

   iii. Stay pure in my thoughts and speech with him/her

   iv. Dress modestly when I go out

   v. Pray for him/her every night

4. **ACADEMIC** (Learning in school and otherwise)

a. Get scholarship to (*fill in*) university/college

   i. Turn in application by February 1

   ii. Take SAT or ACT prep course in October

   iii. Take SAT or ACT twice: November/January

b. Make the honor roll

   i. Do homework before spending time on computer and TV

   ii. Study for at least two hours for every chemistry test

    –Ask Bobby for help or study with Mom

   iii. Turn in all English papers two days early

    –Get teacher's comments and revise paper for due date

c. Read one spiritual book cover to cover by May 1

   i. Read for at least thirty minutes on Sundays

   ii. Ask Fr. (*name*) or youth minister for suggestions

d. Learn to cook five good meals by May 1

   i. Help Mom with dinner on Tuesdays

   ii. Cook Dad's birthday dinner in March

   iii. Start gathering tips and recipes to try online

5. **PERSONAL** (My personal goals that may not fall into the other areas)

a. Buy a used truck by January 1

   i. Save $4,500 (have $3,000 now)

    –Work six hours a week

    –Save seventy-five percent of allowance

   ii. No impulse buying on weekends

b. Learn to play the guitar by next school year

   i. Call Mrs. (*name*) about lessons by Sept 10

   ii. Practice every day after school for twenty mins

c. Serve kids at Spina Bifida camp in summer

   i. Get two letters of recommendation by March 1 (Ask Mr. J & Fr. X)

d. Stay pure in all areas of my life

   i. No spending the night at (*name*)'s house

   ii. Stay in close contact with (*name*) to hold her/him accountable and to stay accountable to them as well

1. SPIRITUAL (Taking care of my spirit; drawing closer to Jesus)

_____

2. PHYSICAL (Taking care of my body; using it well)

_____

3. SOCIAL (Building and maintaining good family, friend, and dating relationships)

_____

4. ACADEMIC (Learning in school and otherwise)

_____

5. PERSONAL (My personal goals that may not fall into the other areas)

About the Authors

Brian Butler served as the Associate Director for Youth Catechesis in the Archdiocese of New Orleans for two years, has taught theology and coordinated campus ministry at the high school level for five years, and has twelve years of experience in youth ministry. Currently, he coordinates a comprehensive vocation formation program for the Diocese of Houma-Thibodaux in Louisiana. Brian is the co-founder of Dumb Ox Productions Inc., a non-profit organization that offers retreats, speakers, and resources focusing on chastity and vocation formation for teenagers. He is the co-author of *The Bible Thumper* (vols. 1 & 2), holds a bachelor's degree in communications from the University of New Orleans, and is in the process of completing a master's degree in theology at Notre Dame Seminary School of Theology. Brian enjoys music, sports, and spending time with his wife, Lisa, and their three children.

Jason Evert speaks to more than 100,000 students each year an apologist and chastity speaker for Catholic Answers. He is the author of six books, including *If You Really Loved Me* and *Pure Love*, which challenge young people to embrace the virtue of chastity. As the founder of Catholic Answer's Pure Love Club, he is internationally-recognized as a leading chastity speaker and teacher. Jason earned a master's degree in theology, and undergraduate degrees in counseling and theology, with a minor in philosophy from the Franciscan University of Steubenville. He and his wife, Crystalina, are the parents of two young boys.

Crystalina Evert has shared her inspirational testimony to hundreds of thousands of teens around the world as a member of the Catholic Answers Speakers' Bureau. She is the author of the book *Pure Womanhood* and is a frequent guest on radio programs throughout the country. Together, she and Jason host the EWTN series, *The Pure Life*. Their other television appearances include Fox News, *Donahue*, WGN, and the BBC. They also serve on the board of directors for the National Abstinence Clearinghouse, and were presented with the 2003 Impact Award by the National Abstinence Clearinghouse in recognition of their success with teens in America.

Notes

Note: Date references (e.g., "October 29, 1980") refer to a particular address by Pope John Paul II on the Theology of the Body.

INTRODUCTION

1 Butch Hancock of the Flatlanders.

2 Christopher West, *Theology of the Body for Beginners* (West Chester, PA: Ascension Press, 2004), p. 95

CHAPTER 1

1 In Greek thought, the "logos" was also understood to be a unifying principle that held the world together. The logos was a connecting link between God and man. This is why, in the Gospel of John, Jesus is referred to as the "Word" (in the original Greek, "logos" is used). Jesus is the unifying link between heaven and earth, between God and man. This places Jesus Christ (who is God and man) at the heart of theology, at the center of the study of God.

2 Christopher West, *Theology of the Body for Beginners,* p. 21

3 Christopher West, *Theology of the Body for Beginners,* pp. 7-8, 24-26, 130

4 *Gaudium et Spes,* 22

5 February 20, 1980

6 *Fides et Ratio* 1.2

7 *Fides et Ratio,* greeting.

8 October 29, 1980

9 John 1:14

10 See *GS* 22 [emphasis added]

11 Monsignor Luigi Giussani, *At the Origin of the Christian Claim, p 87, quoting* Romano Guardini, La Coscienza (Brescia, Italy: Morcelliana, 1961), p. 52

Did You Know?

i *Divorce: Facts, Figures and Consequences,* prepared by Dr. Anne-Marie Ambert, York University, for the Vanier Institute of the Family, 1998

ii Heritage Foundation: Melissa G. Pardue, Robert E. Rector, and Shannan Martin; Backgrounder #1718, January 14, www.heritage.org/Research/Family/bg1718.cfm

iii Bumpass, L.L., and Lu, H.-H. Increased cohabitation changing children's family settings. Research on Today's Issues, NICHD, 13, September, 2002

iv Meg Meeker, Epidemic: *How Teen Sex Is Killing Our Kids* (Washington, D.C.: Regnery Publishing Company, 2002), p. 12

CHAPTER 2

1 Thomas Lickona, "The Neglected Heart: The Emotional Dangers of Premature Sexual Involvement." *American Educator* (Summer 1994): p. 37, citing Josh McDowell and Dick Day, *Why Wait: What You Need to Know About the Teen Sexuality Crisis* (San Bernardino: Here's Life Publishers, 1987)

2 A study from the Marriage and Family Life Office in the Archdiocese of Denver recently revealed that ninety-one percent of engaged couples were sexually active prior to getting married, with roughly sixty-six percent of them living together.

3 *Message of the Holy Father to the Youth of the World on the Occasion of the XIX World Youth Day,* February 22, 2004

4 Karol Wojtyla, *Love and Responsibility* (San Francisco: Ignatius Press, 1993), p. 172

5 *Gaudium et Spes,* 24

6 *Love and Responsibility,* p. 41

7 To see how God uses one great mind to build on the thought of another, read Pope Benedict XVI's first encyclical, *Deus Caritas Est* ("God is Love"). Here, Benedict builds on the thoughts of John Paul II and describes God's love for us as not only *agape* but *eros* as well. God loves us not only with unconditional love (*agape*), but with a passionate love (*eros*). In fact, if you pay close attention, you will notice that much of this encyclical is rooted in and building upon many of the ideas that John Paul II taught in the Theology of the Body.

8 C. S. Lewis, *The Great Divorce* (New York: MacMillan Publishing Company, 1946), p. 103

9 *Redemptor Hominis,* 10

10 *Love and Responsibility,* p. 169

11 Ibid, pp. 170-171

12 Ibid, p. 155

13 Ibid, p. 156

14 Ibid, p. 149

15 Ibid, p. 143

16 Ibid, p. 144

17 Christopher West, *Good News About Sex & Marriage* (Cincinnati, OH: St. Anthony Messenger Press, 2000), p. 229

18 *Love and Responsibility,* p. 171

Did You Know?

i "Teenage Sexual Abstinence and Academic Achievement," by Robert Rector and Kirk A. Johnson, Ph.D., Conference Paper, October 27, 2005

CHAPTER 3

1 November 24, 1982

2 Louis Reard, a lingerie salesman, was the inventor of the bikini.

3 March 18, 1981

4 Karol Wojtyla, *Love and Responsibility,* p. 181

5 *Love and Responsibility,* p. 183

CHAPTER 4

1 Michael Collopy, *Works of Love are Works of Peace* (San Francisco: Ignatius Press, 1996), p. 197

2 Pope John Paul II, to the youth of the world on the occasion of the 19th World Youth Day, 2004

Did You Know?

i *America's Adults and Teens Sound Off About Teen Pregnancy: An Annual National Survey, National Campaign to Prevent Teen Pregnancy,* December 16, 2003

CHAPTER 5

1 This analogy regarding a car, its design to run on a certain fuel, and its correlation to our freedom being based upon the truth of who we are created to be is commonly used by Christopher West in his books and speaking engagements.

2 *Letter to Families (1994),* 14

3 *Fides et Ratio,* 90

4 *Veritatis Splendor,* 32

5 *Redemptor Hominis,* 12

6 *Gaudium et Spes,* 22

Did You Know?

i *American Journal of Preventive Medicine*

CHAPTER 6

1 Christopher West, *Theology of the Body for Beginners* (West Chester, PA: Ascension Press, 2004), p. 90

2 April 29, 1981

3 *Love and Responsibility,* p. 38

4 May 6, 1981

5 April 29, 1981

6 May 6, 1981

7 Christopher West, *God's Plan for a Joy-Filled Marriage,* Talk #4 (West Chester, PA: Ascension Press, 2005)

8 Adapted from a prayer by Christopher West, *Theology of the Body for Beginners,* p 50

Did You Know?

i   United Nations Development Programme. *1998 Human Development Report.* (New York: United Nations, 1998)

ii Roberts, D. F. & Christenson, P. G. Popular music in childhood and adolescence. In Singer, D. G., Singer, J. L. (eds.), *Handbook of Children and the Media* (Thousand Oaks, CA: Sage Publications, Inc., 2001), pp. 395-414. Found at: www.mediafamily.org/facts/facts_music.shtml

iii R. E. J. Ryder, " 'Natural Family Planning' Effective Birth Control Supported by the Catholic Church," British Medical Journal 307 (September 18, 1993), pp. 723–726

CHAPTER 7

1   Hogan, Fr. Richard and Fr. John LeVoir, *Covenant of Love*, p. 47

2   Asuncion, Paraguay, May 18, 1988. As quoted in The *Meaning of Vocation*, pp. 18-19

3   Auckland, New Zealand, November 22, 1986. As quoted in *The Meaning of Vocation*, p. 19

4   Boston, USA, October, 1, 1979. As quoted in *The Meaning of Vocation*, pp. 19-20

5   St. Bernard, *Serm. XVIII in Cantica*

6   The example of the "dirt eater" used to support a rational argument against homosexual acts is from Thomas Storck's article, "Is Opposition to Homosexual Activity Irrational?" *New Oxford Review*, May 1997

7   For more information and research on this issue, consult the NARTH website www.narth.com.

Did You Know?

i   *Archives of Sexual Behavior*, Volume 31, Number 3, pp 289-293, by G.G. Gallup Jr. ; R.L. Burch ; S.M. Platek

CHAPTER 8

1   Dave Roever, *Scarred* (Fort Worth, TX: Roever Communications, 1995), p. 42

2   *Scarred*, p. 112

3   May 5, 1982

4   August 18, 1982

5   September 1, 1982

6   February 20, 1980

7   *Love and Responsibility*, p. 134

8   From a *Catholic World News* article entitled "A Culture of Inverted Sexuality," by Patrick F. Fagan, Dec. 21, 2001. Available online at: www.cwnews.com/news/viewstory.cfm?recnum=20831

9   Ibid.

10 Ibid.

11 "Forgetting Religion," *Washington Post* editorial, March 22, 1931

12 Patrick F. Fagan, "A Culture of Inverted Sexuality"

13 Available online at: www.mkgandhi.org/momgandhi/chap59.htm, cited as (H, 17-4-1937, p. 84).

14 Numerous studies have been conducted around the world showing the effectiveness of Natural Family Planning (NFP) to be in the high nineties, percentage-wise. For example, the Fairfield Study, which was done in five nations with 1,022 couples (who had no serious reason to avoid pregnancy) from 1970–1972 found a method effectiveness of ninety-nine percent (nine pregnancies in 14,416 months). Frank J. Rice and Claude A. Lanctot, "Results of a Recent Study of the Sympto-Lhermal Method of Natural Family Planning," *Linacre Quarterly* 45:4 (November, 1978), 388-391. [Fairfield Study statistic found online, with others at: www.ccli.org. There are various methods used under the single title of Natural Family Planning, and they can be used to avoid or achieve pregnancy. More statistics and information on various models is available at: www.creightonmodel.com, www.popepaulvi.com and www.billings-centre.ab.ca].

15 *Neural Oxytocinergic systems as Genomic Targets for Hormones and as Modulators of Hormone-Dependant Behaviors*, (New York: Rockefeller University, 1999)

16 Eric J. Keroack, M.D., FACOG and Dr. John R. Diggs Jr., M.D., "Bonding Imperative," A Special Report from the Abstinence Medical Council.

CHAPTER 9

1   This classic story has been retold by many. This retelling is based on the story as told by Lorraine Peterson in her book *If God Loves Me, Why Can't I Get My Locker Open?* (Minneapolis: Bethany Fellowship, 1980), p. 19

2   *Message of the Holy Father to the Youth of the World on the Occasion of the XIX World Youth Day*, February 22, 2004

3   April 7, 1982

4   *Ecclesia de Eucharistia*, 1

5   Christopher West, *Theology of the Body for Beginners*, p. 66

6   March 24, 1982

CHAPTER 10

1   Message at World Youth Day 2004, March 1, 2004

2   John Paul II, Address in Rome Italy, October 16, 1987

CHAPTER 11

1   *Love and Responsibility*, p. 171

2   General Audience, June 27, 1984

3   Crystalina Evert, *Pure Womanhood* (San Diego: Catholic Answers, 2005), pp. 21-22

4   November 24, 1982

5   Fulton Sheen, *The World's First Love* (San Francisco: Ignatius Press), p. 10

6   *Catechism of the Catholic Church,* 1127

7   *Lumen Gentium,* 48

8   Wojtyla, *op. cit.,* p. 134

9   Dr. Les Parrott III and Dr. Leslie Parrott, *Saving Your Marriage Before it Starts* (Grand Rapids, MI: Zondervan Publishing House, 1995), p. 41

10 St. Josemaria Escriva, *The Way* (Princeton, NJ: Scepter Press, 1982), Introduction, par. 4

Did You Know?

i   Brent C. Miller, J. Kelly McCoy, and Terrence D. Olson, "Dating Age and Stage as Correlates of Adolescent Sexual Attitudes and Behavior," *Journal of Adolescent Research* 1, no. 3 (1986), pp. 361-71

ii 2001 Youth Risk Behavior Survey

iii Vital and Health Statistics: Series 23, Number 24. December 2004. "Teenagers in the United States: Sexual Activity, Contraceptive Use, and Childbearing, 2002." U.S. Department of Health and Human Services, Centers for Disease Control and Prevention

CHAPTER 12

1   Blessed Pier Giorgio Frassati, as quoted in *My Brother Pier Giorgio: His Last Days,* by Luciana Frassati (New Hope, KY: New Hope Publications, 2002), p. 22

2   John Paul II, World Youth Day, 2002

3   Antananarivo, Madagascar, April 29, 1989. As quoted in *The Meaning of Vocation*, p. 28

4   John Paul II, January 26, 1999, Kiel Center, St. Louis, Missouri

Recommended Resources

The following list contains some excellent resources for teenagers and young adults to help you learn more about the Theology of the Body, as well as the truth and meaning of human sexuality, gender, and related issues.

Books and Resources on the Theology of the Body

Books

- *God's Plan for You: Life, Love, Marriage, and Sex* by David Hajduk. Available from Pauline Books and Media, 1-800-668-2078. www.daughtersofstpaul.com.

- *Man and Woman He Created Them: A Theology of the Body* by Pope John Paul II, translated and introduced by Michael M. Waldstein. Available from Pauline Books and Media, 1-800-668-2078. www.daughtersofstpaul.com.

- *Men and Women are from Eden* by Dr. Mary Healy. Available from St. Anthony's Messenger Press. 1-800-488-0488. www.americancatholic.org

- *Theology of the Body for Beginners* by Christopher West. Available from Ascension Press, 1-800-376-0520. www.ascensionpress.com

Audio/Video Resources

- Ascension Press, P.O. Box 1990, West Chester, PA 19380. 1-800-376-0520. www.ascensionpress.com

- Our Father's Will Communications, P.O. Box 815, Minooka, IL 60447. 1-815-828-5094. www.ourfatherswillcommunications.com

- The Gift Foundation, P.O. Box 95, Carpentersville, IL 60110. 1-800-421-GIFT. www.giftfoundation.org

Books and Resources on Chastity, Dating, Sexuality, and Gender

Books

- *Arms of Love* by Carmen Marcoux. Available from Courtship Now. (306) 934-3511. www.courtshipnow.com

- *Every Woman's Journey: Answering "Who am I" for the Feminine Heart.* Available from Our Father's Will Communications. 1-866-333-OFWC (6392). www.theologyofthebody.net

- *If You Really Loved Me* by Jason Evert. Available from Catholic Answers. 1-888-291-8000. www.pureloveclub.com

- *Love and Responsibility* by Karol Wojtyla (Pope John Paul II). Available from Ignatius Press. 1-800-651-1531. www.ignatius.com

- *Pure Love* (booklet) by Jason Evert. Available from Catholic Answers. 1-888-291-8000. www.pureloveclub.com

- *Pure Womanhood* (booklet) by Crystalina Evert. Available from Catholic Answers. 1-888-291-8000. www.pureloveclub.com

- *Real Love:* Answers to Your Questions on Dating, Marriage and the Real Meaning of Sex by Mary Beth Bonacci. Available from Ignatius Press. 1-800-651-1531. www.ignatius.com

- *Sex and Love: What's a Teenager to Do?* by Mary Beth Bonacci. Available from Ignatius Press. 1-800-651-1531. www.ignatius.com

Audio/Video Resources

- *Dating and Courtship* by Kimberly Hahn. Available from Lighthouse Catholic Media. 1-866-526-2151. www.LighthouseCatholicMedia.com

- *How to Teach Chastity to Teens* by Barbara McGuigan. Available from Lighthouse Catholic Media. 1-866-526-2151. www.LighthouseCatholicMedia.com

- *The Pornography Plague* by Jeff Cavins. Available from Ascension Press. 1-800-376-0520. www.ascensionpress.com

- *Romance without Regret* by Jason and Crystalina Evert. Available from Catholic Answers. 1-888-291-8000. www.pureloveclub.com

- *Winning the Battle for Sexual Purity* by Christopher West. Available from Ascension Press. 1-800-376-0520. www.ascensionpress.com

- *Women: God's Masterpiece* by Christopher West. Available from Ascension Press. 1-800-376-0520. www.ascensionpress.com

Organizations/Apostolates

Homosexuality/Chastity Support

- Courage, 210 W. 31st Street, New York, NY 10001. (212) 268-1010. www.couragerc.net

- National Association for Research and Therapy of Homosexuality (NARTH), 16633 Ventura Blvd, Suite 1340, Encino, CA 91436. (818) 789-4440. www.narth.com

Natural Family Plan/Contraception Alternatives

- Billings Ovulation Method Association, USA, 316 North 7th Avenue, St. Cloud, MN 56303. (320) 252-2100. www.boma-usa.org

- Couple to Couple League, P.O. Box 111184, Cincinnati, OH 45211-1184. (513) 471-2000. www.ccli.org

- Family of the Americas, P.O. Box 1170, Dunkirk, MD 20754. (301) 627-3346. www.familyplanning.net

- NFP Outreach, 3366 NW Expressway, Bldg. D, Suite 630, Oklahoma City, OK 73112. (405) 942-4084. www.nfpoutreach.org

- Northwest Family Services, 4805 N.E. Glisan Street, Portland, OR 97213. (503) 215-6377. www.nwfs.org

- One More Soul, 616 Five Oaks Ave., Dayton, OH 45406. 1-800-307-SOUL. www.omsoul.com

- Pope Paul IV Institute for the Study of Human Reproduction, 6901 Mercy Road, Omaha, NE 68106. (402) 390-6600. www.popepaulvi.org

Pornography Recovery/Healing

- Covenant Eyes. 1-877-479-1119. www.covenanteyes.com

- Family Life Center (Steve Wood), 21202 Olean Blvd., Unit D-6., Port Charlotte, FL 33952. (941) 764-7725. www.dads.org

- Porn No More, The Serenellians, P.O. Box 1096, Maple Falls, WA 98266. www.PornNoMore.com

- True Knights. 1-800-950-2008. www.trueknights.org.

Post-Abortion Healing

- Project Rachel. Available in most major cities. Do a web search by typing "Project Rachel" and your city to find out more information.

- Rachel's Vineyard. (610) 354-0555. www.rachelsvineyard.org

Teen Chastity

- Family Honor, Inc., 2927 Devine Street, Suite 130, Columbia, SC 29205. (803) 929.0858. www.familyhonor.org

- Generation Life, Inc. (215) 885-8760. www.generationlife.org

- Dumb Ox Productions, Inc. (Brian Butler), 310 Saint Philip Street, Thibodaux, LA 70301. (985) 446-2606. www.dumboxproductions.com

- Pure Love Club (seminars, research, chastity clubs). To learn more, call Catholic Answers at 1-888-291-8000. www.pureloveclub.com

- Real Love Productions, Inc. (Mary Beth Bonacci), 191 University Blvd, Denver, CO 80206. Phone: 1-888-NOPIZZA (667-4992). www.reallove.net

- Life-Vision Communications (Janelle), Box 1238, Lloydminster, AB, S9V 1G1. (780) 808-4142. www.janelle.cc

Theology of the Body—Educational Organizations

- John Paul II Institute, 415 Michigan Avenue NE, Washington, DC 20017. Phone: 202-526-3799. www.jpii.edu

- Theology of the Body Institute, P.O. Box 5005, West Chester, PA 19380. (610) 696-7795, ext. 206. www.tobinstitute.org

- Women of the Third Millennium (Katrina Zeno), P.O. Box 23673, Tempe, AZ 85285. (480) 720-5715. www.wttm.org

Unplanned Pregnancy Assistance

- Birthright. 1-800-550-4900. www.birthright.org. Offices in major cities and many smaller towns.

- The Nurturing Network, P.O. Box 1489, White Salmon, WA 98672. (509) 493-4026. www.nurturingnetwork.org

If you are aware of any resource or organization we have missed in this resources section, please let us know by emailing us at TOBforTeens@ascensionpress.com or by writing us at Ascension Press, P.O. Box 1990, West Chester, PA 19380. We will make every effort to add the resource to an upcoming edition of the text.

Prayers

Teacher's Prayer Before Class

You, O God, are my strength, my patience, my light and my counsel. It is you who make responsive to me the students confided to my care. Abandon me not to myself for one moment. For my own conduct and for that of my students, grant me the spirit of wisdom and understanding, the spirit of knowledge and piety, the spirit of holy fear of you, and an ardent zeal to procure Your glory. I unite my efforts to that of Jesus Christ, the master teacher, and I beg the Most Blessed Virgin, St. Joseph, and St. John the Baptist de La Salle to assist me in the exercise of my teaching ministry. Amen.

(Adapted from Robert J. Kealey, Ed.D., The Prayer of Catholic Educators *[Washington, D.C: National Catholic Educational Association, 1987], p. 1 .)*

Prayer to St. Michael the Archangel (for spiritual protection)

Saint Michael the Archangel, defend us in battle. Be our protection against the wickedness and snares of the devil. May God rebuke him, we humbly pray; and do Thou, O Prince of the Heavenly Host—by the power of God—cast into hell, Satan and all the evil spirits, who roam throughout the world seeking the ruin of souls. Amen.

Prayer to Saint Joseph to Know One's Vocation

O Great Saint Joseph, you were completely obedient to the guidance of the Holy Spirit. Obtain for me the grace to know the state of life that God in His providence has chosen for me. Since my happiness on earth, and perhaps even my final happiness in heaven, depends on this choice, let me not be deceived in making it. Obtain for me the light to know God's Will, to carry it out faithfully, and to choose the vocation which will lead me to a happy eternity. Amen.

Prayer to Implore Favors Through the Intercession of the Servant of God, Pope John Paul II

O Blessed Trinity, we thank You for having graced the Church with Pope John Paul II and for allowing the tenderness of Your Fatherly care, the glory of the Cross of Christ, and the splendor of the Spirit of love to shine through him. Trusting fully in your infinite mercy and in the maternal intercession of Mar, he has given us a living image of Jesus the Good Shepherd, and has shown us that holiness is the necessary measure of ordinary Christian life and is the way of achieving eternal communion with You. Grant us, by his intercession, and according to Your will, the graces we implore, hoping that he will soon be numbered among Your Saints. Amen.

(With ecclesiastical approval; Camillo Cardinal Ruini, Vicar General of His Holiness for the Diocese of Rome; © Libreria Editrice Vaticana)

Prayer of Repentance

O my crucified God, behold me at your feet; do not cast me out now that I appear before you as a sinner. I have offended you exceedingly in the past, my Jesus, but it shall be so no longer. Before you, O Lord, I place all my sins. I have now considered your own sufferings and see how great is the worth of that precious blood that flows from your veins. O my God, at this hour close your eyes to my want of merit, and since you have been pleased to die for my sins, grant me forgiveness for them all, that I may no longer feel the burden of my sins, for this burden, dear Jesus, oppresses me beyond measure.

Assist me, my Jesus, for I desire to become good whatsoever it may cost; take away, destroy, utterly root out all that you find in me contrary to your holy will. At the same time, I pray you, Lord Jesus, to enlighten me that I may be able to walk in your holy light. Amen.

–St. Gemma Galgani

Meditations for Confession

In failing to confess, Lord, I would only hide you from myself, not myself from you.

–St. Augustine of Hippo

To the penitent he provides a way back, he encourages those who are losing hope! Return to the Lord and give up sin, pray to him and make your offenses few. Turn again to the Most High and away from sin.

–Sir. 17:19–21 (NAB)

When You Come to Confession

Before we sin, the devil tells us that God is lenient and merciful toward our weakness. But after we sin, he tries to drive us into despair by convincing us that God would never love us again. In reality, we should contemplate God as a judge before we sin and as a loving Father if we sin. This is a simple principle, but the devil deceives millions by reversing it. If we're tempted to despair after sinning, remember the words of St. John Vianney: "Our sins are nothing but a grain of sand alongside the great mountain of the mercy of God."

Do not avoid confession if you keep committing the same sins. Rather, follow the advice of St. Francis de Sales, who said, "Have patience with all the world, but first of all with yourself." Also, do not avoid confession because you fear that your sins are too bad to confess. The Bible tells us, "His mercies never come to an end; they are new every morning" (Lam. 3:22–23).

St. Maria Faustina Kowalska recommended three things to the person preparing for confession:

1. *Sincerity and openness:* "An insincere, secretive soul risks great dangers in the spiritual life, and even the Lord Jesus himself does not give himself to such a soul on a higher level."

2. *Humility:* "A soul does not benefit from the sacrament of confession if it is not humble. Pride keeps it in darkness. The soul neither knows how, nor is it willing, to probe with precision the depths of its own misery. It puts on a mask and avoids everything that might bring it recovery."

3. *Obedience:* "A disobedient soul will win no victory, even if the Lord Jesus himself, in person, were to hear its confession."

By giving us the sacrament of Reconciliation, God does not want to cause us embarrassment or humiliation. He wishes to comfort us. But we must allow him. When writing to the youth of the world, Pope John Paul II reminds us that "in order to see Jesus, we first need to let Him look at us!"

Examination of Conscience

According to St. Ignatius Loyola, "There are five points in this method of making the general examination of conscience:

1. Give thanks to God for favors received.
2. Ask for grace to know your sins and to rid yourself of them.
3. Demand an account of your soul from the time of rising to the present examination. Go over one hour after another, one period after another. The thoughts should be examined first, then the words, and finally the deeds.
4. Ask pardon of God our Lord for your faults.
5. Resolve to amend with the grace.

Close with an Our Father.

Using the Ten Commandments to Prepare for Confession

1. *I am the Lord your God; you shall have no strange gods before me.*
   - Is God the center of your life, or do you let things such as money, work, your image, popularity, a relationship, pleasure, or superstition to replace God as your chief concern?
   - Have you used magic, horoscopes, or psychics?
   - Are you indifferent or ungrateful toward God? If you have difficulties with the faith, do you make an effort to find answers?

2. *You shall not take the name of the Lord your God in vain.*
   - Have you used God's name to curse other people?
   - Have you been careless with his name, using it as a joke?
   - Have you used his name as an exclamation when you're angry or surprised?
   - Have you used obscene language?

3. *Remember to keep holy the Lord's Day.*
   - Do you honor God, especially on Sunday and holy days of obligation?
   - Have you deliberately, without just cause, missed Mass on these days, arrived late, or left Mass early?
   - Have you shown reverence at the Mass by modest dress and behavior?
   - At Mass, do you pay attention to Christ and his sacrifice for you, or does your mind wander?
   - Have you received Communion while in a state of mortal sin?
   - Do you make Sunday a day of rest and avoid unnecessary work?

4. *Honor your father and your mother.*
   - Have you been disobedient, dishonest, or disrespectful to your parents?
   - Do you cause them undue worry?
   - Do you treat your siblings with respect and love?
   - Do you show respect and obedience to those who have authority over you?

5. *You shall not kill.*
   - Do you respect human life from conception to natural death?
   - Have you ever been responsible or partly responsible for the death of another (including abortion)?
   - Have you been drunk?
   - Have you used drugs?
   - Have you ever endangered your life or the lives of others by driving recklessly or driving under the influence of alcohol or drugs?
   - Have you hurt others through insults or gossip?
   - Could you repeat in front of Jesus the things you have said about others?
   - Have you hurt your own body?

6. *You shall not commit adultery.*
   - Have you engaged in any form of sexual activity outside of marriage, such as masturbation, pornography, lust, premarital sex, prostitution, rape, homosexual acts, or contraception?
   - Do you watch television shows, listen to music, read magazines, or play games that are not pure?

7. *You shall not steal.*
- Have you taken or stolen what does not belong to you?
- Have you deliberately damaged the property of another?
- Have you cheated anyone from having what was due to him?
- Do you always respect public property?
- Are you selfish?
- Are you lazy or wasteful of your time? Do you work diligently, or do you spend your employer's time doing personal things?
- Do you neglect the poor?

8. *You shall not bear false witness against your neighbor.*
- Have you lied?
- Have you damaged the reputation of another by unkind words, gossip, or negative humor?
- Have you betrayed another by revealing secrets that were entrusted to you?
- Have you cheated on exams? Do you act hypocritically?
- Do you brag?

9. *You shall not covet your neighbor's wife.*
- Do you harbor thoughts of sexual desire for anyone who is not your spouse?
- Do you put yourself in occasions of sexual temptation?
- Do you expose others to sexual temptations through immodest dress, impure speech, or crude behavior?

10. *You shall not covet your neighbor's goods.*
- Instead of delighting in God's generosity to you, are you jealous of the talents and possessions others have?
- Do you wish the misfortune of others so that you will profit?
- Are you selfish, envious, materialistic, or self-centered, failing to have concern for others?

Using the Beatitudes (see Mt 5:3–12) to Prepare for Confession

While the Ten Commandments tell us what to avoid, the Beatitudes tell us what to become. By examining our Lord's Sermon on the Mount, you can take a deeper look at the state of your soul before confession.

Blessed are the poor in spirit, for theirs is the kingdom of heaven.
- Do you trust God with all of your heart, preferring him to everything?
- Do you abandon yourself to God's Providence, giving him your anxieties in exchange for his joy?

Blessed are those who mourn, for they shall be comforted.
- Do you have real sorrow in your heart for your sins?
- If you do not, do you at least pray for that?
- Do you wallow in your own problems or seek out and comfort those who are lonely, rejected, or suffering?

Blessed are the meek, for they shall inherit the earth.
- Are you haughty and proud or humble like Christ?
- If you are gifted in academics, sports, music, or some other talent, do you give God the glory?
- Are you a servant?
- Do you follow God in order to please him with a sincere heart, or are you self-seeking?
- Do you look down upon certain people, or do you treat others with equal respect, attention, and love?

Blessed are those who hunger and thirst for righteousness, for they shall be satisfied.
- Do you long for God's will to be done, or do I pursue my own interests apart from him?
- Are you lukewarm in my faith, being satisfied with mediocrity?

Blessed are the merciful, for they shall obtain mercy.
- Are you mindful of how much God has forgiven you, or are you quick to condemn and slow to forgive others the harm that they have caused you?
- Are you resentful?
- Are you sympathetic to the needs of others?
- Do you pray and work for the salvation of souls?

Blessed are the pure in heart, for they shall see God.
- Have you not only rejected thoughts of lust but prayed to have a pure heart and live a life of purity?
- Have you glorified God with your body? Do you act like your body is a temple of the Holy Spirit?

Blessed are the peacemakers, for they shall be called sons of God.
- Do you not only avoid causing harm but strive to bring peace and reconciliation into the lives of others?

Blessed are those who are persecuted for righteousness' sake, for theirs is the kingdom of heaven.
- Do you have the courage to do the will of God?
- If mocked for living according to God's laws, do you give in?

Blessed are you when men revile you and persecute you and utter all kinds of evil against you falsely on my account. Rejoice and be glad, for your reward is great in heaven, for so men persecuted the prophets who were before you.
- Do you spread the faith and refuse to compromise it?
- Do you not only refuse to use the Lord's name in vain but seek to correct those who do?

- Have you been ashamed of Jesus, or do you challenge your friends who are falling into sin?

How to Go to Confession

While some churches have confession available every day, most have the sacrament available on Saturday afternoons or by appointment. When you arrive, take some time to examine your conscience. Ask the Holy Spirit to help you to remember where you've fallen away from God. Using the methods above will help you to do this. You could also say a prayer for the priest before entering the confessional. When you enter, the priest may begin by greeting you or reading Scripture. You may respond by saying: "Bless me, Father, for I have sinned. It has been [the number of days, weeks, months, or years] since my last confession." You may also use your own words if you like, but you should give the priest an idea of how long it has been since your last confession.

After stating your sins (including how often they occurred), it is good to add: "I am sorry for these sins and all the sins of my life." The priest will give you a penance—usually a prayer to say, a Scripture passage to read, or a charitable act to perform. He will then invite you to say an act of contrition. You may offer the following one or use your own words to express sorrow for your sins:

"O my God, I am heartily sorry for having offended you, and I detest all my sins because of your just punishments. But I am sorry most of all because they offend you who are all good and worthy of all my love. I firmly resolve, with the help of your grace, to sin no more and to avoid the near occasions of sin. Amen." You also might use a simple act of contrition such as "God, be merciful to me, a sinner" (see Luke 18:9–14).

After the priest sees that you are genuinely repentant, he will give you absolution, saying:
"God, the Father of mercies, through the death and resurrection of his Son has reconciled the world to himself and sent the Holy Spirit among us for the forgiveness of sins; through the ministry of the Church may God give you pardon and peace, and I absolve you from your sins in the name of the Father and of the Son and of the Holy Spirit."

Finally, the priest may say: "Go in peace." And you say: "Thanks be to God." Or he may say: "Give thanks to the Lord, for he is good." And you say: "His mercy endures forever."

Although these steps using the Ten Commandments and the Beatitudes may seem a bit intimidating, don't be worried about following a perfect formula. What God looks at is the sincerity of your heart. If you have not been to confession in a while, let the priest know this, and he'll guide you through the sacrament.